Parallel Computing Architectures and APIs

IoT Big Data Stream Processing

Parallel Computing Architectures and APIs

IoT Big Data Stream Processing

Vivek Kale

CRC Press is an imprint of the
Taylor & Francis Group, an informa business
A CHAPMAN & HALL BOOK

CRC Press
Taylor & Francis Group
52 Vanderbilt Avenue,
New York, NY 10017

Printed on acid-free paper

International Standard Book Number-13: 978-1-138-55391-0 (Hardback)

Visit the Taylor & Francis Web site at
http://www.taylorandfrancis.com

and the CRC Press Web site at
http://www.crcpress.com

To my family friends Charudutta ("Charu") and Shobha Palkar

with whom we reconnected after a gap of almost 30 years

Contents

Section I Genesis of Parallel Computing

Section II Road to Parallel Computing

Section V Internet of Things Big Data Stream Processing

Preface

A basic trade-off exists between the use of one or a small number of complex processors, at one extreme, and a moderate to very large number of simpler processors, at the other. When combined with a high bandwidth, the interprocessor communication facility leads to significant simplification in the design process. However, two major roadblocks prevent the widespread adoption of such moderately to massively parallel architectures: the interprocessor communication bottleneck and the difficulty and high cost of algorithm/software development.

One of the most important reasons for studying parallel computing architectures is to learn how to extract the best performance from parallel systems. Specifically, you must understand its architectures so that you will be able to exploit those architectures during programming via the standardized application programming interfaces.

Until the last few decades, the business of the global economy was, essentially, manufacturing. The focus on goods rather than services led to a product-focused, mass-market marketing strategy resulting in a high cost of acquiring new customers, and a low cost for customers switching to other brands. There has always been a focus on customer needs, but with the advent of computers, there has been a shift away from producing goods or providing services, toward discovering and meeting the needs of the individual customer. Don Peppers and Martha Rogers pioneered the concept of one-to-one marketing made possible by the advent of computer-assisted database marketing. Businesses with highly diversified customer needs and highly differentiated customer valuations were expected to benefit from one-to-one customized marketing. This paradigm of one-to-one marketing has been further extended inward onto the production systems via Industry 4.0.

In the eighteenth century, the first industrial revolution, Industry 1.0, was characterized by mechanical production powered by water and steam. The industrial revolution in the twentieth century, Industry 2.0, introduced mass production, based on the division of labor and powered by electrical energy. In the 1970s, Industry 3.0 was set in motion by embedded electronics and information technology (IT) for further automation of production. Industry 4.0 (especially in Europe; Industrial Internet in the United States), reflects the rise of a basket of new digitally-enabled industrial technologies i.e. digital manufacturing that enable realization of the manufacturing of individual products in a batch size of one while maintaining the economic conditions of mass production i.e. *mass customization.*

Internet of Things (IoT) is the foundation of Industry 4.0. With the advent of IoT, a new class of applications has emerged that requires managing data streams, that is, data composed of a continuous, real-time sequence of items. Streaming applications have gained prominence for both business and technical reasons. Businesses and government agencies increasingly want to analyze data much sooner than is possible with the traditional model of storing data in a data warehouse and performing the analysis off-line. Technologically, data is now available from a wide variety of monitoring devices, including sensors that are extremely cheap. Data from such devices is potentially unbounded and needs to be processed in real time. Application domains requiring data stream management include military, homeland security, sensor networks, financial applications, network management, website performance tracking, and real-time credit card fraud detection.

The Internet of Things refers to a network of inter-connected things, objects, or devices on a massive scale connected to the Internet. These objects being smart sense their surroundings, and gather and exchange data with other objects. Based on the gathered data, the objects make intelligent decisions to trigger an action or send the data to a server over the Internet and wait for its decision. The Internet of Things aims to integrate and collect information from and offer services to a diverse spectrum of physical things used in different domains. "Things" are everyday objects for which the Internet of Things offers a virtual presence on the Internet, allocates a specific identity and virtual address, and adds capabilities to self-organize and communicate with other things without human intervention. To ensure a high quality of services, additional capabilities can be included such as context awareness, autonomy, and reactivity.

For applications such as sensor networks, network monitoring, microblogging, web exploring, social networking, and so on, a big data input stream has the characteristics of high speed, real time, and large volume. These data sources often take the form of continuous data streams, and timely analysis of such a data stream is very important as the life cycle of most of this data is very short. The volume of data is so high that there is not enough space for storage, and not all data needs to be stored. Thus, the storing and then computing batch computing model does not fit at all for such requirements. Increasingly, data in big data environments is beginning to have the feature of streams, and big data stream computing has emerged as a panacea for computing data online within real-time constraints.

Stream computing is a computing paradigm that reads data from collections of software or hardware sensors in stream form and computes such continuous data streams, where the output results are also in the form of a real-time data stream. Thus,

- Data stream is a sequence of datasets
- Continuous data stream is an infinite sequence of datasets
- Parallel data stream has more than one stream to be processed at the same time

Stream computing is an effective way of supporting big data by providing extremely low-latency velocities with massively parallel processing architectures. It is becoming the fastest and most efficient way to obtain useful knowledge from big data stream, allowing organizations to react quickly when problems appear or to predict new trends in the immediate future.

What Makes This Book Different?

An incredible amount of sensing data is being generated around the world every second. The amount of data generated is so large that it is difficult not only to manage but also process using traditional data management tools. Such data is referred to as big data. To tackle the challenge of processing big data, Google developed the MapReduce framework, which needs to process millions of web pages every second. Over the last five years with the availability of several open-source implementations of this framework such as Hadoop, it has become a dominant framework for solving big data processing problems. Batch processing refers to the computational analysis of bounded datasets. In practical terms, this means that those datasets are available and retrievable as a whole from some form of storage. We know the size of the dataset at the start of the computational process and the duration of that process is limited in time.

However, for processing sensing data that is continuously being generated, it was observed that volume is not the only challenge of such big data processing and that the velocity of data generation is also an important challenge that needs to be tackled.

The limitation of the previous approach in managing and analyzing high volume and velocity data in real time has led to the development of sophisticated new distributed techniques and technologies. The processing of data with such features is defined as data stream processing or stream processing. Stream processing refers to the computational analysis of unbounded datasets; it is concerned with the processing of data as it arrives to the system. Given the unbounded nature of data streams, the stream processing systems need to run constantly for as long as the stream is delivering new data, which is theoretically forever.

This book focuses on Internet of Things big data stream processing. Evidently, this would be majorly enabled by cloud computing characterised by multi-tenancy, scalability, rapid elasticity, measured provisioning, etc. The cloud plays an important role within the big data world, but this book does not discuss cloud computing systems as none of the stream processing systems surveyed (see Chapter 20: Section 20.2) allow the use of cloud computing resources, which can scale up and down according to the volume and velocity of the data that needs to be processed. For a detailed discussion on the cloud computing technologies, refer to the companion volume *Guide to Cloud Computing for Business and Technology Managers* (Kale 2015).

The characteristic features of this book are

- Devolves uniprocessors in terms of a ladder of abstractions to ascertain (say) performance characteristics at a particular level of abstraction.
- Explains the limitations of uniprocessor high performance because of Moore's law.
- Introduces the basics of processors, networks, and distributed systems.
- Explains the characteristics of parallel systems, parallel computing models, and parallel algorithms.
- Explains the three primary categorical representatives of parallel computing architectures, namely, shared memory, message passing, and stream processing.
- Introduces the three primary categorical representatives of parallel programming application programming interfaces, namely, OpenMP, MPI, and CUDA.
- Provides an overview of the Internet of Things, wireless sensor networks, sensor data processing, big data, and stream processing.
- Provides an introduction to 5G communications, Edge and Fog computing.

The uniqueness of envisaged concepts like *sensor farms* is to change the traditional individual view to a collective view that treats universally-deployed RFID tags-sensor combinations (combos) as a new infrastructure—a new wireless platform on which novel applications can be developed. The newer paradigms also reinterprets the traditional supply chain (SC) in terms of the flow of decisions, information, and materials, leading to the trifurcation of conventional SC networks into decision networks (like fourth-party logistics [4PLs]), information networks (like wireless sensor networks [WSN] and sensor farms), and logistics networks (like third-party logistics [3PLs]). In their new avatar of the trifurcated SC networks, supply chain management (SCM) will chart *blue ocean* opportunities powered by artificial intelligence (AI) solutions for the decision networks, and, big data stream processing and fusion solutions for the information and logistic networks. The author wanted to write a book presenting the vision of parallel computing-enabled SCM systems—the outcome is the book that you are reading now. Thank you!

How Is This Book Organized?

Chapter 1 examines the hardware components of a typical computer (central processing unit, memory, storage, graphics processing unit, etc.) focusing on issues that are relevant for algorithm design and software development to ultimately achieve efficient program execution and computer performance. To set the context for understanding computer performance issues, the chapter introduces the concept of hardware and software logical equivalence, and discusses the *stack of abstraction*. The chapter also introduces the concept of application programming interfaces.

Chapter 2 discusses aspects of processor physics especially the relation between the speed of processing and the power problem. It looks at the various trade-offs including area versus delay, delay versus power, and area versus delay versus power. The chapter then elaborates on Moore's law, which identifies the trend that "computing power doubles every 2 years."

Section I presents an overview of the genesis of parallel computing. Chapters 3 through 5 introduce the basics of processors, networking, and distributed systems, respectively.

Section II with Chapters 6 through 8 introduces the overarching concepts of parallel systems that characterize parallel computing as a whole. Chapter 6 presents Flynn's taxonomy for parallel computers defining the single instruction, single data; single instruction, multiple data; multiple instruction, single data; and multiple instruction, multiple data architectures. General-purpose multiprocessor systems (multiple instruction, multiple data computers) are further subdivided into two major subtypes: *shared memory multiprocessor* systems and *distributed memory multicomputers*. Chapter 7 discusses parallel computation models that are helpful in analyzing and designing algorithms, as well as in determining performance metrics used for the evaluation of algorithms. Chapter 8 describes various aspects of parallel algorithms.

Section III with Chapter 9 introduces the overarching concepts of parallel computing performance that characterize any parallel computing architecture as a whole. Chapters 10 through 12 explain the primary parallel computing architectures, namely, shared memory, message passing, and stream processing.

Section IV with Chapter 13 provides an overview of parallel programming application programming interfaces. Chapters 14 through 16 explain the primary categorical representatives of parallel computing application programming interfaces, namely, OpenMP, MPI, and CUDA.

Section V covers components of an Internet of Things big data stream processing systems. Chapters 17 through 20 explain the corresponding technologies of the Internet of Things, sensor data processing, big data computing, and stream processing.

In the Epilogue to the book, with the reader's indulgence, the author explores the idea of quantum computing. The requirements of massive parallelism envisaged in the future is achievable more effectively through quantum computing.

Who Should Read This Book?

All stakeholders of an Internet of Things big data stream processing project can benefit from reading this book. In contemporary organizations, CIOs are the decision makers of

IT-related issues—but they don't battle alone; IT teams have technical members who whet what vendors and/or consultants recommend. This book should be useful not only for CIOs but also their business-IT and IT teams while undertaking big data stream processing projects using parallel computing.

The approach adopted in this book will be useful to any professional who must present a case for realizing the Internet of Things–driven solutions or to those who are involved in executing an Internet of Things–driven computing project.

The book is targeted at the following categories of stakeholders:

- Executives and business and operational managers
- Business development, product management, and commercial managers
- Functional and technical members
- Business analysts, enterprise architects, and solution architects
- Project managers and module leaders
- Technical managers and professionals interested in parallel computing, Internet of Things, big data, and stream processing.
- Students of engineering, management, and computer and technology courses interested in business and digital transformations

  The pervasiveness of computing devices containing multicore CPUs and GPUs, including home and office PCs, laptops, and mobile devices, is making even common users dependent on parallel processing. It is no longer sufficient for even basic programmers to acquire only the traditional sequential programming skills. The preceding trends point to the need for imparting a broad-based skill set in Parallel and Distributed Computing (PDC) technology. Every computer science (CS) and computer engineering (CE) undergraduate student should achieve a basic skill level in parallel and distributed computing (PDC). This book addresses the lack of adequate textbook support for integrating PDC-related topics into undergraduate courses, especially in the early curriculum.
- General readers interested in the phenomenon of parallel computing.

Vivek Kale
Mumbai, India

You may want to read through the author's related books, especially *Agile Network Businesses: Collaboration, Coordination, and Competitive Advantage*, *Big Data Computing: A Guide for Business and Technology Managers*, *Creating Smart Enterprises: Leveraging Cloud, Big Data, Web, Social Media, Mobile and IoT Technologies* and *Digital Transformation of Enterprise Architecture*.

Acknowledgments

I would like to thank all those who have helped me with their clarifications, criticism, and valuable information during the writing of this book.

Thanks again to Aastha Sharma for making this book happen and guiding it through to completion.

I owe the largest debt of gratitude to my wife, Girija, and our two (now adult) daughters, Tanaya and Atmaja. Girija has taught me more about the world than anyone else and without whom life itself would be impossible. Most importantly, my efforts would not have been equal to this task had they not been generously supported, encouraged, and understood by my wife, Girija.

Vivek Kale
Mumbai, India

Author

Vivek Kale has more than two decades of professional IT experience during which he has handled and consulted on various aspects of enterprise-wide information modeling, enterprise architectures, business process redesign, and e-business architectures. He has been Group CIO of Essar Group, the steel/oil and gas major of India, as well as Raymond Ltd., the textile and apparel major of India. He is a seasoned practitioner in enhancing business agility through the digital transformation of business models, enterprise architecture, and business processes, and enhancing IT-enabled enterprise intelligence (EQ). He has authored books on cloud computing and big data computing. He is also author of *Big Data Computing: A Guide for Business and Technology Managers* (CRC Press 2016), *Agile Network Businesses: Collaboration, Coordination, and Competitive Advantage* (CRC Press 2017), and *Digital Transformation of Enterprise Architecture* (CRC Press 2020).

1

Uniprocessor Computers

This introductory chapter commences by discussing the various types of computers, namely, microcomputers, midrange computers, mainframe computers, and supercomputers. A general uniprocessor computer system is composed of hardware, software, and network. In order to implement efficient computer programs, it is essential to understand the basic hardware structure of computers. This chapter examines the hardware components of a typical computer (central processing unit [CPU], memory, storage, graphics processing unit [GPU], etc.), focusing on issues that are relevant for algorithm design and software development to ultimately achieve efficient program execution and computer performance. A typical computer is composed of several important components that are connected to the computer's motherboard, including the CPU, the GPU, the memory, and the disk drive.

To set the context for understanding computer performance issues, the chapter introduces the concept of hardware and software logical equivalence, and discusses the *stack of abstraction* consisting of a modeling-level, algorithm-level, high-level, assembly-level, system or instruction set architecture (ISA) level, machine or microarchitecture-level, control or logic-level, and device-level architecture. The chapter concludes by introducing the concept of application programming interfaces (APIs). The API defines the set of instructions the hardware is designed to execute and gives the application access to the ISA.

1.1 Types of Computers

Today's computer systems come in a variety of sizes, shapes, and computing capabilities. The Apollo 11 spacecraft that enabled men to land on the moon and return safely to Earth was equipped with a computer that assisted them in everything from navigating to systems monitoring, and it had a 2.048 MHz CPU built by the Massachusetts Institute of Technology (MIT). Today's standards can be measured in 4 GHz in many home personal computers (PCs; megahertz [MHz] is 1 million computing cycles per second, while gigahertz [GHz] is 1 billion computing cycles per second). Further, the Apollo 11 computer weighed 70 pounds versus today's powerful laptops weighing as little as 1 pound—we have come a long way. Rapid hardware and software developments and changing end-user needs continue to drive the emergence of new computer models, from the smallest handheld personal digital assistant/cell phone combinations to the largest multiple CPU mainframes for enterprises. Categories such as microcomputer, midrange, mainframe, and supercomputer systems are still used to help us express the relative processing power and number of end users that can be supported by different types of computers. These are not precise classifications, and they do overlap each other.

1.1.1 Microcomputers

Microcomputers are the most important category of computer systems for both business and household consumers. Although usually called a personal computer, or PC, a microcomputer is much more than a small computer for use by an individual as a communication device. The computing power of microcomputers now exceeds that of the mainframes of previous computer generations, at a fraction of their cost. Thus, they have become powerful networked professional workstations for business professionals.

1.1.2 Midrange Computers

Midrange computers are primarily high-end network servers and other types of servers that can handle the large-scale processing of many business applications. Although not as powerful as mainframe computers, they are less costly to buy, operate, and maintain, and thus meet the computing needs of many organizations. Midrange systems first became popular as minicomputers in scientific research, instrumentation systems, engineering analysis, and industrial process monitoring and control. Minicomputers were able to easily handle such functions because these applications are narrow in scope and do not demand the processing versatility of mainframe systems. Today, midrange systems include servers used in industrial process control and manufacturing plants and play major roles in computer-aided manufacturing (CAM). They can also take the form of powerful technical workstations for computer-aided design (CAD) and other computation and graphics-intensive applications. Midrange systems are also used as front-end servers to assist mainframe computers in telecommunications processing and network management.

Midrange systems have become popular as powerful network servers (computers used to coordinate communications and manage resource sharing in network settings) to help manage large Internet websites, corporate intranets and extranets, and other networks. Internet functions and other applications are popular high-end server applications, as are integrated enterprise-wide manufacturing, distribution, and financial applications. Other applications, such as data warehouse management, data mining, and online analytical processing, are contributing to the demand for high-end server systems.

1.1.3 Mainframe Computers

Mainframe computers are large, fast, and powerful computer systems; they can process thousands of million instructions per second (MIPS). They can also have large primary storage capacities with main memory capacity ranging from hundreds of gigabytes to many terabytes. Mainframes have downsized drastically in the last few years, dramatically reducing their air-conditioning needs, electrical power consumption, and floor space requirements—and thus their acquisition, operating, and ownership costs. Most of these improvements are the result of a move from the cumbersome water-cooled mainframes to a newer air-cooled technology for mainframe systems.

Mainframe computers continue to handle the information processing needs of major corporations and government agencies with high transaction processing volumes or complex computational problems. For example, major international banks, airlines, oil companies, and other large corporations process millions of sales transactions and customer inquiries every day with the help of large mainframe systems. Mainframes are still used for computation-intensive applications, such as analyzing seismic data from oil field explorations or simulating flight conditions in designing aircraft.

Mainframes are also widely used as super servers for large client/server networks and high-volume Internet websites of large companies. Mainframes are becoming a popular business computing platform for data mining and warehousing, as well as electronic commerce applications.

1.1.4 Supercomputers

Supercomputers are a category of exceedingly powerful computer systems specifically designed for scientific, engineering, and business applications requiring extremely high speeds for massive numeric computations. Supercomputers use the parallel processing architectures of interconnected microprocessors (which can execute many parallel instructions). They can easily perform arithmetic calculations at speeds of billions of floating-point operations per second (gigaflops)—a floating-point operation is a basic computer arithmetic operation, such as addition, on numbers that include a decimal point. Supercomputers that can calculate in trillions of floating-point operations per second (teraflops), which use massively parallel processing (MPP) designs of thousands of microprocessors, are now in use.

The market for supercomputers includes government research agencies, large universities, and major corporations. They use supercomputers for applications such as global weather forecasting, military defense systems, computational cosmology and astronomy, microprocessor research and design, and large-scale data mining.

1.2 Computer System

A typical desktop computer system is representative of a whole spectrum of computer systems.

1.2.1 Hardware

A typical desktop computer has a system unit, which is the case or box that houses, for example:

- Motherboard
- Other printed circuit boards
- Storage devices
- Power supply
- Peripheral devices

The motherboard is the main printed circuit board, and holds the computer's processor chip(s), read-only memory (ROM) chips, random-access memory (RAM) chips, and several other key electronic components.

The processor is an important part of a computer, and can be a single chip or a collection of chips.

- ROM chips typically contain a small set of programs that start the computer, run system diagnostics, and control low-level input and output activities. The instructions in the ROM chips are permanent, and the only way to modify them is to reprogram the ROM chips.
- RAM chips are volatile and hold programs and data that are temporary in nature.

These programs are collectively called the basic input output system (BIOS) in PCs.

Each printed circuit board houses a number of chips, some of which are soldered and the rest are plugged into the board. The latter permits the user to upgrade the computer components.

Chipsets: Chipsets provide hardware interfaces for the processor to interact with other devices, such as dynamic random-access memory (DRAM) and graphics cards.

A battery powered real-time clock chip keeps track of the current date and time.

The system unit is generally designed in such a way that it can be easily opened to add or replace modules. The different components in the system unit are typically connected using a bus, which is a set of wires for transferring electrical signals. Circuits etched into the boards act like wires, providing a path for transporting data from one chip to another.

The motherboard also typically contains expansion slots—the number of expansion slots in the motherboard determines its expandability. Expansion slots are sockets into which expansion cards such as a video card, sound card, and internal modem can be plugged. An expansion card has a card edge connector with metal contacts, which when plugged into an expansion slot socket, connects the circuitry on the card to the circuitry on the motherboard:

- A sound card contains circuitry to convert digital signals from the computer into sounds that play through speakers or headphones that are connected to the expansion ports of the card.
- A modem card connects the computer to a telephone system to transport data from one computer to another over phone lines.
- A network card, on the other hand, provides the circuitry to connect a computer to other computers on a local area network (LAN).

Each logical command from the processor must typically be decomposed into long sequences of low-level commands to trigger the actions to be performed by the corresponding device and to supervise the progress of the operation by testing the device's status.

Each device keyboard, mouse, printer, monitor, etc., requires special controller circuitry, termed a *device controller*, for transferring data from the processor and memory to the device, and vice versa. A device controller is designed either as a chip that is placed in the motherboard or as a printed circuit board that is plugged into an expansion slot of the motherboard.

Peripheral devices are connected to their respective controllers in the system unit using special cables to sockets called expansion ports. The ports are located on the backside of the system unit and provide connections through holes in the back of the system unit. Ports are of two types:

- Serial ports transfer a single bit at a time, and are commonly used to connect mouse and communication equipment to the computer.
- Parallel ports transfer several bits simultaneously and are commonly used to connect printers to the computer.

Storage devices: Storage devices are typically mounted in the system unit. Those involving removable media such as the floppy disk drive, the CD-ROM drive, and the ZIP drive are mounted on the front side of the system unit, and the hard disk drives are typically mounted inside the system unit. Commonly used storage devices are floppy disk drives, hard disk drives, CD-ROM drives, and ZIP drives:

- A floppy disk drive is a device that reads and writes data on floppy disks. A typical floppy disk drive uses 3 1/2-inch floppy disks, each of which can store up to 1.44 MB.
- A hard disk drive can store billions of bytes on a nonremovable disk platter.
- A CD-ROM drive is a storage device that uses laser technology to read data from a CD-ROM.

Input/output (I/O) devices:

1. The primary input devices are
   - The keyboard looks similar to that of a typewriter, with the addition of number keys and several additional keys that control computer-specific tasks.
   - The mouse is useful in manipulating objects depicted on the screen.
   - The microphone is useful in audio input in the form of verbal commands, dictation, and so on.
2. The primary output devices are
   - The monitor is a display device that forms an image by converting electrical signals from the computer into points of colored light on the screen. Its functioning is very similar to a television picture tube, but it has a much higher resolution so that a user sitting at close quarters can clearly see computer-generated data such as text and images.
   - Printer.
   - Speakers.

1.2.2 Software

A desktop computer typically comes with pre-installed software composed of

- Application software: Application programs are designed to satisfy end-user needs by operating on input data to perform a given job, for example, to prepare a report, update customer master, or print customer bills. There are two types of application software:
  - Packaged software includes programs prewritten by professional programmers, and are typically offered for sale on a floppy disk or CD-ROM.
  - Custom software includes programs written for highly specialized tasks such as scheduling or analytics or optimization.
- Systems software: Systems software enables the application software to interact with the computer, and helps the computer manage its internal and external resources. Systems software is required to run applications software. Systems software can be classified into

- Utility programs, which are generally used to support, enhance, or expand the development of application programs. Examples include editors and programs for merging files.
- Compiler or language translator program, which translates a program written in a high-level language (HLL) such as C into machine language, which the hardware can directly execute. Thus, a compiler provides the end user with the capability to write programs in a HLL.
- The operating system (OS) is an important part of most computer systems because it exerts a major influence on the overall function and performance of the entire computer. OSs allocate and control the use of all hardware resources: the processor, the main memory, and the peripheral devices. They also add a variety of new features, above and beyond what the hardware provides:
  - The shell provides the end user with a more capable machine, in that the computer system provides direct capability to specify commands by typing them on a keyboard.
  - The graphical user interface (GUI) goes one step further by providing the user with a graphical view of the desktop, and letting the user enter commands by clicking on icons.
  - The multitasking feature of the OS provides the user with the capability to run multiple tasks "concurrently."
  - The file system of the OS provides the user with a structured way of storing and accessing "permanent" information.

Most application programs need to access IO devices and storage devices such as disks, terminals, and printers. Computer systems provide an abstract interface to the application programs, called a *device driver*, which performs the required low-level IO activity. Whereas an application program uses generic commands, a device requires specific device driver software, because each device has its own specific commands—the device driver receives generic commands from the application program and converts them into specialized commands for the device, and vice versa.

1.2.3 Network

A computer network is a collection of computers and other devices that communicate to share data, hardware, and software. Each device on a network is called a node.

Networks are of various types:

- A LAN is a network that is located within a relatively limited area such as a building or campus, in medium-sized and large businesses, educational institutions, and government offices.
- A wide area network (WAN) is a network that covers a large geographical area.

Different types of networks provide different services, use different technology, and require users to follow different procedures. Popular network types include Ethernet, Token Ring, ARCnet, FDDI, and ATM.

A computer connected to a network can use all of its local resources, such as the hard drive, software, data files, and printer. It can also access network resources including network servers and network printers. Network servers that in turn can serve as

- The *file server*, which serves as a common repository for storing program files and data files that need to be accessible from multiple workstations or client nodes on the network. When an individual client node sends a request to the file server, it supplies the stored information to the client node. Thus, when the user of a client workstation attempts to execute a program, the client's OS sends a request to the file server to get a copy of the executable program. Once the server sends the program, it is copied into the memory of the client workstation, and the program is executed in the client.

  The file server can also supply data files to clients in a similar manner.
- The *application server*, which runs application software on request from other computers, and forwards the results to the requesting client.

A network interface card (NIC) connects a computer to a network. This interface card sends data from the workstation out over the network and collects incoming data for the workstation. The NIC for a desktop computer can be plugged into one of the expansion slots in the motherboard. Different types of networks require different types of NICs: the NIC for a laptop computer is usually a Personal Computer Memory Card International Association (PCMCIA) card.

A network OS controls the computer network in terms of the flow of data, maintaining security, and keeping track of user accounts. Commonly used OSs such as UNIX, Windows XP, and Windows Vista already include network OS capability. There are also software packages such as Novell Netware that are designed exclusively for use as a network OS. A network OS usually has two components:

- The server software is installed in the server workstation and has features to control file access from the server hard drive, manage the print queue, and track network user data such as userids and passwords.
- The client software, which is installed on the local hard drive of each client workstation, is essentially a device driver for the NIC. When the client workstation boots up, the network client software is activated and establishes the connection between the client and the other devices on the network.

1.3 Hardware and Software Logical Equivalence

Hardware consists of tangible objects such as integrated circuits, printed circuit boards, cables, power supplies, memories, and printers. Software, in contrast, consists of abstract ideas, algorithms, and their computer representations, namely programs.

Hardware and software functionality is interchangeable—what can be executed by hardware can also be executed by an equivalent software simulation. The decision to put certain functions in hardware and others in software is based on such factors as cost, speed, reliability, flexibility, and frequency of expected changes. These decisions change with trends in technology and computer usage.

Thus, any instruction executed by the hardware can also be simulated in the software. Similarly, any operation performed by the software can also be built directly into the hardware. In general, new functionality is first introduced in the software, as it is likely to undergo many changes. As the functionality becomes more standard and is less likely to change, it is migrated to the hardware.

The boundary between the software and the hardware is of particular interest to systems programmers and compiler developers. In the very first computers, this boundary—the ISA—was quite clear; the hardware presented the programmer with an abstract model that took instructions from a serial program one at a time and executed them in the order in which they appeared in the program. Over time, however, this boundary blurred considerably, as more and more hardware features were exposed to the software, and, in turn, the hardware design itself began to involve more and more software programming techniques. Nowadays, it is often difficult to tell software and hardware apart, especially at the intervening boundary.

Computer systems have undergone dramatic changes since their inception a few decades ago. However, it is difficult to say whether it is the hardware that drives the software or if it is the other way around. Both are intimately tied to each other; trends in one do affect the other and vice versa:

- Clock speed: Clock speed had been steadily increasing over the last several decades; however, the current trend hints toward a state of saturation. The IBM dual-core Power6 processor released in 2007 operates at an astonishing 4.7 GHz clock.
- Low-power systems: In the late 1990s, as the number of transistors as well as the clock speed steadily increased, power consumption—especially power density—began to increase at an alarming rate. High power densities translated to higher temperatures, necessitating expensive cooling technologies. Today, power consumption has become a first-order design constraint, and power-aware hardware designs are commonplace.
- Large memory systems: Memory size has continuously been increasing steadily, mirroring the downward trend in price per bit. However, memory access time increases with size, necessitating the use of cache memories to reduce average memory latencies. Nowadays, it is commonplace to see multilevel cache organizations in general-purpose computers.
- Multicore processors: The current trend is to incorporate multiple processor cores on the same die. These cores execute multiple threads of execution in parallel.

1.4 Ladder of Abstraction

The reason why performance has consistently been doubling every two years for the past few decades is because of a layered approach adopted in computer engineering (see Chapter 2: Section 2.4). Per this approach, the computer is viewed as a hierarchy of abstractions; it becomes easier to master the complexity of computers and to design computer systems in a systematic, organized way. Each layer from devices to architecture, to OSs/computer languages, and to applications is optimized independently.

Thus, the study of a computer system is effectively the study of an ensemble of abstractions. Computer software and hardware can be viewed as a series of *architectural abstractions* or *virtual machines* (VMs). This abstraction (or specification) is like a contract: it defines how the system behaves. The abstraction defines how the outside world interacts with the system. The implementation, on the other hand, defines how the system is built, as seen from the inside.

Different users see different (virtual) machines depending on the level at which they use the computer. The user who interacts with a computer system at a particular abstraction level has a view of what its capabilities are at this level, and this view results directly from the functions that the computer can perform at this level. For instance, a HLL programmer sees a VM that is capable of executing statements specified in a HLL. An assembly language programmer, on the other hand, sees a different machine with registers and memory locations that can execute instructions specified in an assembly language. The ISA provides a level of abstraction that allows the same (machine language) program to be run on a family of computers having different implementations (i.e., microarchitectures).

Programs developed for a particular abstraction level can be executed in different platforms—which differ in speed, cost, and power consumption but implement the same abstract machine. Appropriate interfaces are used to specify the interaction between different abstractions. This implementation is done by translating or interpreting the steps or instructions of one level using instructions or facilities from the lower level. A particular computer designer or user needs to be familiar only with the level at which he/she is using the computer. For instance, a programmer writing a C program can assume that the program will be executed on a VM that directly executes C programs. The programmer need not be concerned about how the VM implements C's semantics.

Each architectural abstraction is a set of rules that describes the logical function of a computer as observable by a program running on that abstract machine. The architecture does not specify the details of exactly how its functions will be performed; it only specifies the architecture's functionality. Implementation issues related to functionality are left to the lower-level machines. The job of the computer architect is to define the hardware/software interface and to exploit technology trends to translate them into computer performance, reduced power consumption, reliability, etc.

1.4.1 Modeling-Level Architecture

At this level, the computer system is viewed as a machine that can solve well-defined computer problems, that is, problems that can be represented and manipulated inside a computer. This process involves representing the real-life problem's data by some form of data that can be manipulated by a computer. Modeling often implies simplification, the replacement of a complex and detailed real-world situation by a comprehensive model that captures the essence of the problem, "abstracting away" the details whose effect on the problem's solution is minimal.

1.4.2 Algorithm-Level Architecture

At this level, the computer system is viewed as a machine that can execute algorithms.

The basic actions involved in a computer algorithm are

- Specify data values (using abstract data types).
- Perform calculations and assign data values.
- Test data values and select alternate courses of action including repetitions.
- Terminate the algorithm.

Algorithm efficiency: Computer theorists are mainly concerned with discovering the most efficient algorithms for a given class of problems. The algorithm's efficiency relates its resource usage, such as execution time or memory consumption, to the size of its input data, n. The efficiency is stated using the "Big O" notation, O(n) (see Section 8.1.1).

Algorithm development is always done for a specific algorithm-level architecture having an underlying computational model. A computational model conceptualizes computation in a particular way by specifying the kinds of primitives, relationships, and events that can be described in an algorithm:

- Primitives: They represent the simplest objects that can be expressed in the model. Examples of primitives found in most computational models are constants and variables.
- Methods of combination: They specify how the primitives can be combined with one another to obtain compound expressions.
- Methods of abstraction: They specify how compound objects can be named and manipulated as units.

These models of computation are equivalent in the sense that any problem that has a solution in one model is also solvable in any one of the other models.

Three basic computational models are currently in use:

1. Imperative (or state) computational model: The imperative model of computation is based on the execution of a sequence of instructions that modify the machine state comprising variables in the high-level architecture, or registers and memory locations in the assembly-level architecture. It is based on the Turing machine model of effective computability: the Turing machine model can express anything that is computable. An imperative program consists of a sequence of statements or instructions and side effect–prone functions; the execution of each statement (or instruction) would cause the machine to change the value of one or more elements of its state, thereby taking the machine to a new state. Consequently, program development consists of specifying a sequence of state changes to arrive at the solution.

   The imperative model has been the most widely used model; it is the closest to modeling the computer hardware, making it the most efficient model in terms of execution speed. Commonly used programming languages such as C, C++, FORTRAN, and COBOL are based on this computational model.

2. Functional (or applied) computational model: The functional model has its foundation in mathematical logic. In this model, computing is based on recursive function theory (RFT), an alternative (and equivalent) model of effective computability. As with the Turing machine model, RFT can express anything that is computable. Two prominent computer scientists who pioneered this computational model are Stephen Kleene and Alonso Church.

   The functional model consists of a set of values, functions, and the application of side effect–free functions. A side effect–free function is one in which the entire result of a computation is produced by the return value(s) of the function. Side effect–free functions can only access explicit input parameters—there are no global variables in a fully functional model. And, in the canonical functional models, there are no assignment statements either.

Functions may be named and may be composed with other functions. Functions can take other functions as arguments and return functions as results. Programs consist of definitions of functions, and computations are application of functions to values. A classic example of a programming language that is built on this model is LISP.

3. Logic (or rule-based) computational model: The logic model of computation is a formalization of the logical reasoning process. It is based on relations and logical inference. An algorithm in this model involves a collection of rules, in no particular order. Each rule consists of an enabling condition and an action. The execution order is determined by the order in which the enabling conditions are satisfied. The logic model is related to relational databases and expert systems. A programming language designed with this model in mind is Prolog.

Some other computational models suggested for improvement of either computer or programmer performance are

1. Concurrent model: In this model, an algorithm consists of multiple processes or tasks that may exchange information. The computations may occur concurrently or in any order. The model is primarily concerned with methods for synchronization and communication between processes. The concurrent model may also be implemented within any of the other computational models. Concurrency in the imperative model can be viewed as a generalization of control. Concurrency is particularly attractive within the functional and logic models, as subexpression evaluation and inferences may then be performed concurrently. Hardware description languages (HDLs) such as Verilog and VHDL use the concurrency model, as they model hardware components, which tend to operate concurrently.
2. Object-oriented model: In this model, an algorithm consists of a set of objects that compute by exchanging messages. Each object is bound up with a value and a set of operations that determine the messages to which it can respond. Functions are thus designed to operate on objects. Objects are organized hierarchically. That is, complex objects are designed as extensions of simple objects; the complex object will "inherit" the properties of the simple object. The object-oriented model may be implemented within any of the other computational models. Imperative programming languages that use the object-oriented approach are C++ and Java.

1.4.3 High-Level Architecture

At this level, the computer system is viewed as a machine that can execute programs written in HLLs such as C, C++, FORTRAN, Java, and Visual Basic. This implies embodying the algorithm as a program as per the syntax and semantics of a high-level programming language.

This level is used by application programmers and systems programmers who take algorithms and formally express them in a HLL. Programs written in HLLs are translated to a lower level by translators known as compilers. Several LISP machines were developed in the 1970s and 1980s by different vendors to directly execute LISP programs.

1.4.4 Assembly-Level Architecture

At this level, the computer system is viewed as a machine that implements the high-level architecture. The language used to write programs at this level is called an assembly language, which is a symbolic form for the language used in the immediate lower level, namely the ISA.

Assembly-level architecture effectively implements the notion of storage locations such as registers and memory. Its instructions are also more primitive than HLL statements. An instruction may, for instance, add two registers, move data from one memory location to another, or determine if a data value is greater than zero.

1.4.5 System or Instruction Set Architecture-Level Architecture

At this level, the computer system is viewed as a machine that can execute programs written in machine language. The memory model, IO model, and register model in the ISA are virtually identical to those in the assembly-level architecture. However, when specifying register and memory addresses in machine language, they are specified in binary encoding. The instructions in the ISA are also mainly binary encodings of the instructions present in the assembly-level architecture. Programs written in an assembly language are translated to machine language using a program called assembler.

The most commonly found ISA is the IA-32 ISA (or x86) introduced by Intel Corporation in 1979. Other ISAs that are in use today are IA-64, MIPS, Alpha, PowerPC, SPARC, and PA-RISC. ISAs that include fewer operations and addressing modes are often called reduced instruction set computer (RISC) ISAs. Those with a large repertoire of operations and addressing modes are often called complex instruction set computer (CISC) ISAs.

1.4.6 Machine or Microarchitecture-Level Architecture

At this level, the computer system is viewed as a machine that can interpret machine language instructions. A microarchitecture specification includes the resources and techniques used to realize the ISA specification, along with the way the resources are organized to realize the intended cost and performance goals. At this level, the viewer sees hardware objects such as the instruction fetch unit, register files, arithmetic logic units (ALUs), latches, cache memory, memory systems, IO interfaces, and interconnections, where

A *register file* is a collection of registers from which a single register can be read or written by specifying a register number.

An *ALU* is a combinational logic circuit that is capable of performing simple arithmetic and logical operations that are specified in machine language instructions.

The register file, ALU, and other components are connected using bus-type or point-to-point interconnections to form a *data path*. The basic operation of the data path consists of fetching an instruction from the main memory, decoding its bit pattern to determine what it specifies, and carrying out its execution by

- Fetching the required operands.
- Using the ALU to operate on the operand values.
- Storing back the result in the specified register or memory location.

The actual interpretation of the machine language instructions is done by a control unit, which controls and coordinates the activities of the data path. It issues commands to the data path to fetch, decode, and execute machine language instructions one by one.

There is a fundamental break at the ISA. Whereas the architectures above it are usually implemented by translation, the ISA and the architectures below it are always implemented by interpretation.

1.4.7 Control or Logic-Level Architecture

At this level, the computer system is viewed as a machine that can realize the computer microarchitecture in terms of actual microcode or digital logic and circuit designs using gates that accept one or more digital *inputs* and produce as *output* some logical function of the inputs:

- Several gates can be connected to form a multiplexer, decoder, programmable logic array (PLA), or other combinational logic circuits such as an adder. The outputs of an adder, subtractor, and other functional units can be passed through a multiplexer to obtain an ALU.
- A few gates can be connected together with some feedback arrangement to form a flip-flop or 1-bit memory, which can be used to store a 0 or a 1. Several flip-flops can be organized to form a register, and several registers can be organized to form a register file.
- Memory systems are built in a similar manner, but on a much larger scale.

Thus, the logic-level architecture uses a hierarchical approach to implementing the individual blocks of the microarchitecture.

Digital computers are typically designed as synchronous or clocked sequential circuits, meaning that they use clock signals to coordinate and synchronize the different activities in a computer. Changes in the machine state occur only at discrete times that are coordinated by the clock signals. Thus, the basic speed of a computer is determined by the time of one clock period. The clock speed of the processor used in the original IBM PC was 4.77 MHz. The clock speeds in current state-of-the-art computers range from 1 to 3.8 GHz. If all other specifications are identical, higher clock speeds mean faster processing.

1.4.8 Device-Level Architecture

At this level, the computer system is viewed as a machine that can realize logic-level architecture in terms of logic circuits using individual transistors and wires. Different types of transistor devices are available, for example, bipolar junction transistors (BJT) and metal-oxide-semiconductor field-effect transistors (MOSFET). Digital computer applications invariably use MOSFETs with different design styles. The most prevalent style is the complementary metal-oxide semiconductor (CMOS) approach, which uses a P-type metal-oxide semiconductor (PMOS) network and a complementary N-type metal-oxide semiconductor (NMOS) network.

One possible way of designing a device-level architecture involves taking the logic-level architecture and implementing it as follows: connect a few transistors together to form device-level circuitry that implements logic gates such as inverter, AND, OR, NAND, and NOR. Then, implement each logic gate in the logic-level architecture by the equivalent device-level circuitry.

Instead of attempting to implement the logic-level architecture, the very-large-scale integration (VLSI) designer takes the microarchitecture and implements the functional blocks in the microarchitecture with device-level circuitry. By bypassing the logic-level architecture, this approach leads to a more efficient design.

1.5 Application Programming Interfaces

Modern computing systems can be expressed in terms of the reference model described in Figure 1.1. The highest level of abstraction is represented by the API, which interfaces applications to libraries and/or the underlying OS. The application binary interface (ABI) separates the OS layer from the applications and libraries, which are managed by the OS. The ABI covers details such as low-level data types, alignment, and call conventions, and defines a format for executable programs. System calls are defined at this level. This interface allows the portability of applications and libraries across OSs that implement the same ABI. At the bottom layer, the model for the hardware is expressed in terms of the ISA, which defines the instruction set for the processor, registers, and memory, and interrupts management. The ISA is the interface between the hardware and software, and it is important to the OS developer (system ISA) and developers of applications who directly manage the underlying hardware (user ISA).

The API defines the set of instructions the hardware was designed to execute and gives the application access to the ISA. It includes HLL library calls, which often invoke system calls. A process is the abstraction for the code of an application at execution time; a thread is a lightweight process. The API is the projection of the system from the perspective of the HLL program and the ABI is the projection of the computer system seen by the process. Consequently, the binaries created by a compiler for a specific ISA and a specific OS are not portable. Such code cannot run on a computer with a different ISA or on computers with the same ISA but different OSs.

However, it is possible to compile a HLL program for a VM environment, where portable code is produced and distributed and then converted dynamically by binary translators to the ISA of the host system. A dynamic binary translation converts blocks of guest

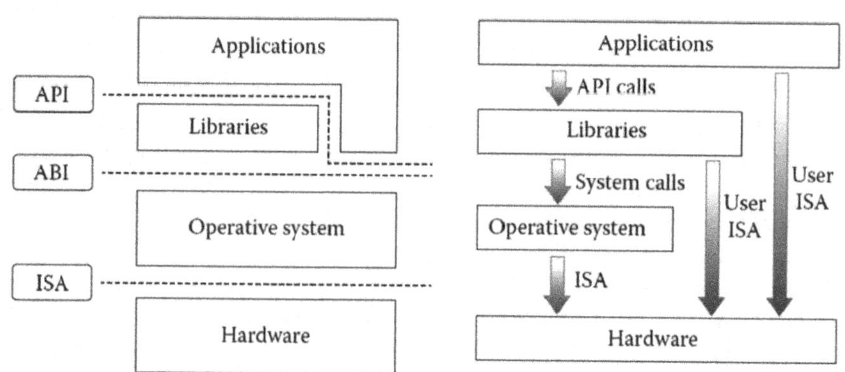

FIGURE 1.1
Layering and interfaces between the layers of a computer system.

instructions from the portable code to the host instruction and leads to a significant performance improvement as such blocks are cached and reused.

For any operation to be performed in the application-level API, ABI and ISA are responsible for making it happen. The high-level abstraction is converted into machine-level instructions to perform the actual operations supported by the processor. The machine-level resources, such as processor registers and main memory capacities, are used to perform the operation at the hardware level of the CPU. This layered approach simplifies the development and implementation of computing systems and simplifies the implementation of multitasking and the coexistence of multiple executing environments. In fact, such a model not only requires limited knowledge of the entire computing stack, but it also provides ways to implement a minimal security model for managing and accessing shared resources. For this purpose, the instruction set exposed by the hardware has been divided into different security classes that define who can operate them, namely, privileged and nonprivileged instructions.

Privileged instructions are those that are executed under specific restrictions and are mostly used for sensitive operations, which expose (behavior sensitive) or modify (control sensitive) the privileged state. For instance, behavior-sensitive instructions are those that operate on the I/O, whereas control-sensitive instructions alter the state of the CPU registers. Nonprivileged instructions are those instructions that can be used without interfering with other tasks because they do not access shared resources. For instance, this category contains all the floating, fixed-point, and arithmetic instructions.

All the current systems support at least two different execution modes: supervisor mode and user mode. The first mode denotes an execution mode in which all the instructions (privileged and nonprivileged) can be executed without any restriction. This mode, also called master mode or kernel mode, is generally used by the OS (or the hypervisor) to perform sensitive operations on hardware-level resources. In user mode, there are restrictions to control the machine-level resources. If code running in user mode invokes the privileged instructions, hardware interrupts occur and trap the potentially harmful execution of the instruction.

1.6 Summary

This introductory chapter began by discussing the various types of computers, namely, microcomputers, midrange computers, mainframe computers, and supercomputers. A general uniprocessor computer system is composed of hardware, software, and network. It examined the hardware components of a typical computer (CPU, memory, storage, GPU, etc.), focusing on issues relevant for algorithm design and software development to ultimately achieve efficient program execution and computer performance. A typical computer is composed of several important components that are connected to the computer's motherboard, including the CPU, the GPU, the memory, and the disk drive. The chapter then introduced the concept of hardware and software logical equivalence and discussed the *stack of abstraction* consisting of modeling-level, algorithm-level, high-level, assembly-level, system or ISA level, machine or microarchitecture-level, control or logic-level, and device-level architecture. The chapter concluded by introducing the concept of APIs. The API defines the set of instructions the hardware was designed to execute and gives the application access to the ISA.

2

Processor Physics and Moore's Law

The chapter commences with a discussion on aspects of processor physics, especially the relation between the speed of processing and the power problem. The chapter then looks at the various trade-offs, including area versus delay, delay versus power, and area versus delay versus power. The chapter proceeds to elaborate on Moore's law, which identifies the trend that "computing power would double every 2 years." The chapter concludes by combining the power wall, memory wall, and instruction-level parallelism (ILP) wall with the performance wall. In light of the performance wall, Moore's law is transformed to state that *the number of cores will double every two years* (or every fabrication technology).

2.1 Speed of Processing and Power Problem

The design of hardware is carried out in various stages, at different levels of abstraction. Among the two phases in the life of a program, namely development and execution, hardware designers are concerned with the execution phase. Well-designed hardware structures are those that have adequate performance/throughput and a long battery life (if running off a battery), and are compact and affordable. Other issues that have become important, depending on the computing environment, are binary compatibility, reliability, and security.

When designing hardware, the important factors are

- Performance

A key design parameter in hardware design is the speed with which computer systems execute programs. This can be measured in terms of *response time* and *throughput*.

Replacing a processor with a faster one would invariably decrease the program execution time (ET) as well as improve throughput. However, improving the throughput of a computer system does not necessarily result in a reduced response time. For instance, the throughput of a computer system improves when we incorporate additional processing cores and use these cores to execute independent tasks, but that does not decrease the ET of any single program.

Whereas the response time refers to how long the computer takes to do an activity, throughput refers to how much the computer does in unit time. The speed of a program execution can be measured in terms of

1. Response time: The response time is measured by the time elapsed from the initiation of some activity until its completion. A frequently used response time metric is program ET, which specifies the time the computer takes to execute the program once.

The ET of a program can be expressed as the product of three quantities:

- The number of instructions executed or the instruction count (IC).
- The average number of clock cycles required to execute an instruction or cycles per instruction (CPI).
- The duration of a clock cycle or cycle time (CT).

Thus,

$$ET = IC \times CPI \times CT$$

Although the resulting ET can give a fair estimate of the ET, it can be rendered invalid because of inaccuracies in any one of the constituent factors:

- The IC of a program may vary depending on the data values supplied as input to the program.
- The CPI obtained may vary depending on what other programs are simultaneously active in the system.
- The computer systems may dynamically adjust the clock CT (dynamic frequency scaling) in order to reduce the power consumption.

2. Throughput: Throughput specifies the number of programs, jobs, or transactions the computer system completes per unit time.

If the system completes C programs during an observation period of T seconds, its throughput X is measured as C/T programs/seconds. For processors, a more commonly used throughput measure is the number of instructions executed in a clock cycle, referred to as its instructions per cycle (IPC).

- Power consumption

  Power is an important issue because it directly translates into heat production. Most integrated circuits will fail to work correctly if the temperature rises beyond a few degrees. Power consumption has two components:

  - Dynamic power consumption relates to power consumed when there is switching activity (or change of state) in a system. Dynamic power is directly proportional to the extent of switching activity in the system and the clock frequency of operation. It is also proportional to the capacitance in the circuits and wires, and to the square of the supply voltage of the circuits.
  - Static power consumption relates to power consumed even when there is no switching activity in the system. Static power consumption occurs due to leakage currents in the system. With continued scaling in transistor technology—reduction in transistor sizes—static power consumption is becoming comparable to dynamic power consumption. Static power consumption is also related to the supply voltage. Therefore, to develop low-power systems, computer hardware designers strive to reduce the supply voltage of the circuits as well as to reduce the amount of hardware complexity used to perform the required functionality.

- Price

  All things being equal, between two comparable computer systems, price will be an important factor. The major factors affecting the price are

- Design cost
- Manufacturing cost
- Profit margin

All of these are impacted by the sales volume. In general, price increases exponentially with the complexity of the system. Thus, it is imperative to reduce hardware complexity at all costs.

- Size
  Size is an important design consideration, especially for laptops and embedded systems.

2.2 Area, Delay, and Power Consumption

This section provides an overview of techniques for determining area, delay, and energy consumption. Since these three are not independent, the latter half of the section discusses their dependencies, that is, the trade-offs between them.

2.2.1 Area Consumption

Over the years, as chip area and transistor densities have grown steadily, area consumption has remained one of the primary design constraints, because it directly impacts the cost of processing and yield.

The total area used for a circuit can be classified into

- Gate area consumption: Depending on the level of detail available, the different methods and techniques used are
  - Transistor counting technique: This estimate gives a lower bound of the total area (area due to interconnect and gaps between cells is not taken into account). If a net list is available, the area of the design can be estimated by counting the number of transistors used and by multiplying the result with the area of a single transistor.
  - Complexity-based techniques: Different measures and approaches exist to express the area complexity in terms of the known properties of the function to be implemented. For instance, it is assumed that the area complexity of a Boolean function corresponds to the minimum number of gates required to implement the function and thus can serve as a valid estimate of the gate count. Once the area for the combinatorial part of a design has been estimated, the area needed for the registers and other memory elements is also considered. However, to accommodate typical very long instruction word (VLIW) circuits, the model is extended by adding information about the area of the Boolean function. In order to apply this technique to multi-output Boolean functions, a multi-output function is transformed into an equivalent single-output function—the transformation amounts to adding a multiplexer to the

circuit and calculating the linear measure for the result. Finally, the additional area of the multiplexer is considered.

- Rent's rule: An empirical method to predict the area of a circuit is based on the number of pins T of the circuit given by Rent's rule defined by

$$G = \left(\frac{T}{t}\right)^{\frac{1}{p}}$$

- where the Rent coefficient t is interpreted as the average number of terminals required by a single gate and p is known as the Rent exponent. An estimate of the area can be made based on the number of pins of the circuit:

$$T = t \cdot G^p$$

- Interconnect consumption: An a priori estimation technique for interconnects, called Donath's method, recursively applies Rent's rule to estimate the average lengths, $\bar{l}_k$, and the expected number of interconnections, $\bar{n}_k$, at each level k of the design hierarchy. Using these, the average length, $\bar{L}$, of the interconnect is calculated as

$$\bar{L} = \frac{\sum_{k=0}^{K-1} \bar{n}_k \bar{l}_k}{\sum_{k=0}^{K-1} \bar{n}_k}$$

Donath's model can be refined to accommodate placement information corresponding to gates that are interconnected being placed closer together. This would result in lower length interconnections.

The estimation of interconnect consumption is important as it directly impacts the three main design constraints:

- *Area consumption: The wires have to be placed somewhere on the chip. Especially structures such as busses require a large area.*
- *Delay consumption: The propagation delay is directly dependent on the length of the wires.*
- *Power consumption: The capacitance and resistance of the wires are dependent on the length of the wires, thus longer wires require more energy to transport a signal value.*

2.2.2 Delay Consumption

For all systems, timing is a critical design constraint; in particular, real-time systems are expected to generate a response within a specified maximum delay after applying a stimulus. This section focuses on the delay estimation for synchronous circuits.

The delay or ET of a synchronous circuit can be expressed in two ways:

- The CT, which is the period of the fastest clock that can be applied to the circuit, without introducing errors.
- The latency, which is the time required to execute operations, expressed in terms of clock cycles.

Delay estimation techniques can be subdivided into two main categories:

- Delay estimation for individual resources constituting the system

  In synchronous circuits, sources of delay are

  - Gate delay is the time it takes a gate to switch from one level to another.

    With the lowering of the supply voltage, the gate delay increases as

$$\tau_{\Delta} = \frac{C_L \cdot V_{\Delta}}{\beta(V_G - V_T)^a} \approx \frac{C_L}{\beta \cdot \gamma^a V_{dd}^{a-1}}$$

where:

V_G is the gate voltage
V_T is the threshold voltage of the transistor
β is a transistor-dependent parameter
V_{dd} is the supply voltage

Using $V_{\Delta} \approx V_{dd}$ and $V_G - V_T \approx \gamma V_{dd}$, the gate delay is inversely proportional with the supply voltage:

$$\tau_{\Delta} a \frac{1}{V_{dd}^{a-1}}$$

Thus, the gate delay can be lowered by increasing the supply voltage, that is, by increasing the driving power. However, this has an even more serious impact on the power consumption of a circuit.

  - Propagation delay is the time needed to transport a signal over a certain distance on a chip. With ever-decreasing feature sizes and ever higher switching speeds, the propagation delay becomes increasingly important. Resistance–capacitance (RC) trees are commonly used to model an interconnect.

- Delay estimation for the whole system

  As soon as the CT and latencies of the resources have been estimated, an estimate can be made of the delay of a system composed of those resources. In most cases, the execution order of the resources is not yet known and therefore a schedule has to be made—different scheduling strategies evoke different delays. Once the schedule is known, the latency of the circuit is known. Additionally, if the CT is known, an estimate is available for the total delay of the whole system.

The scheduling problem can be formulated as follows: given a set of tasks and resources, an ordering of tasks and assignment to resources has to be found while satisfying a set of given constraints; constraints can be applied separately or simultaneously. Constraints can be anything ranging from minimizing total latency, restricting the number of resources, to hard deadlines for certain tasks.

Depending on the constraints, different scheduling strategies are applicable:

- Unconstrained scheduling aims to find the minimum latency schedule. There are no constraints, either on the number of resources or on the time limits to be met. Unconstrained minimum latency scheduling can be solved in polynomial time by applying the as soon as possible (ASAP) scheduling algorithm.

- Time-constrained scheduling enforces only time constraints. The number of resources is not limited. There are two types of time-constrained scheduling:
  - Latency-constrained scheduling specifies a global maximum latency constraint. This scheduling problem can be solved by running the ASAP algorithm and by verifying that its solution meets the latency constraint.
  - Scheduling under timing constraints specifies additional constraints for the individual resources. These timing constraints can be either absolute or relative. Scheduling under absolute timing constraints can be solved using the Bellman–Ford algorithm.
- Resource-constrained scheduling arises from resource-limited circuits, typically incurred by constraints on the total chip area. The number of resources necessary to implement a circuit largely determines the area used by the circuit. Therefore, resource-constrained scheduling can be used to find delay versus area trade-offs (Section 1.3.1).

Resource-constrained scheduling is intractable, but several exact algorithms and heuristics exist to come up with an approximate solution in reasonable time including:

- Integer linear programming algorithms
- List scheduling
- Force-directed scheduling

2.2.3 Power Consumption

Several power estimation techniques exist for very-large-scale integration (VLSI) and can be applied at different levels in the design flow. In order to properly design for low power, one needs feedback in the form of power estimation techniques. A number of approaches are available to estimate the power consumption of a design.

Except for the technique of direct measurement of the power consumption, all techniques rely on models of the power dissipation in an IC. Power dissipation in complementary metal-oxide semiconductor (CMOS) ICs can be divided into three main categories.

- Static power dissipation: Under ideal conditions, a CMOS circuit does not dissipate any power when it is not switching. However, in reality, a certain amount of power is always lost due to a number of mechanisms such as leakage currents and substrate injection currents. These currents cause a static power dissipation component in CMOS circuits.
- Dynamic power dissipation: Capacitance charging is the dominating factor in power dissipation in CMOS circuits. Every time switching occurs, parasitic capacitances are either charged or discharged. The energy required to charge the capacitors is drawn from the power supply. Hence, power is dissipated when capacitances are charged. The amount of dissipated power depends on the size of the parasitic capacitances and the voltage swing.
- Activity-based power dissipation: Dynamic power dissipation is the dominating factor in the total power dissipation of a circuit. The energy needed to charge these capacitances gives an estimate of the dissipation in the circuit.
- Capacitance charging:

The energy dissipation due to the charging of capacitances in CMOS gates is given by

$$E = E_{\mathrm{C}} + E_{\mathrm{R}} = C_{\mathrm{L}} V_{\mathrm{dd}} V_{\Delta}$$

Assuming the voltage swing approximately equals the supply voltage, that is, $V_{\Delta} \approx V_{\mathrm{dd}}$, leads to

$$E \approx C_{\mathrm{L}} V_{\mathrm{dd}}^{2}$$

Thus, the approximate dissipated energy only depends on the capacitive load and the supply voltage, it is not impacted by the gate-specific or transistor-specific parameters such as the channel width or length of a field-effect transistor (FET).

- Load capacitance: If an output of a gate switches from a low to a high level, the capacitances that have to be charged are
  - Output capacitance of the gate
  - Input capacitances of the connected gates
- Wire capacitances of the interconnect

Thus, the total capacitance charged by gate C_{L} is

$$C_{\mathrm{L}} = C_{\mathrm{out}}^{O} + C_{\mathrm{wire}} + C_{\mathrm{in}}$$

where:

C_{out}^{O} is the output capacitance of the driving gate
C_{wire} is the capacitance due to the interconnect
C_{in} the total input capacitance of the gates being driven

Considering that the interconnect capacitance is modeled by an output wire capacitance, C_{wire}^{O}, and the sum of the input wire capacitances, $C_{\mathrm{wire}}^{I_i}$, and the input capacitance of the gates being driven is given by the sum of the input capacitances of every gate, $C_{\mathrm{in}}^{I_i}$, the total capacitance charged by gate C_{L} becomes

$$C_{\mathrm{L}} = C_{\mathrm{out}}^{O} + C_{\mathrm{wire}}^{O} + \sum_{i=1}^{N} \left(C_{\mathrm{wire}}^{I_i} + C_{\mathrm{in}}^{I_i} \right)$$

Thus, the total switched capacitance of a circuit can be calculated by summing the switched input, output, and wire capacitances per gate.

- Circuit-level power dissipation: The total energy dissipated in a large integrated circuit is given by

$$E = \sum_{i=1}^{N} a_i C_{\mathrm{L}_i} V_{\mathrm{dd}}^{2}$$

where:

N is the number of nodes in the circuit
a_i is the number of times the ith node switches from a low to a high level
C_{L_i} is the load capacitance of node i

The load capacitance is approximated by the average load capacitance given by

$$C_{L_i} \approx \bar{C}_L = \frac{C}{N}$$

where C represents the total capacitance.
Substituting for in the earlier equation gives the total energy consumed by the circuit:

$$E \approx \frac{1}{N}\sum_{i=1}^{N} a_i C V_{dd}^2 = \alpha C V_{dd}^2$$

where:

- a is the average switching activity of the circuit
- C is the average total switched capacitance
- V_{dd} is the supply voltage

- System-level power dissipation: A major obstacle in estimating the energy or power consumption at a high level is that, in general, detailed structural information of the design is still lacking. This kind of information is usually only available after scheduling, and the final net list only after a full synthesis step. Although they are more accurate, it takes too much time to compute these estimates so they cannot be used for a quick estimate in an iterative process.

However, if a design is constructed using fixed sub-circuits, the time needed to estimate the cost figures of a sub-circuit once may be acceptable with respect to the overall design time. If the sub-circuits have been used in a previous design, these numbers might even be available beforehand.

Nevertheless, if only the functional description is available, simulation is currently the most obvious way to quickly estimate the power consumption of a design.

2.3 Area, Latency, and Power Trade-offs

The area, delay, and power of a circuit are strongly interdependent. As a result, design constraints are often in conflict and trade-offs have to be made (Figure 2.1).

2.3.1 Area versus Delay Trade-off

Traditionally, area and delay have been the primary cost and performance measures of a design. Even though power consumption has emerged as an important design issue recently, trade-offs between area and delay continue to be of importance in most designs.

- Circuit techniques

  Circuit techniques are used to modify the area and delay of a given circuit without changing the circuit behavior.

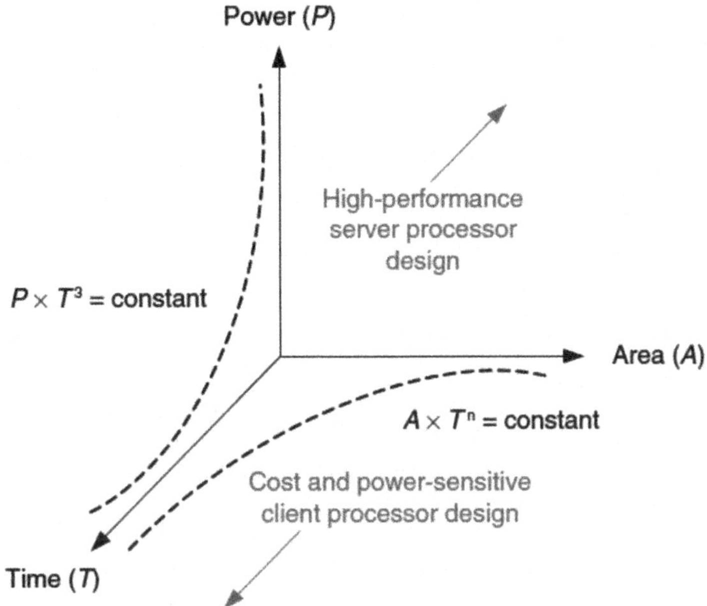

FIGURE 2.1
Processor design trade-offs.

- Retiming is the process of modifying a synchronous network by shifting, adding, or deleting registers. Retiming can be applied to achieve different optimization goals:
  - CT minimization involves the reduction delay of the longest path (not interrupted by registers) in the circuit. This is done by shifting the registers such that the longest path is shortened or replaced by another path, thereby reducing the path delay.
- Area minimization involves leveraging retiming itself for area minimization, as adding or removing registers, respectively, increases or decreases the area of the circuit.

Since, CT and area minimization are interdependent, combined area and delay optimization requires combinatorial optimization to remove combinatorial bottlenecks in the circuit followed by retiming to meet the CT requirements.

- Pipelining is a technique used to increase the throughput of a circuit, which is defined as the number of data samples processed per clock cycle. While pipelining does not reduce the delay of a circuit per se, given an increased throughput after pipelining, the CT of the circuit can be lowered to get the same overall processing rate (data samples per time unit). However, pipelining is not free and invariably increases the area of the circuit because of the extra registers and control logic needed.

- Area-time (AT) bounds

  Based on three different categories of information processing capabilities of a circuit with a certain area A and a certain execution delay T, the three categories of lower bounds are

- Limited memory: A circuit can only *remember* a limited number of bits from one time step to the next. This number of bits is proportional to the area. Thus,

$$A = \text{constant}$$

- Limited input/output (IO): A circuit can only process and generate a limited number of inputs and outputs. This number is proportional to the product of the area and the delay. Thus,

$$AT = \text{constant}$$

  For instance, to read n-input ports, one needs n-input terminals for a single time unit, or only one input port for n time units.

- Limited information exchange: The amount of information that can flow from one part of the area to the other in a single time unit is limited to the square root of the area. Thus, the total information flow is limited to the product of the square root of the area and the delay. Thus,

$$AT^2 = \text{constant}$$

An equivalent interpretation is that the number of interconnections (wires) is limited to the square root of the area (i.e., the largest possible value for the shortest side of a rectangular area).

Experimentally, the first two bounds have been ascertained to be fairly good approximations. However, in the case of the third bound, almost all experiments showed the following relationship:

$$AT^r = \text{constant},$$

where r varies between 1.2 and 1.5.

2.3.2 Delay versus Power Trade-off

The average power used by the circuit is defined by

$$P = \frac{E}{T}.$$

Using the approximate value of the total energy E consumed by a circuit in T time, gives

$$P = a\frac{CV_{\text{dd}}^2}{T}.$$

This expression clearly shows the dependence between the power usage, the supply voltage, and the execution delay of the circuit.

Once a circuit is implemented, its power can be reduced by

- Frequency scaling

Power can be reduced by increasing the execution delay T.

In a synchronous circuit the frequency f is given by

$$f = \frac{1}{T}$$

which results in

$$P \propto f$$

Thus, the power linearly depends on the frequency and it can be reduced linearly by decreasing the frequency.

- Voltage scaling

  Scaling down the supply voltage of the circuit, the corresponding power scales quadratically. As indicated earlier, with the lowering of the supply voltage, the gate delay increases as

$$\tau_\Delta \propto \frac{1}{V_{\mathrm{dd}}^{\alpha-1}}$$

  As a result, the power is reduced even more, ultimately resulting in a cubic dependency on the supply voltage:

$$P \propto V_{\mathrm{dd}}^3$$

The voltage cannot be reduced indefinitely because when the supply voltage approaches the threshold voltages of the transistors, the robustness of the transistors against noise is severely lowered and proper circuit behavior is compromised.

2.3.3 Area versus Delay versus Power Trade-off

The chapter has discussed factors regarding power consumption for already implemented circuits and consequently the area was assumed to be fixed. However, if the area is not fixed, the influence of the area on the capacitance and delay must also be taken into account.

The equation for AT bounds can be generalized to

$$AT^r = \gamma \text{ and } P = a\frac{CV_{\mathrm{dd}}^2}{T}.$$

where r and γ are constants.

There are two optional scenarios depending on whether the supply voltage is kept constant or is scaled:

- Constant voltage: The average total capacitance in the circuit can be assumed to be linearly dependent on the total area of the circuit.

  This gives the area and power as the function of the delay:

$$A = \frac{\gamma}{T^r}, \quad P = a\mu_c\gamma\frac{V_{\mathrm{dd}}^2}{T^{r+1}}$$

- Scaled voltage: Assuming
  - The average latency per gate T_g is given by

$$T_g = \frac{C_g}{\beta V_{dd}}$$

where C_g is the average load capacitance per gate and β is a constant.

  - The total delay of the circuit is linearly dependent on the gate delay:

$$T = c_T T_g$$

where c_T is some constant.

The total capacitance is linearly dependent on the product of the average gate capacitance and the area:

$$C_{aV} = \mu_s C_g A$$

where μ_s is another constant.

The latency, area, and power as a function of the supply voltage or delay is given by

$$T = \frac{c_T C_g}{\beta V_{dd}}, \quad A = \frac{\gamma}{T^r}, \quad P = a\mu_s\gamma\left(\frac{cT}{\beta}\right)^2 \frac{C_g^3}{T^{r+3}}$$

2.4 Moore's Law

On April 19, 1965, Gordon Moore, cofounder of Intel Corporation, published an article in *Electronics Magazine* entitled "Cramming More Components onto Integrated Circuits," in which he identified and conjectured a trend that computing power would double every two years (this was termed Moore's law in 1970 by Calvin Mead, CalTech professor and VLSI pioneer). This law has been able to reliably predict both the reduction in costs and the improvements in the computing capability of microchips, and those predictions have held true (Figure 2.2).

In 1965, the amount of transistors that fitted on an integrated circuit could be counted in tens. In 1971, Intel introduced the 4004 microprocessor with 2300 transistors. In 1978, when Intel introduced the 8086 microprocessor, the IBM PC was effectively born (the first IBM PC used the 8088 chip), which had 29,000 transistors. In 2006, Intel's Itanium 2 processor carried 1.7 billion transistors. In the next two years, we will have chips with over 10 billion transistors. What does this mean? Transistors are now so small that millions could fit on the head of a pin. While all this was happening, the cost of these transistors was also exponentially falling, as per Moore's prediction (Figure 2.3).

In real terms, this means that a mainframe computer from the 1970s that cost over US$1 million had less computing power than an iPhone has today. The next generation of smartphone that we will be using in the next two to three years will have 1 GHz processor

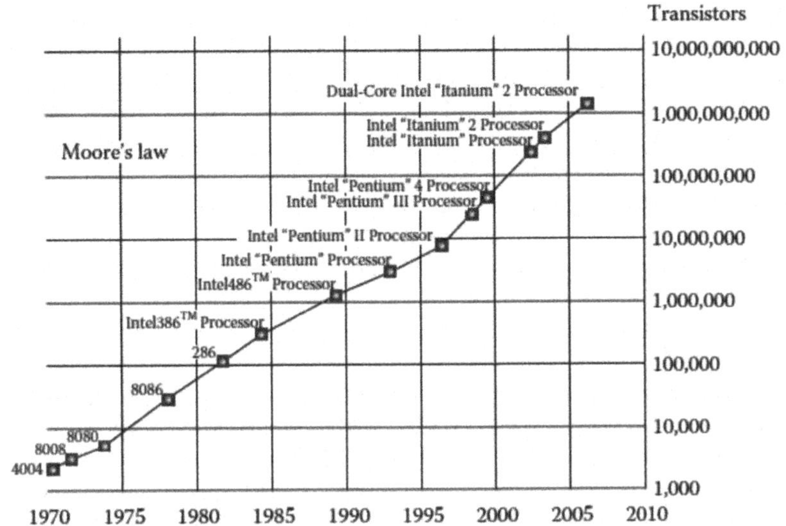

FIGURE 2.2
Increase in the number of transistors on an Intel chip.

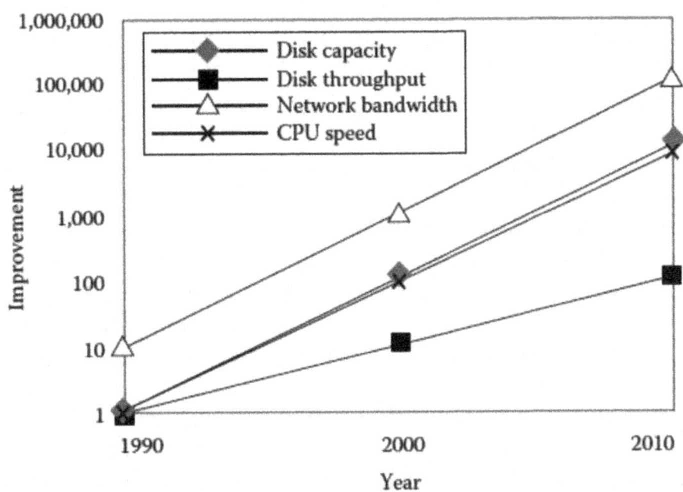

FIGURE 2.3
Hardware trends in the 1990s and the last decade.

chips, which is roughly one million times faster than the Apollo Guidance Computer. Theoretically, for a number of reasons, Moore's law will run out of steam somewhere in the not too distant future. Firstly, the ability of a microprocessor silicon-etched track or circuit to carry an electrical charge has a theoretical limit.

At some point when these circuits get physically too small and can no longer carry a charge or the electrical charge bleeds, we will have a design limitation problem. Secondly, as successive generations of chip technology are developed, manufacturing costs increase. In fact, Gordon Moore had said that each new generation of chips requires a doubling in cost of the manufacturing facility as tolerances become tighter. At some point, it will theoretically become too costly to develop the manufacturing plants that produce these chips. The usable limit for semiconductor process technology will be reached when chip process geometries shrink to be smaller than 20 nanometers (nm), to 18 nm nodes. At these nodes, the industry will start getting to the point where semiconductor manufacturing tools are too expensive to depreciate with volume production; that is, their costs will be so high that the value of their lifetime productivity will never justify it. Lastly, the power requirements of chips are also increasing. More power being equivalent to more heat equivalent to bigger batteries implies that at some point, it becomes increasingly difficult to power these chips while putting them on smaller platforms.

2.4.1 Leveraging Moore's Law

Moore's law has been leveraged to offer continually increasing single-thread microprocessor performance. For instance, in the 90 nm CMOS technology node, several companies were able to produce multi-instruction issuing superscalar microprocessors with 64-bit addressing and up to a megabyte of cache memory running in excess of 2 GHz. The dramatic increase in operating frequency and micro-architectural complexity was accompanied by a significant increase in power consumption. Overall, this sets practical limits on how much power a given central processing unit (CPU) socket can effectively handle in an economically feasible way.

Although Moore's law continued to offer more integrated transistors with each new technology node, the prospects of deeper pipelining to increase frequency, more advanced micro-architectural structures to increase ILP, and larger caches to increase locality characteristics were all at the point of diminishing returns with respect to their costs. This led computer architects and designers to look beyond the microprocessor core for ways to improve performance and value.

An immediate area of focus was the memory system. While there has always been a recognized balance between data availability from the memory system and computation, the gap between the cycle time of commodity dynamic random-access memory (DRAM) chips and those of microprocessors had widened significantly. This gap created very long latencies for accesses from the memory system to the microprocessor core—if the data cannot be supplied at an appropriate rate and/or time, a processor's powerful execution capability is immaterial. Frequent waits for memory data return can significantly degrade the overall performance of the system.

Consequently, computer architects have focused a great deal of attention on improving the performance of the overall memory system. The use of on-chip multilevel cache hierarchies allowed designers to deploy larger overall cache footprints without disrupting the sensitive power and size constraints of the innermost L1 caches. The deployment of various hardware- and software-based prefetching mechanisms enabled the speculative access of memory ahead of the demand usage to minimize wait time and latency. The optimization of the memory controller to support more outstanding requests and to schedule requests that take maximum advantage of the DRAM-banked structures enabled designers to shave additional latency from these critical memory references (see Section 3.3.4 and 3.3.5).

Although these memory system optimizations offered some important performance improvements, they also hit the inevitable limits of diminishing returns. As each new technology node continued to offer more transistors, computer architects were compelled to find new ways to make the most effective use of them. Considering that many higher-end computer systems had made good use of multiple CPU chips to form symmetric multiprocessor (SMP) systems for decades, the integration of multiple microprocessor cores on the chip signaled the start of the chip multiprocessing (CMP) era in computer architecture.

2.4.1.1 Reconfigurable Computing

The job of the computer architect is to define the hardware/software interface and to exploit technology trends to translate them into enhanced computer performance and reliability, reduced power consumption, etc. For decades, computer architects translated the abundance of transistors afforded by Moore's law (doubling of the performance every two years) into performance. The reason why this was so successful is because of a layered approach that had been followed in computer engineering (see Chapter 1: Section 1.4), which isolated changes in any particular layer from all other layers. Unfortunately, in the past decade this very successful run has come to an abrupt end, and the main reason for this is power consumption. Reconfigurable computing now becomes a viable option because its benefits (power efficiency) outweigh its disadvantages.

The inability to scale a single core to further exploit ILP in a power-efficient manner turned computer architecture toward multicore and many-core architectures. However, the multicore revolution by itself cannot solve the power problem because of the *single-core architecture*–type inefficiencies that reappear as the number of cores is scaled up: multicore are unable to extract sufficient speedup from parallel programs (see "Amdahl's law" in Section 3.2.1). The response to this newer challenge is heterogeneous architectures where specific functions are accelerated (performance) by dedicated hardware (power efficiency). These architectures are fast becoming the dominant paradigm after multicore.

The catalyst for the proliferation of heterogeneous architectures is a possible development in the near future, called dark silicon. Given a fixed power budget, only a small portion of the chip will be powered up at any point in time. This, however, allows unprecedented flexibility for specialization, because a large number of accelerators can be built on the same chip to be woken up only when needed.

Beyond tuning the architecture for the domain, astonishing efficiency gains can be obtained if the architecture is matched to the problem. Graphics processors have long leveraged this application–architecture synergy by applying massively data-parallel processors to an inherently data-parallel problem, thereby achieving 10–100× gains in efficiency.

2.5 Performance Wall

Up to the early 2000s, the approach taken by manufacturers such as Intel was to design a highly complex superscalar processor with techniques for simultaneous operation coupled with using a state-of-the-art fabrication technology to obtain the highest chip density and clock frequency. However, this approach was coming to an end. With clock frequencies reaching almost 4 GHz, technology was not going to provide a continual path upward because of the laws of physics and increasing power consumption that come with increasing clock frequency and transistor count.

For decades, architects translated Moore's law into performance, but we are now close to hitting three major walls.

2.5.1 Power Wall

The power consumption of a chip has a static component (leakage currents) and a dynamic component due to switching. Dynamic power consumption is proportional to the clock frequency, the square of the voltage switched, and the capacitive load. Therefore, each increase in clock frequency will directly increase the power consumption. Voltages have been reduced as a necessary part of the decreased feature sizes of the fabrication technology, reducing the power consumption. As the feature size of the chip decreases, the static power becomes more significant and can be 40% of the total power. By the mid-2000s, it had become increasing difficult to limit the power consumption while improving clock frequencies and performance.

The power wall reflects the inability to significantly reduce power consumption (and more importantly power density). The power wall is likely to lead us to a "dark silicon" future where the majority of the transistors on a chip will have to be turned off because of power constraints.

2.5.2 Memory Wall

The memory wall reflects the fact that current memory technology can be fast or vast, but not both at the same time; this leads to a complex memory hierarchy that is also plagued with its own significant limitations.

The *memory wall* is caused by the increasing difference between the processor speed and the memory access times. The semiconductor main memory has not kept up with the increasing speed of processors. Some of this can be alleviated by using caches and often nowadays multilevel caches, but still it poses a major obstacle.

2.5.3 Instruction-Level Parallelism Wall

The *instruction-level parallelism* wall is caused by the increasing difficulty to exploit more parallelism within an instruction sequence.

All these walls combine leading to the performance wall:

Power wall + Memory wall + Instruction-Level parallelism wall = Performance wall

for a sequential processor.

This motivates the emergence of the multicore approach for using the ever-increasing number of transistors on a chip. Moore's law originally predicted that the number of transistors on an integrated circuit chip would double approximately every two years. Now, Moore's law gets transformed to state that *the number of cores will double every two years* (or every fabrication technology).

2.6 Summary

This chapter commenced by discussing aspects of processor physics, especially the relation between the speed of processing and the power problem. The chapter then looked at the various trade-offs including area versus delay, delay versus power, and area versus delay versus power. The chapter then elaborated on Moore's law, which identifies the trend that "computing power would double every 2 years." The chapter concluded by combining the power wall, memory wall, and ILP wall into the performance wall. In light of the performance wall, Moore's law gets transformed to state that *the number of cores will double every two years* (or every fabrication technology).

Section I

Genesis of Parallel Computing

This section presents an overview of the genesis of parallel computing.

Chapter 3 looks at the characteristics of uniprocessors and measures to enhance their performance: improving the central processing unit (CPU) performance, increasing the processor clock frequency, parallelizing the arithmetic logic unit (ALU) structure, pipelining, memory hierarchy, cache memory, very long instruction word (VLIW) processors, superscalarity, instruction-level parallelism (ILP), multicore architectures, and multithreading.

Chapter 4 discusses network principles (such as protocols, protocol layers, and protocol suites), types of networks (personal area network [PAN], local area network [LAN], metropolitan area network [MAN], wide area network [WAN]), and both network models (Open Systems Interconnection [OSI] and Transmission Control Protocol/Internet Protocol [TCP/IP] reference models).

Chapter 5 provides an introduction to distributed systems. The unification of parallel and distributed computing allows one to harness a set of networked and heterogeneous computers and present them as a unified resource. Architectural styles help categorize and provide reference models for distributed systems. The fundamental deployment blocks of any distributed system are system architectural styles concerned with the physical deployment of such systems, and software architectural styles that define the logical organization of components and their roles. Message-based communication is the most relevant abstraction for interprocess communication (IPC) and forms the basis for several IPC techniques, which is a fundamental element in distributed systems. It is the element that ties together separate processes and allows them to be seen as a unified whole.

3

Processor Basics

Understanding the performance of programs is very complex today because writing a program with the aim of improving its performance involves a good deal of knowledge about the underlying principles and the organization of a given computer. The performance of a program is a combination of excellent algorithms, their good codification using a computer language, the compiler that serves to translate programs to machine instructions, and the efficacy of the computer in executing those instructions, which may include input/output (I/O) operations (see Chapter 1: Section 1.4.5).

To cope with today's complex computer systems, hardware and software designers use hierarchical layers where each layer hides details from the above layer. In general, the goal is to find a language that facilitates building the hardware and the compiler that maximizes performance while minimizing cost (see Chapter 1: Section 1.4).

3.1 Processor

A processor is characterized by its word length, operation frequency, and memory capacity.

- *Word length* indicates the number of bits that a computer system can handle to perform low-level operations, in particular; modern personal computers use 32 and 64 bits. However, there are other kinds of computer systems based on microcontroller units (MCUs), or in digital signal processors (DSPs) that use 4, 8, 24, and 32 bits of word length.
- Clock frequency is a measure that indicates the speed of executing the basic operations of a particular computer system; it is measured in Hertz. Although high clock speeds are associated with faster code execution, this does not necessarily mean a performance increase because the processor temperature rises, reducing the computational performance. Nowadays, multicore technology is used to obtain a good performance in the frequency ranges of 1–4 GHz.
- Memory refers to any kind of storing device of binary data, such as transistors, capacitors, and other electronic components. The memory together with the central processing unit (CPU) is regarded as one of the most important factors in the overall computer performance. It can be external to the CPU such as the random-access memory (RAM), or within the circuitry of the CPU itself such as registers and the L1 cache. *Primary* and *secondary* storage have been used, respectively, to denote memory and mass storage devices such as hard drives. Memory serves to store programs and data while the CPU is processing them, and is known as RAM. It is typically an integrated circuit (IC) or a package of ICs that are used to store binary data.

- Volatile memory is not permanent; the stored data is lost when power is removed.
    - Dynamic RAM (DRAM): DRAMs are asynchronous and have been used in personal computers (PCs) since IBM PC days. They do not need to be synchronized to the system clock, which controls how often the processor can receive data; they work fine in low-speed memory bus systems but are not nearly as suitable for use in high-speed (>66 MHz) memory systems.
    - Synchronous DRAM (SDRAM): SDRAM is synchronized to the system clock; SDRAMs are much faster than asynchronous DRAMs and are used to improve the performance of the system. SDRAMs are inexpensive to produce since the circuits inside them use one transistor and one capacitor to create a memory cell to represent a single bit of data. The capacitors of the SDRAM need to be recharged (refreshed) thousands of times per second to maintain the content, and these refreshment cycles produce slow access time.
- Static RAM (SRAM): SRAM consists of flip-flops, with each flip-flop composed of four to six transistors in a special arrangement of wires, and each can hold 1 bit of memory. An advantage of SRAM is that it does not need to be refreshed, resulting in much faster access times. A disadvantage is that it needs more space on chip than SDRAM since each memory cell requires more components. Consequently, the user gets less memory per chip, making SRAM chips larger and more expensive than SDRAM chips. Typical use of SRAM is the computer's L2 cache. SRAM can be purchased in ICs in the form of a dual in-line package (DIP) or module packages similar to dual in-line memory modules (DIMMs). The market for SRAM is mainly reserved for electronic hobbyists and IC manufacturers, because this kind of memory is of no practical use to the average PC consumer as the L2 cache in a PC cannot be upgraded.
- Non-volatile memory; the stored data remains even after power has been removed.
    - Electrically erasable programmable read-only memory (EEPROM) IC chips are built in such a way that they can trap electrons inside the circuit, which allows it to hold onto its data without an external power supply. EEPROM data can be accessed (read/write) 1 byte at a time.
    - Flash memory is a particular type of EEPROM; flash memory is logically structured like a storage device, with data divided into sectors of 512-byte blocks; consequently, data is read/write 512 bytes at a time. Flash memory is often used in portable electronics, such as smartphones, digital cameras, and digital music devices. This technology is also useful for computer basic input/output systems (BIOS) and personal computer memory cards.

3.2 Aspects of Processor Performance

3.2.1 Potential for Speedup

The central question is how much faster does the multiprocessor system perform over a single processor system.

This can be reflected in the speedup factor, $S(p)$ given by

$$S(p) = \frac{\text{Execution time using a single processor}}{\text{Execution time using a multiprocessor with p processors}}$$

$$= \frac{t_s}{t_p}$$

where:
t_s is the execution time on a single processor
t_p is the execution time on a system with p processors

A speedup factor of p with p processors is called linear speedup. Conventional wisdom is that the speedup factor should not be greater than p because if a problem is divided into p parts, each executed on one processor of a p-processor system and $t_p < t_s/p$, then the same parts could be executed one after the other on a single processor system in time less than t_s.

When evaluating the speedup factor, the best-known equivalent sequential algorithm employing a single processor must be used because the parallel algorithm is unlikely to perform as well on a single processor. The classical way of evaluating sequential algorithms is by using the time complexity notation, but it is less effective for a parallel algorithm because of uncertainties such as communication times between cooperating parallel processes.

In 1967, Amdahl explored what the maximum speedup would be when a sequential computation is divided into parts and these parts are executed on different processors. Amdahl assumed that a computation has sections that cannot be divided into parallel parts and these must be performed sequentially on a single processor, and other sections that can be divided equally among the available processors.

This is not comparing the best sequential algorithm with a particular parallel algorithm—it is comparing a particular computation mapped onto a single computer and mapped onto a system having multiple processors.

Let f be the fraction of the whole computation that must be executed sequentially, that is, it cannot be divided into parallel parts. Hence, the fraction that can be divided into parts is $1 - f$. If the whole computation executed on a single computer in time t_s, ft_s is indivisible and $(1 - f)t_s$ is divisible. The ideal situation is when the divisible section is divided equally among the available processors and then this section would be executed in time $(1-f)t_s/p$, where p is the number of processors. The total execution time using p processors is $ft_s + (1-f)t_s/p$.

The speedup factor is given by Amdahl's law:

$$S(p) = \frac{t_s}{ft_s + (1-f)t_s/p} = \frac{1}{f + (1-f)/p} = \frac{p}{1 + (p-1)f}$$

The significant implication of Amdahl's law is that as p increases and tends to infinity, $S(p)$ tends to a limit of $1/f$. In other words, suppose the sequential part is 5% of the whole, the maximum speedup obtainable is 20 *irrespective of the number of processors.*

3.2.2 Scalability

Scalability is usually used to indicate a hardware design that allows the system to be increased in size to obtain a more *efficient* performance; this is described as hardware or architectural scalability. Equivalently, scalability can also be used to indicate an (parallel) algorithmic design that allows the data to be increased in size to obtain a more *effective* performance. Increasing the problem size improves the relative performance because it entails greater parallelism.

All multiprocessor systems are architecturally scalable; however, as processors are added to the system, the interconnection networks need to be upgraded to tackle envisaged greater communication delays, increased contentions, and reductions in system efficiency. The underlying goal of most multiprocessor designs is to achieve scalability and this is reflected in the variety of interconnection networks that have been devised. If p is the number of processors and n is the number of input data elements in a problem, both p and n can be altered to improve performance. Altering p alters the size of the computer system and altering n alters the size of the problem.

Gustafson argued that when a problem is ported onto a multiprocessor system, larger problem sizes can be considered, that is, the same problem but with a larger number of data values. The starting point for Gustafson's law is the computation on the multiprocessor rather than on the single computer. In Gustafson's analysis, the parallel execution time is kept constant, which we assume to be some acceptable time for waiting for the solution. The computation on a multiprocessor is composed of a fraction that is computed sequentially, (say) f', and a fraction that contains parallel parts, $(1-f')$.

The corresponding *scaled speedup fraction* $S'(p)$ is given by

$$S'(p)=\frac{f't_p+(1-f')pt_p}{t_p}=p+1(1-p)f'$$

The fraction f' is the fraction of the computation on the multiprocessor that cannot be parallelized. Different from f previously, f' is the fraction of the computation on a single computer that cannot be parallelized.

The significant implication of Gustafson's law is that it should be possible to get high speedup if we scale up the problem size. In other words, as stated earlier, with Amdahl's law with $f=5\%$, the speedup computes to 10.26, whereas with Gustafson's law if f' is 5%, the scaled speedup computes to 19.05 with only 20 processors; Gustafson quotes results obtained in practice of very high speedup close to linear on a 1024-processor hypercube.

3.2.3 Speedup versus Communication Overhead

The potential benefit of parallel computing is typically measured by the time it takes to complete a task on a single processor versus the time it takes to complete the same task on N parallel processors. This is expressed in terms of speedup given by

$$S(N)=\frac{T_p(1)}{T_p(N)}.$$

Communication between the processor and the memory takes time due to the speed mismatch between the processor and the memory (see Section 3.3.5). For parallel computing systems, communication between the processors to exchange data involves transferring data or messages across the interconnection network.

Communication between processors is fraught with several problems:

- Memory wall
- Memory bandwidth
- Memory collisions
- Interconnection network delay

Delays involved in processing an algorithm on a parallel processor system are

$T_r\,(N)$	Memory read	Delay to read data from memory shared by N processors
$T_w\,(N)$	Memory write	Delay to write data from memory shared by N processors
$T_c\,(N)$	Communicate	Delay to communicate between a pair of processors when there are N processors in the system
$T_p\,(N)$	Process data	Delay to process the algorithm using N parallel processors

Consider a parallel algorithm consisting of N independent tasks that can be executed either on a single processor or on N processors. Assuming that data travels between the processors and the memory, and that there is no interprocessor communication due to the task independence, then

the time required to travel between the processors and the memory, in the absence of interprocessor communication due to the task independence, is estimated as

$$T_p(1) = N\tau_p \text{ and } T_{p(N)} = \tau_p.$$

If τ_m is the memory access time to read one block of data and each task requires one block of input data, then N tasks would require to read N blocks. The time needed by the parallel processors to read data from the memory is estimated as

$$T(1) = N\tau_m \text{ and } T_r(N) = aT_r(1) = aN\tau_m$$

where:

$a = 1/N$ for distributed memory

$a = 1$ for shared memory without collisions

$a > N$ for shared memory with collisions

The interprocessor communication overhead involving reading and writing data into the memory is given by

$$T_c(N) = \beta N\tau_m$$

where:

$\beta \geq 0$ and depends on the algorithm and how the memory is organized.

$\beta = 0$ for a single processor, where there is no data exchange or when the processors in a multiprocessor system do not communicate while evaluating the algorithm.

β could be equal to $\log_2 N$ or even N. This could be the case when the parallel algorithm programmer or hardware designer did not fully consider the cost of interprocessor or interthread communications.

The time required for writing back the results to the memory is estimated as

$$T_w(1) = N\tau_m \text{ and } T_w(N) = aT_w(1) = aN\tau_m$$

For a single processor, the total time to complete a task, including memory access overhead, is given by

$$T_{\text{total}}(1) = T_r(1) + T_p(1) + T_w(1) = N(2\tau_m + \tau_p)$$

When communication overhead is also considered, the total time to complete a task is given by

$$T_{\text{total}}(N) = T_r(N) + T_p(N) + T_w(N) = 2Na\tau_m + \tau_p$$

The speedup factor is given by

$$S(N) = \frac{T_{\text{total}}(1)}{T_{\text{total}}(N)} = \frac{2aN\tau_m + N\tau_p}{2Na\tau_m + \tau_p}.$$

Memory mismatch ratio R can be defined as the ratio of the memory access time required to read one block of data to the time for processing one block of data:

$$R = \frac{\tau_m}{\tau_p}$$

τ_p is expected to be orders of magnitude smaller than τ_m depending on the granularity of the subtask being processed and the speed of the memory.

Using R, the speedup factor is given by

$$S(N,R) = \frac{2aRN + N}{2aRN + 1}$$

when

$RN << 1$, speedup is maximum
$RN > 0.1$, speedup decreases rapidly
$R = 1$, speedup is minimum

Memory design and communication between processors or threads are very important factors. For multicore processors that contain all the processors on the same chip, communication occurs at a much higher speed compared with multiprocessors, where communication takes place across chips. For multicore processors, τ_m is reduced by orders of magnitude for multicore systems especially for small R values.

3.3 Enhancing Uniprocessor Performance

The basic computer system is a single processor (uniprocessor) system based on the Von Neumann model, which is inherently sequential: the entire task to solve a problem is executed by the CPU one instruction at a time. The drawbacks of such a computer have been overcome by adopting various measures that are described in the following sections.

This section discusses the techniques used to enhance the performance of a uniprocessor.

3.3.1 Improving CPU Performance

Regarding integration, Moore's law continues the scaling trend by improving transistor performance, increasing transistor integration capacity to implement more complex architectures, and reducing power consumption per logic operation to keep heat dissipation within limits. The microarchitecture of multicore processors also follows Moore's law since the cores are contained within a processor chip. The performance increases because the microarchitecture alone is governed by Pollack's rule, which states that the increase is roughly proportional to the square root increase in complexity; hence, efforts that devote r Base Core Equivalent (BCE) resources will result in the sequential performance of $\sqrt{r}$. If the logic of a processor core is doubled, then it delivers only 40% more performance; in contrast, a multicore processor has the potential to provide near linear performance improvement with complexity and power.

3.3.2 Increasing Processor Clock Frequency

The performance of a computer system can be increased by increasing the clock rate, that is, by reducing the time of every clock cycle and, hence, the execution time. In the previous few decades, the clock rate increased at an exponential rate but it hit the power wall because the power increases cubically with the clock rate (see Chapter 2: Section 2.3.2).

In search for a way out of this power–performance dilemma, some attempts have been made to simplify processor designs by giving up some architectural complexity in favor of more simplified ideas. Using the additional transistors for larger caches is one option, but again there is a limit beyond which a larger cache will not pay off any more in terms of performance. Multicore processors, that is, several CPU cores on a single die or socket, are the solution chosen by all major manufacturers today (see Section 3.3.9).

Increasing the system clock frequency allows the computer to execute more instructions per unit time. Logic gates need time to switch states and system buses need time to be charged or discharged through bus drivers; the type of gate circuits also dictates the clock speed, such as using the complementary metal-oxide semiconductor (CMOS) or domino logic or current-mode logic. These delays are closely tied to the underlying silicon technology, such as the N-type metal-oxide semiconductor (NMOS), CMOS, and bipolar.

As discussed in Section 2.2.3, there is a fundamental limit to how fast a chip can run based on dynamic power dissipation, approximately given by

$$E \approx aCV_{\mathrm{dd}}^2$$

where:

a is the average switching activity of the circuit
C is the average total switched capacitance
V_{dd} is the supply voltage

Engineers developed many techniques to reduce the power consumption of the chip while raising the clock frequency. One obvious solution was to reduce the value of C through a finer lithographic process resolution. A bigger impact resulted when the chip power supply voltage was reduced from 5.0 to 2.2 V and then 1.2 V.

3.3.3 Parallelizing Arithmetic Logic Unit (ALU) Structure

An example of using parallelism to enhance performance is the multiplication operation. Before the advent of very-large-scale integration (VLSI), early computers used the adder in the ALU to do multiplication through the add–shift technique.

Assume the two numbers to be multiplied, a and b, have the following binary representations:

$$C = a \times b$$

$$= \sum_{i=0}^{n-1}\sum_{j=0}^{n-1} 2^{i+j} a_i b_j = \sum_{i=0}^{n-1}\left(\sum_{j=0}^{n-1} 2^{i+j} a_i b_j\right)$$

where a_i, $b_i = \{0, 1\}$.

This can be thought of as the parallel implementation of the multiplication operation. The last form is the bit-serial implementation where the partial products are added over two stages: first along the j index and then the results are added over the i index.

Figure 3.1a shows the bit-serial multiplication technique for the case $n=4$. After $n=4$ clock cycles, the $2n$-bit product $a \times b$ is available with the n-bit high word stored in the accumulator and the n-bit low word stored in the right shift register. The time required to perform the bit-serial multiplication is roughly estimated as

$$T_{\text{serial}} = nT_{\text{add}} = n^2 T_{fa}$$

where:

T_{add} is the n-bit carry ripple adder delay
T_{fa} is the 1-bit full adder delay

With VLSI technology, it became feasible to incorporate a parallel multiplier in the ALU and consequently to speed up the processor. Figure 3.1b shows the parallel multiplication technique and structure for the case $n=4$. Most of the parallel multiplier structure is composed of a two-dimensional array of cells that generate the partial product bits simultaneously. At the bottom is a carry ripple adder.

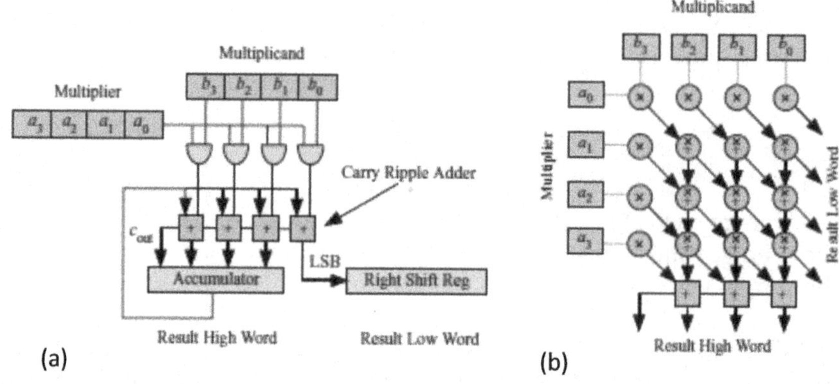

FIGURE 3.1
(a) Bit-serial binary multiplication and (b) parallel binary multiplication.

The gray squares with a + symbol indicate a 1-bit full adder. The gray circles with a + and × symbol indicate an AND gate connected to a 1-bit full adder. The array of AND gates is responsible for generating all the bits of the partial products a_ib_j. The array of adders is responsible for adding up all these partial products.

The diagonal lines indicate lines of equal binary weight, and the vertical lines indicate the path for the carry-out signals.

The time required to perform the parallel multiplication operation is

$$T_{\text{parallel}} \approx 2(n-1)T_{fa}$$

Thus, the time required for parallel multiplication is n times smaller than the bit-serial multiplication delay. However, this comes at a cost of additional hardware.

3.3.4 Pipelining

A central architectural design approach widely adopted to achieve increased performance is by using pipelining. Pipelining involves dividing the processing of an instruction into a series of sequential steps and providing a separate unit within the processor for each step. Speedup comes about when multiple instructions are executed in series. Normally, each unit operates for the same time, performing its actions for each instruction as it passes through, and the pipeline operates in lock-step synchronous fashion.

For a pipeline of depth m, executing N independent steps, subsequent operations take $N+m-1$ steps. We can thus calculate the expected speedup versus a general-purpose unit that needs m cycles to generate a single result:

$$\frac{T_{\text{seq}}}{T_{\text{pipe}}} = \frac{mN}{N+m-1}$$

which is proportional to m for large N.

The throughput is

$$\frac{N}{T_{\text{pipe}}} = \frac{1}{1+\dfrac{m-1}{N}}$$

This approaches 1 for large N. It is evident that the deeper the pipeline, the larger the number of independent operations must be to achieve reasonable throughput because of the overhead caused by the wind-up phase.

In order to get at least p results per cycle $(0<p\leq 1)$, the corresponding N is given as

$$p = \frac{1}{1+\dfrac{m-1}{N_c}} \Rightarrow N_c = \frac{(m-1)p}{1-p}$$

Thus, $p=0.5$ gives $N_c=m-1$. Consequently, this immediately identifies a potential performance bottleneck in codes that use short, tight loops. In superscalar or even vector processors, the situation becomes even worse as multiple identical pipelines operate in parallel, leaving shorter loop lengths for each pipe.

3.3.5 Memory Hierarchy

The processor is, of course, only one part of the overall system design. Memory is required. The main semiconductor memory operates much slower than the processor (the memory wall), partly because of its size and partly because of the dynamic memory design used for high capacity and lower costs. Hence, high-speed cache memory is added near the processor to hold recently used information that can be accessed much more quickly than from the main memory. The cache memory has to operate much faster than the main memory and uses a different circuit design. Speed, capacity, and cost in a semiconductor are related. As the memory capacity is increased on a memory chip, the tendency is for the device to operate slower for a given technology in addition to its cost increasing. This leads to a memory hierarchy with multiple levels of cache memory, that is, an L1 cache, an L2 cache, and possibly an L3 cache, between the processor and the main memory. Each level of cache is slower and larger than the previous level and usually includes the information held in the previous level (although not necessarily, depending on the design).

Consequently, in computer systems the memory is organized hierarchically; it consists of multiple levels of memory with different speeds and sizes. The faster memories are more expensive per bit than the slower memory and thus smaller. A memory hierarchy can have multiple levels, but data is copied only between two adjacent levels at a time. The processor's closer level is smaller and faster (because it uses more expensive technology) than the lower level.

Since the major reason for having a memory hierarchy is performance, the time to service hits and misses is very important. The time to access the upper level of the memory hierarchy is known as the hit time—it includes the time needed to determine if the access is a *hit* or a *miss*. The time to replace a block in the upper level with the corresponding block from the lower level, plus the time to deliver this block to the processor is known as the *miss penalty*.

Three primary technologies are used in building memory hierarchies. The main memory is implemented from DRAM, while levels closer to the processor (caches) use SRAM. The third technology used to implement the larger and slowest level in the hierarchy is the magnetic disk.

3.3.5.1 Cache Memory

All modern computers make use of cache memory. In most cases, it is implemented on the same die as the microprocessor that forms the processor. To close the gap further between the high clock speeds of modern processors and the relatively long time required to access DRAM, many processors have incorporated an additional level of caching. This second level can be located on the same chip or in a separate set of SRAMs out of the chip processor; it is accessed if a miss occurs in the primary cache. In the two-level cache structure, the primary cache allows concentrating on minimizing the hit time to yield a shorter clock cycle while the secondary cache allows concentrating on the miss rate to reduce the penalty of long memory access time.

3.3.6 Very Long Instruction Word (VLIW) Processors

This technique is considered fine-grain parallelism since the algorithm is now parallelized at the instruction level, which is the finest level of detail into which one could hope to divide an algorithm. A VLIW implies that several instructions or opcodes are sent to the

CPU to be executed simultaneously. Picking the instructions to be issued in one VLIW is done by the compiler. The compiler must ensure that there is no dependency between the instructions in a VLIW and that the hardware can support executing all the issued instructions. This presents a potential advantage over instruction pipelining since instruction scheduling is done before the code is actually run.

3.3.7 Superscalarity

A superscalar processor is able to simultaneously execute several instructions from independent instruction pipelines. Superscalar processors have a dynamic scheduler that examines the instructions in the instruction cache/memory and decides which ones to be issued to each instruction pipeline. Dynamic scheduling allows out-of-order instruction issue and execution.

Superscalarity is a capacity of the CPU to provide more than one result per clock cycle; it is mainly based on hardware replication, and it is a special form of parallel execution. If a processor is designed to be capable of executing more than one instruction, that is, producing more than one "result" per cycle, this objective is reflected in many aspects of its design:

- Multiple instructions can be fetched and decoded concurrently (3–6 nowadays).
- Address and other integer calculations are performed in multiple integer (add, mult, shift, mask) units (2–6). This is closely related to the previous point, because feeding these units requires code execution.
- Multiple floating-point pipelines can run in parallel.
- Caches are fast enough to sustain more than one load or store operation per cycle, which is reflected in the number of available execution units for loads and stores (2–4).

Superscalarity is a special form of parallel execution and a variant of instruction-level parallelism (ILP). Out-of-order execution and compiler optimization must work together in order to fully exploit superscalarity.

Even on the most advanced architectures, it is extremely hard for compiler-generated code to achieve a throughput of more than two or three instructions per cycle. This is why applications with very high performance demands sometimes still resort to the use of assembly language.

3.3.8 Instruction-Level Parallelism

SISD architecture is based on the key principles of the serial computer or uniprocessor, where during execution of one program instruction, one data element is processed. Since the mid-1980s, uniprocessor architectures have included techniques that have allowed pipelined overlapping in instruction execution, thereby providing a technique called instruction-level parallelism.

The established approaches for implementing ILP in uniprocessor designs are

- Hardware-based techniques including the dynamic-time detection of program sections that can be parallelized. This is the dominant solution used in CPUs in desktop and server computing.

- Software compiler–based techniques, where optionality for parallelism is examined during software compilation being typical for CPUs in the single program, multiple data (SPMD) class of computing.

Essential concepts in these optimization approaches include:

- *Pipelining*: Pipelining is a sequential process in CPUs where sequential stages of instruction fetch and decode, execute, and write the result back to memory. For maximum process efficiency, each of these stages needs to be continuously populated by a succession of the next program instruction.
- *Data dependency*: Many of the instructions can be data dependent of the result of the previous instruction execution. If the successive command in the pipeline requires the result from the previous instruction execution, this may stall the program execution.

Both techniques apply a great degree of intelligence in analyzing and optimizing the program instructions toward ILP in program execution, including loop unrolling, branch prediction, and dynamic scheduling with renaming. ILP is strictly a hardware SISD practice occurring inside a processing unit. The increase in the CPU processing performance followed Moore's law (see Section 2.4) until 2005, when the amount of required electrical computation power and related mandatory system maintenance forced chip manufacturers to start shifting toward multiprocessor designs. The era of continuous evolution in ILP in uniprocessors came to an end and a shift to other parallel paradigms—such as single instruction, multiple data (SIMD) and multiple instruction, multiple data (MIMD)—in search of ever greater performance started (see Section 6.1).

3.3.9 Multicore Architectures

To leverage multicore technology, it is crucial to use the hardware resources by means of efficient parallel programming. Multicore technology imposes certain challenges, most of them concerning the reduction in the main memory bandwidth and cache memory size per core.

The technical motivation behind multicore is based on the observation that, for a given semiconductor process technology, the power dissipation of modern CPUs is proportional to the third power of clock frequency f (actually it is linear in f and quadratic in supply voltage V_{dd}, but a decrease in f allows for a proportional decrease in V_{dd}). Thus, lowering f and V_{dd} can dramatically reduce power dissipation (Chapter 1: Section 1.3.3).

Assuming that a single core with clock frequency, f, has a performance of p and a power dissipation of W, some relative change in performance:

$$\varepsilon_p = \Delta p / p$$

will emerge for a relative clock change of

$$\varepsilon_f = \Delta f_c / f_c.$$

$|\varepsilon_f|$ is an upper limit for $|\varepsilon_p|$, which in turn will depend on the applications considered. The power dissipation is

$$W + \Delta W = \left(1 + \varepsilon_f\right)^3 W$$

Reducing the clock frequency opens the possibility to place more than one CPU core on the same die (or, more generally, into the same package) while keeping the same power envelope as before. For *m slow* cores, this condition is expressed as

$$(1+\varepsilon_f)^3 m = 1 \Rightarrow \varepsilon_f = m^{-1/3} - 1$$

The overall performance of the multicore chip:

$$p_m = (1+\varepsilon_p)pm$$

should at least match the single-core performance so that

$$\varepsilon_p > \frac{1}{m} - 1$$

is a limit on the performance penalty for a relative clock frequency reduction of ε_f that should be obtainable for the multicore to remain a viable option.

The simplest way to devise a multicore is to place separate CPU dies in a common package.

Figure 3.2 shows monoprocessor and multiprocessor systems with and without multicores.

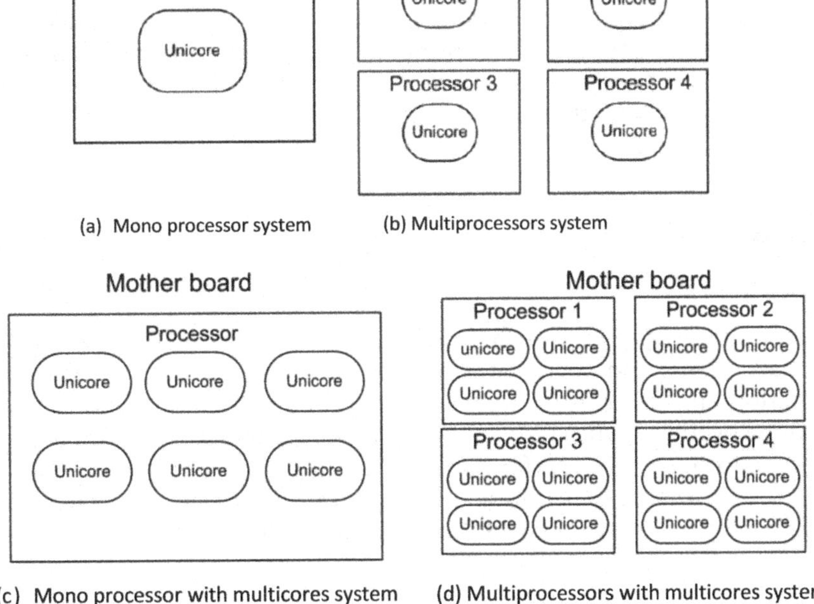

FIGURE 3.2
Processor systems.

3.3.10 Multithreading

Most processors are heavily pipelined and have the potential to deliver a high performance if the pipelines can actually be used. Factors that can inhibit the efficient use of pipelines include

- Dependencies
- Memory latencies
- Insufficient loop length
- Unfortunate instruction mix
- Branch misprediction

All these factors lead to frequent pipeline bubbles, and a large part of the execution resources remains unutilized. The tendency to design longer pipelines in order to raise clock speeds and the general increase in complexity add to the problem. Consequently, processors become hotter (dissipate more power) without a proportional increase in average application performance—an effect that can only be partially compensated by the multicore transition.

Processors have threading capabilities known as hyper-threading or simultaneous multithreading (SMT). Multithreaded processors have multiple architectural states that embrace all data, status, and control registers, including stacks and instruction pointers. Execution resources such as arithmetic units, caches, queues, and memory interfaces are not duplicated. Due to its multiple architectural states, the CPU appears to be composed of several cores (sometimes called logical processors) and can thus execute several instructions streams (threads) in parallel, no matter if they belong to the same program or not. Here, the hardware is responsible for keeping track of which instructions belong to which architectural state; therefore, all threads share the same execution resources.

As all threads share the same execution resources, it is possible to fill bubbles in a pipeline due to stalls in one thread with instructions (or parts thereof) from another. If there are multiple pipelines that can run in parallel, and one thread leaves one or more of them in an idle state, another thread can also use them.

3.4 Summary

The chapter commenced with the characteristics of processors such as word length, clock frequency, and volatile and non-volatile memory. The chapter then described aspects of processor performance such as the potential for speedup, scalability, and speedup versus communication overhead. The latter half of the chapter looked at enhancing uniprocessor performance: improving CPU performance, increasing processor clock frequency, parallelizing the ALU structure, pipelining, memory hierarchy, cache memory, VLIW processors, superscalarity, ILP, multicore architectures, and multithreading.

4

Networking Basics

The merging of computers and communications has had a profound influence on the way computer systems are organized. Although data centers holding thousands of Internet servers are becoming common, the once-dominant concept of the computer center as a room with a large computer to which users brought their work for processing is now totally obsolete. The old model of a single computer serving all of an organization's computational needs has been replaced by one in which a large number of separate but interconnected computers do the job. These systems are called computer networks.

Two computers are said to be networked if they are able to exchange information. The connection need not be via a copper wire; fiber optics, microwaves, infrared, and communication satellites can also be used. Networks come in many sizes, shapes, and forms, as we will see later. They are usually connected together to make larger networks, with the Internet being the most well-known example of a network of networks.

Computer network and a distributed system: The key distinction between them is that in a distributed system, a collection of independent computers appears to its users as a single coherent system. Usually, it has a single model or paradigm that it presents to the users. Often, a layer of software on top of the operating system, called middleware, is responsible for implementing this model. A well-known example of a distributed system is the World Wide Web (www). It runs on top of the Internet and presents a model in which everything looks like a document (web page). On the other hand, in a computer network, coherence, model, and software are absent. Users are exposed to the actual machines, without any attempt by the system to make the machines look and act in a coherent way. If the machines have different hardware and different operating systems, that is fully visible to the users. If a user wants to run a program on a remote machine, it entails logging onto that machine and running it there. In effect, a distributed system is a software system built on top of a network. The software gives it a high degree of cohesiveness and transparency. Thus, the distinction between a network and a distributed system lies with the software (especially the operating system), rather than with the hardware. Nevertheless, there is considerable overlap between the two subjects. For example, both distributed systems and computer networks need to move files around. The difference lies in who invokes the movement, the system or the user.

4.1 Network Principles

4.1.1 Protocol

The term *protocol* is used to refer to a well-known set of rules and formats to be used for communication between processes in order to perform a given task. There are two important parts to the definition of a protocol:

- A specification of the sequence of messages that must be exchanged.
- A specification of the format of the data in the messages.

The existence of well-known protocols enables the separate software components of distributed systems to be developed independently and implemented in different programming languages on computers that may have different order codes and data representations. A protocol is implemented by a pair of software modules located in the sending and receiving computers. For example, a transport protocol transmits messages of any length from a sending process to a receiving process. A process wishing to transmit a message to another process, issues a call to a transport protocol module, passing it a message in the specified format. The transport software then concerns itself with the transmission of the message to its destination, subdividing it into packets of some specified size and format that can be transmitted to the destination via the network protocol—another, lower-level protocol. The corresponding transport protocol module in the receiving computer receives the packet via the network-level protocol module and performs inverse transformations to regenerate the message before passing it to a receiving process.

4.1.2 Protocol Layers

Network software is arranged in a hierarchy of layers. Each layer presents an interface to the layers above it that extends the properties of the underlying communication system. A layer is represented by a module in every computer connected to the network. Each module appears to communicate directly with a module at the same level in another computer in the network; however, in reality, data is not transmitted directly between the protocol modules at each level. Instead, each layer of network software communicates by local procedure calls with the layers above and below it. On the sending side, each layer (except the topmost, or application layer) accepts items of data in a specified format from the layer above it and applies transformations to encapsulate the data in the format specified for that layer before passing it to the layer below for further processing. On the receiving side, the converse transformations are applied to data items received from the layer below before they are passed to the layer above. The protocol type of the layer above is included in the header of each layer, to enable the protocol stack at the receiver to select the correct software components to unpack the packets. The data items are received and passed upward through the hierarchy of software modules, being transformed at each stage until they are in a form that can be passed to the intended recipient process.

4.1.3 Protocol Suite

A complete set of protocol layers is referred to as a protocol suite or a protocol stack, reflecting the layered structure. Figure 4.1 shows a protocol stack that conforms to the seven-layer Reference Model for Open Systems Interconnection (OSI) adopted by the International Organization for Standardization (ISO). The OSI reference model was adopted in order to encourage the development of protocol standards that would meet the requirements of open systems. The purpose of each level in the OSI reference model is summarized in Table 4.1. As its name implies, it is a framework for the definition of protocols and not a definition for a specific suite of protocols.

Protocol suites that conform to the OSI model must include at least one specific protocol at each of the seven levels that the model defines (Table 4.1).

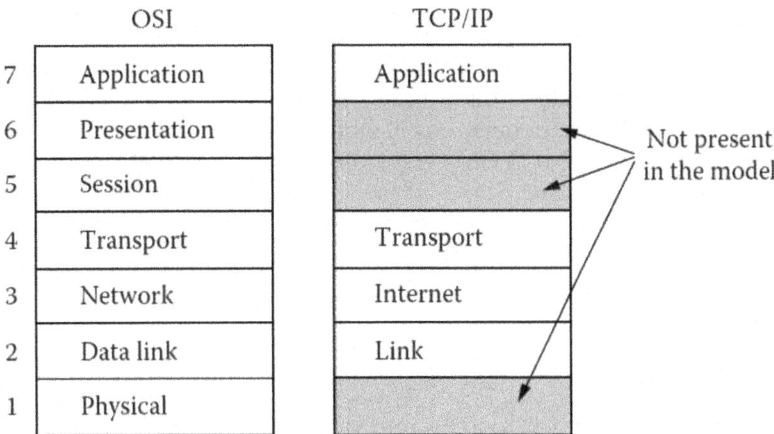

FIGURE 4.1
OSI versus TCP/IP network reference model.

TABLE 4.1
OSI Layers or Stack

Layer	Description	Examples
Application	Protocols at this level are designed to meet the communication requirements of specific applications, often defining the interface to a service.	http, FTP, SMTP, COBRA HOP
Presentation	Protocols at this level transmit data in a network representation that is independent of the representations used in individual computers, which may differ. Encryption is also performed in this layer, if required.	TLS security, COBRA data representation
Session	At this level, reliability and adaption measures are performed, such as the detection of failures and automatic recovery.	SIP
Transport	This is the lowest level at which messages (rather than packets) are handled. Messages are addressed to communication ports attached to processes. Protocols in this layer may be connection oriented or connectionless.	TCP, LDP
Network	Transfers data packets between computers in a specific network. In a WAN or an Internetwork, this involves the generation of a route passing through routers. In a single LAN, no routing is required.	IP, ATM virtual circuits
Data link	Responsible for the transmission of packets between nodes that are directly connected by a physical link. In a WAN, transmission is between pairs of routers and hosts. In a LAN, it is between any pair of hosts.	Ethernet MAC, ATM cell transfer, PPP
Physical	The circuits and hardware that drive the network. It transmits sequences of binary data by analogue signaling, using the amplitude or frequency modulation of electrical signals (on cable circuits), light signals (on fiber-optic circuits), or other electromagnetic signals (on radio and microwave circuits).	Ethernet baseband signaling, ISDN

4.1.4 Datagram

A datagram is essentially another name for a data packet. The term *datagram* refers to the similarity of this delivery mode to the way in which letters and telegrams are delivered. The essential feature of datagram networks is that the delivery of each packet is a one-shot process; no setup is required, and once the packet is delivered, the network retains no information about it.

4.2 Types of Networks

There is no generally accepted taxonomy into which all computer networks fit, but two dimensions stand out as important: transmission technology and scale. We will now examine each of these in turn. Broadly speaking, two types of transmission technology are in widespread use: broadcast links and point-to-point links.

Point-to-point links connect individual pairs of machines. To go from the source to the destination on a network made up of point-to-point links, short messages, called packets in certain contexts, may have to first visit one or more intermediate machines. Often, multiple routes of different lengths are possible, so finding good routes is important in point-to-point networks. Point-to-point transmission with exactly one sender and exactly one receiver is sometimes called unicasting. In contrast, on a broadcast network, the communication channel is shared by all the machines on the network; packets sent by any machine are received by all the others. An address field within each packet specifies the intended recipient. Upon receiving a packet, a machine checks the address field. If the packet is intended for the receiving machine, that machine processes the packet; if the packet is intended for some other machine, the packet is ignored.

Broadcast systems usually also allow the possibility of addressing a packet to all destinations by using a special code in the address field. When a packet with this code is transmitted, it is received and processed by every machine on the network. This mode of operation is called broadcasting. Some broadcast systems also support transmission to a subset of the machines, which is known as multicasting. An alternative criterion for classifying networks is by scale. Distance is important as a classification metric because different technologies are used at different scales. At the top are personal area networks (PANs), networks that are meant for one person. Next are longer-range networks. These can be divided into local (LANs), metropolitan (MANs), and wide area networks (WANs), each with increasing scale. Finally, the connection of two or more networks is called an Internetwork. The worldwide Internet is certainly the best-known (but not the only) example of an Internetwork.

4.2.1 Personal Area Networks

PANs let devices communicate over the range of a person. A common example is a wireless network that connects a computer with its peripherals. Almost every computer has an attached monitor, keyboard, mouse, and printer. Without using wireless, this connection must be done with cables. Many new users have a hard time finding the right cables and plugging them into the right little holes (even though they are usually color coded) that most computer vendors offer the option of sending a technician to the user's home to do it. To help these users, some companies got together to design a short-range wireless network, called Bluetooth, to connect these components without wires. The idea is that if your devices have Bluetooth, then you need no cables. You just put them down, turn them on, and they work together. For many people, this ease of operation is a big plus. PANs can also be built with other technologies that communicate over short ranges, such as radio-frequency identification (RFID) on smartcards and library books.

4.2.2 Local Area Networks

Wireless LANs are very popular these days, especially in homes, older office buildings, cafeterias, and other places where it is too much trouble to install cables. A LAN is a privately owned network that operates within and nearby a single building such as a home, office, or factory. LANs are widely used to connect personal computers and consumer electronics to allow them share resources (e.g., printers) and exchange information. When LANs are used by companies, they are called enterprise networks.

In these systems, every computer has a radio modem and an antenna that it uses to communicate with other computers. In most cases, each computer talks to a device in the ceiling called an access point (AP), wireless router, or base station, and relays packets between wireless computers and also between them and the Internet. However, if other computers are close enough, they can communicate directly with one another in a peer-to-peer configuration.

There is a standard for wireless LANs called IEEE 802.11, popularly known as Wi-Fi, which has become very widespread. It runs at speeds anywhere from 11 to hundreds of megabytes per second. Wired LANs use a range of different transmission technologies. Most of them use copper wires, but some use optical fiber. LANs are restricted in size, which means that the worst-case transmission time is bounded and known in advance. Knowing these bounds helps with the task of designing network protocols. Typically, wired LANs run at speeds of 100 Mbps to 1 Gbps, have low delay (microseconds or nanoseconds), and make very few errors. Newer LANs can operate at up to 10 Gbps. Compared to wireless networks, wired LANs exceed them in all dimensions of performance. It is just easier to send signals over a wire or a fiber than through the air.

The topology of many wired LANs is built from point-to-point links. IEEE 802.3, popularly called Ethernet, is, by far, the most common type of wired LAN. In switched Ethernet, each computer speaks the Ethernet protocol and connects to a box called a switch with a point-to-point link, hence the name. A switch has multiple ports, each of which can connect to one computer. The job of the switch is to relay packets between computers that are attached to it, using the address in each packet to determine which computer to send it to. Switched Ethernet is a modern version of the original classic Ethernet design that broadcasts all the packets over a single linear cable. At most, one machine could successfully transmit at a time, and a distributed arbitration mechanism was used to resolve conflicts. It used a simple algorithm: computers could transmit whenever the cable was idle. If two or more packets collided, each computer just waited a random time and tried later. To build larger LANs, switches can be plugged into each other using their ports.

Both wireless and wired broadcast networks can be divided into static and dynamic designs, depending on how the channel is allocated. A typical static allocation would be to divide time into discrete intervals and use a round-robin algorithm, allowing each machine to broadcast only when its time slot comes up. Static allocation wastes channel capacity when a machine has nothing to say during its allocated slot, so most systems attempt to allocate the channel dynamically (i.e., on demand). Dynamic allocation methods for a common channel are either centralized or decentralized. In the centralized channel allocation method, there is a single entity, for example, the base station in cellular networks, which determines who goes next. It might do this by accepting multiple packets and prioritizing them according to some internal algorithm. In the decentralized channel allocation method, there is no central entity; each machine must decide for itself whether to transmit. You might think that this approach would lead to chaos, but it does not. Later, we will study many algorithms designed to bring order out of the potential chaos.

4.2.3 Metropolitan Area Networks

A MAN covers a city. The best-known examples of MANs are the cable television networks available in many cities. These systems grew from earlier community antenna systems used in areas with poor over-the-air television reception. In those early systems, a large antenna was placed on top of a nearby hill and a signal was then piped to the subscriber's house. Cable television is not the only MAN, though. Recent developments in high-speed wireless Internet access have resulted in another MAN, which has been standardized as IEEE 802.16 and is popularly known as WiMAX.

4.2.4 Wide Area Networks

A WAN spans a large geographical area, often a country or continent. Each of these offices contains computers intended to run user (i.e., application) programs. The rest of the network that connects these hosts is called the communication subnet, or just subnet for short. The job of the subnet is to carry messages from host to host. In most WANs, the subnet consists of two distinct components: transmission lines and switching elements. Transmission lines move bits between machines. They can be made of copper wire, optical fiber, or even radio links. Most companies do not have transmission lines lying about, so instead, they lease the lines from a telecommunications company. Switching elements, or just switches or routers, are specialized computers that connect two or more transmission lines. When data arrives on an incoming line, the switching element must choose an outgoing line on which to forward it.

The WAN, as we have described, looks similar to a large wired LAN, but there are some important differences that go beyond long wires. Usually in a WAN, the hosts and subnet are owned and operated by different people. Second, the routers will usually connect different kinds of networking technology. Lastly, subnet(s) can be entire LANs themselves. This means that many WANs will in fact be Internetworks or composite networks that are made up of more than one network.

Rather than lease dedicated transmission lines, a company might connect its offices to the Internet. The virtual private network (VPN) allows connections to be made between offices as virtual links that use the underlying capacity of the Internet. Compared to the dedicated arrangement, a VPN has the usual advantage of virtualization, which is that it provides flexible reuse of a resource (Internet connectivity), and the usual disadvantage of virtualization, which is a lack of control over the underlying resources.

4.3 Network Models

Now that we have discussed layered networks in the abstract, it is time to look at some examples. We will discuss two important network architectures: the OSI reference model and the Transmission Control Protocol/Internet Protocol (TCP/IP) reference model. Although the protocols associated with the OSI model are no longer used, the model itself is actually quite general and still valid, and the features discussed at each layer are still very important. The TCP/IP model has the opposite properties: the model itself is of little use but the protocols are widely used.

4.3.1 OSI Reference Model

The OSI model (minus the physical medium) is shown in Figure 4.1. This model is based on a proposal developed by the ISO as a first step toward international standardization of the protocols used in the various layers. The model is called the ISO OSI reference model because it deals with connecting open systems—that is, systems that are open for communication with other systems. We will just call it the OSI model for short.

The OSI model has seven layers. The principles that were applied to arrive at the seven layers can be briefly summarized as follows:

- A layer should be created where a different abstraction is needed.
- Each layer should perform a well-defined function.
- The function of each layer should be chosen with an eye toward defining internationally standardized protocols.
- The layer boundaries should be chosen to minimize the information flow across the interfaces.
- The number of layers should be large enough that distinct functions need not be thrown together in the same layer out of necessity and small enough that the architecture does not become unwieldy.

We describe each layer of the model in turn, starting at the bottom layer. Note that the OSI model itself is not a network architecture because it does not specify the exact services and protocols to be used in each layer. It just tells what each layer should do. However, ISO has also produced standards for all the layers, although these are not part of the reference model itself. Each one has been published as a separate international standard. The model (in part) is widely used, although the associated protocols have long been forgotten.

- Physical layer

  The physical layer is concerned with transmitting raw bits over a communication channel. Design issues have to do with making sure that when one side sends a 1 bit, it is received by the other side as a 1 bit, not as a 0 bit. Typical questions here are what electrical signals should be used to represent a 1 and a 0, how many nanoseconds a bit lasts, whether transmission may proceed simultaneously in both directions, how the initial connection is established, how it is torn down when both sides are finished, how many pins the network connector has, and what each pin is used for. These design issues largely deal with mechanical, electrical, and timing interfaces, as well as the physical transmission medium, which lies below the physical layer.

- Data link layer

  The main task of the data link layer is to transform a raw transmission facility into a line that appears free from undetected transmission errors. It does so by masking the real errors so the network layer does not see them. It accomplishes this task by having the sender break up the input data into data frames (typically a few hundred or a few thousand bytes) and transmit the frames sequentially. If the service is reliable, the receiver confirms correct receipt of each frame by sending back an acknowledgement frame.

Another issue that arises in the data link layer (and most of the higher layers as well) is how to keep a fast transmitter from drowning a slow receiver in data. Some traffic regulation mechanism may be needed to let the transmitter know when the receiver can accept more data.

Broadcast networks have an additional issue in the data link layer: how to control access to the shared channel. A special sublayer of the data link layer, the medium access control sublayer, deals with this problem.

- Network layer

  The network layer controls the operation of the subnet. A key design issue is determining how packets are routed from source to destination. Routes can be based on static tables that are wired into the network and rarely changed, or more often, they can be updated automatically to avoid failed components. They can also be determined at the start of each conversation, for example, a terminal session, such as a log-in to a remote machine. Finally, they can be highly dynamic, being determined anew for each packet to reflect the current network load. If too many packets are present in the subnet at the same time, they will get in one another's way, forming bottlenecks. Handling congestion is also a responsibility of the network layer, in conjunction with higher layers that adapt the load they place on the network. More generally, the quality of the service provided (delay, transit time, jitter, etc.) is also a network layer issue.

  When a packet has to travel from one network to another to get to its destination, many problems can arise. The addressing used by the second network may be different from that used by the first one. The second network may not accept the packet at all because it is too large. The protocols may differ, and so on. It is up to the network layer to overcome all these problems to allow heterogeneous networks to be interconnected. In broadcast networks, the routing problem is simple, so the network layer is often thin or even nonexistent.

- Transport layer

  The basic function of the transport layer is to accept data from above it, split it up into smaller units if need be, pass these to the network layer, and ensure that the pieces all arrive correctly at the other end. Furthermore, all this must be done efficiently and in a way that isolates the upper layers from inevitable changes in the hardware technology over the course of time. The transport layer also determines what type of service to provide to the session layer and, ultimately, to the users of the network. The most popular type of transport connection is an error-free, point-to-point channel that delivers messages or bytes in the order in which they were sent. However, other possible kinds of transport service exist, such as the transporting of isolated messages with no guarantee about the order of delivery and the broadcasting of messages to multiple destinations. The type of service is determined when the connection is established.

As an aside, an error-free channel is impossible to achieve; what people really mean by this term is that the error rate is low enough to ignore in practice.

The transport layer is a true end-to-end layer; it carries data all the way from the source to the destination. In other words, a program on the source machine carries on a conversation with a similar program on the destination machine, using the message headers and control messages. In the lower layers, each protocol is between a machine and its immediate neighbors, and not between the ultimate source and destination machines, which may be separated by many routers. The difference between layers one to three, which are chained, and layers four to seven, which are end to end, is illustrated in Figure 2.1.

- Session layer

  The session layer allows users on different machines to establish sessions between them. Sessions offer various services, including dialog control (keeping track of whose turn it is to transmit), token management (preventing two parties from attempting the same critical operation simultaneously), and synchronization (checkpointing long transmissions to allow them to pick up from where they left off in the event of a crash and subsequent recovery).

- Presentation layer

  Unlike the lower layers, which are mostly concerned with moving bits around, the presentation layer is concerned with the syntax and semantics of the information transmitted. In order to make it possible for computers with different internal data representations to communicate, the data structures to be exchanged can be defined in an abstract way, along with a standard encoding to be used on the wire. The presentation layer manages these abstract data structures and allows higher-level data structures (e.g., banking records) to be defined and exchanged.

- Application layer

  The application layer contains a variety of protocols that are commonly needed by users. One widely used application protocol is the HyperText Transfer Protocol (http), which is the basis for the World Wide Web. When a browser wants a web page, it sends the name of the page it wants to the server hosting the page using http. The server then sends the page back. Other application protocols are used for file transfer, electronic mail, and network news.

4.3.2 TCP/IP Reference Model

Let us now turn from the OSI reference model to the reference model used in the grandparent of all wide area computer networks, the Advanced Research Projects Agency Network (ARPANET), and its successor, the worldwide Internet. The ARPANET was a research network sponsored by the US Department of Defense (DoD). It eventually connected hundreds of universities and government installations, using leased telephone lines. When satellite and radio networks were later added, the existing protocols had trouble interworking with them, so a new reference architecture was needed. Thus, from nearly the beginning, the ability to connect multiple networks in a seamless way was one of the major design goals. This architecture later became known as the TCP/IP reference model, after its two primary protocols. Given the DoD's concern that some of its precious hosts, routers, and Internetwork gateways might get blown to pieces at a moment's notice by an attack from the Soviet Union, another major goal was that the network be able to survive loss of subnet hardware, without existing conversations being broken off. In other words, the DoD wanted connections to remain intact as long as the source and destination machines were functioning, even if some of the machines or transmission lines in between were suddenly put out of operation. Furthermore, since applications with divergent requirements were envisioned, ranging from transferring files to real-time speech transmission, a flexible architecture was needed.

4.3.2.1 Link Layer

All these requirements led to the choice of a packet-switching network based on a connectionless layer that runs across different networks. The lowest layer in the model, the link layer, describes what links such as serial lines and classic Ethernet must do to meet the needs of this connectionless Internet layer. It is not really a layer at all, in the normal sense of the term, but rather an interface between hosts and transmission links. Early material on the TCP/IP model has little to say about it.

4.3.2.2 Internet Layer

The Internet layer is the linchpin that holds the whole architecture together. Its job is to permit hosts to inject packets into any network and have them travel independently to the destination (potentially on a different network). They may even arrive in a completely different order than they were sent, in which case, it is the job of higher layers to rearrange them, if in-order delivery is desired. Note that Internet is used here in a generic sense, even though this layer is present in the Internet.

The analogy here is with the (snail) mail system. A person can drop a sequence of international letters into a mailbox in one country, and with a little luck, most of them will be delivered to the correct address in the destination country. The letters will probably travel through one or more international mail gateways along the way, but this is transparent to the users. Furthermore, that each country (i.e., each network) has its own stamps, preferred envelope sizes, and delivery rules is hidden from the users. The Internet layer defines an official packet format and protocol called the Internet Protocol (IP), plus a companion protocol called the Internet Control Message Protocol (ICMP) that helps it function. The job of the Internet layer is to deliver IP packets where they are supposed to go. Packet routing is clearly a major issue here, as is congestion (though IP has not proven effective at avoiding congestion).

4.3.2.3 Transport Layer

The layer above the Internet layer in the TCP/IP model is now usually called the transport layer. It is designed to allow peer entities on the source and destination hosts to carry on a conversation, just as in the OSI transport layer. Two end-to-end transport protocols have been defined here. The first one, the Transmission Control Protocol (TCP), is a reliable connection-oriented protocol that allows a byte stream originating on one machine to be delivered without error on any other machine in the Internet. It segments the incoming byte stream into discrete messages and passes each one on to the Internet layer. At the destination, the receiving TCP process reassembles the received messages into the output stream. The TCP also handles flow control to make sure a fast sender cannot swamp a slow receiver with more messages than it can handle.

The second protocol in this layer, the User Datagram Protocol (UDP), is an unreliable, connectionless protocol for applications that do not want TCP's sequencing or flow control and wish to provide their own. It is also widely used for one-shot, client–server-type request–reply queries and applications in which prompt delivery is more important than accurate delivery, such as transmitting speech or video. Since the model was developed, IP has been implemented on many other networks.

4.3.2.4 Application Layer

The TCP/IP model does not have session or presentation layers as there was no perceived need for them. Instead, applications simply include any session and presentation functions that they require. Experience with the OSI model has proven this view correct: these layers are of little use to most applications.

On top of the transport layer is the application layer. It contains all the higher-level protocols. The early ones included virtual terminal (TELetype NETwork [TELNET]), file transfer (FTP), and electronic mail (Simple Mail Transfer Protocol [SMTP]). Many other protocols have been added to these over the years. Some important ones include the Domain Name System (DNS) for mapping host names onto their network addresses; http, the protocol for fetching pages on the World Wide Web; and Real-Time Protocol (RTP), the protocol for delivering real-time media such as voice or movies.

OSI versus TCP/IP reference model: The OSI model was devised before the corresponding protocols were invented. This ordering meant that the model was not biased toward one particular set of protocols, a fact that made it quite general. The downside of this ordering was that the designers did not have much experience with the subject and did not have a good idea of which functionality to put in which layer. For example, the data link layer originally dealt only with point-to-point networks. When broadcast networks came around, a new sublayer had to be hacked into the model. Furthermore, no thought was given to Internetworking. With TCP/IP, the reverse was true: the protocols came first, and the model was really just a description of the existing protocols. There was no problem with the protocols fitting the model. They fit perfectly. The only trouble was that the model did not fit any other protocol stacks. Consequently, it was not especially useful for describing other non-TCP/IP networks.

4.4 Interconnection Networks

The overall performance of a cluster system can be determined by the speed of its processors and the interconnection network. Many researchers argue that the interconnection network is the most important factor that affects cluster performance. Regardless of how fast the processors are, communication among processors, and hence scalability of applications, will always be bounded by the network bandwidth and latency. The bandwidth is an indication of how fast a data transfer may occur from a sender to a receiver. Latency is the time needed to send a minimal size message from a sender to a receiver.

In the early days of clusters, the Ethernet was the main interconnection network used to connect nodes. Many solutions have been introduced to achieve high-speed networks. Key solutions in high-speed interconnects include:

- Gigabit Ethernet
- Myrinet
- Quadrics

TABLE 4.2

Comparison of Various Interconnection Networks

Interconnection Network	Data Rate	Switching	Routing
Ethernet	10 Mbit/s	Packet	Table based
Fast Ethernet	100 Mbit/s	Packet	Table based
Gigabit Ethernet	1 Gbit/s	Packet	Table based
Myrinet	1.28 Gbit/s	Wormhole	Source path
Quadrics	7.2 Gbyte/s	Wormhole	Source path

While the Ethernet resides at the low end of the performance spectrum, it is considered a low-cost solution. Other solutions add communication processors on the network interface cards, which provide programmability and performance. Table 4.2 shows the relative performance and other features of different high-speed networks.

4.4.1 Ethernet

The Ethernet is a packet-switched LAN technology introduced by Xerox PARC in the early 1970s. The Ethernet was designed to be a shared bus technology where multiple hosts are connected to a shared communication medium. All hosts connected to an Ethernet receive every transmission, making it possible to broadcast a packet to all hosts at the same time. The Ethernet uses a distributed access control scheme called Carrier Sense Multiple Access with Collision Detect (CSMA/CD). Multiple machines can access an Ethernet at the same time. Each machine senses whether a carrier wave is present to determine whether the network is idle before it sends a packet. Only when the network is not busy sending another message can transmission start. Each transmission is limited in duration and there is a minimum idle time between two consecutive transmissions by the same sender.

Each computer connected to an Ethernet network is assigned a unique 48-bit address, known as its Ethernet address. Ethernet manufacturers assign unique Ethernet addresses as they produce hardware interfaces. The Ethernet address, which is also called a media access (MAC) address, is fixed in machine-readable form on the host interface hardware. The address can specify the physical address of one network interface, the network broadcast address, or a multicast. In addition to its MAC address, an interface must recognize a broadcast address (all 1s) and the group addresses in the case of multicast. The Ethernet interface hardware is usually given the set of addresses to recognize by the operating system during boot time. The host interface hardware, which receives a copy of every packet that passes by, will use the destination address to determine the packets that should be passed to the host. Other packets addressed to other hosts will be ignored.

In the early days of LAN technology, an Ethernet speed of 10 million bits per second (10 Mbps) (10Base-T) was quite sufficient. However, with the dramatic increase in central processing unit (CPU) speed and advances in network technology, a 10 Mbps Ethernet became an obvious bottleneck. Fast Ethernet, which uses twisted-pair wiring, was later introduced with a speed of 100 Mbps (100Base-T). Dual-speed Ethernet (10/100 Ethernet) was also introduced to accommodate both 10 and 100 Mbps connections. By the late 1990s, demand increased for even higher-speed Ethernet; consequently, Gigabit Ethernet was introduced. Gigabit Ethernet (1000Base-T) extended the Ethernet technology to a bit rate of1 Gbps.

In order to achieve an acceptable level of performance and to eliminate any potential bottleneck, there must be some balance between the Ethernet speed and the processor speed. The initial Beowulf prototype cluster in 1994 was built with DX4 processors and 10 Mbit/s Ethernet. The network configuration of a high-performance cluster is dependent on

- The size of the cluster.
- The relationship between processor speed and network bandwidth.
- The current price list for each of the components.

4.4.2 Switches

A switch is used to establish connections from the input ports to the output ports. An $n_1 \times n_2$ switch consists of n_1 input ports, n_2 output ports, links connecting each input to every output, control logic to select a specific connection, and internal buffers. Although n_1 and n_2 do not have to be equal, in practice and in most cases they have the same value, which is usually a power of two.

These connections can be

- One-to-one, which represent point-to-point connections; when only one-to-one connections are allowed, the switch is called crossbar.
- One-to-many, which represent multicast or broadcast.
- Many-to-one causes conflicts at the output ports and therefore needs arbitration to resolve conflicts if allowed.

An $n \times n$ crossbar switch can establish $n!$ connections. To allow only one-to-one connections, the first input port should have n choices of output ports, the second input port will have $(n - 1)$ choices, the third input port will have $(n - 2)$ choices, and so on. Thus, the number of one-to-one connections is $n * (n - 1) * (n - 2) * \ldots 2 * 1 = n!$. If we allow both one-to-one as well as one-to-many in an $n \times n$ switch, the number of connections that can be established is n^n. For example, a binary switch has two input ports and two output ports. The number of one-to-one connections in a binary switch is two (straight and crossed), while the number of all allowed connections is four (straight, crosses, lower broadcast, and upper broadcast).

Routing can be achieved using two mechanisms:

- Source-path routing: The entire path to the destination is stored in the packet header at the source location. When a packet enters the switch, the outgoing port is determined from the header. Used routing data is stripped from the header and routing information for the next switch is now in front.
- Table-based routing: The switch must have a complete routing table that determines the corresponding port for each destination. When a packet enters the switch, a table lookup will determine the outgoing port.

Figure 4.2 illustrates the difference between source-path routing and table-based routing in the case when a packet enters an 8-port switch at port 0. In the source-path case, the header contains the entire path and the next port is port 6. In the table-based case, the destination address dest-id is looked up in the routing table and port 6 is followed.

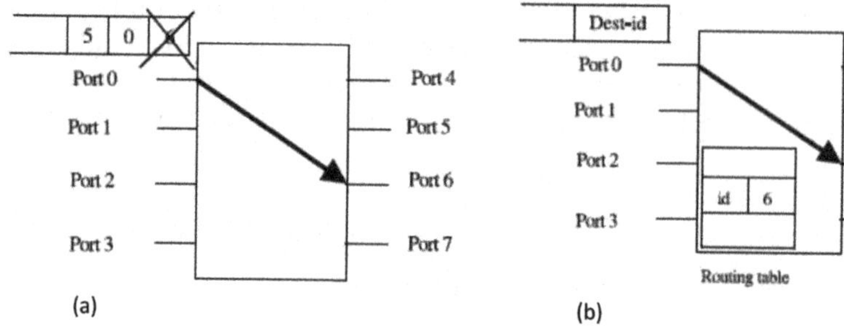

FIGURE 4.2
(a) Source-path routing and (b) table-based routing.

4.5 Summary

The merging of computers and communications has had a profound influence on the way computer systems are organized. The old model of a single computer serving an organization's entire computational needs has been replaced by one in which a large number of separate but interconnected computers do the job. These systems are called computer networks. The chapter commenced with network principles (such as protocols, protocol layers, and protocol suite), types of networks (PAN, LAN, MAN, WAN), and both network models: OSI and TCP/IP reference models. The chapter concluded by introducing interconnection networks.

5

Distributed Systems Basics

The centralized approach to processing data, in which users access a central database on a central computer through personal computers (PCs) and workstations, dominated organizations from the late 1960s through the mid-1980s because there was no alternative approach to compete with it. The introduction of reasonably priced PCs during the 1980s, however, facilitated the placement of computers at various locations within an organization; users could access a database directly at those locations. Networks connected these computers, so users could access not only data located on their local computers, but also data located anywhere across the entire network.

This chapter addresses issues involved in distributed systems.

5.1 Distributed Systems

Distributed systems consist of a collection of heterogeneous but fully autonomous components that can execute on different computers. While each of these components has full control over its constituent subparts, no master component possesses control over all the components of a distributed system. Thus, for each of these systems to appear as a single and integrated whole, the various components need the ability to interact with each other via predefined interfaces through a computer network.

The characteristic global features of a successful distributed system are

- Distributed systems are heterogeneous arising from the need to (say) integrate components on a legacy IBM mainframe, with the components newly created to operate on a UNIX workstation or Windows NT machine.
- Distributed systems are scalable in that when a component becomes overloaded with too many requests or users, a replica of the same component can be instantiated and added to the distributed system to share the load among them. Moreover, these instantiated components can be located closer to the local users and other interacting components to improve the performance of the overall distributed system.
- Distributed systems execute components concurrently in a multithreaded mode via multiply invoked components corresponding to the number of simultaneously invoked processes.
- Distributed systems are fault-tolerant in that they duplicate components on different computers so that if one computer fails, another can take over without affecting the availability of the overall system.
- Distributed systems are more resilient in that whereas distributed systems have multiple points of failure, the unaffected components are fully operational even though some of the components are not functional or are malfunctioning. Moreover, the distributed system could invoke another instance of the failed

components along with the corresponding state of the process (characterized by the program counter, the register variable contents, and the state of the virtual memory used by the process) to continue with the process.

- Distributed systems demonstrate invariance or transparency with reference to characteristics such as
  - Accessibility, either locally or across networks to the components
  - Physical location of the components
  - Migration of components from one host to another
  - Replication of components including their states
  - Concurrency of components requesting services from shared components
  - Scalability in terms of the actual number of requests or users at any instance
  - Performance in terms of the number and type of available resources
  - Points of failure, be it a failure of the component, network, or response

The terms parallel systems and distributed systems are often used interchangeably; however, the term distributed refers to a wider class of systems, while the term parallel implies a subclass of tightly coupled systems. Distributed systems encompasses any architecture or system that allows the computation to be broken down into units and executed concurrently on different computing elements, whether these are processors on different nodes, processors on the same computer, or cores within the same processor. Distributed often implies that the locations of all the constituting computing elements are not the same and such elements might be heterogeneous in terms of their hardware and software features. Classic examples of distributed computing systems are computing grids or Internet computing systems, which combine the biggest variety of architectures, systems, and applications in the world.

Parallel systems refers to a model in which the computation is divided among several processors sharing the same memory. The architecture of a parallel computing system is often characterized by the homogeneity of its components: each processor is of the same type and it has the same capability as the others. The shared memory has a single address space, which is accessible to all processors. Parallel programs are then broken down into several units of execution that can be allocated to different processors and can communicate with each other by means of the shared memory.

Originally, parallel systems used to include only those architectures that featured multiple processors sharing the same physical memory and computer. However, current parallel systems are considered to include all those architectures that are based on the concept of shared memory regardless of whether this is physically colocated or created with the support of libraries, specific hardware, and a highly efficient networking infrastructure. For example, a cluster in which the nodes are connected through an InfiniBand network and configured with a distributed shared memory system can also be considered a parallel system.

5.1.1 Distributed Computing

Distributed computing studies the models, architectures, and algorithms used for building and managing distributed systems. A distributed system is a collection of independent computers that appears to its users as a single coherent system. Distributed systems are primarily focused on the aggregation of distributed resources and unified usage. This is accomplished by communicating with other computers only by exchanging messages.

A distributed system is the result of the interaction of several components across the entire computing stack from hardware to software. The hardware and operating system layers make up the bare-bones infrastructure of one or more data centers, where racks of servers are deployed and connected together through high-speed connectivity. This infrastructure is managed by the operating system, which provides the basic capability of machine and network management. The core logic is then implemented in the middleware that manages the virtualization layer, which is deployed on the physical infrastructure in order to maximize its utilization and provide a customizable runtime environment for applications. The middleware provides different facilities and functionalities per the requirement of the end customers and users. These facilities range from virtual infrastructure building and deployment to application development and runtime environments.

The different layers constituting the distributed system stack are

- Hardware layer: At the very bottom layer, computer and network hardware constitute the physical infrastructure; these components are directly managed by the operating system, which provides the basic services for interprocess communication (IPC), process scheduling and management, and resource management in terms of file system and local devices. Taken together, these two layers become the platform on top of which specialized software is deployed to turn a set of networked computers into a distributed system.
- Operating system layer: The use of well-known standards at the operating system level and even more at the hardware and network levels allows easy harnessing of heterogeneous components and their organization into a coherent and uniform system. For example, network connectivity between different devices is controlled by standards, which allow them to interact seamlessly. At the operating system level, IPC services are implemented on top of standardized communication protocols such Transmission Control Protocol/Internet Protocol (TCP/IP), User Datagram Protocol (UDP), or others.
- Middleware layer: The middleware layer leverages such services to build a uniform environment for the development and deployment of distributed applications. This layer supports the programming paradigms for distributed systems. By relying on the services offered by the operating system, the middleware develops its own protocols, data formats, and programming language or frameworks for the development of distributed applications. All of them constitute a uniform interface to distributed application developers that is completely independent from the underlying operating system and hides all the heterogeneities of the bottom layers.
- Application layer: The topmost layer is represented by the applications and services designed and developed to use the middleware. These can serve several purposes and often expose their features in the form of graphical user interfaces (GUIs) accessible locally or through the Internet via a web browser.

Architectural styles for distributed systems are helpful in understanding the different roles of components in the system and how they are distributed across multiple computers.

Architectural styles are of two types:

- System architectural style
- Software architectural style

5.1.1.1 System Architectural Styles

System architectural styles cover the physical organization of components and processes over a distributed infrastructure. They provide a set of reference models for the deployment of such systems and help engineers not only have a common vocabulary in describing the physical layout of systems but also quickly identify the major advantages and drawbacks of a given deployment and whether it is applicable for a specific class of applications.

These reference models can be further enhanced or diversified according to the specific needs of the application to be designed and implemented.

- N-tier architecture

  In the 1980s, the prior monolithic architecture began to be replaced by the client/server architecture, which split applications into two pieces in an attempt to leverage new inexpensive desktop machines. Distributing the processing loads across many inexpensive clients allowed client/server applications to scale more linearly than single host/single process applications could, and the use of off-the-shelf software such as relational database management systems (RDBMS) greatly reduced the application development time. While the client could handle the user interface and data display tasks of the application, and the server could handle all the data management tasks, there was no clear solution for storing the logic corresponding to the business processes being automated. Consequently, the business logic tended to split between the client and the server; typically, the rules for displaying data became embedded inside the user interface, and the rules for integrating several different data sources became stored procedures inside the database. Whereas this division of logic made it difficult to reuse the user interface code with a different data source, it also made it equally difficult to use the logic stored in the database with a different front-end user interface (such as ATM and mobile) without being required to redevelop the logic implemented in the earlier interface. Thus, a customer service system developed for a particular client system (such as a 3270 terminal, a PC, or a workstation) would have great difficulty in providing telephony and Internet interfaces with the same business functionality.

  The client/server architecture failed to recognize the importance of managing the business rules applicable to an enterprise independent of both the user interface and the storage and management of enterprise data. The three-tiered application architecture of the 1990s resolved this problem by subdividing the application into three distinct layers:

  - Data management, which stores and manages data independent of how it is processed and displayed by the other layers.
  - Business logic, which implements the business logic to process data independent of how it is stored or displayed by the other two layers.
  - Presentation, which formats and displays the data independent of the way it is interpreted/processed and stored by the other two layers.

  With the advent of the Internet in the past few years, the three tiers were split even further to accommodate the heterogeneity in terms of the user interfaces, processing systems, or databases existing in various parts of an enterprise.

  The power of the n-tier architecture derives from the fact that instead of treating components as integral parts of systems, components are treated as stand-alone entities, which can provide services for applications. Applications exist only as a cooperating constellation of components, and each component in turn can simultaneously be part of many different applications.

- Peer-to-peer

  The peer-to-peer model introduces a symmetric architecture in which all the components, called peers, play the same role and incorporate both the client and server capabilities of the client/server model. More precisely, each peer acts as a server when it processes requests from other peers and as a client when it issues requests to other peers. With respect to the client/server model that partitions the responsibilities of the IPC between server and clients, the peer-to-peer model attributes the same responsibilities to each component. Therefore, this model is quite suitable for highly decentralized architecture, which can scale better along the dimension of the number of peers. The disadvantage of this approach is that the management of the implementation of algorithms is more complex than in the client/server model.

5.1.1.2 Software Architectural Styles

Software architectural styles are based on the logical arrangement of software components. They are helpful because they provide an intuitive view of the whole system, despite its physical deployment.

- Data-centered architectures

  The repository architectural style is the most relevant reference model in this category. It is characterized by two main components: the central data structure, which represents the current state of the system, and a collection of independent components, which operate on the central data. The ways in which the independent components interact with the central data structure can be very heterogeneous. In particular, repository-based architectures differentiate and specialize further into subcategories according to the choice of control discipline to apply for the shared data structure.

  Data-centered architectures are of two types:

  - Databases systems. In this case, the dynamic of the system is controlled by the independent components, which, by issuing an operation on the central repository, trigger the selection of specific processes that operate on data.
  - Blackboard systems. In this case, the central data structure itself is the main trigger for selecting the processes to execute; knowledge sources representing the intelligent agents sharing the blackboard react opportunistically to changes in the knowledge base—almost in the same way that a group of specialists brainstorm in a room in front of a blackboard.

The blackboard architectural style is characterized by three main components:

- Knowledge sources. These are the entities that update the knowledge base that is maintained in the blackboard.
- Blackboard. This represents the data structure that is shared among the knowledge sources and stores the knowledge base of the application.
- Control. The control is the collection of triggers and procedures that govern the interaction with the blackboard and update the status of the knowledge base.

Blackboard models have become popular and widely used for artificial intelligent applications in which the blackboard maintains the knowledge about a domain in the form of assertions and rules, which are entered by domain experts. These operate through a control shell that controls the problem-solving activity of the system. Particular and successful applications of this model can be found in the domains of speech recognition and signal processing.

- Dataflow architectures

  In the case of dataflow architectures, it is the availability of data that controls the computation. With respect to the data-centered styles, in which the access to data is the core feature, dataflow styles explicitly incorporate the pattern of data flow, since their design is determined by an orderly motion of data from component to component, which is the form of communication between them. Styles within this category differ in one of the following ways: how the control is exerted, the degree of concurrency among components, and the topology that describes the flow of data.

  Dataflow architectures are optimal when the system to be designed embodies a multistage process, which can be clearly identified as a collection of separate components that need to be orchestrated together. Within this reference scenario, components have well-defined interfaces exposing input and output ports, and the connectors are represented by the data streams between these ports.
- Batch sequential style. The batch sequential style is characterized by an ordered sequence of separate programs executing one after the other. These programs are chained together by providing as input for the next program the output generated by the last program after its completion, which is most likely in the form of a file. This design was very popular in the mainframe era of computing and still finds applications today. For example, many distributed applications for scientific computing are defined by jobs expressed as sequences of programs that, for example, pre-filter, analyze, and post-process data. It is very common to compose these phases using the batch sequential style.
- Pipe-and-filter style. The pipe-and-filter style is a variation of the previous style for expressing the activity of a software system as a sequence of data transformations. Each component of the processing chain is called a filter, and the connection between one filter and the next is represented by a data stream. With respect to the batch sequential style, data is processed incrementally and each filter processes the data as soon as it is available on the input stream. As soon as one filter produces a consumable amount of data, the next filter can start its processing. Filters generally do not have state, nor know the identity of either the previous or the next filter, and they are connected with in-memory data structures such as first-in/first-out (FIFO) buffers or other structures. This particular sequencing is called pipelining and introduces concurrency in the execution of the filters.

  A classic example of this architecture is the microprocessor pipeline, whereby multiple instructions are executed at the same time by completing a different phase of each of them. We can identify the phases of the instructions as the filters, whereas the data streams are represented by the registries that are shared within the processors. Another example are the UNIX shell pipes (i.e., cat <file-name>| grep<pattern>| wc -l), where the filters are the single shell programs composed together and the connections are their input and output streams that are chained together. Applications of this architecture can also be found in the compiler design (e.g., the lex/yacc model is based on a pipe of the following phases | scanning | parsing | semantic analysis | code generation), image and signal processing, and voice and video streaming.

- Call and return architectures

  This category identifies all systems that are organized into components mostly connected together by method calls. The activity of systems modelled in this way is characterized by a chain of method calls whose overall execution and composition identify the execution of one or more operations. The internal organization of components and their connections may vary. Nonetheless, it is possible to identify three major subcategories, which differentiate by the way the system is structured and how methods are invoked: top-down style, object-oriented style, and layered style.

  - Top-down style. This architectural style is quite representative of systems developed with imperative programming, which leads to a divide-and-conquer approach to problem resolution. Systems developed according to this style are composed of one large main program that accomplishes its tasks by invoking subprograms or procedures. The components in this style are procedures and subprograms, and connections are method calls or invocation. The calling program passes information with parameters and receives data from return values or parameters. Method calls can also extend beyond the boundary of a single process by leveraging techniques for remote method invocation, such as remote procedure call (RPC) and all its descendants. The overall structure of the program execution at any point in time is characterized by a tree, the root of which constitutes the main function of the principal program. This architectural style is quite intuitive from a design point of view but hard to maintain and manage in large systems.
  - Layered style. The layered system style allows the design and implementation of software systems in terms of layers, which provide a different level of abstraction of the system. Each layer generally operates with at most two layers: one that provides a lower abstraction level and one that provides a higher abstraction layer. Specific protocols and interfaces define how adjacent layers interact. It is possible to model such systems as a stack of layers, one for each level of abstraction. Therefore, the components are the layers and the connectors are the interfaces and protocols used between adjacent layers. A user or client generally interacts with the layer at the highest abstraction, which, in order to carry its activity, interacts and uses the services of the lower layer. This process is repeated (if necessary) until the lowest layer is reached. It is also possible to have the opposite behavior: events and callbacks from the lower layers can trigger the activity of the higher layer and propagate information up through the stack.

The advantages of the layered style are

- It supports a modular design of systems and allows us to decompose the system according to different levels of abstractions by encapsulating together all the operations that belong to a specific level.
- It enables layers to be replaced as long as they are compliant with the expected protocols and interfaces, thus making the system flexible.

- The main disadvantage is its lack of extensibility, since it is not possible to add layers without changing the protocols and the interfaces between layers. This also makes it complex to add operations. Examples of layered architectures are the modern operating system kernels and the International Standards Organization/Open Systems Interconnection (ISO/OSI) or the TCP/IP stack.
- Object-oriented style. This architectural style encompasses a wide range of systems that have been designed and implemented by leveraging the abstractions of object-oriented programming (OOP). Systems are specified in terms of classes and implemented in terms of objects. Classes define the type of components by specifying the data that represents their state and the operations that can be done over this data. One of the main advantages over the top-down style is that there is a coupling between the data and the operations used to manipulate it. Object instances become responsible for hiding their internal state representation and for protecting their integrity while providing operations to other components. This leads to a better decomposition process and more manageable systems. The disadvantages of this style are mainly two: each object needs to know the identity of an object if it wants to invoke operations on it, and shared objects need to be carefully designed in order to ensure the consistency of their state.

- Virtual architectures

  The virtual machine class of architectural style is characterized by the presence of an abstract execution environment (generally referred as a virtual machine) that simulates features that are not available in the hardware or software. Applications and systems are implemented on top of this layer and become portable over different hardware and software environments as long as there is an implementation of the virtual machine with which they interface. The general interaction flow for systems implementing this pattern is the following: the program (or the application) defines its operations and state in an abstract format, which is interpreted by the virtual machine engine. The interpretation of a program constitutes its execution. In this scenario, it is quite common for the engine to maintain an internal representation of the program state. Very popular examples within this category are rule-based systems, interpreters, and command-language processors.

  Virtual machine architectural styles are characterized by an indirection layer between applications and the hosting environment. This design has the major advantage of decoupling applications from the underlying hardware and software environment; however, at the same time, it introduces some disadvantages, such as a slowdown in performance. Other issues might be related to the fact that, by providing a virtual execution environment, specific features of the underlying system might not be accessible.

  - Rule-based style. This architecture is characterized by representing the abstract execution environment as an inference engine. Programs are expressed in the form of rules or predicates that hold true. The input data for applications is generally represented by a set of assertions or facts that the inference engine uses to activate rules or to apply predicates, thus transforming data. The output can either be the product of the rule activation or a set of assertions that holds true for the given input data. The set of rules or predicates identifies the knowledge base that can be queried to infer properties about the system. This approach is quite peculiar, since it allows expressing a system or a domain in terms of its behavior rather than in terms of the components. Rule-based systems are very popular in the field of artificial intelligence. Practical applications can be found in the field of process control, where rule-based systems are used to monitor the status of physical devices by being fed from the sensory data collected and processed by PLCs1 and by activating alarms when specific conditions on the sensory data apply. Another interesting use of rule-based systems can be found in the networking domain: network intrusion detection systems (NIDS) often rely on a set of rules to identify abnormal behaviors connected to possible intrusions in computing systems.

- Interpreter style. The core feature of the interpreter style is the presence of an engine that is used to interpret a pseudo-program expressed in a format acceptable to the interpreter. The interpretation of the pseudo-program constitutes the execution of the program itself. Systems modelled according to this style exhibit four main components: the interpretation engine that executes the core activity of this style, an internal memory that contains the pseudo-code to be interpreted, a representation of the current state of the engine, and a representation of the current state of the program being executed. This model is quite useful in designing virtual machines for high-level programming (Java, C#) and scripting languages (Awk, PERL, and so on). Within this scenario, the virtual machine closes the gap between the end-user abstractions and the software/hardware environment in which such abstractions are executed.

- Independent components

  This class of architectural style models systems in terms of independent components that have their own life cycles, which interact with each other to perform their activities. There are two major categories within this class—communicating processes and event systems—which differentiate in the way the interaction among components is managed.

  - Communicating processes. In this architectural style, components are represented by independent processes that leverage IPC facilities for coordination management. This is an abstraction that is quite suitable for modeling distributed systems that, being distributed over a network of computing nodes, are necessarily composed of several concurrent processes. Each of the processes provides other processes with services and can leverage the services exposed by the other processes. The conceptual organization of these processes and the way in which the communication happens vary according to the specific model used, either peer-to-peer or client/server. Connectors are identified by the IPC facilities used by these processes to communicate.
  - Event systems. In this architectural style, the components of the system are loosely coupled and connected. In addition to exposing operations for data and state manipulation, each component also publishes (or announces) a collection of events with which other components can register. In general, other components provide a callback that will be executed when the event is activated. During the activity of a component, a specific runtime condition can activate one of the exposed events, thus triggering the execution of the callbacks registered with it. Event activation may be accompanied by contextual information that can be used in the callback to handle the event. This information can be passed as an argument to the callback or by using some shared repository between components. Event-based systems have become quite popular, and support for their implementation is provided either at the application programming interface (API) level or the programming language level.

The main advantage of such an architectural style is that it fosters the development of open systems: new modules can be added and easily integrated into the system as long as they have compliant interfaces for registering to the events. This architectural style solves some of the limitations observed for the top-down and object-oriented styles:

- The invocation pattern is implicit, and the connection between the caller and the callee is not hard-coded; this gives a lot of flexibility since the addition or removal of a handler to events can be done without changes in the source code of applications.
- The event source does not need to know the identity of the event handler in order to invoke the callback.

The disadvantage of such a style is that it relinquishes control over system computation. When a component triggers an event, it does not know how many event handlers will be invoked and whether there are any registered handlers. This information is available only at runtime and, from a static design point of view, becomes more complex to identify the connections among components and to reason about the correctness of the interactions.

5.1.1.3 Technologies for Distributed Computing

Middleware is system services software that executes between the operating system layer and the application layer and provides services. It connects two or more applications, thereby providing connectivity and interoperability to the applications. Middleware is not a silver bullet that will solve all integration problems. Due to overhyping in the 1980s and early 1990s, the term middleware has lost popularity but it has come back in the last few years. Today, the middleware concept, however, is even more important for integration, and all integration projects will have to use one or many different middleware solutions. Middleware is mainly used to denote products that provide the glue between applications, which is distinct from simple data import and export functions that might be built into the applications themselves.

All forms of middleware are helpful in easing the communication between different software applications. The selection of middleware influences the application architecture, because middleware centralizes the software infrastructure and its deployment. Middleware introduces an abstraction layer in the system architecture and thus considerably reduces the complexity. On the other hand, each middleware product introduces a certain communication overhead into the system, which can influence performance, scalability, throughput, and other efficiency factors. This is important to consider when designing the integration architecture, particularly if our systems are mission critical and are used by a large number of concurrent clients.

Middleware is connectivity software that is designed to help manage the complexity and heterogeneity inherent in distributed systems by building a bridge between different systems, thereby enabling communication and the transfer of data. Middleware could be defined as a layer of enabling software services that allows application elements to interoperate across network links, despite differences in underlying communications protocols, system architectures, operating systems, databases, and other application services. The role of middleware is to ease the task of designing, programming, and managing distributed applications by providing a simple, consistent, and integrated distributed programming environment. Essentially, middleware is a distributed software layer, or platform, that lives above the operating system and abstracts over the complexity and heterogeneity of the underlying distributed environment with its multitude of network technologies, machine architectures, operating systems, and programming languages.

The middleware layers are interposed between applications and Internet transport protocols. The middleware abstraction comprises two layers. The bottom layer is concerned with the characteristics of protocols for communicating between processes in a distributed system and how data objects, for example, a customer order, and data structures used in application programs can be translated into a suitable form for sending messages over a communications network, taking into account that different computers may rely on heterogeneous representations for simple data items. The layer above is concerned with IPC mechanisms, while the layer above that is concerned with non-message- and message-based forms of middleware. Message-based forms of middleware provide asynchronous messaging and event notification mechanisms to exchange messages or react to events over electronic networks. Non-message-based forms of middleware provide synchronous communication mechanisms designed to support client–server communication.

Middleware uses two basic modes of message communication:

- Synchronous or time dependent: The defining characteristic of a synchronous form of execution is that message communication is synchronized between two communicating application systems, both of which must be up and running, and that the execution flow at the client's side is interrupted to execute the call. Both sending and receiving applications must be ready to communicate with each other at all times. A sending application initiates a request (sends a message) to a receiving application. The sending application then blocks its processing until it receives a response from the receiving application. The receiving application continues its processing after it receives the response.
- Asynchronous or time independent: With asynchronous communication, an application sends (requestor or sender) a request to another while it continues its own processing activities. The sending application does not have to wait for the receiving application to complete and for its reply to come back. Instead, it can continue processing other requests. Unlike the synchronous mode, both application systems (sender and receiver) do not have to be active at the same time for processing to occur.

The basic messaging processes inherently utilize asynchronous communication. There are several benefits to asynchronous messaging:

- Asynchronous messaging clients can proceed with application processing independently of other applications. Loose coupling of senders and receivers optimizes system processing by not having to block sending client processing while waiting for the receiving client to complete the request.
- Asynchronous messaging allows batch and parallel processing of messages. The sending client can send as many messages to the receiving clients without having to wait for the receiving clients to process previously sent messages. On the receiving end, different receiving clients can process the messages at their own speed and timing.
- There is less demand on the communication network because the messaging clients do not have to be connected to each other or the message-oriented middleware (MOM) while messages are processed. Connections are active only to put messages to the MOM and get messages from the MOM.

- The network does not have to be available at all times because of the timing independence of client processing. Messages can wait in the queue of the receiving client if the network is not available. MOM implements asynchronous message queues at its core. It can concurrently service many sending and receiving applications.

Despite its performance drawbacks, synchronous messaging has several benefits over asynchronous messaging. The tightly coupled nature of synchronous messaging means the sending client can better handle application errors in the receiving client. If an error occurs in the receiving client, the sending client can try to compensate for the error. This is especially important when the sending client requests a transaction to be performed in the receiving client. The better error handling ability of synchronous messaging means it is easier for programmers to develop synchronous messaging solutions. Since both the sending and receiving clients are online and connected, it is easier for programmers to debug errors that might occur during the development stage. Since most developers are also more familiar with programming using synchronous processing, this also facilitates the development of synchronous messaging solutions over asynchronous messaging solutions.

When speaking of middleware products, we encompass a large variety of technologies. The most common forms of middleware are

- Database access technologies
  - Microsoft Open Database Connectivity (ODBC)
  - Java Database Connectivity (JDBC)
- Asynchronous middleware
  - Store and Forward Messaging
  - Publish/Subscribe Messaging
  - Point-to-Point Queuing
  - Event-driven Processing Mechanism
- Synchronous middleware
  - Remote Procedure Call (RPC)
  - Remote Method Invocation (RMI)
- Message-oriented middleware (MOM)
  - Integration Brokers
  - Java Messaging Service (JMS)
- Request/reply messaging middleware
- Transaction processing monitors (TPMs)
- Object request brokers (ORBs)
  - OMG CORBA ORB compliant
  - Java RMI and RMI-IIOP (Internet Inter-ORB Protocol)
  - Microsoft COM/DCOM/COM+/.NET Remoting/WCF
- Application servers
- Service-oriented architecture
  - Web services using WSDL, UDDI, SOAP, and XML
  - RESTful services

- Enterprise service buses (ESBs)
- Enterprise systems

For a detailed discussion on the foregoing technologies, refer to the companion volume *Guide to Cloud Computing for Business and Technology Managers* (Kale 2015).

5.2 Distributed System Benefits

The motivation for using a distributed system is some or all of the following requirements:

- Inherently distributed computations: In many applications such as a money transfer in banking, or reaching a consensus among parties that are geographically distant, the computation is inherently distributed.
- Resource sharing: Resources such as peripherals, complete datasets in databases, special libraries, as well as data (variable/files) cannot be fully replicated at all sites because it is often neither practical nor cost-effective. Further, they cannot be placed at a single site because access to that site might prove to be a bottleneck. Therefore, such resources are typically distributed across the system. For example, distributed databases partition the datasets across several servers, in addition to replicating them at a few sites for rapid access as well as reliability.
- Access to geographically remote data and resources: In many scenarios, the data cannot be replicated at every site participating in the distributed execution because it may be too large or too sensitive to be replicated. For example, payroll data within a multinational corporation is both too large and too sensitive to be replicated at every branch office/site. It is therefore stored at a central server, which can be queried by branch offices. Similarly, special resources such as supercomputers only exist in certain locations, and to access such supercomputers, users need to log in remotely.
- Enhanced reliability: A distributed system has the inherent potential to provide increased reliability because of the possibility of replicating resources and executions, as well as the reality that geographically distributed resources are not likely to crash/malfunction at the same time under normal circumstances. Reliability entails several aspects:
    - Availability, that is, the resource should be accessible at all times.
    - Integrity, that is, the value/state of the resource should be correct, in the face of concurrent access from multiple processors, as per the semantics expected by the application.
    - Fault-tolerance, that is, the ability to recover from system failures, where such failures may be defined to occur in one of many failure models.
- Increased performance/cost ratio: By resource sharing and accessing geographically remote data and resources, the performance/cost ratio is increased. Although higher throughput has not necessarily been the main objective behind using a distributed system, nevertheless, any task can be partitioned across the various computers in the distributed system. Such a configuration provides a better performance/cost ratio than using special parallel machines.

- Scalability: As the processors are usually connected by a wide-area network, adding more processors does not pose a direct bottleneck for the communication network.
- Modularity and incremental expandability: Heterogeneous processors can be easily added into the system without affecting the performance, as long as those processors are running the same middleware algorithms. Similarly, existing processors can be easily replaced by other processors.

5.3 Distributed Computation Systems

A distributed computation system consists of a set of processors that are connected by a communication network. The communication network provides the facility of information exchange among processors. A communication delay is finite but unpredictable. The processors do not share a common global memory and communicate solely by passing messages over the communication network. There is no physical global clock in the system to which processes have instantaneous access. The communication medium may deliver messages out of order; messages may be lost, garbled, or duplicated due to timeout and retransmission; processors may fail; and communication links may go down. The system can be modeled as a directed graph in which vertices represent the processes and edges represent unidirectional communication channels.

A distributed application runs as a collection of processes on a distributed system. A distributed program is composed of a set of n asynchronous processes $p_1, p_2, \ldots, p_i, \ldots, p_n$, that communicate by message passing over the communication network. Without loss of generality, we assume that each process is running on a different processor. The processes do not share a global memory and communicate solely by passing messages. Let C_{ij} denote the channel from process p_i to process p_j and let m_{ij} denote a message sent by p_i to p_j. The communication delay is finite and unpredictable. Also, these processes do not share a global clock that is instantaneously accessible to these processes.

Process execution and message transfer are asynchronous—a process may execute an action spontaneously and a process sending a message does not wait for the delivery of the message to be complete.

The global state of a distributed computation is composed of the states of the processes and the communication channels. The state of a process is characterized by the state of its local memory and depends upon the context. The state of a channel is characterized by the set of messages in transit in the channel.

The execution of a process consists of a sequential execution of its actions. The actions are atomic and the actions of a process are modeled as three types of events, namely, internal events, message send events, and message receive events. Let e_i^x denote the xth event at process p_i. The occurrence of events changes the states of respective processes and channels, thus causing transitions in the global system state. An internal event changes the state of the process at which it occurs. A send event (or a receive event) changes the state of the process that sends (or receives) the message and the state of the channel on which the message is sent (or received). An internal event only affects the process at which it occurs.

The evolution of a distributed execution is depicted by a space–time diagram. Figure 5.1 shows the space–time diagram of a distributed execution involving three processes. The horizontal line represents the progress of the process; the dot indicates an event; and

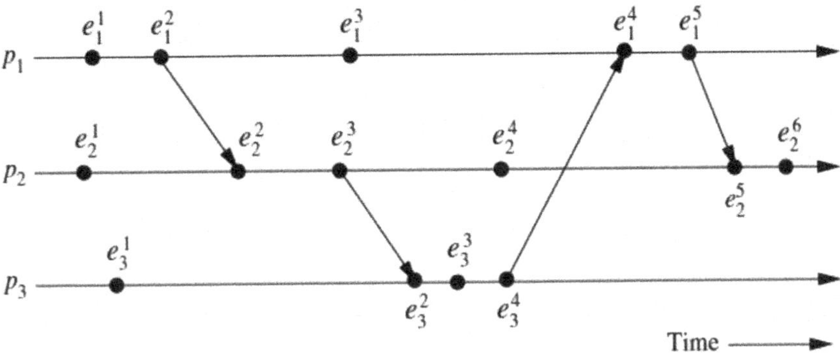

FIGURE 5.1
Space–time diagram of a distributed execution.

the slant arrow indicates a message transfer. Generally, the execution of an event takes a finite amount of time; however, since we assume that an event execution is atomic (hence, indivisible and instantaneous), it is justified to denote it as a dot on a process line. In Figure 5.1, for process p_1, the second event is a message send event, the third event is an internal event, and the fourth event is a message receive event.

5.4 Summary

In this chapter, we provided an introduction to distributed computing. Distributed systems constitute a large umbrella under which several different software systems are classified. The unification of parallel and distributed computing allows one to harness a set of networked and heterogeneous computers and present them as a unified resource. Architectural styles help categorize and provide reference models for distributed systems. More precisely, system architectural styles are more concerned with the physical deployment of such systems, whereas software architectural styles define logical organizations of components and their roles. These two styles are the fundamental deployment blocks of any distributed system. Message-based communication is the most relevant abstraction for IPC and forms the basis for several techniques of IPC, which is a fundamental element in distributed systems; it is the element that ties together separate processes and allows them to be seen as a unified whole.

Section II

Road to Parallel Computing

This section introduces parallel systems. Chapters 6 through 8 introduce the overarching concepts of parallel systems that characterize parallel computing as a whole.

Chapter 6 presents Flynn's taxonomy for parallel computers defining the server set identifier (SSID), single instruction, multiple data (SIMD), multiple instruction, single data (MISD), multiple instruction, multiple data (MIMD) architectures. General-purpose multiprocessor systems (MIMD computers) are further subdivided into two major subtypes: *shared memory multiprocessor systems* and *distributed memory multicomputers*. The chapter concludes by discussing the characteristics of parallel systems such as coupling, parallelism, concurrency, and granularity, and aspects of distributed communications such as synchronous/asynchronous primitives and blocking/non-blocking primitives.

Chapter 7 discusses parallel computation models that are helpful for analyzing and designing algorithms, as well as in determining performance metrics used for the evaluation of algorithms. A computational model can be used to evaluate algorithms independently of their implementation in a specific programming language and of the use of a specific computer system. In the case of the shared memory model, every processor shares and has access to a global memory. The chapter discusses, within the shared memory model, the random-access machine (RAM) and parallel random-access machine (PRAM) models under the class of theoretical models, and bulk synchronous parallel (BSP) and LogP models under the class of practical models. Similarly, within the interconnected network models, it discusses mesh, mesh of trees, cubes, cubes connected cycles, etc., under the class of theoretical models, and cluster and grids under the class of practical models. In dataflow computers, an operation to be executed is governed by the availability of its operands, and not by the current instruction of a program.

Chapter 8 describes various aspects of parallel algorithms. The chapter commences by looking at classes of problems that are solvable through parallelization. It then describes various types of parallelization, namely, functional, data, recursive, exploratory, and speculative parallelization. The amount of work to be performed within a task determines the grain size: depending on whether the grain size of tasks is small or large, the computation is termed, respectively, fine-grained or coarse-grained. Load balancing deals with minimizing the parallel program run-time that is achieved by the uniform distribution of computations across available processors. In the last part, the chapter exemplifies the process of developing a parallel algorithm for a particular model.

6

Parallel Systems

The chapter commences with Flynn's taxonomy for parallel computers, defining the single instruction, single data (SISD), single instruction, multiple data (SIMD), multiple instruction, single data (MISD), and multiple instruction, multiple data (MIMD). The MIMD are further classified based on their memory structure (global or distributed) and the mechanism used for communication/synchronization (shared variables or message passing) into global memory, message passing (GMMP), global memory, shared variables (GMSV), distributed memory message, passing (DMMP), and distributed memory, shared variable DMSV. Flynn's taxonomy also gives rise to levels of parallelisms, viz. task-level, data-level, instruction-level, and bit-level parallelism. Instruction-level parallelism allows the compiler and the processor to overlap the execution of multiple instructions or even to change the order in which instructions are executed. Pipelining is an excellent example of this form of parallel processing. General-purpose multiprocessor systems (MIMD computers) can also be divided into two major subtypes: *shared memory multiprocessor* systems and *distributed memory multicomputers.*

Scalability suffers in the case of shared memory systems for a large number of processors because the connection to the common memory becomes a bottleneck. In a distributed memory system, each processor has its own main memory and such processor–memory pairs operate as individual computers that are interconnected. The programming model for such a distributed memory system is usually a message-passing model in which messages pass information between the computers.

6.1 Flynn's Taxonomy for Parallel Computer Architectures

In 1966, M. J. Flynn proposed a four-way classification of computer systems based on the notions of instruction streams and data streams. Flynn's classification has become standard and is widely used. Flynn coined the abbreviations SISD (single instruction stream, single data stream), SIMD, MISD, and MIMD (pronounced "sis-dee," "sim-dee," and so forth) for the four classes of computers shown in Figure 6.1, based on the number of instruction streams (single or multiple) and data streams (single or multiple) (Flynn 1996): Computers in the

- SISD class represent ordinary "uniprocessor" machines.
- SIMD class, with several processors directed by instructions issued from a central control unit, are sometimes characterized as "array processors."
- MISD class have not found widespread application, but one can view them as generalized pipelines in which each stage performs a relatively complex operation (as opposed to ordinary pipelines found in modern processors where each stage does a very simple instruction-level operation).

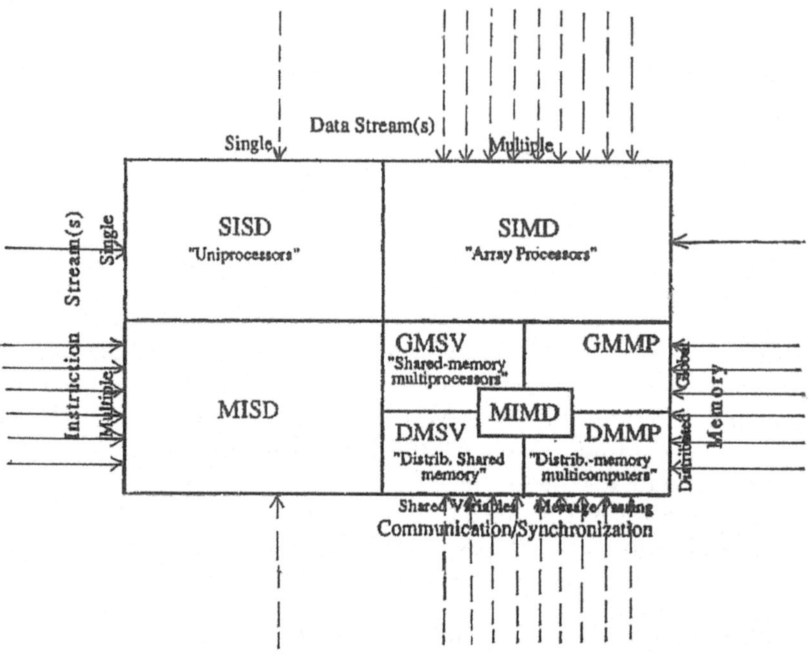

FIGURE 6.1
The Flynn–Johnson classification of computer systems.

- MIMD are further classified based on their memory structure (global or distributed) and the mechanism used for communication/synchronization (shared variables or message passing) into the following categories:
  - GMMP global memory message passing, which is not widely used.
  - GMSV global memory, shared variables, which is loosely referred to as (shared memory) multiprocessors.
  - DMMP distributed memory, message passing, which is known as (distributed memory) multicomputers.
  - DMSV distributed memory, shared variables, in which combines the ease of implementing distributed memory with the ease of programming the shared variable scheme is sometimes called distributed shared memory. When all processors in an MIMD-type machine execute the same program, the result is sometimes referred to as single program, multiple data (SPMD [spim-dee]).

Additional suggested architectures are

- Single program stream, single data stream (SPSD). This is equivalent to the SISD hardware architecture, where a computer program is progressed by a sequential program stream addressing a shared data source. The program may be parallelized by the functionality available in the functional unit such as instruction-level parallelism and pipelining.
- Multiple program streams, single data stream (MPSD). This model of parallel computation is rare and is typically engaged only in software testing.

- Single program stream, multiple data streams (SPMD). In this model, a single instruction stream (the program) is devised and executed on several independent processing units simultaneously, each accessing different elements on the same data stream.
- Multiple program streams, multiple data streams (MPMD). Multiple, different cooperating programs are executed in parallel, each executing non-overlapping sections in the data stream. Independent programs use novel synchronization procedures to accomplish the tasks cooperatively.

These numerous models of computing architectures exploit parallelism in various ways, each enabling parallel computation with differing scalability.

Parallelism within an application can be at several levels:

- Large grain (or task level)
- Medium grain (or data level)
- Fine grain (or instruction level)
- Very fine grain (bit level)

Thus, Flynn's taxonomy is representative of the hardware architecture at many different levels:

- Task-level parallelism in a multiprocessor system is synonymous with Flynn's MIMD architecture, which occurs when each central processing unit (CPU) executes a different process on the same or different data. The varying threads can execute the same or completely different code. In any case, varying threads must communicate with one another as they work. Communication takes place usually to pass data from one thread to the next as part of a workflow. Task parallelism emphasizes the distributed (parallelized) nature of the processing (i.e., threads), as opposed to the data (data parallelism). Most real programs fall somewhere on a continuum between task parallelism and data parallelism. Most supercomputers fall into this category.
- Data-level parallelism is synonymous with Flynn's SIMD architecture—single instruction (all processing units perform identical instructions) and multiple data (each processing unit can operate on varying data elements). Data-level parallelism is accomplished when each processor performs the same task on different data inputs. In some circumstances, one thread may control operations on several different pieces of data. In other situations, threads may control the operation, but they may execute the same code. Data-level parallelism emphasizes the distributed (parallelized) nature of the data, as opposed to the processing (task parallelism). Most modern computers, particularly those with graphics processing units (GPUs), employ SIMD instructions and execution units.
- Instruction-level parallelism performs many concurrent operations in a single computer program:
  - $R3 \leftarrow R1 + R2$
  - $R6 \leftarrow R4 + R5$
  - $R7 \leftarrow R3 + R6$

The third operation is dependent on the prior two operations being complete. However, the first two operations are independent operations, so they can be calculated at the same time. The most efficient compiler and processor design would identify and take advantage of as much of this parallelism as possible. Ordinary programs are typically written under a sequential execution model where instructions execute one after the other and in the order specified by the programmer.

- Bit-level parallelism is a form of parallel computing based on increasing processor word size. It is done by performing the arithmetic on two numbers, bit by bit. The addition, for example, of two 32-bit numbers was performed in 32 machine cycles, by very simple circuitry capable only of adding one bit to another. Quite possibly, the earliest use of parallelism in computers was to perform the operations on all bits simultaneously in parallel.

Instruction-level parallelism allows the compiler and the processor to overlap the execution of multiple instructions or even to change the order in which instructions are executed. Pipelining is an excellent example of this form of parallel processing. The idea of pipelining is that as each instruction completes a step, the following instruction moves into the stage just vacated. Thus, when the first instruction is completed, the next one is already one stage short of completion. Data hazard occurs when a processor fetches data c and f. Since c and f have not been written back, the fetch may access the wrong data (previously stored in c and f, not the current ones). This is called read after write (RAW).

6.2 Types of Parallel Computers

General-purpose multiprocessor systems (MIMD computers) can be divided into two types:

6.2.1 Shared Memory Multiprocessor Systems

These are a direct extension of a single processor system. In a single processor system, the processor accesses the main memory for program instructions and data (Figure 6.2a). In a shared memory multiprocessor system, multiple processors are arranged to have access to a single main memory. This is a very convenient configuration from a programming perspective as the data generated by one processor and stored in the main memory is immediately accessible by other processors. As in a single processor system, cache memory is present to reduce the need to continually access the main memory, and commonly there are two or three levels of cache memory.

Memory can either be shared or distributed (Figure 6.2a and b). Shared memory is typically composed of one of the following two architectures: uniform memory access (UMA) or nonuniform memory access (NUMA). Regardless of the specific architecture, shared memory is generally accessible to all processors in a system, and multiple processors may operate independently and continue to share the same memory. Figure 6.3a illustrates the UMA architecture. Multiple CPUs are capable of accessing one memory resource. This is also referred to as a symmetric multiprocessor (SMP). In contrast, NUMA is often made by physically linking two or more SMPs: one SMP is capable of directly accessing the memory of another SMP (see Figure 6.3b).

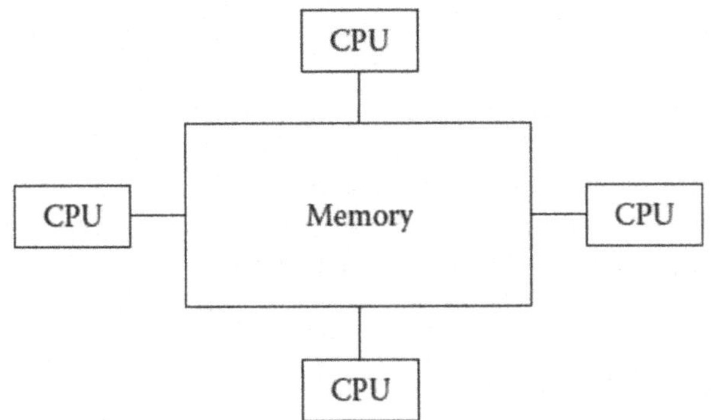

(a) Shared memory systems

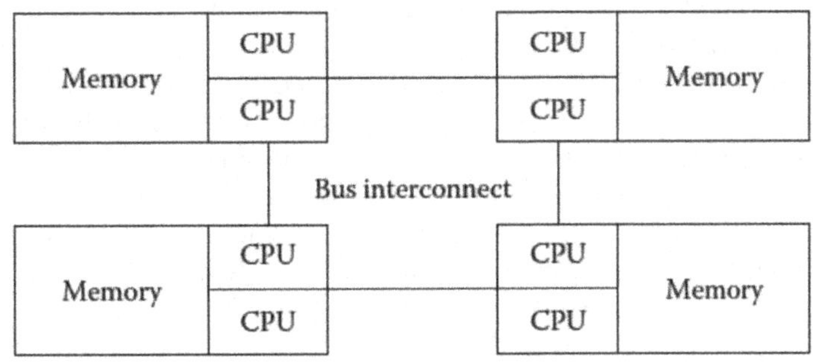

(b) Distributed systems

FIGURE 6.2
Parallel computing architectures.

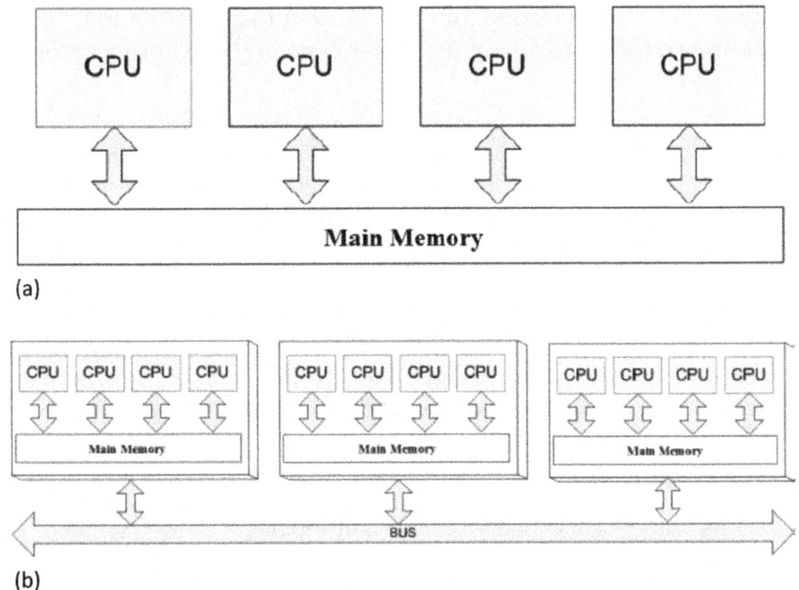

FIGURE 6.3
(a) UMA-shared memory and (b) NUMA-shared memory.

Multicore processors, at least with a small number of cores, usually employ shared memory configuration.

However, for a large number of processors, scalability suffers in the case of shared memory systems because the connection to the common memory becomes a bottleneck. There are several possible programming models for a shared memory system that mostly revolve around using threads (which are independent parallel code sequences within a process).

6.2.2 Distributed Memory Multicomputers

Distributed memory multicomputers are an alternative to shared memory, especially for larger systems. In a distributed memory system, each processor has its own main memory and such processor–memory pairs operate as individual computers that are interconnected (Figure 6.2b). Beginning in the late 1980s, it became feasible to use networked computers as a parallel computing platform. In the 1990s, it became cost-effective to interconnect low-cost commodity computers (PCs) with commodity interconnects (Ethernet) to form a high-performance computing cluster, and this approach continues today. The programming model for such a distributed memory system is usually a message-passing model in which messages pass information between computers. Generally, the programmer inserts message-passing routines in his/her code. The most widely used suite of message-passing libraries for clusters is the message-passing interface (MPI).

Similar to shared memory systems, distributed memory systems vary widely, but share a common characteristic. Distributed memory systems require a communication network to connect inter-processor memory. In this type of architecture, processors have access to their own memory and do not share memory with another SMP. If a processor needs information from another data store, it has to communicate how and when it is to be accessed. This sharing generally comes about through a simple Ethernet connection. Hybrids of this technology have also been developed and are referred to as distributed shared memory architecture. However, this type of architecture is generally used in supercomputers.

With the advent of multicore computer systems, a cluster of multicore computers can form a very high-performance computing platform. The programming model for such a cluster may be a hybrid model with threads on each multicore system and message passing between systems. For example, one can easily use both OpenMP for creating threads and an MPI for message passing in the same C/C++ program.

Distributed memory computers can also extend to incorporate computers that are not physically close. Grid computing refers to a computing platform in which computers are geographically distributed and interconnected (usually through the Internet) to form a collaborative resource. Grid computing tends to focus on collaborative computing and resource sharing.

6.2.2.1 *Interconnection Network (IN)*

Multiprocessors INs can be classified based on a number of criteria:

- Mode of operation (synchronous versus asynchronous)
- Control strategy (centralized versus decentralized)

- Switching techniques (circuit versus packet)
- Topology (static versus dynamic)
- Mode of operation

  INs are classified according to the mode of operation as

  - In a synchronous mode of operation, a single global clock is used by all components in the system such that the whole system is operating in a lock-step manner. While synchronous systems tend to be slower compared to asynchronous systems, they are race and hazard free.
  - In an asynchronous mode of operation, handshaking signals are used in order to coordinate the operation of asynchronous systems; it does not require a global clock.
- Control strategy

  INs can be classified according to the control strategy as

  - In centralized control systems, a single central control unit is used to oversee and control the operation of the components of the system. However, the function and reliability of the central control unit can become the bottleneck in a centralized control system.
  - In decentralized control systems, the control function is distributed among different components in the system.

  While the crossbar is a centralized system, the multistage INs are decentralized.

- Switching techniques

  INs can be classified according to the switching mechanism as

  - In the circuit switching mechanism, a complete path has to be established prior to the start of communication between a source and a destination. The established path will remain in existence during the whole communication period.
  - In a packet switching mechanism, communication between a source and a destination takes place via messages that are divided into smaller entities, called packets. On their way to the destination, packets can be sent from one node to another in a store-and-forward manner until they reach their destination.

  While packet switching tends to use the network resources more efficiently compared to circuit switching, it suffers from variable packet delays.

- Topology

  An IN topology is a mapping function from a set of processors and memories onto the same set of processors and memories; it describes how to connect processors and memories to other processors and memories. A fully connected topology is a mapping in which each processor is connected to all other processors in the computer. All multiprocessor systems can be distinguished by their IN topology.

Shared memory systems can be designed using bus-based or switch-based INs. The simplest IN for shared memory systems is the bus. However, the bus may get saturated if multiple processors are trying to access the shared memory (via the bus) simultaneously. A typical bus-based design uses caches to solve the bus contention problem. Other shared memory designs rely on switches for interconnection. For example, a crossbar switch can be used to connect multiple processors to multiple memory modules.

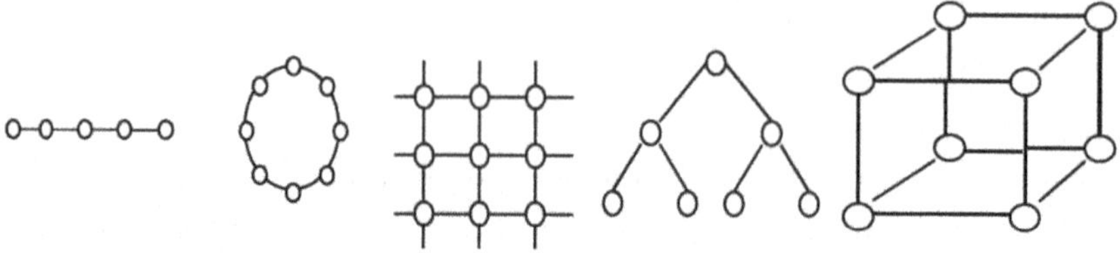

FIGURE 6.4
Examples of static topologies: (a) linear array, (b) ring, (c) mesh, (d) tree, and (e) hypercube.

TABLE 6.1
Performance Characteristics of Static INs

Network	Degree	Diameter	Cost (# Links)
Linear array	2	$N-1$	$N-1$
Binary tree	3	2([log2N] – 1)	$N-1$
n-cube	log2N	log2N	$nN/2$
2-D mesh	4	—	$2(N-n)$

Message-passing INs can be divided into static and dynamic. Static networks form all connections when the system is designed rather than when the connection is needed. In a static network, messages must be routed along established links. Figure 6.4 shows a selection of popular static topologies: linear array, ring, mesh, tree, and hypercube.

Table 6.1 tabulates the performance characteristics of static INs.

Dynamic INs establish a connection between two or more nodes on the fly as messages are routed along the links. The number of hops in a path from source to destination node is equal to the number of point-to-point links a message must traverse to reach its destination. In either static or dynamic networks, a single message may have to hop through intermediate processors on its way to its destination. Therefore, the ultimate performance of an IN is greatly influenced by the number of hops taken to traverse the network.

Figure 6.5 shows examples of dynamic networks.

- Figure 6.5a shows the single-stage IN that is a simple dynamic network that connects each of the inputs on the left side to some, but not all, of the outputs on the right side through a single layer of binary switches represented by the rectangles. The binary switches can direct the message on the left-side input to one of two possible outputs on the right side.
- Figure 6.5b shows the multistage IN (MIN) that is the outcome of cascading enough single-stage networks together. The connection from the source 010 to the destination 010 is highlighted as a bold path. These are dynamic INs because the connection is made on the fly, as needed. In order to connect a source to a destination, we simply use a function of the bits of the source and destination addresses as instructions for dynamically selecting a path through the switches. For example, to connect source 111 to destination 001 in the omega network, the switches in the first and second stage must be set to connect to the upper output port, while the switch at the third stage must be set to connect to the lower output port (001).

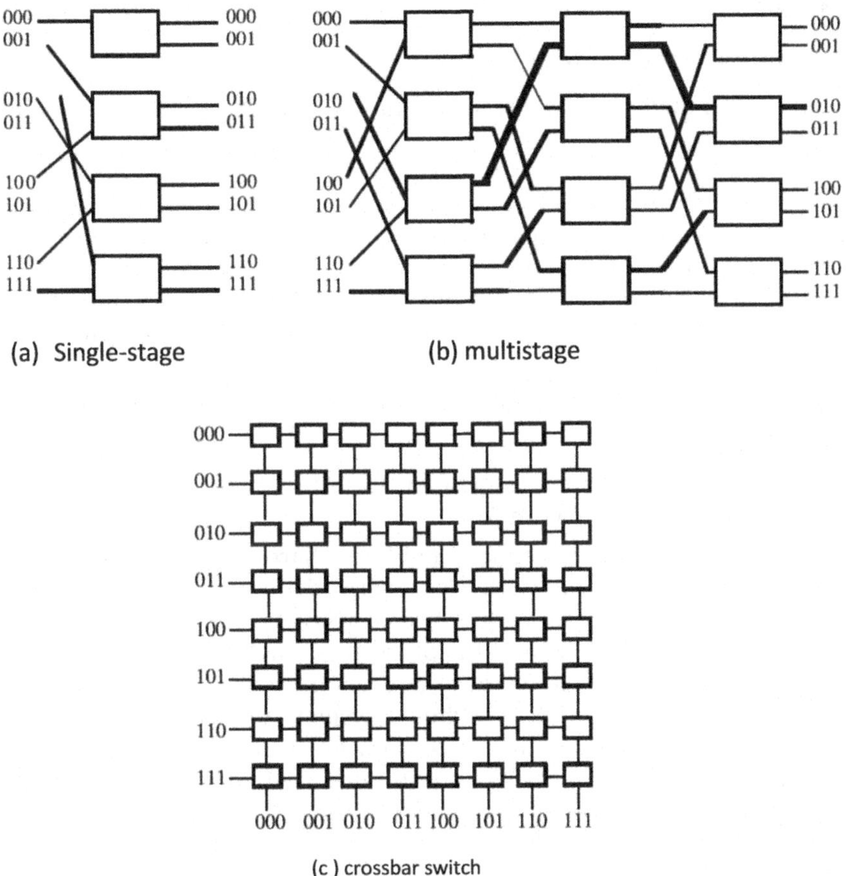

FIGURE 6.5
Examples of dynamic topologies.

- Figure 6.5c shows the crossbar switch that provides a path from any input or source to any other output or destination by simply selecting a direction on the fly. For example, to connect row 111 to column 001 requires only one binary switch at the intersection of the 111 input line and the 011 output line to be set.

Table 6.2 tabulates the performance characteristics of dynamic INs.

TABLE 6.2
Performance Characteristics of Dynamic INs

Network	Delay	Cost (Complexity)
Bus	$O(N)$	$O(1)$
Multiple bus	$O(mN)$	$O(m)$
MINs	$O(\log N)$	$O(N\log N)$

6.3 Characteristics of Parallel Systems

6.3.1 Coupling, Parallelism, Concurrency, and Granularity

- Coupling

  The degree of coupling among a set of hardware or software modules is measured in terms of the interdependency and binding and/or homogeneity among the modules. When the degree of coupling is high (low), the modules are said to be tightly (loosely) coupled. SIMD and MISD architectures generally tend to be tightly coupled because of the common clocking of the shared instruction stream or the shared data stream.

  Here, we briefly examine various MIMD architectures in terms of coupling:

  - Tightly coupled multiprocessors (with UMA shared memory).
  - Tightly coupled multiprocessors (with NUMA shared memory or that communicate by message passing).
  - Loosely coupled multicomputers (without shared memory) physically colocated. These may be bus-based (e.g., networks of workstations (NOW) connected by a local area network [LAN] or Myrinet card) or use a more general communication network, and the processors may be heterogeneous. In such systems, processors neither share memory nor have a common clock, and hence may be classified as distributed systems; however, the processors are very close to one another, which is characteristic of a parallel system. As the communication latency may be significantly lower than in wide area distributed systems, the solution approaches to various problems may be different for such systems than for wide area distributed systems.
  - Loosely coupled multicomputers (without shared memory and without a common clock) that are physically remote. These correspond to the conventional notion of distributed systems.

- Parallelism or speedup of a program on a specific system

  This is a measure of the relative speedup of a specific program on a given machine. The speedup depends on the number of processors and the mapping of the code to the processors. It is expressed as the ratio of time $T(1)$ with a single processor, to time $T(n)$ with n processors.

- Parallelism within a parallel/distributed program

  This is an aggregate measure of the percentage of time that all the processors are executing CPU instructions productively, as opposed to waiting for communication (either via shared memory or message passing) operations to complete. The term is traditionally used to characterize parallel programs. If the aggregate measure is a function of only the code, then the parallelism is independent of the architecture.

- Concurrency of a program

  This is similar to the parallelism of a program, but is used in the context of distributed programs. The parallelism/concurrency in a parallel/distributed program can be measured by the ratio of the number of local (non-communication and non-shared memory access) operations to the total number of operations (including the communication or shared memory access operations).

- Granularity of a program

  The ratio of the amount of computation to the amount of communication within the parallel/distributed program is termed *granularity*. If the degree of parallelism is coarse-grained (fine-grained), there are relatively many more (fewer) productive CPU instruction executions, compared to the number of times the processors communicate either via shared memory or message passing and wait to get synchronized with the other processors.

  Programs with fine-grained parallelism are best suited for tightly coupled systems including:

  - SIMD and MISD architectures
  - Tightly coupled MIMD multiprocessors (that have shared memory)
  - Loosely coupled multicomputers (without shared memory) that are physically colocated

If programs with fine-grained parallelism were run over loosely coupled multiprocessors that are physically remote, the latency delays for the frequent communication over the wide area network (WAN) would significantly degrade the overall throughput. As a corollary, it follows that on such loosely coupled multicomputers, programs with a coarse-grained communication/message-passing granularity will incur substantially less overhead.

6.3.2 Shared Memory Systems versus Message-Passing Systems

Shared memory systems are those in which there is a (common) shared address space throughout the system. Communication among processors takes place via shared data variables, and control variables for synchronization among the processors. In shared memory systems, how synchronization can be achieved is exemplified by semaphores and monitors that were originally designed for shared memory uniprocessors and multiprocessors.

All multicomputer (NUMA as well as message passing) systems that do not have a shared address space provided by the underlying architecture and hardware necessarily communicate by message passing.

Programmers find it easier to program using shared memory than message passing. The abstraction called shared memory is sometimes provided to simulate a shared address space; for a distributed system this abstraction is called distributed shared memory. Implementing this abstraction incurs certain cost but it simplifies the task for the application programmer.

- Shared memory system emulating message-passing system

  The shared address space can be partitioned into disjoint parts, one part being assigned to each processor. "Send" and "receive" operations can be implemented by writing to and reading from the destination/sender processor's address space, respectively. Specifically, a separate location can be reserved as the mailbox for each ordered pair of processes. A $P_i - P_j$ message passing can be emulated by a *write* by P_i to the mailbox and then a *read* by P_j from the mailbox. In the simplest case, these mailboxes can be assumed to have unbounded size. The *write* and *read* operations need to be controlled using synchronization primitives to inform the receiver/sender after the data has been sent/received.

- Message-passing system emulating shared memory system

  This involves effectively obtaining "write" and "read" operations by actually using *send* and *receive* operations. Each shared location can be modeled as a separate process: "write" to a shared location is emulated by sending an update message to the corresponding owner process; "read" to a shared location is emulated by sending a query message to the owner process. As accessing another processor's memory requires *send* and *receive* operations, this emulation is expensive. Although emulating shared memory might seem to be more attractive from a programmer's perspective, it is only an abstraction. Thus, the latencies involved in "read" and "write" operations may be high even when emulating shared memory because the "read" and "write" operations are finally implemented by using network-wide communication under the covers.

An application can, of course, use a combination of shared memory and message passing. In an MIMD message-passing multicomputer system, each "processor" may be a tightly coupled multiprocessor system with shared memory. Within the multiprocessor system, the processors communicate via shared memory.

6.3.3 Distributed Communication

6.3.3.1 Blocking/Non-blocking, Synchronous/Asynchronous Primitives

The blocking/non-blocking and synchronous/asynchronous primitives are defined as follows:

- Synchronous primitives

  A Send or a Receive primitive is synchronous if both the Send() and Receive() handshake with each other. The processing for the Send primitive completes only after the invoking processor learns that the other corresponding Receive primitive has also been invoked and that the receive operation has been completed. The processing for the Receive primitive completes when the data to be received is copied into the receiver's user buffer.

- Asynchronous primitives

  A Send primitive is said to be asynchronous if control returns to the invoking process after the data item to be sent has been copied out of the user-specified buffer. It does not make sense to define asynchronous Receive primitives.

- Blocking primitives

  A primitive is blocking if control returns to the invoking process after the processing for the primitive (whether in synchronous or asynchronous mode) completes.

- Non-blocking primitives

  A primitive is non-blocking if control returns to the invoking process immediately after invocation, even though the operation has not completed. For a non-blocking Send, control returns to the process even before the data is copied out of the user buffer. For a non-blocking Receive, control returns to the process even before the data may have arrived from the sender.

- A Send primitive Send() has at least two parameters—the destination and the buffer in the user space, containing the data to be sent. Similarly, a Receive primitive Receive() has at least two parameters—the source from which the data is to be received (this could be a wildcard) and the user buffer into which the data is to be received.
- For the Send primitive, the two ways of sending data are
  - The buffered option, which is the standard option, copies the data from the user buffer to the kernel buffer. The data is later copied from the kernel buffer onto the network.
  - The unbuffered option, the data gets copied directly from the user buffer onto the network.
  - For the Receive primitive, the buffered option is usually required because the data may already have arrived when the primitive is invoked, and needs a storage place in the kernel.

For non-blocking primitives, a return parameter on the primitive call returns a system-generated handle that can be later used to check the status of the completion of the call. The process can check for the completion of the call in two ways:

- It can keep checking (in a loop or periodically) if the handle has been flagged or posted.
- It can issue a Wait with a list of handles as parameters. The Wait call usually blocks until one of the parameter handles is posted.

The various versions of the primitives are

- *Blocking synchronous Send*: The data gets copied from the user buffer to the kernel buffer and is then sent over the network. After the data is copied to the receiver's system buffer and a *Receive* call has been issued, an acknowledgement back to the sender causes control to return to the process that invoked the *Send* operation and completes the *Send*.
- *Non-blocking synchronous Send*: Control returns back to the invoking process as soon as the copy of data from the user buffer to the kernel buffer is initiated. A parameter in the non-blocking call also gets set with the handle of a location that the user process can later check for the completion of the synchronous *Send* operation. The location gets posted after an acknowledgement returns from the receiver. The user process can keep checking for the completion of the non-blocking synchronous *Send* by testing the returned handle, or it can invoke the blocking *Wait* operation on the returned handle.
- *Blocking asynchronous Send*: The user process that invokes the *Send* is blocked until the data is copied from the user's buffer to the kernel buffer. (For the unbuffered option, the user process that invokes the *Send* is blocked until the data is copied from the user's buffer to the network.)

- *Non-blocking asynchronous Send*: The user process that invokes the *Send* is blocked until the transfer of the data from the user's buffer to the kernel buffer is initiated. (For the unbuffered option, the user process that invokes the *Send* is blocked until the transfer of the data from the user's buffer to the network is initiated.) Control returns to the user process as soon as this transfer is initiated, and a parameter in the non-blocking call also gets set with the handle of a location that the user process can check later using the *Wait* operation for the completion of the asynchronous *Send* operation. The asynchronous *Send* completes when the data has been copied out of the user's buffer. Checking for the completion may be necessary if the user wants to reuse the buffer from which the data was sent.
- *Blocking Receive*: The *Receive* call blocks until the data expected arrives and is written in the specified user buffer. Then, control is returned to the user process.
- *Non-blocking Receive*: *The Receive* call will cause the kernel to register the call and return the handle of a location that the user process can later check for the completion of the non-blocking *Receive* operation. This location gets posted by the kernel after the expected data arrives and is copied to the user-specified buffer. The user process can check for the completion of the non-blocking *Receive* by invoking the *Wait* operation on the returned handle. (If the data has already arrived when the call is made, it would be pending in some kernel buffer, and still needs to be copied to the user buffer.)

A synchronous *Send* lowers the efficiency within the process and, conceptually, blocking primitives are easier to use.

6.3.3.2 Processor Synchrony

Processor synchrony indicates that all the processors execute in lock-step with their clocks synchronized. As this synchrony is not attainable in a distributed system, what is more generally indicated is that for a large granularity of code, usually termed a step, the processors are synchronized. This abstraction is implemented using some form of barrier synchronization to ensure that no processor begins executing the next step of code until all the processors have completed executing the previous steps of code assigned to each of the processors.

6.3.4 Synchronous versus Asynchronous Executions

An asynchronous execution is a computation or execution in which

- There is no processor synchrony and there is no bound on the drift rate of processor clocks.
- Message delays (transmission + propagation times) are finite but unbounded.
- There is no upper bound on the time taken by a process to execute a step.

A synchronous execution is a computation or execution in which

- Processors are synchronized and the clock drift rate between any two processors is bounded.

- Message delivery (transmission + delivery) times are such that they occur in one logical step or round.
- There is a known upper bound on the time taken by a process to execute a step.
- Emulating an asynchronous system by a synchronous system

An asynchronous program (written for an asynchronous system) can be emulated on a synchronous system fairly trivially as the synchronous system is a special case of an asynchronous system—all communication finishes within the same round in which it is initiated.

- Emulating a synchronous system by an asynchronous system

A synchronous program (written for a synchronous system) can be emulated on an asynchronous system using a tool called a synchronizer.

6.4 Summary

The chapter commenced with Flynn's taxonomy for parallel computers, defining the SSID, SIMD, MISD, and MIMD. The MIMD were further classified based on their memory structure (global or distributed) and the mechanism used for communication/synchronization (shared variables or message passing) into GMMP, GMSV, DMMP, and DMSV. Flynn's taxonomy also gives rise to levels of parallelisms, viz. task-level, data-level, instruction-level, and bit-level parallelism. Instruction-level parallelism allows the compiler and the processor to overlap the execution of multiple instructions or even to change the order in which instructions are executed. Pipelining is an excellent example of this form of parallel processing. General-purpose multiprocessor systems (MIMD computers) can also be divided into two major subtypes: *shared memory multiprocessor* systems and *distributed memory* multicomputers.

Scalability suffers in the case of shared memory systems for a large number of processors because the connection to the common memory becomes a bottleneck. In a distributed memory system, each processor has its own main memory and such processor–memory pairs operate as individual computers that are interconnected. The programming model for such a distributed memory system is usually a message-passing model in which messages pass information between computers. The chapter concluded by discussing the characteristics of parallel systems such as coupling, parallelism, concurrency, and granularity, and aspects of distributed communications such as synchronous/asynchronous primitives and blocking/non-blocking primitives.

7

Parallel Computing Models

Parallel models of computation are helpful when analyzing and designing algorithms, as well as in determining performance metrics used for the evaluation of algorithms. Models of computation should be independent of hardware; they should not be associated with a specific computer architecture or with a class of such architectures especially so in the field of parallel computing where the diversity of architectures is high. Algorithms developed adopting these models should be implementable and executable on computers with different architectures.

7.1 Shared Memory Models

7.1.1 Theoretical Models

A computational model can be used to evaluate algorithms independently of an implementation in a specific programming language and of the use of a specific computer system. To be useful, a computational model must abstract from many details of a specific computer system while retaining those characteristics that have a larger influence on the execution time of algorithms.

7.1.1.1 RAM Model

The random-access machine (RAM) model captures the essential features of traditional sequential computers. The RAM model is composed of a single processor and a memory with sufficient capacity; each memory location can be accessed in a random (direct) way. In each time step, the processor performs one instruction as specified by a sequential algorithm. Instructions for (read or write) access to the memory as well as for arithmetic or logical operations are provided. The RAM model provides a simple model that abstracts from many details of real computers, such as a fixed memory size and the existence of a memory hierarchy with caches, complex addressing modes, or multiple functional units; however, the RAM model can also be used to perform a runtime analysis of sequential algorithms to describe their asymptotic behavior, which is meaningful for real sequential computers.

7.1.1.2 PRAM Model

A parallel random-access machine (PRAM) consists of a bounded set of identical processors {P1,…, Pn}, which are controlled by a global clock. Each processor is a RAM that can access the common memory to read and write data, and a local memory to store private data. Each processor can access any location in the common memory in unit time, which is the same time needed for an arithmetic operation.

There is no direct connection between processors. Instead, communication can only be performed via the common memory.

All processors execute the same program synchronously. The PRAM executes computation steps one after another. In each step, each processor:

- Reads data from the common memory or its private memory (read phase).
- Performs a local computation.
- Writes a result back into the common memory or into its private memory (write phase).

Since each processor can access any location in the common memory, memory access conflicts can occur when multiple processors access the same memory location at the same time. Such conflicts can occur both in the read phase and the write phase of a computation step.

Depending on how these read conflicts and write conflicts are handled, variant PRAM models defined are

- exclusive read, exclusive write (EREW) PRAM model forbids simultaneous read accesses as well as simultaneous write accesses to the same memory location by more than one processor. Thus, in each step, each processor must read from and write into a different memory location (like other processors).
- concurrent read, exclusive write (CREW) PRAM model allows simultaneous read accesses by multiple processors to the same memory location in the same step, but simultaneous write accesses are forbidden within the same step.
- exclusive read, concurrent write (ERCW) PRAM model allows simultaneous write accesses, but forbids simultaneous read accesses within the same step.
- concurrent read, concurrent write (CRCW) PRAM model allows both simultaneous read and write accesses within the same step.

If simultaneous write accesses are allowed as for the CRCW PRAM model, write conflicts to the same memory location must be resolved to determine the result of multiple processors trying to write to the same memory location in the same step. The different resolutions schemes proposed are

- *Common model* requires that all processors writing simultaneously to a common location write the same value.
- *Arbitrary model* allows an arbitrary value to be written by each processor; if multiple processors simultaneously write to the same location, an arbitrarily chosen value will succeed.
- *Priority model* assigns priorities to the processors and in the case of simultaneous writes, the processor with the highest priority succeeds.
- *Combining model* assumes that the values written simultaneously to the same memory location in the same step are combined by summing them up and the combined value is written.

In the PRAM model, the cost of an algorithm is defined as the number of PRAM steps to be performed for the execution of an algorithm. As previously described, each step consists of a read phase, a local computation, and a write phase. Usually, the costs are specified as an asymptotic execution time with respect to the size of the input data.

The variants of the PRAM model differ in computational power. Informally, a PRAM model is computationally stronger, or more powerful, if it enables the development of faster algorithms to solve select problems at comparatively lower limitations that must be met during the execution of algorithms. In this perspective, PRAM models can be arranged with respect to increasing computational power as follows:

EREW, CREW, common CRCW, arbitrary CRCW, priority CRCW, combining CRCW

The arrangement shows that the weakest model is EREW, and the strongest is combining CRCW. Moreover, any algorithm that runs in an EREW also runs in a CREW; an algorithm that runs in a CREW also runs in a common CRCW, etc. A more precise relationship between the models can be established by investigating the possibility of simulating some models by others.

A theoretical runtime analysis based on the PRAM model provides useful information on the asymptotic behavior of parallel algorithms. However, the PRAM model has its limitations concerning a realistic performance estimation of application programs on real parallel machines because of assumptions such as

- Each processor can access any location in the common memory in unit time. Real parallel machines do not provide memory access in unit time. Large variations in memory access time often occur, and accesses to a global memory or to the local memory of other processors are usually much slower than accesses to the local memory of the accessing processor.

  Real parallel machines use a memory hierarchy with several levels of caches with different access times. This cannot be modeled with the PRAM model. Therefore, the PRAM model cannot be used to evaluate the locality behavior of the memory accesses of a parallel application program.
- Synchronous execution of the processors.
- Absence of collisions when multiple processors access the common memory simultaneously.

Because of these structures, several extensions of the original PRAM model have been proposed.

7.1.2 Practical Models

7.1.2.1 Bulk Synchronous Parallel (BSP) Model

The BSP model has been proposed as a bridging model between hardware architecture and software development: the idea is to provide a standard on which both hardware architects and software developers can agree. Thus, software development can be decoupled from the details of a specific architecture, and software does not have to be adapted when porting it to a new parallel machine.

The BSP model is an abstraction of a parallel machine with a physically distributed memory organization. A parallel computer consists of a number of components (processors), each of which can perform processing or memory functions. The components are connected by a router (interconnection network [IN]), which can send point-to-point messages between pairs of components. There is also a synchronization unit, which supports the synchronization of all or a subset of the components.

A computation in the BSP model is composed of a sequence of supersteps within which

- Each component performs local computations that can be performed in one time unit. At the end of each superstep, a barrier synchronization is performed.
- Each component participates in point-to-point message transmissions. The effect of message transmissions becomes visible in the next time step, that is, a receiver of a message can use the received data but not before the next superstep.

  In each superstep, the router can implement arbitrary *h*-relations capturing communication patterns, where each processor sends or receives at most *h* messages.

The granularity of the computations is determined by a periodicity parameter *L*, which determines the length of the supersteps in time units:

- A lower bound for *L* is set by the hardware.
- An upper bound for *L* is set by the parallel program to be executed such that in each superstep, computations with approximately *L* steps can be assigned to each processor. The BSP model allows that the value of *L* can be controlled by the program to be executed, even at runtime.

A computation in the BSP model can be characterized by four parameters:

p: The number of (virtual) processors used within the supersteps to perform computations.

s: The execution speed of the processors expressed as the number of computation steps per second that each processor can perform, where each computation step performs an (arithmetic or logical) operation on a local data element.

l: The number of steps that are required for the execution of a barrier synchronization.

g: The number of steps that are required on average for the transfer of a memory word in the context of a *h*-relation.

The execution time $T_{\text{superstep}}$ of a single superstep is given by

$$T_{\text{superstep}} = \max_{\text{processors}} w_i + h \cdot g + l$$

The BSP model is a general model that can be used as a basis for different programming models. To support the development of efficient parallel programs with the BSP model, the BSPLib library has been developed, which provides operations:

- For the initialization of a superstep.
- For performing communication operations.
- For participating in the barrier synchronization at the end of each superstep.

There are several concerns about the BSP model:

- The length of the supersteps must be sufficiently large to accommodate arbitrary *h*-relations. This has the effect that the granularity cannot be decreased below a certain value.

- Messages sent within a superstep can only be used in the next superstep, even if the IN is fast enough to deliver messages within the same superstep.
- The BSP model expects hardware support for synchronization at the end of each superstep. Such support may not be available for some parallel machines.

Because of these concerns, the BSP model has been extended to the LogP model to provide more realistic modeling of real parallel machines.

7.1.2.2 LogP Model

Like the BSP model, the LogP model is based on the assumption that a parallel computer consists of a set of processors with local memory that can communicate by exchanging point-to-point messages over an IN. Thus, the LogP model is also intended for modeling parallel computers with a distributed memory.

The communication behavior of a parallel computer is described by four parameters:

L: The upper bound on the latency of the network capturing the delay observed when transmitting a small message over the network.

o: The management overhead that a processor needs for sending or receiving a message; during this time, a processor cannot perform any other operation.

g: The gap or minimum time interval between consecutive send or receive operations of a processor.

P: The number of processors of the parallel machine.

All parameters except P are measured in time units or as multiples of the machine cycle time. It is assumed that

- The network has a finite capacity, which means that between any pair of processors at most $[L/g]$ messages are allowed to be in transmission at any time. If a processor tries to send a message that would exceed this limit, it is blocked until the message can be transmitted without exceeding the limit.
- The processors exchange small messages that do not exceed a predefined size. Larger messages must be split into several smaller messages. The processors work asynchronously with each other. The latency of any single message cannot be predicted in advance, but is bounded by L if there is no blocking because of the finite capacity.

The execution time of an algorithm in the LogP model is determined by the maximum of the execution times of the participating processors. Access by a processor P1 to a data element that is stored in the local memory of another processor P2 takes time $2 \cdot L + 4 \cdot o$; half of this time is needed to bring the data element from P2 to P1, the other half is needed to bring the data element from P1 back to P2. A sequence of n messages can be transmitted in time $L + 2 \cdot o + (n-1) \cdot g$.

A drawback of the original LogP model is that it is based on the assumption that the messages are small and that only point-to-point messages are allowed. More complex communication patterns must be assembled from point-to-point messages. To release the restriction to small messages, the LogP model has been extended to the LogGP model that contains an additional parameter G (gap per byte). This parameter specifies the transmission time per byte for long messages. The bandwidth available per processor is $1/G$. The time for the transmission of a message with n bytes takes $o + (n-1)G + L + o$.

The LogGP model has been successfully used to analyze the performance of message-passing programs.

The LogGP model has been further extended to the LogGPS model by adding a parameter S to capture synchronization that must be performed when sending large messages. The parameter S is the threshold for the message length above which synchronization between sender and receiver is performed before message transmission starts.

7.2 Interconnection Network Models

The network model is composed of a number of processors that operate according to the RAM model. Processors can operate either synchronously or asynchronously, but typically the asynchronous mode is assumed; there is no shared memory in the model. In order to exchange data, processors are connected by bidirectional communication channels, or links, that form an *interconnection network.* Processors communicate and coordinate their activities by sending messages through links of an IN. The transfer of messages is implemented by routing procedures running on all processors and cooperating with each other.

The network model defines the way the processors are connected to each other, which is called the IN *topology.* A graph can be an alternative diagram of a network model, that is, the IN topology can be described by means of a graph whose vertices represent processors, and edges represent bidirectional links between processors.

The parameters that determine a topology's suitability for parallel computation are

- *Diameter of a network* is the maximum distance measured by the number of links (edges) between any two processors or nodes (vertices) of a network. A network is the better the smaller diameter it has, because in the worst case a message must be routed over the number of links equal to the diameter of a network.
- *Degree of a network* is the maximum number of neighbor links of a vertex in a network. If this degree is small, then the communication procedures performing message routing are simple and thus more efficient, since a smaller number of channels are required to be controlled by a routing procedure. How the diameter and degree of a network change is crucial when the number of processors increases. In this respect, a network is considered good if as the number of processors p increases, the diameter of the network grows at most logarithmically with p, and its degree remains constant, wherein this constant is small.
- *Edge connectivity* is a measure of the multiplicity of paths between the vertices of a network. It is defined as the minimum number of edges that must fail—be removed from a network—to make it disconnected. The greater the edge connectivity, the better the network resistance to damage. Moreover, in networks with higher connectivity there is less contention of processes for communication resources.
- *Bisection width of a network* is the minimum number of edges that must be removed from the network to split it into two equal subnetworks. The product of a bisection width and a data transfer rate in a single channel, called bisection bandwidth, specifies the number of bits that can be transferred per unit time between the halves of a network. This bandwidth should be as large as possible.

- *Cost of a network* can be defined in several ways. In the simplest case, the measure of a cost is the total number of links of a network.

For an accrual topology, there is a tradeoff between the various parameters because their effect is mutually contradictory. For instance, a network should possibly be sparse, that is, with a number of edges $O(p)$, because then it is inexpensive to implement. On the other hand, while consisting of a small number of edges, it should have good communication properties, that is, a small diameter and large bisection width and edge connectivity—which is mutually contradictory and also expensive!

A completely connected network corresponds to the topology where there is an edge between each pair of vertices. The diameter of such a network equals one that provides fast communication between vertices. The degree increases linearly as the network is scaled, which is a huge drawback. The cost of a completely connected network measured by the number of edges (communication links) is given by

$$p(p-1)/2 = O\left(p^2\right)$$

where p is the number of vertices (processors). This cost is too high to make the network suitable for practical implementation.

7.2.1 Theoretical Models

7.2.1.1 Mesh

In a k-dimensional (i.e., k-D) mesh, almost every vertex is connected by edges (links) with $2k$ other vertices; its vertices are arranged in an array:

$$P\left[1 \ldots n_1, 1 \ldots n_2, \ldots, 1 \ldots n_k\right]$$

where $\prod_{i=1}^{k} n_i = p$.

Thus, a vertex $P[i_1, i_2, \ldots, i_j, \ldots, i_k]$ is connected to vertices $P[i_1, i_2, \ldots, i_j \pm 1, \ldots, i_k]$ for $j = 1, 2, \ldots, k$ if such vertices exists.

Figure 7.1 depicts a diagram of a 1-D mesh where each vertex (except for the two vertices at the ends) have two neighbors. Completing a network with wraparound connections yields a *ring*, or a 1-D *torus*.

The advantages of a 1-D mesh are a small degree (=2) and ease of scaling, whereas the disadvantage is a large network diameter ($=p-1$).

Figure 7.2a and b depict a 2-D mesh of degree 4 and diameter $O\left(\sqrt{p}\right)$. Figure 7.2c shows a 3-D mesh. The advantage of 2-D and 3-D meshes is that they allow easy mapping of computations carried out on regular structures. For example, they enable linear algebra

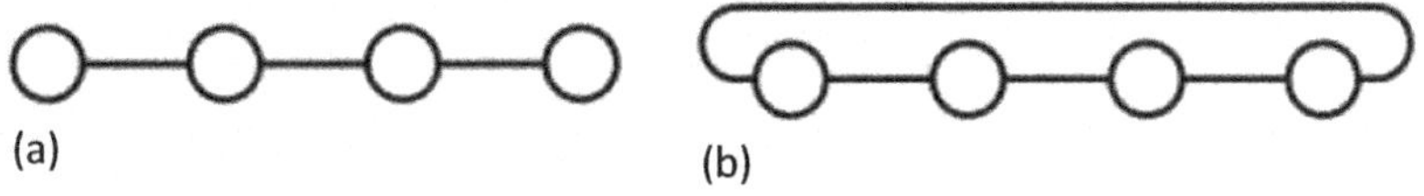

FIGURE 7.1
(a) 1-D mesh and (b) ring or 1-D torus.

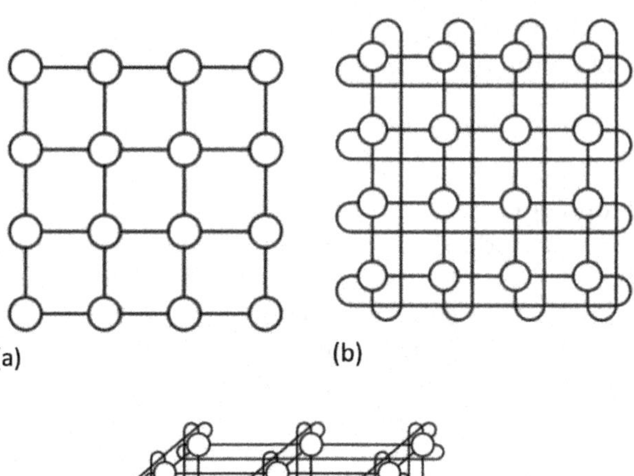

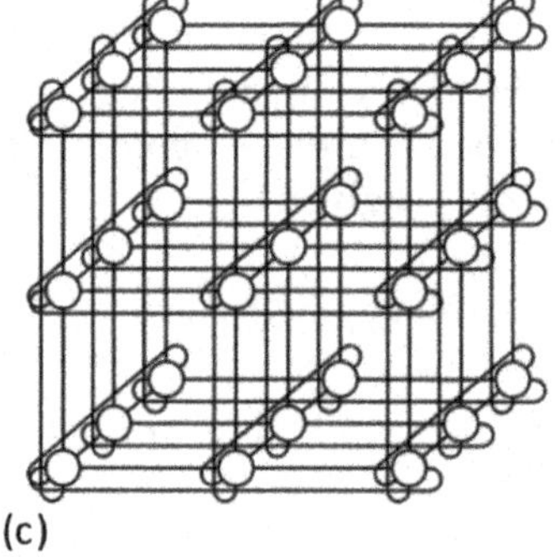

FIGURE 7.2
(a) 2-D mesh 4×4, (b) 2-D torus 4×4, and (c) 3-D torus 3×3×3.

computations involving matrix operations, or computations in computer graphics, where an image plane is partitioned into regular pieces processed by individual processors.

7.2.1.2 Mesh of Trees

A 2-D $n \times n$ mesh is a 2-D mesh of trees. It is created by removing edges of a mesh and adding vertices and edges such that in each row and column of a mesh a complete binary tree is formed (Figure 7.3). The diameter of a 2-D mesh of trees is equal to ($4 \log n$) and its degree is 3.

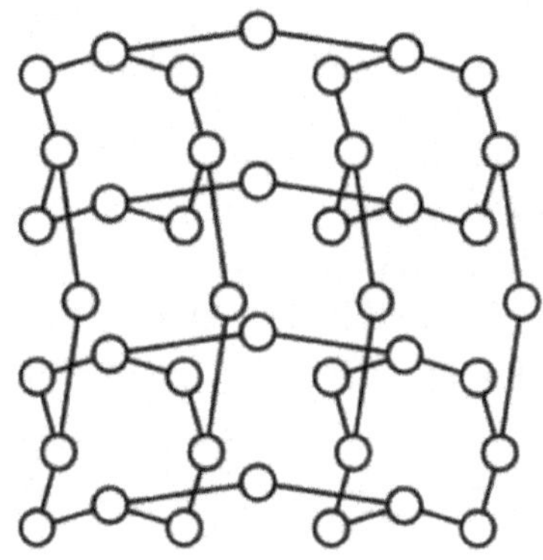

FIGURE 7.3
2-D mesh of trees 4×4.

7.2.1.3 Cube

Mesh may contain any number of vertices on each dimension. Fixing this number to two results in a *cube*, or *hypercube*, topology. A *k*-D cube consists of $p=2^k$ for $k \geq 0$ vertices numbered 0, 1,…, $2k-1$.

If the number of vertices is represented in a binary notation, $\omega \in \{0,1\}^k$, then two vertices are considered to be connected by an *edge*, if the bit strings w and $w^{\prime}$ corresponding to the numbers of these vertices differ only at one position.

Figure 7.4a–e shows how

- 0-D cube consists of a single vertex ($p=2^0$)
- 1-D cube consists of two 0-D cubes
- 2-D cube consists of two 1-D cubes
- 3-D cube consists of three 2-D cubes
- 4-D cube consists of four 3-D cubes

Since edges are connections between vertices whose numbers differ at 1 bit, the vertices of 3-D cubes composing a 4-D cube are connected in such a way that vertex 0000 of the left 3-D cube is connected to vertex 1000 of the right 3-D cube, vertex 0001 is connected to vertex 1001, and so on, right up to the pair of vertices 0111 and 1111 (Figure 7.4e).

In this topology, the diameter of a cube is equal to its dimension $k=\log p$ and the degree of a cube is equal to $\log p$, which is a disadvantage because this degree can be large for multidimensional cubes.

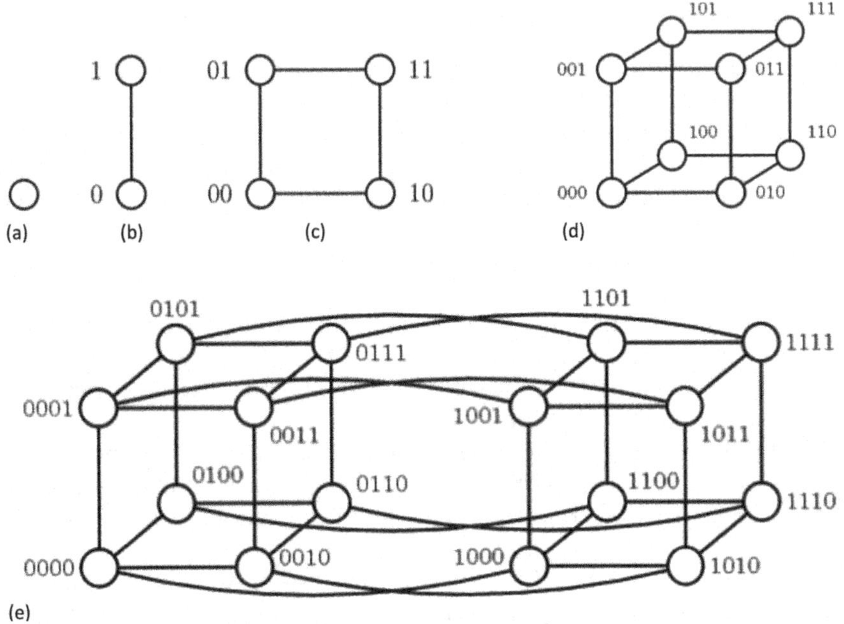

FIGURE 7.4
(a) 0-D cube, (b) 1-D cube, (c) 2-D cube, (d) 3-D cube, and (e) 4-D cube.

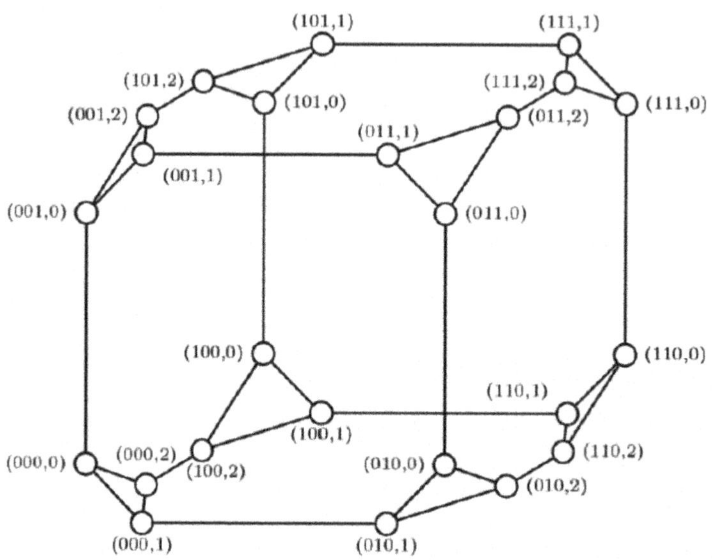

FIGURE 7.5
3-D cube-connected cycles.

A cube is not as easily scalable as compared with (say) a 1-D mesh. To extend a k-dimensional cube into a $(k+1)$-dimensional cube, $2k$ processors are needed. For instance, scaling a 4-D cube into a 5-D cube, we need to double it, which requires adding 16 processors.

7.2.1.4 Cube-Connected Cycles

As noted previously, the disadvantage of a cube is the logarithmic increase in degrees of vertices when a cube is scaled. This disadvantage does not occur for a k-dimensional network of cube-connected cycles (CCC), which is formed by replacing each vertex of a k-dimensional cube with a cycle consisting of k vertices (Figure 7.5). A CCC network has the diameter $O(\log p)$, where p is the number of vertices in a network, and the degree of 3.

7.2.1.5 Butterfly

A k-dimensional butterfly consists of $k+1$ stages numbered 0, 1, 2,…, k. At each stage of a network there are 2^k vertices numbered 0, 1,…, $2k-1$. A vertex corresponds to a pair $(i, w) = (i, w_k - 1\ w_k - 2, \ldots, w_0)$ that specifies the location of the vertex in the network, where i is the network stage and w is the k-bit

binary number identifying the network column. The vertices (i, w) and $(\tilde{\imath}', w')$ are connected by an edge, if $\tilde{\imath}' = I + 1$, and either $w = w'$ or strings w and w' differ only at the i'th bit. The network name is derived from the characteristic layout of its edges that resembles a butterfly wing.

As shown in Figure 7.6a, a 3-D butterfly network consists of two 2-D networks of the same type. Adopting a similar scheme for network combining, we can recursively create a $(k+1)$-D network out of two k-D networks for any k. The degree of a k-D butterfly network is 4, and its diameter equals $2k = O(\log p)$, where $p = (k+1)2^k$ is the number of vertices in a network.

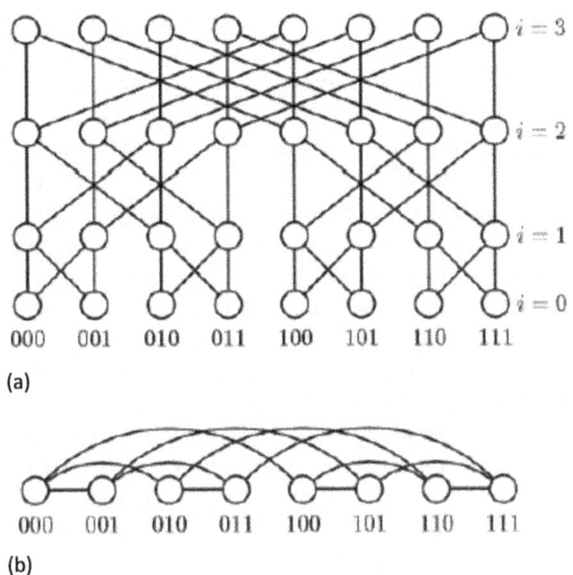

FIGURE 7.6
(a) 3-D butterfly and (b) transformation of a 3-D butterfly into a 3-D cube.

TABLE 7.1
Selected Parameters of Interconnection Network Topologies

Network Type	Diameter	Max. Degree	Bisection	Edge Connect.	Cost
Completely connected	1	$p-1$	$p2/4$	$p-1$	$p(p-1)/2$
1-D net	$p-1$	2	1	1	$p-1$
1-D torus	$[p/2]$	2	2	2	p
2-D torus	$2[\sqrt{p}/2]$	4	$2\sqrt{p}$	4	$2p$
2-D mesh	$2(\sqrt{p}-1)$	4	$\sqrt{p}$	2	$2(p-\sqrt{p})$
Mesh of trees $n \times n$ $(p=n(3n-2))$	$4 \log n$	3	n	2	$4n(n-1)$
k-D cube $(p=2k)$	$\log p$	$\log p$	$p/2$	$\log p$	$(p \log p)/2$
Cube-connected cycles ($p=k2k$ for $k \geq 3$)	$2k-1+[k/2]$	3	$p/(2k)$	3	$3p/2$
Butterfly $(p=(k+1)2k)$	$2k$	4	$p/(2k)$	3	$2p$

Note: p is the number of vertices in a network.

If the vertices in each column of a k-D butterfly network are merged, and the multiple edges are replaced by a single edge, we get a k-D cube (Figure 7.6b).

Table 7.1 presents selected parameters of the previously discussed network topologies.

7.2.2 Practical Models

7.2.2.1 Cluster

The 1990s witnessed a significant shift from expensive and specialized parallel machines to more cost-effective clusters of PCs and workstations. The advances in network technology and the availability of low-cost and high-performance commodity workstations have driven this shift. Clusters provide an economical way of achieving high performance. Enterprises that could not afford the expensive proprietary supercomputers have found an affordable alternative in clusters.

A cluster is a collection of stand-alone computers connected using some IN. Each node in a cluster could be a workstation, a personal computer, or even a multiprocessor system. A node is an autonomous computer that may be engaged in its own private activities while simultaneously cooperating with other units in the context of some computational task. Each node has its own input/output systems and its own operating system. When all nodes in a cluster have the same architecture and run the same operating system, the cluster is called homogeneous, otherwise, it is heterogeneous. The IN could be a fast local area network (LAN) or a switch. To achieve high-performance computing, the IN must provide high-bandwidth and low-latency communication.

The nodes of a cluster may be constantly dedicated to the cluster; hence, computation can be performed on the entire cluster. Dedicated clusters are normally packaged compactly in a single room. With the exception of the front-end node, all nodes are headless with no keyboard, mouse, or monitor. Dedicated clusters usually use high-speed networks such as fast Ethernet and Myrinet. Alternatively, nodes owned by different individuals on the Internet could participate in a cluster only part of the time. In this case, the cluster can utilize the idle central processing unit (CPU) cycles of each participating node if the owner grants permission.

In addition to providing high-performance computing, clusters can also be used to provide a high-availability environment. High availability can be achieved when only a subset of the nodes is used in the computation and the rest are used as a backup in case of failure. In cases when one of the main objectives of the cluster is high availability, the middleware will also support features that enable the cluster services for recovery from failure and fault tolerance among all nodes of the cluster. For example, the middleware should offer the necessary infrastructure for checkpointing. A checkpointing scheme makes sure that the process state is saved periodically. In the case of node failure, processes on the failed node can be restarted on another working node.

7.2.2.2 Grids

While clusters are collections of computers tied together as a single system, grids consist of multiple systems that work together while maintaining their distinct identities. A grid denotes middleware infrastructure, tools, and applications concerned with integrating geographically distributed computational resources. Owing to the decentralized and heterogeneous nature of a grid, the middleware that glues the different components is more complicated compared with that of clusters. Resembling an electric power grid, the computing grid is expected to become a pervasive computing infrastructure that supports large-scale and resource-intensive applications. Grid resources, which span the entire globe, include hardware, software, data, and instruments.

An important concept in grids is the virtual organization, which offers a unified view of resources. Although the resources in a grid might be in separate administrative domains, they are made available as virtual local resources to any node on the grid. A user signing on at one location would view computers at other remote locations as if they were part of the local system. Grid computing works by pooling the resources available, and then allocating them to individual tasks as the need arises. Resources are returned to the pool upon completion of the task. A grid gives an illusion of a big virtual computer capable of carrying out enormous tasks. The challenge is to allow meaningful sharing of resources without compromising local autonomy.

The support of grids requires innovative solutions to a number of challenging issues including:

- Resource management
- Resource monitoring
- Interoperability
- Security
- Billing and accounting
- Communication
- Performance

There are several examples of grid platforms and tools such as Globus. The Globus Toolkit is an enabling technology for the grid. It allows users to securely share computing power, databases, and other tools online across corporate, institutional, and geographic boundaries, without sacrificing local autonomy. The toolkit includes software services and libraries for resource monitoring, discovery, and management, plus security and file management. It also includes software for communication, fault detection, and portability. The Globus Toolkit has grown through an open-source strategy. Version 1.0 was introduced in 1998.

7.3 Dataflow Model

Conventional sequential computers are based on the RAM model, which is controlled by a sequence of instructions stemming from the *flow of control* in a program being executed. Both the type of operations carried out as well as their order are governed by successive program instructions. Data plays a passive role in computation, it is simply fetched at times when it becomes necessary for the operation. In order to perform a computation in parallel, the RAM model is extended to support the pipelined instruction execution and simultaneous work of many processors (or multiple RAM models).

In dataflow computers, an operation to execute is governed not by the current instruction of a program but by the availability of its operands. A *dataflow computer* simultaneously performs all operations that can be currently done, that is, whose operands are known. Therefore, data plays an active role in computation, as its availability establishes the operation and the time when it is executed. In a multiprocessor computer, parallel computation is specified by a programmer by indicating which sequences of operations can be executed concurrently. In a dataflow computer, the possibilities of parallel execution are not specified explicitly—they come from dependencies between data, since the input data of operations is the output data (results) of operations carried out previously.

Computing with conventional CPUs (control flow cores) involves a control flow processor containing a latency-critical loop. Data is read from the memory into the processor core, where operations are performed and the results are written back to the memory. Modern processors contain many levels of caching, forwarding, and prediction logic to improve the efficiency of this paradigm; however, the model is inherently sequential with its performance limited by the speed at which data can move around this loop.

A dataflow engine (DFE) operates differently. Data is streamed from the memory onto the chip where operations are performed and the data is forwarded directly from one functional unit ("dataflow core") to another as the results are needed, without ever being written to the off-chip memory until the chain of processing is complete. Each dataflow core computes only a single type of operation (e.g., an addition or multiplication) and is thus simple, so thousands can fit on one chip with every dataflow core computing simultaneously. Unlike in the control flow core where operations are computed at different points in time on the same functional units ("computing in time"), the complete dataflow computation is laid out spatially on the chip ("computing in space").

One analogy for moving from control flow to dataflow is the Ford car manufacturing model, where expensive, highly skilled craftsmen (control flow cores) have been replaced by a factory line: moving cars through a sea of single-skill workers (dataflow cores).

Dependencies in the dataflow are resolved statically at compile time, and because there are no new dependencies present at runtime the whole DFE can be deeply pipelined (1,000–10,000 stages). Every stage of the pipeline computes in parallel with the dataflow architecture maintaining a throughput of one result per cycle. This DFE structure can then be emulated on large field programmable gate arrays (FPGAs). A static dataflow machine doesn't require techniques such as branch prediction (since there aren't any branches) or out-of-order scheduling (parallelism is explicit). And since data is always available on-chip for as long as it is needed, general-purpose caches are not needed with the minimum amount of buffering memory automatically utilized as necessary. This saves the silicon area and power budget. By eliminating these extraneous functions, the full resources of the chip are dedicated to performing computations.

The advantage of the DFE is based on the elimination of sequentially iterated instruction streams and the reduction in memory accesses for both instructions and data. Instead of using indexed register files and hierarchical caching memory, the intermediate values and variables for the computation are stored in sparsely distributed registers that are close to the physical operators. Deep pipelining of the DFE provides high parallelism and sustained high throughput when computing repeated operations on large data volumes, but means that DFEs are less optimized for single operations on small amounts of data.

Thus, it is typically appropriate to combine a DFE with one or more control flow CPU cores:

- DFEs handle the computation of large-scale streaming operations in an application.
- Control flow cores manage dynamic events and control.

Despite an interesting idea underlying flow computation, and multiple research conducted in the field from the beginning of the 1970s, dataflow computers have not become competitive in comparison with conventional computers. The reason for this is the enormous hardware complexity of dataflow computers, as well as the difficulties in expressing their computation and developing appropriate programming language compilers. Others believe that the reason for their failure is non-deterministic (asynchronous) operation, arguing that conventional computers achieved success, among others, due to the synchronous arrangement of their work based on a central clock. Proponents contend that in the future, building dataflow computers will be profitable thanks to advances in the manufacturing technology of very-large-scale integration (VLSI) circuits and the results of further work on ways to express dataflow computation.

Deterministic versus non-deterministic executions:

A deterministic receive primitive specifies the source from which it wants to receive a message. A non-deterministic receive primitive can receive a message from any source—the message delivered to the process is the first message that is queued in the local incoming buffer, or the first message that comes in subsequently if no message is queued in the local incoming buffer. A distributed program that contains no non-deterministic receives has a deterministic execution; otherwise, if it contains at least one non-deterministic receive primitive, it is said to have a non-deterministic execution. Each execution defines a partial order on the events in the execution.

Even in an asynchronous system, for any deterministic (asynchronous) execution, repeated re-execution will reproduce the same partial order on the events. This is a very useful property for applications such as debugging and the detection of unstable predicates, and for reasoning about global states.

Given any non-deterministic execution, any re-execution of that program may result in a very different outcome, and any assertion about a non-deterministic execution can be made only for that particular execution. Different re-executions may result in different partial orders because of variable factors such as

- *Lack of an upper bound on message delivery times and unpredictable congestion.*
- *Local scheduling delays on the CPUs due to timesharing.*

Therefore, non-deterministic executions are difficult to reason about.

7.4 Summary

A computational model can be used to evaluate algorithms independently of an implementation in a specific programming language and of the use of a specific computer system. In the case of a shared memory model, every processor shares and has access to a global memory. The chapter commenced with the shared memory model, describing the RAM and PRAM models. The RAM model captures the essential features of traditional sequential computers. In the case of practical models, the chapter discussed BSP and LogP models. The BSP model has been proposed as a bridging model between hardware architecture and software development: the idea is to provide a standard on which both hardware architects and software developers can agree. The LogP model is based on the assumption that a parallel computer consists of a set of processors with local memory that can communicate by exchanging point-to-point messages over an IN.

An IN model is composed of a number of processors. In order to exchange data, these processors are connected by bidirectional communication channels, or links, that form an IN; there is no shared memory in the model. The chapter discussed the theoretical models of mesh, mesh of trees, cube, CCCs, and butterfly. Practical models discussed include cluster and grid.

In dataflow computers, an operation to be executed is governed not by the current instruction of a program but by the availability of its operands. In a dataflow computer, the possibilities of parallel execution are not specified explicitly—they come from dependencies between data, since the input data of operations is the output data (results) of operations carried out previously.

8

Parallel Algorithms

A problem that needs to be solved is subdivided into a number of subproblems or tasks. Similarly, the corresponding algorithm is also subdivided into a number of subcomponents. Normally, the components cooperate with each other using the intermediate results of computation as well as synchronizing their action. The desired output of the parallel algorithm is an amalgamation of results computed by the algorithm components.

The process of designing a parallel algorithm consists of four steps:

- Subdividing a computational problem into tasks that can be executed simultaneously, and developing sequential algorithms for individual tasks.
- Analyzing computation granularity.
- Minimizing the cost of the parallel algorithm.
- Assigning tasks to processors executing the parallel algorithm.

8.1 Classes of Problems Solvable through Parallelization

In computational complexity theory, problems are divided into several complexity classes according to their running times on a single processor system or a deterministic Turing machine.

- Tractable problems: Problems whose running times are upper bounded by polynomials in n are said to belong to the P class and are generally considered to be *tractable*. Even if the polynomial is of a high degree such that a large problem requires years of computation on the fastest available supercomputer, there is still hope that with improvements in the algorithm or in computer performance, a reasonable running time may be obtained.
- Intractable problems: Problems for which the best-known deterministic algorithm runs in exponential time are *intractable*. A problem of this kind for which, when given a solution, the correctness of the solution can be verified in polynomial time, is said to belong to the non-deterministic polynomial (NP) class.

A deterministic algorithm is one that will return the same answer no matter how many times it is called on the same data. Moreover, it will always take the same steps to complete the task when applied to the same data.

An example of an NP problem is the subset-sum problem: Given a set of n integers and a target sum s, determine if a subset of the integers in the given set adds up to s. This problem looks deceptively simple, yet no one knows how to solve it other than by trying practically all of the 2n subsets of the given set. An efficient general algorithm for solving this problem is not known. Neither has anyone been able to prove that an efficient (polynomial-time) algorithm for the subset-sum problem does not exist.

Defining the class of NP-complete problems means that any problem in NP can be transformed, by a computationally efficient process, to any one of these problems. The subset-sum problem is known to be NP-complete. Thus, if one ever finds an efficient solution to the subset-sum problem, this is tantamount to proving P=NP. On the other hand, if one can prove that the subset-sum problem is not in P, then neither is any other NP-complete problem.

Problems exist that are not even in NP, meaning that even verifying that a claimed solution to such a problem is correct is currently intractable. An NP-hard problem is one that we do not know to be in NP, but we do know that any NP problem can be reduced to it by a polynomial-time algorithm. The name of this class implies that such problems are at least as hard as any NP problem.

Thus, the proof that a problem of interest is NP-complete consists of two parts:

- Proving that it is in NP by showing that a given solution for it can be verified in polynomial time.
- Proving that it is NP-hard by showing that some NP-complete (and thus any NP) problem can be reduced to it.

In fact, the P=? NP question is an open problem of complexity theory. A positive answer to this question would mean that the subset-sum and a host of other "hard" problems can be solved efficiently even if we do not yet know how to do it. A negative answer, on the other hand, would imply that problems exist for which efficient algorithms can never be found. Despite a lack of proof in either direction, researchers in complexity theory believe that, in fact, P≠NP.

8.1.1 Parallelizable Tasks

Parallel processing is generally of no avail for solving NP problems. Parallel processing is primarily useful for speeding up the execution time of the problems in P. Here, even a factor of 1000 speedup can mean the difference between practicality and impracticality (running time of several hours versus one year). Nick's Class (NC) of efficiently parallelizable problems in P might be defined as those problems that can be solved in a time period that is at most polylogarithmic in the problem size n, that is, $T(p)=O(\log^k n)$ for some constant k, using no more than a polynomial number $p=O(n^l)$ of processors.

A weaker form of NC, known as the parallel computation thesis, is stated as follows:

> *Anything that can be computed on a Turing machine using polynomially (polylogarithmically) bounded space in unlimited time can be computed on a parallel machine in polynomial (polylogarithmic) time using an unlimited number of processors, and vice versa.*

The problem with this thesis is that it places no bounds on computational resources other than time. The significance of NC, and its popularity, stems from its establishing simultaneous bounds on time and hardware resources, while at the same time being relatively insensitive to architectural and technological variations in parallel machine implementations.

The question NC=?P is an open problem of parallel complexity theory. A P-complete problem in P is a problem such that any other problem in P can be transformed to it in polylogarithmic time using a polynomial number of processors. So, if a polylogarithmic-time algorithm with a polynomial number of processors is ever found for any P-complete problem, then all problems in P are efficiently parallelizable and NC = P. Some of these problems have been around for years and studied extensively by numerous researchers. Thus, the lack of efficient algorithms for these problems strongly supports the conclusion that NC ≠ P.

Asymptotic running times describe how the execution time of an algorithm increases with the size of the input. The notation for the asymptotic running time uses functions whose domains are the natural numbers N. The function describes the essential terms for the asymptotic behavior and ignores less important terms such as constants and terms of lower increase.

Given two functions $f(n)$ and $g(n)$ of an independent variable n (usually the problem size), we define the relationships O (big-oh), Ω (big-omega), and Θ (theta) between them as follows:

The O-notation, Ω-notation, *and* Θ-notation, *which describe boundaries of the increase of the running time.*

The asymptotic upper bound is given by the O-notation*:*

$$O(g(n)) = \{f(n) \mid \text{there exists a positive constant } c \text{ and } n_0 \in N,$$

$$\text{such that for all } n \geq n_0 : 0 \leq f(n) \leq cg(n)\}$$

The asymptotic lower bound is given by the Ω-notation*:*

$$\Omega(g(n)) = \{f(n) \mid \text{there exists a positive constant } c \text{ and } n_0 \in N,$$

$$\text{such that for all } n \geq n_0 : 0 \leq cg(n) \leq f(n)\}$$

The bounds of the function from above and below is given by the Θ-notation*:*

$$\Theta(g(n)) = \{f(n) \mid \text{there exists positive constants } c_1, c_2 \text{ and } n_0 \in N,$$

$$\text{such that for all } n \geq n_0 : 0 \leq c_1 g(n) \leq f(n) \leq c_2 g(n)\}$$

Consequently, the growth rate of $f(n)$ is …. that of $g(n)$; the blank can be filled in with the relational symbol (<, ≤, =, ≥, >) corresponding to the defined relations:

<	$f(n) = o(g(n))$	$\lim_{n\to\infty} f(n)/g(n) = 0$ {read little-oh of $g(n)$}
≤	$f(n) = O(g(n))$	{big-oh}
=	$f(n) = \Theta(g(n))$ or $\theta(g(n))$	{theta}
≥	$f(n) = \Omega(g(n))$	{big-omega}
>	$f(n) = \omega(g(n))$	$\lim_{n\to\infty} f(n)/g(n) = \infty$ {little-omega}

Figure 8.1 illustrates the boundaries for the O-notation, Ω-notation, and Θ-notation.

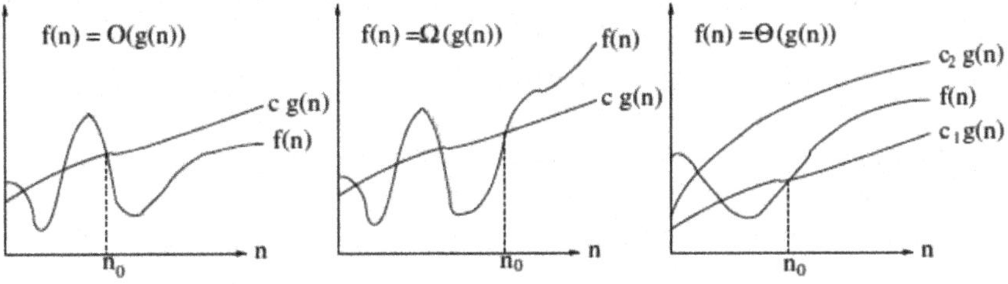

FIGURE 8.1
Graphical representation of the notions of asymptotic complexity.

8.2 Types of Parallelization

The degree of problem (program) concurrency is defined as the number of subproblems extracted in the problem that can potentially be solved in parallel, or as the number of tasks executed simultaneously in the parallel or concurrent program. The greater the degree of problem concurrency, the better it is suited for parallel execution.

Designing an efficient parallel program is also easier when relationships between tasks, that is the frequency of communication and the synchronization of their operation, are small. This is the case when the tasks are independent of each other and in the course of execution they do not need to communicate. It is enough to convey to tasks the data to be processed and then collect and combine the computed results.

8.2.1 Functional Parallelization

Subdivision of the problem into tasks (or subproblems) is referred to as *functional parallelization*. Subdivision into separate functions is used in the following example in which each task is designed to implement a separate function whose goal is to strike off composite numbers that are multiples of a given prime.

The tasks are dependent on each other, as in some of them the data computed is used by other tasks. These dependencies between tasks, requiring certain tasks to be executed before other tasks, can be represented by an acyclic-directed graph called a *task dependence graph*.

The algorithm or method of Sieve of Eratosthenes can be used to find the primes in the interval $[2\ldots n]$ for some natural n.

The first number 2 is recorded as the first prime number and then the multiples of 2 are struck off the list (sieved) starting from the square of this number, that is from $2^2=4$, since these multiples are not prime.

After removal of 4, a nonstruck-off number greater than the last prime (that is 2) is 3. It is recorded as the next prime and the multiples of 3 starting from $3^2=9$ are struck off. The tasks of striking off the multiples of 2 and 3 from the interval $[2\ldots n]$ can be carried out simultaneously.

After removal of 9, a nonstruck-off number greater than the last prime (that is 3) is 5. It is recorded as the next prime and the multiples of 5 starting from 25 are struck off. The tasks of striking off the multiples of 2, 3, and 5 from the interval $[2\ldots n]$ can be carried out simultaneously.

The Sieve of Eratosthenes ends when all the tasks are finished and the penultimate task finds a prime satisfying the condition $r_k^2 > n$ or else $r_k > \sqrt{n}$. The result of solving the problem is all numbers left in the interval $[2\ldots n]$.

Figure 8.2a shows a task-dependency graph (TDG) for the problem of finding primes. In task A_i for $i=1, 2,\ldots, k-1$ a consecutive prime $r_{i+1}(r_2=3, r_3=5$, and so on) is evaluated by striking off the multiple of r_i. The prime found is sent to task A_{i+1}. A task A_k checks whether $r_k^2 > n$, while task S collects information about the completion of all tasks and decides whether to finish computation.

Figure 8.2a shows that the maximum degree of problem concurrency, equal to the number of A_i tasks, increases with n. This degree is governed by an index k derived from

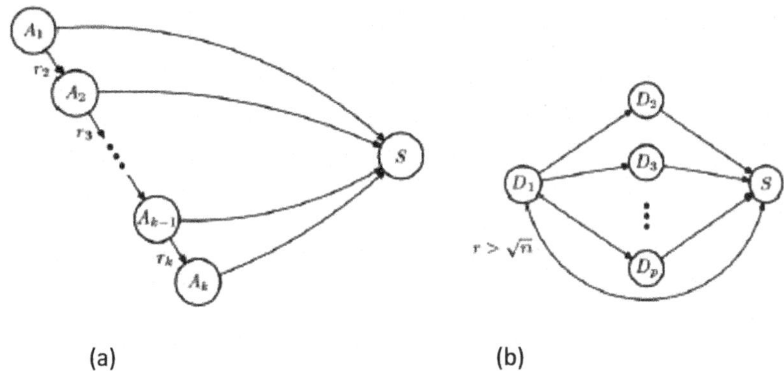

FIGURE 8.2
(a) Task-dependency graph for functional parallelization and (b) task-dependency graph for data parallelization.

inequality $r_k^2 > n$. For a fixed n, the number of tasks that can be performed in parallel is limited. Consequently, the speedup that can be achieved by applying the discussed algorithm is also limited.

In the functional subdivision used in the problem of finding primes using the Sieve of Eratosthenes, each of the extracted tasks (functions) performs sieving of composite numbers that are multiples of a given prime.

8.2.2 Data Parallelization

Data subdivision is the most common method to extract tasks that can be executed in parallel. It is frequently used when large amounts of data are processed. The benefits of conducting parallel computing are then significant and sometimes only this type of computing guarantees processing data in reasonable time.

Subdivision is concerned with

- Input data
- Intermediate data
- Output data

When designing a parallel algorithm, all possible partitions of data should be analyzed in order to choose the one that leads to efficient computing.

- Input data

The subdivision of input data is based on partitioning this data into a number of equal parts. Each of these parts is processed by a separate task; typically, the tasks perform the same computation on the assigned parts of the data and evaluate on the basis of its own part a certain amount of output data. The subdivision of input data is used in the following example in which the tasks find the primes in the assigned parts of input data of sizes $[n/p]$.

Given n input items, they can be broken down into p parts for $p < n$ of size at most $[n/p]$ and assigned to particular tasks. In each of the p tasks, all the necessary functions on portions of data assigned to a task are carried out.

In the problem of finding prime numbers employing the Sieve of Eratosthenes, an interval [2...p] can be divided into p subintervals: $[2...[n/p]]$, $[[n/p]+2...[n/p]]$,..., $[(p-1)[n/p]...n]$. In each task associated with a given subinterval the multiples of consecutive primes, that is, 2, 3, 5, and so on, are struck off.

If we assume that p is sufficiently smaller than $\sqrt{n}$, then the primes less than $\sqrt{n}$ and the first prime greater than $\sqrt{n}$ will be found by the task assigned to subinterval $[2...[n/p]]$.

The task D_1 sends consecutively determined primes to other tasks ($D_2, D_3, \ldots, D_p$) and it also sends a signal to task S about the end of computation when a prime greater than $\sqrt{n}$ is detected (Figure 8.2b). The problem solution is nonstruck-off numbers in the subintervals processed by all tasks.

The degree of concurrency of the parallel algorithm constructed using data parallelization is p, for p satisfying $1<p<n$.

- Output data

The subdivision of output data assumes that the respective parts of this data are computed by the tasks in parallel. This is possible if each element of the output data can be determined independently as a function of the input data.

The problem of multiplication of matrices a and b of sizes $n \times n$, that is, $c=ab$ can be obtained by performing multiplication of submatrices of size approximately $[n/2] \times [n/2]$, as follows:

$$\left[\begin{array}{c|c} a_{1,1} & a_{1,2} \\ \hline a_{2,1} & a_{2,2} \end{array}\right] \times \left[\begin{array}{c|c} b_{1,1} & b_{1,2} \\ \hline b_{2,1} & b_{2,2} \end{array}\right] = \left[\begin{array}{c|c} c_{1,1} & c_{1,2} \\ \hline c_{2,1} & c_{2,2} \end{array}\right]$$

The output data, that is matrix c, is composed of four submatrices, each of which can be computed by a separate task. The subdivision of the problem into four tasks is based on the subdivision of the output data as indicated below:

A disadvantage of both subdivisions is a relatively low degree of concurrency equal to 4. It is easy to point out that decomposition can also be done on the basis of *intermediate data,* that is, taking into account the products of the submatrices appearing earlier. These products can be evaluated by separate tasks in the first stage, and in the second stage the selected pairs of intermediate results can be combined into the final one. Such a subdivision based on the intermediate data has a higher degree of concurrency equal to 8.

However, in this case the need for synchronization of computation arises due to the dependencies between groups of tasks for the two stages.

8.2.3 Recursive Parallelization

Recursive subdivision is used in cases where the problem is solved by the *divide-and-conquer* method. In every step of this method, the problem is divided into a number of independent subproblems, or tasks. In most circumstances, the tasks are smaller instances of the original problem. The tasks are executed in a similar manner and their division into subsequent subtasks ends when they are so simple that they can be resolved in a trivial way. When all the tasks are executed, their results are combined into the solution to the original problem.

An example of the application of the divide-and-conquer method is a recursive algorithm to find both the minimum and maximum elements in a given array a. In line 10, the central index is determined that splits the array into two equal parts a[i...k] and a[k + 1...j]. On this basis, the problem is subdivided into two tasks that are executed in parallel. The aim of the tasks is to find both the minimum and maximum elements in their parts of the array. On any next level of recursion, the number of parallel tasks doubles, and so the degree of concurrency increases. The described recursive subdivision enables solving the problem of finding both the minimum and maximum elements in time $O(\log n)$, assuming that the necessary number of processors are available, while a sequential algorithm is executed in time $O(n)$.

```
procedure min_max(a[I...j])
begin
   if j-i+1=2 then
      if a[i]<a[j] then
         return (a[i],a[j]);
      else
         return (a[j],a[i]);
      end
   else
      k:= (j+i-1)/2
      (min1, max1):= min_max(a[i...k]);
      (min2, max2):= min_max(a[k+1...j]);
      return (MIN(min1, min2), MAX(max1,max2)));
   end
end
```

8.2.4 Exploratory Parallelization

This type of subdivision is used for problems where a space of solutions is to be searched: the space is divided into parts explored in parallel by a set of tasks. When one of the tasks finds a solution, it sends a signal to other tasks to finish the computation. An example is the problem of finding the way through a maze that does not pass any of the maze fields repeatedly, starting from the input field (In) and ending with the output field (Out) The problem of finding the path through a maze can be formulated in a number of ways. The simplest of them asks to find any path leading from the input to the output of the maze. A parallel algorithm ends its operation when any of the tasks (processors) finds an acceptable path. The cost of the corresponding computation, which is proportional to the part of a solution space that is searched, may be less or greater than the cost of a corresponding sequential computation—depending on the *position* of the solution in a solution tree.

The problem of maze traversal can also be formulated with the requirement of finding the shortest (or longest) path. In this case, the whole solution tree must be searched. A parallel algorithm will then outperform a sequential one, if only the work related to searching the subtrees is deployed evenly among the tasks.

8.2.5 Speculative Parallelization

Suppose we have a problem Z in which first a task A is executed and depending on a certain condition checked at the end of task A, one of the tasks B_1, B_2, or B_3 is performed (Figure 8.3). If task A does not transfer any input data to tasks B_i, only making the decision as to which of them should be followed, then the tasks A and B_i can be implemented in parallel with four processors.

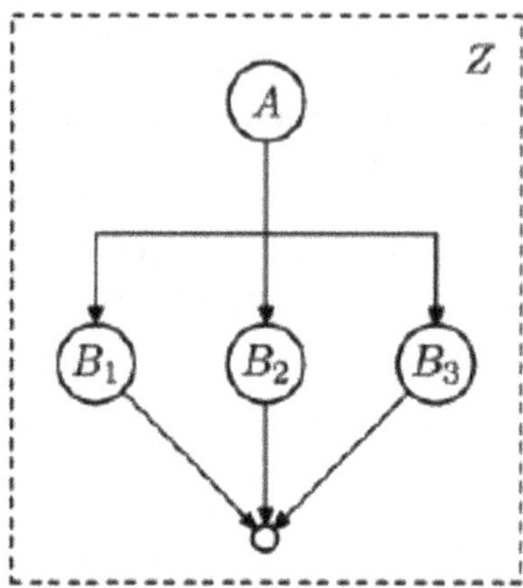

FIGURE 8.3
Parallel execution A, B_1, B_2, and B_3.

After finishing the tasks, depending on the results acquired in task A, the computation is continued with the results obtained by the appropriate task B_i. The results achieved in the other two tasks are rejected. This procedure is called speculative decomposition since while starting the execution of tasks B_i, it is known in advance that the results of all the other tasks will be discarded. However, this ensures a faster solution of problem Z, because instead of a sequential execution of task A and then the appropriate task B_i, these tasks are performed in parallel.

The described approach can be applied in case statements, where task A involves the computation of the value of a selector and tasks are multiple "branches" of a case statement.

8.3 Granularity of Parallelization

The degree of concurrency is related to the notion of the granularity of computation. When a problem is subdivided into many small tasks, it is termed *fine granularity*. When the problem is subdivided into a small number of large tasks, it is termed *coarse granularity*. From another perspective, the amount of work to be performed within a task determines the grain size: depending on whether the grain size of tasks is small or large, the computation is termed, respectively, *fine-* or *coarse-grained*.

In order to minimize the execution time of an algorithm, granularity should be as fine as possible. The execution time of small tasks by a large number of processors is short, and as a consequence high speedup is achieved. Although a high degree of concurrency and a concomitant granularity favor the use of parallelism, this can be adversely affected by the accompanying communication costs. If the algorithm has been implemented by adopting the network model, communication costs are unavoidable and these costs commonly grow with the number of (communicating) tasks. This implies that the degree of concurrency and granularity should be properly determined to achieve optimal speedup.

8.4 Assigning Computational Tasks to Processors

Load balancing deals with minimizing the parallel program runtime that is achieved by the uniform distribution of computations across available processors. In other words, the aim is to minimize the time period during which processors are idle. Once the problem has been subdivided into tasks (subproblems) and algorithms for particular tasks have been developed, the computations need to be spread across the available processors. Assuming that the number of tasks is at least equal to the number of processors, the goal is to assign tasks to processors in such a way that the execution time of a parallel program consisting of a number of tasks is as short as possible.

Assuming that the number of tasks and their execution times are known, minimization of the runtime of a parallel program belongs to the class of NP-complete problems. Among them is the scheduling problem formulated as follows. Given n tasks with execution times $\tau_1, \tau_2, \ldots, \tau_n$ and an integer m, assign the tasks to m processors for execution so that the time for completion of the work, termed the *length of a schedule*, is minimum.

The perfect balancing of processor workloads is not easy to achieve for several reasons:

- Difficulty in evaluating the execution times of tasks. These times may depend on the input data or the intermediate results acquired. The number of tasks to complete can also be difficult to evaluate before the beginning of computation.
- Differential computational speeds of processors across heterogeneous computers. The computational speed depends on the processor type, the kind of operations executed (floating- or fixed-point), the software libraries used, etc.
- Impact of communication between tasks on the implementation of computation. Although the nominal data rate of interconnection network (IN) links is frequently known, the transfer time of data may depend on the network load.
- Communication between tasks that are concurrent processes is non-deterministic. This is, for example, due to the necessity to be served by processors of the emerging system events signaled by priority interrupts.

Processor load balancing can be achieved using a static or dynamic method. The choice of the method depends on the nature of the parallel program, that is, on the specifics of its tasks and the interaction between them.

Parallel computers are equipped with hierarchical memories in which references to local memory cells (located closer to the reference point) take shorter time than to nonlocal memory cells (located farther away from the reference point). So, in parallel algorithms the number of references to local memories should be maximized, while the number of references to nonlocal memories minimized—in particular to the cells of shared memory. If the elements of some data structure are used repeatedly, the preferred solution can be to copy the structure from the shared memory (or other nonlocal memory) to a local memory and repeatedly refer to elements in this memory. This process is referred to as data replication.

In the case of distributed memory, transferring data between tasks (processors) is achieved via an IN. The IN transmission rates are much slower than the computation speed of processors in such networks including clusters consisting of computers or multicore processor computers. In order to reduce the cost of parallel algorithms, the amount of data to be transferred in distributed memory systems should be as small as possible. Additionally, the frequency of data transmissions due to the relatively large latency associated with each transmission should be as small as possible. In general, the number of interactions between tasks should be minimized by (say) integrating a group of small messages into a single message of larger size. Thus, it is advantageous to send messages of larger size but seldom rather than short messages more frequently. Instead of computing data in one task and broadcasting it to other tasks, it can be computed in each task, thus avoiding communication—but at the cost of redundant computation. This process is referred to as computational replication. Accordingly, distributed memory computers can be recommended for coarse-grained algorithms of large grain size and scarce communication.

8.5 Illustrating Design of a Parallel Algorithm

To exemplify the process of developing a parallel algorithm for a particular model, we show how Gaussian elimination can be implemented on a mesh of trees in order to solve a system of linear equations.

The method solves the equation:

$$A * x = b$$

(in matrix form) by applying a sequence of transformations to both A and b such that in the end, A is reduced to the identity matrix I. If the original system contains n equations in n unknowns, then the Gaussian elimination algorithm is made up of n iterations. The aim of the ith iteration is to make all elements in column i of A equal to 0 except for a_{ii}, which becomes 1. This can be accomplished by subtracting multiples of row i from all other rows, and dividing the elements of row i by the pivot a_{ii}. The same transformations are effected on the elements of vector b.

Figure 8.4 illustrates Gaussian elimination on a mesh of trees. The processors are arranged in a mesh-like structure, but they are not connected using regular mesh links. Instead, the processors in each row are connected together to form a binary tree of processors, with the root of the tree being the first processor in that row. Similarly, there is a binary tree of processors for each column of the mesh. This particular way of connecting processors determines the communication patterns. A datum can propagate to all processors on a certain row (or column) in time logarithmic with respect to the number of processors on that row (or column). A fine-grain task is identified with the process of computing the new value for an element of A or b. The maximum degree of parallelism is achieved

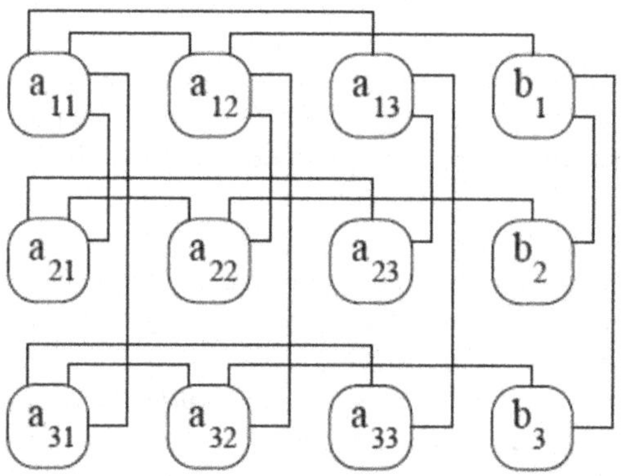

FIGURE 8.4
Gaussian elimination on a mesh of trees.

when each such task is mapped onto one processor in the mesh. The processors in the last column also keep track of the unknowns $x_1, x_2, \ldots, x_n$ and are responsible for swapping x_i and x_j whenever columns i and j in A have to be swapped.

By choosing the finest granularity, we indeed ensure maximum parallelism, but we must pay a certain communication cost among so many small tasks, each assigned to a different processor. Once the processors have the required data, each computes a single value of the A or b matrix. This allows all processors to compute the new values for the elements of A and b simultaneously, in each iteration. But before the actual computation can take place, $O(\log n)$, time is spent in each iteration choosing the pivot and distributing (communicating) the necessary data to the processors.

Thus, $\log n$ fine-grain tasks can be aggregated into one coarse-grain task, which is now charged to compute the new values for $\log n$ elements, sequentially. The overall $O(n \log n)$ running time of the algorithm remains the same, because the time spent on sequential computation is not asymptotically higher than the communication time. Mapping one coarse-grain task to one processor, the problem can still be solved in the same amount of time (asymptotically), but now with fewer processors.

This section exemplified the design methodology for developing parallel algorithms on a model where the processors are arranged in a mesh-like structure, but with the regular mesh links replaced by row and column binary trees. The reason behind choosing this topology is to reduce the diameter of a regular mesh of processors, thereby reducing the communication cost among the processors in the model.

However, this topology has certain disadvantages:

- The new topology does not possess the regularity and modularity that make a mesh of processors so easy to extend.
- The length of the links in a mesh of trees increases with the number of processors in the model, affecting its scalability.

A way to make communications inside a mesh of processors easier, while still retaining the attractive features of the model, is to augment them with a *bus*, which is simply a communication link to which a number of processors are attached in order to transmit and receive data. Depending on the particular technology used to implement them, these buses can be fixed, reconfigurable, or optical.

8.6 Parallel Algorithms for Conventional Computations

Unless the computational environment exhibits some special properties, for example, imposing restrictions on the availability or reliability of data to be processed, any computation is a conventional or traditional one.

8.6.1 Parallel Prefix and Suffix Computations on a Linked List

This section shows that a parallel approach can also be useful when working with pointer-based data structures, such as a linked list. A singly linked list L consists of a number of nodes where each node (except the last one) holds a pointer to the next node in the list

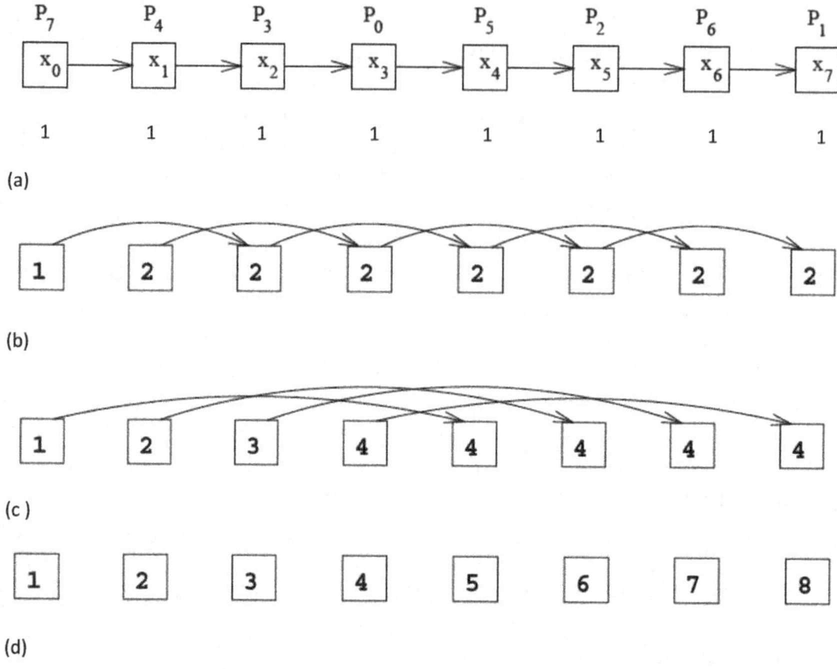

FIGURE 8.5
(a) A singly linked list L, (b) after one iteration, (c) after two iterations, and (d) after three iterations.

(Figure 8.5a). Besides this pointer, a node also usually holds a value (that depends on the application) and other necessary information.

The problem assumes that a linked list L has been stored in the shared memory of a parallel random-access machine (PRAM). Each node is added to the list at a different time, without global knowledge of the data structure constructed so far or the positions where future nodes will be added. The head of the list has sequence number 1, the node pointed at by the head bears sequence number 2, and so on. The list-sequencing problem asks for the sequence number of each node to be computed. Given a pointer to the head of L, one can easily compute the sequence numbers for all nodes in time linear in the size of L, just by following the chain of pointers and adding 1 to the current sequence number at each step. In order to execute this algorithm, a single processor suffices. The question is if more processors are available, whether one can do better than a linear running time.

If the PRAM model has as many processors as there are nodes in L, each processor can know the location of one distinct node in the list and can therefore access any information stored in that node in constant time. For the list-sequencing problem, the values x_j, $1 \leq j \leq n$, stored in each node are initially all equal with 1. The parallel algorithm then consists of repeatedly performing the following step: *each processor adds its own value to the value stored in its successor node and then updates its pointer to the node following its successor.*

The number of final sequence numbers computed at each step doubles. A graphical illustration of the algorithm for the particular case of a list with eight elements is given in Figure 8.5. For a list L having n nodes, $O(\log n)$ steps are required to complete the computation and each step takes constant time. In the end, each node will have its successor pointer set to nil (Figure 8.5d).

Algorithm 8.1

```
for all i in parallel do
     next(i) ← succ(i);
     val ← (i) 1.
end for.
finished ← false;
while (not finished) do
     finished ← true;
     for all i in parallel do
          if next(i) ≠ nil then
               val(next(i)) ← val(i) + val(next(i));
               next(i) ← next(next(i));
               if next(i) ≠ nil then
                  finished ← false.
               Endif
          End if
     End for
end while
```

The algorithmic technique used to solve the list-sequencing problem has far broader applicability than just computing the sequence numbers of the elements composing a linked list. If Algorithm 8.1 is modified such that we replace addition by a generic operator "O," transforming two objects x_i and x_j into an object of the same type x_i O x_j, then what we obtain is an algorithm performing a *prefix computation*. It is so called because the values stored in each node at the end of the algorithm are $x_1, x_1 \text{ O } x_2, x_1 \text{ O } x_2 \text{ O } x_3, \ldots, x_1 \text{ O } x_2 \ldots \text{O } x_n$ from the head of the list down to the last element.

Transforming a prefix computation algorithm into a suffix one is easily achieved by replacing the following line in the modified version of Algorithm 8.1:

$$\text{val}(\text{next}(i)) \leftarrow \text{val}(i)\,\text{O}\,\text{val}(\text{next}(i)) \text{ with } \text{val}(i) \leftarrow \text{val}(i)\,\text{O}\,\text{val}(\text{next}(i)).$$

In suffix computation, the resulting values would be

$$x_1 \text{ O } x_2 \text{ O} \ldots \text{O } x_n, x_2 \text{ O } x_3 \text{ O} \ldots \text{O } x_n, \ldots, \text{O } x_n.$$

Many problems of practical interest can be reduced to a form of *prefix* or *suffix* computation; so having an efficient parallel algorithm to deal with these two generic computations is of great importance.

If we now instantiate "O" back to "+" and initialize all values with 1, then instead of the list-sequencing problem we are now solving the list-ranking problem, where we have to compute the rank of each node as its distance from the end of the list.

8.7 Parallel Algorithms for Unconventional Computations

When it comes to tackling a computational problem with unconventional characteristics, a parallel approach may yield even better results. In some cases, the performance of the parallel algorithm, expressed in terms of the speedup or quality-up achieved, is superlinear in the number of processors used in the parallel computer, relative to what the best sequential algorithm can offer. In other cases, the inherently parallel nature of the problem renders a sequential machine (or even one with insufficient processing elements) useless, and consequently, a sequential solution fails altogether.

8.8 Summary

The chapter commenced with looking at classes of problems that are solvable through parallelization. It then described various types of parallelization, namely, functional, data, recursive, exploratory, and speculative parallelization. The amount of work to be performed within a task determines the grain size: depending on whether the grain size of tasks is small or large, the computation is termed *fine-* or *coarse-grained,* respectively. Load balancing deals with minimizing the parallel program runtime that is achieved by the uniform distribution of computations across available processors. The last part of the chapter exemplified the process of developing a parallel algorithm for a particular model.

Section III

Parallel Computing Architectures

This sections looks at parallel computing architectures. Chapters 10 through 12 explain the primary parallel computing architectures, namely, shared memory, message passing, and stream processing, respectively.

Chapter 9 introduces the overarching concepts of parallel computing performance that characterize any parallel computing architecture as a whole.

Chapter 10 discusses architectural aspects of shared memory systems. Shared memory systems form a major category of multiprocessors. In this category, all processors share a global memory. Communication between tasks running on different processors is performed through writing to and reading from the global memory. All inter-processor coordination and synchronization are also accomplished via the global memory. The chapter discusses the main challenges of shared memory systems, namely, contention and cache coherence problems. Local caches are typically used to alleviate the bottleneck problem. The introduction of caches creates consistency problems among caches and between memory and caches. Cache coherence schemes can be subdivided into snooping protocols and directory-based protocols. However, scalability remains the main drawback of a shared memory system.

Chapter 11 discusses the architectural aspects of message-passing systems. Message-passing systems provide alternative methods for communication and the movement of data among multiprocessors (compared to shared memory multiprocessor systems). A message-passing system typically combines local memory and the processor at each node of the interconnection network. There is no global memory so it is necessary to move data from one local memory to another by means of message passing. There are, however, a number of problems associated with message-passing systems, including communication overhead and the difficulty of programming. The chapter discusses the architecture and the network models of message-passing systems. The chapter then sheds some light on routing and network switching techniques.

Chapter 12 discusses the architectural aspects of stream processing. The principles of the stream architecture are based on the key properties of many performance-demanding applications and the characteristics of modern very-large-scale integration (VLSI) technology. Stream processors are designed for the strengths of modern VLSI technology with minimum execution overheads, providing efficiency on par with application-specific solutions such as Application-Specific Integrated Circuits (ASICs). The stream architecture focuses on the effective management of locality (state), bandwidth (communication), and throughput optimization rather than latency.

9

Parallel Computing Architecture Basics

High-Performance Distributed Computing (HPDC) refers to any computational activity that requires many computers to execute a task. The major applications of HPDC include data storage and analysis, data mining, simulation and modeling, scientific calculations, bio-informatics, big data challenges, and complex visualizations.

Early high-performance computing (HPC) systems were more concerned with executing code on parallel architectures aligned with distributed systems. Now, the focus has shifted to enabling transparent and efficient utilization of the infrastructural capabilities of distributed computing architectures such as clusters/grids/clouds.

9.1 High-Performance Distributed Computing

Over the past years, distributed systems have gained substantial importance. The reasons for their growing importance are manifold:

- Geographically distributed environment: The most apparent idea of distributed systems is the physical distribution of computers around the globe. For example, in the case of banks that are present in multiple locations to handle the accounts of its customers. Banks are truly connected, also called globalized, if they can monitor interbank transactions, monitor and record fund transfers from globally dispersed automated teller machines (ATMs), and access customer accounts around the globe, etc. Another example is the Internet that takes the nadir point in functioning as a distributed system. Furthermore, the mobility of users has added a new dimension to geographic distribution.
- Resource sharing: A resource represents both software and hardware. The ubiquitous nature of distributed systems is due to the resource sharing facility. Resource sharing is a commonplace activity with networked resources available today. Hardware resources such as printers, files, and more specifically to functionality such as search engines are routinely shared. From the hardware provision standpoint, sharing resources such as printers and disks reduces costs, but users are interested in sharing on a much higher level, for example, their applications and everyday activities. A user is interested in sharing web pages rather than the hardware they are implemented on; similarly, users are more interested in sharing applications such as search engines and currency converters than the servers on which these applications depend. It is important to recognize that strategies to implement resource sharing vary widely in their scope depending on how users work together; for example, a search engine serves users throughout the world, while a closed group of users collaborates directly by sharing documents.

- Computation speed: An increased computation speed forms perhaps the most important motivation for considering distributed architectures. There is a physical limit to how much a uniprocessor can compute in unit time. While Very Long Instruction Word (VLIW) architectures provide a boost to the processing power by introducing parallelism at the instruction level, these techniques do not scale well beyond a certain level. An alternative to this approach is to stack multiple processors and divide the problem set into smaller problems and assign these to individual processors that can operate concurrently. This method is scalable and the processing power can be gradually increased by stacking more processors. This forms a simpler and economic alternative to purchasing a single large uniprocessor. In recent times, big data computations have led to the birth of software systems that can break the problem into smaller bits and spread them across the network for multicore computations due to the distributed nature of the data.
- Fault tolerance. The software built around a single, powerful uniprocessor is prone to complete collapse if the processor fails, and this is risky. It is preferable to compromise a bit on the processing by using distributed systems, when a failure cripples a fraction of the processing element with a chance for graceful degradation and improved tolerance. This method can also enhance the reliability and availability of the system by incorporating the redundant processing elements. In many cases, a system can have triple modular redundancy where three identical functional units are used to perform the same computation and the correct answer is typically determined by a majority vote. In other fault-tolerant distributed systems, processors cross-check one another at predefined checkpoints, catering to automatic failure detection, diagnosis, and eventual recovery. Thus, a distributed system provides an excellent opportunity for incorporating fault tolerance and graceful degradation.

9.2 Performance Evaluation

Computer systems are evaluated based on several measures of performance. The measure used depends on the machine being evaluated for a particular application involving certain types of operations: the measures are based on a representative mix of operations depending on their occurrences in the application. The corresponding performance rating used could either be the *peak rate* (i.e., the million instructions per second [MIPS] rating the central processing unit [CPU] cannot exceed) or the more realistic *average* or *sustained* rate. Sometimes, a comparative rating that compares the average rate of the machine to that of other well-known reference machines (e.g., IBM MIPS and VAX MIPS) is also used.

Some of the common measures of performance are

- Million instructions per second (MIPS)
- Million operations per second (MOPS)
- Million floating-point operations per second (megaflops or MFLOPS)
- Billion floating-point operations per second (gigaflops or GFLOPS)
- Trillion floating-point operations per second (teraflops or TFLOPS)

In addition to performance, other factors considered in evaluating architectures are generality (how wide is the range of applications suited for this architecture), ease of use, and expandability or scalability.

Several analytical techniques are used in estimating performance. All these techniques are approximations and as the complexity of the system increases, most of these techniques become unwieldy. A practical method for estimating performance in such cases is by using benchmarks.

9.2.1 Benchmarks

Typically, a particular computer architecture should efficiently execute those features of a programming language that are most frequently used in actual programs. This ability is often measured by benchmarks: benchmarks are considered representative of classes of applications envisioned for the architecture. Benchmarks are useful in evaluating hardware as well as software and single processor as well as multiprocessor systems. They are also useful in comparing the performance of a system before and after certain changes are made. Benchmarks are standardized batteries of programs run on a machine to estimate its performance. The results of running a benchmark on a given machine can then be compared with those on a known or standard machine.

Some common benchmarks are

- Real-world/application benchmarks. These use system- or user-level software code drawn from real algorithms or full applications, commonly used in system-level benchmarking. These usually have large code and data storage requirements.
- Derived benchmarks. These are also called *algorithm-based benchmarks*. These extract the key algorithms and generate realistic datasets from real-world applications, and are used for debugging, internal engineering, and competitive analysis.
- Single processor benchmarks. These are low-level benchmarks used to measure performance parameters that characterize the basic architecture of the computer. These hardware/compiler parameters predict the timing and performance of the more complex kernels and applications. They are used to measure the theoretical parameters that describe the overhead or potential bottleneck, or the properties of some item of hardware.
- Kernel benchmarks. These are code fragments extracted from real programs in which the code fragment is responsible for most of the execution time. They have the advantage of a small code size and a long execution time. Examples are Linpack and Lawrence Livermore loops. The Linpack measures the MFLOPS rating of the machine in solving a system of equations in a FORTRAN environment. The Lawrence Livermore loops measure the MFLOPS rating in executing 24 common FORTRAN loops operating on datasets with 1001 or fewer elements.
- Local benchmarks. These are programs that are site-specific, that is, they include in-house applications that are not widely available. Since the user is most interested in the performance of the machine for his/her applications, local benchmarks are the best means of evaluation.
- UNIX utility and application benchmarks. These are programs that are widely employed by the UNIX user community. The System Performance Evaluation Cooperative Effort (SPEC) benchmark suite belongs to this category and consists of ten scenarios taken from a variety of science and engineering applications. This

suite, developed by a consortium of computer vendors, is for the evaluation of workstation performance. The performance rating is provided in *SPECmarks*.

- Synthetic benchmarks. These are small programs constructed especially for benchmarking purposes. They do not perform any useful computation, but statistically approximate the average characteristics of real programs. Examples are Dhrystone and Whetstone benchmarks.

The *Whetstone benchmark* was originally developed in ALGOL60. Whetstone reflects mostly numerical computing, using a substantial amount of floating-point arithmetic. It is now chiefly used in a FORTRAN version. Its main characteristics are

- A high degree of floating-point data and operations, since the benchmark is meant to represent numeric programs.
- A high percentage of the execution time is spent in mathematical library functions.
- Use of very few local variables, since the issue of local versus global variables was hardly discussed when these benchmarks were developed.
- Instead of local variables, a large number of global variables are used. Therefore, a compiler in which the most heavily used global variables are used as register variables (as in 3) will boost the Whetstone performance.
- Since the benchmark consists of nine small loops, Whetstone has an extremely high code locality. Thus, a near 100% hit rate can be expected even for fairly small instruction caches.

The *Dhrystone benchmark* program set is based on the statistics of actual usage of program features, particularly in systems programming. Following the pioneering work of D. Knuth in the early 1970s, an increasing number of publications provided such statistical data about the actual usage of programming language features. Its characteristics are

- It contains a measurable quantity of floating-point operations.
- A considerable percentage of the execution time is spent in string functions. In the case of C compilers, this number goes up to 40%.
- Unlike Whetstone, Dhrystone contains hardly any loops within the main measurement loop. Therefore, for processors with small instruction caches, almost all the memory accesses are cache misses. But as the cache becomes larger, all the accesses become cache hits.
- Only a small amount of global data is manipulated and the data size cannot be scaled.
- Stanford small programs. Concurrent with the development of the first reduced instruction set computer (RISC) systems, John Hennessy and Peter Nye at Stanford's computer systems laboratory collected a set of small C programs. These programs became popular because they were the basis for the first comparisons of RISC and complex instruction set computer (CISC) processors. They have now been collected into one C program containing eight integer programs (Permutations, Towers of Hanoi, Eight queens, Integer matrix multiplication, Puzzle, Quicksort, Bubble sort, and Tree sort) and two floating-point programs (matrix multiplication and fast Fourier transform).
- The PERFormance Evaluation for Cost-effective Transformations (PERFECT) benchmark suite consists of 13 FORTRAN subroutines spanning four application

areas (signal processing, engineering design, physical and chemical modeling, and fluid dynamics). This suite consists of complete applications (with the input/output [IO] portions removed) and hence constitutes significant measures of performance.

- The Scalable, Language-independent, Ames Laboratory One-minute Measurement (SLALOM) is designed to measure the parallel computer performance as a function of problem size. The benchmark always runs in 1 min. The speed of the system under test is determined by the amount of computation performed in 1 min.
- Parallel benchmarks. These are for evaluating parallel computer architectures. The 1985 workshop at the National Institute of Standards (NIST) recommended the following suites for parallel computers: Linpack, Whetstone, Dhrystone, Livermore loops, Fermi National Accelerator Laboratory codes used in equipment procurement, NASA/Ames benchmark of 12 FORTRAN subroutines, John Rice's numerical problem set, and Raul Mendez's benchmarks for Japanese machines.

Many other benchmark suites are in use and more are being developed. It is important to note that benchmarks provide only a broad performance guideline. It is the responsibility of the user to select the benchmark that comes close to his/her application and further evaluate the machine based on scenarios expected in the application for which the machine is being evaluated.

9.3 Application and Architecture

The degree of parallelism is simply the index of the number of computations that can be executed concurrently. Suppose that the application allows the development of processing algorithms with a degree of parallelism *A*; the language used to code the algorithm allows the representation of algorithms with a degree of parallelism *L*; the compilers produce an object code that retains a degree of parallelism *C*; and the hardware structure of the machine has a degree of parallelism *H*. Then, for processing to be most efficient:

$$H \geq C \geq L \geq A$$

Thus, if the objective is to minimize the computation time of the application at hand, the processing structure that offers the least computation time is the most efficient one.

Thus, in order to obtain the best possible performance from a parallel-processing system, the application is partitioned into a set of tasks that can be executed concurrently. Each task accomplishes a part of the overall computation and typically requires some sort of communication (i.e., to transmit results, to request or provide data items that may be common to both tasks, etc.) with other tasks during execution. The performance of such a parallel-processing system is characterized by

- Level of parallelism: A computation is assumed to consist of a process(es) that is constituted of a task(s), which is constituted of an instruction(s), which is constituted of an operation(s), which is constituted of microcode. Accordingly, the following levels (with decreasing granularity) are typically considered:

    - Process level
    - Task level
    - Instruction level
    - Operation level
    - Microcode level
- Granularity: The granularity of an application module (task) is a function of R, the runtime (execution time) of the task and C, the communication time of the task with other tasks.
    - Coarse granularity exists when R is large compared to C.
    - Medium granularity exists when R is comparable with C.
    - Fine granularity exists when R is very small compared with C.
- Degree of parallelism: The degree of parallelism is simply the index of the number of computations that can be executed concurrently.
- Data dependency: Data dependencies are the result of precedence constraints between operations (or tasks or procedures) imposed by the application. The precedence constraints between the operations are obeyed automatically in a single processor system since only one operation is executed at a time. However, when the application is split into several tasks to be implemented on a multiple processor system, a task requiring a data item will have to wait until another task producing it has indeed produced that item. If several tasks are updating a (shared) variable, the update sequence should be such that the result is the same as that would be obtained when the application is executed by a single processor system. Data dependencies also affect the granularity and the degree of parallelism of the application.

9.3.1 Multiprocessor Architectures

The main objective of multiple processor architectures is to minimize the computation time (i.e., to maximize the throughput of the system) of an application. Ideally, a computer system with N processors should provide a throughput of N times that of a single processor system. This requires that the degree of parallelism of the application is almost N. In practice, the communication between tasks (due to data dependencies), the allocation of tasks to processors, and the control of the execution of multiple tasks generate considerable overhead. Hence, in general, the N-fold speedup previously mentioned is not possible.

However, there are applications that can be partitioned such that there is no communication between tasks. These are called trivially or embarrassingly parallel applications. If the system structure minimizes the task creation and execution overhead, an N-fold throughput can be achieved for these applications.

One obvious way of reducing the overhead is to partition the application into tasks with as large a granularity as possible. Although this minimizes the communication and task management overhead, it reduces the degree of parallelism since there are now fewer tasks that can be executed concurrently. To maximize the degree of parallelism, the application must be partitioned into as large a number of fine-grain tasks as possible. But, this increases the execution overhead. Thus, a compromise is needed between the granularity and the degree of parallelism, to maximize the throughput of the system.

9.4 Maximum Performance Computing Approach

It is widely accepted that the modeling and measurement of application characteristics can be used to optimize the design of a cluster, for example, in terms of relative resources dedicated to computation, memory, and interconnect. The same approach can be extended to every level in a computer system, developing dedicated, problem-specific computer architectures to address different domains of scientific problems in the most efficient way, achieving the maximum performance.

To deliver maximum application performance, a multidisciplinary approach to computing is recommended where a team of natural and computer scientists and engineers work together to codesign a system all the way from the formulation of the computational problem down to the design of the best possible computer architecture for its solution. The essence of this approach is to optimize the scientific algorithm to match the capabilities of the computer at the same time as optimizing the computer to match the requirements of the algorithm. Dataflow computing provides a key part of the solution by combining flexibility with maximum performance and high efficiency. Figure 9.1 shows the process for maximizing application performance with dataflow computing.

The first step is application analysis, the main objective of which is to establish an understanding of the application, the algorithms used, and the potential performance bottlenecks. Application analysis should cover all the layers involved in a computational problem, from the mathematics and algorithms to the low-level computer science and electrical engineering aspects. This includes considerations such as

- Type and regularity of computation
- Ratio of computation and memory access
- Balance between local computation and network communication
- Balance between computation and disk I/O
- Trade-offs between (re)computation and storage

All of these can have a large impact on the final system performance—even if an application has a highly optimized computational kernel, this will have no impact if an application is limited by the speed it can read/write data to disk.

The second step in the process is to transform the application to create a structure that is suitable for acceleration. This includes algorithm-level transformations as well as code transformations, and data layout or representation transformations. The analysis and transformation steps are those that require the largest degree of multidisciplinary codesign cooperation. Natural scientists with expertise in the problem domain can collaborate with computer scientists and engineers to make sure the full range of possibilities is explored.

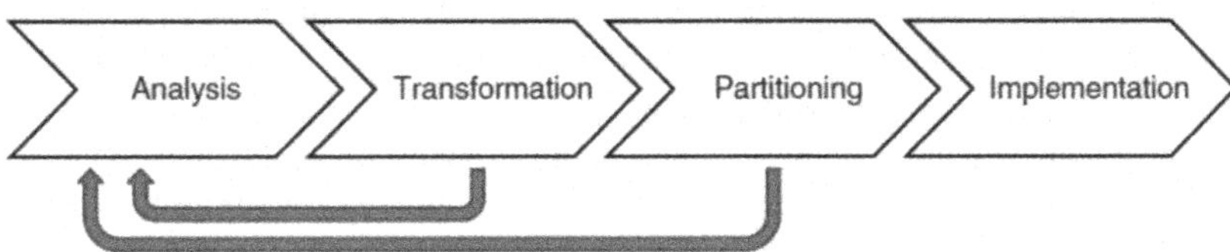

FIGURE 9.1
Process for accelerating applications with dataflow computing.

In the third step, the application is partitioned between the different resources in the computing system. There are two key things to be partitioned: code and data. For program code, we consider multiple code partitioning options that determine where each operation runs—on conventional CPUs or on dataflow engines. We orthogonally consider data access plans—the location of each significant data array used in the computation. For the dataflow engines, data can either be present in the large (tens of gigabytes) off-chip memory or the smaller on-chip memory (typically a few megabytes). For CPUs, data can reside on disk, in the main memory, or in one of several levels of on-chip cache.

Each combination of transformation, code option, and data access plan will provide a certain level of performance in return for a certain amount of implementation effort. This process of analyzing, transforming, and partitioning can be performed iteratively as additional possibilities are explored, and high-level performance modeling can be used to quickly narrow down to a small set of implementation options that are most likely to be successful.

Finally, one particular option can be selected for implementation.

9.5 Parallel Computing Basics

An important aspect of parallel computing is the parallel execution time, which consists of the time for computation on processors or cores and the time for data exchange or synchronization. The parallel execution time should be smaller than the sequential execution time on one processor, so that designing a parallel program is worth the effort. The parallel execution time is the time elapsed between the start of the application on the first processor and the end of the execution of the application on all processors. This time is influenced by the distribution of work to processors or cores, the time for information exchange or synchronization, and idle times in which a processor cannot do anything useful but wait for an event to happen.

In general, a smaller parallel execution time results when the work load is assigned equally to processors or cores, which is called load balancing, and when the overhead for information exchange, synchronization, and idle times is small. Finding a specific scheduling and mapping strategy that leads to a good load balance and a small overhead is often difficult because of many interactions. For example, reducing the overhead for information exchange may lead to load imbalance, whereas a good load balance may require more overhead for information exchange or synchronization.

For a quantitative evaluation of the execution time of parallel programs, cost measures such as *speedup* and *efficiency* are used, which compare the resulting parallel execution time with the sequential execution time on one processor. There are different ways to measure the cost or runtime of a parallel program and a large variety of parallel cost models based on parallel programming models have been proposed and used. These models are meant to bridge the gap between specific parallel hardware and more abstract parallel programming languages and environments.

A first step in parallel programming is the design of a parallel algorithm or program for a given application problem. The design starts with the decomposition of the computations of an application into several parts, called *tasks*, which can be computed in parallel on the cores or processors of the parallel hardware. The *potential parallelism* is an inherent property of an application algorithm and influences how an application can be split into tasks.

The decomposition into tasks can be complicated and laborious, since there are usually many different possibilities of decomposition for the same application algorithm. The size of tasks (e.g., in terms of the number of instructions) is called *granularity* and there is typically the possibility of choosing tasks of different sizes. Defining the tasks of an application appropriately is one of the main intellectual works in the development of a parallel program and is difficult to automate.

The tasks of an application are coded in a parallel programming language or environment and are assigned to *processes* or *threads,* which are then assigned to physical computation units for execution. The assignment of tasks to processes or threads is called scheduling and fixes the order in which the tasks are executed. *Scheduling* can be done by hand in the source code or by the programming environment, at compile time or dynamically at runtime. The assignment of processes or threads onto the physical units, processors, or cores is called *mapping* and is usually done by the runtime system but can sometimes be influenced by the programmer.

The methods of synchronization and coordination in parallel computing are strongly connected with the way in which information is exchanged between processes or threads, and this depends on the memory organization of the hardware. The tasks of an application algorithm can be independent but can also depend on each other, resulting in data or control dependencies of tasks. Data and control dependencies may require a specific execution order of the parallel tasks: If a task needs data produced by another task, the execution of the first task can start only after the other task has actually produced the data and provides the information. Thus, dependencies between tasks are constraints on the scheduling. In addition, parallel programs need synchronization and coordination of threads and processes in order to execute correctly.

The term thread is connected with shared memory and the term process is connected with distributed memory. A coarse classification of the memory organization distinguishes between

- *Shared memory machines*: For shared memory machines, a global shared memory stores the data of an application and can be accessed by all processors or cores of the hardware systems. Information exchange between threads is done by shared variables written by one thread and read by another thread. The correct behavior of the entire program has to be achieved by synchronization between threads, so that the access to shared data is coordinated, that is, a thread reads a data element not before the write operation by another thread storing the data element has been finalized. Depending on the programming language or environment, synchronization is done by the runtime system or by the programmer.
- *Distributed memory machines*: For distributed memory machines, there exists a private memory for each processor, which can only be accessed by this processor and no synchronization for memory access is needed. Information exchange is done by sending data from one processor to another processor via an interconnection network by explicit communication operations.

Specific barrier operations offer another form of coordination that is available for both shared memory and distributed memory machines. All processes or threads have to wait at a barrier synchronization point until all other processes or threads have also reached that point. Only after all processes or threads have executed the code before the barrier, can they continue their work with the subsequent code after the barrier.

9.6 Parallel Computing Paradigms

Over the years, parallel-processing paradigms have evolved along with appropriate architectures. There are three main categories of parallel architectures: shared memory parallel architecture, distributed memory parallel architecture, and parallel accelerator architecture. In shared memory parallel architecture, the main memory is shared by all the processing elements (e.g., cores in the CPU). On the other hand, in distributed memory parallel architecture, the main memory is distributed to different nodes and each processing element can only access part of the main memory. In the past decade, parallel architectures have quickly evolved into new types of parallel accelerators, such as general-purpose graphics processing units (GPGPUs) and Intel Xeon Phi.

The three high-performance computing paradigms are

1. Shared memory parallel architecture
2. Distributed memory parallel architecture
3. Parallel accelerator architecture

9.7 Summary

The chapter commenced by describing high-performance distributed computing. It then described benchmarks for performance evaluation. Benchmarks are a measure of the efficient execution by the computer architecture of those features of a programming language that are most frequently used in actual programs. Benchmarks are considered to be representative of classes of applications envisioned for the architecture. Benchmarks are useful in evaluating hardware as well as software and single processor as well as multiprocessor systems. The chapter then looked at the degree of parallelism of an application, which is simply the index of the number of computations that can be executed concurrently. Modeling and measurement of application characteristics can be used to optimize the design of a cluster, for example, in terms of relative resources dedicated to computation, memory, and interconnect. There are three main categories of parallel architectures: shared memory parallel architecture, distributed memory parallel architecture, and parallel accelerator architecture. We study these in Chapters 10 through 12, respectively.

10

Shared Memory Architecture

Shared memory systems form a major category of multiprocessors. In this category, all processors share a global memory. Communication between tasks running on different processors is performed through writing to and reading from the global memory. All interprocessor coordination and synchronization are also accomplished via the global memory. A shared memory computer system consists of a set of independent processors, a set of memory modules, and an interconnection network, as shown in Figure 6.2.

Two main problems that need to be addressed when designing a shared memory system are

- *Performance degradation due to contention*: Performance degradation might happen when multiple processors are trying to access the shared memory simultaneously. A typical design might use caches to solve the contention problem. However, having multiple copies of data spread throughout the caches might lead to a coherence problem: the copies in the caches are coherent if they are all equal to the same value.
- *Coherence problems*: If one of the processors writes over the value of one of the copies, then the copy becomes inconsistent because it no longer equals the value of the other copies.

In this chapter, we study a variety of shared memory systems and their solutions to the cache coherence problem.

10.1 Shared Memory Paradigm

In shared memory parallel architecture, the main memory is shared by all the processing elements (cores), and every processing element can directly access data stored in the shared memory. Without loss of generality, in the remaining part of the book, we use cores to represent processing elements.

10.1.1 Multicore Architecture

Multicore architecture, where multiple cores are integrated in the same central processing unit (CPU), is the classic shared memory parallel architecture. As shown in Figure 10.1, each core has its own private cache, and all the cores share the last-level cache. All the cores can directly access all the data stored in the main memory; all the cores have the same latency to access the data from the shared memory. Compared with traditional single-core architecture, multicore architecture provides much higher computational capability and is much more energy efficient.

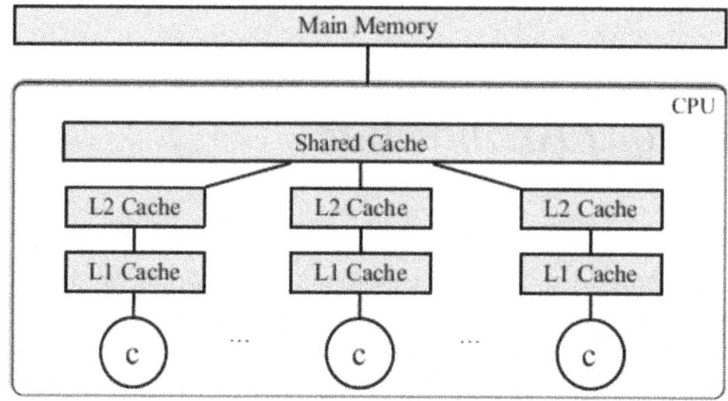

FIGURE 10.1
Classic multicore architecture.

10.1.2 Multi-Socket Multicore Architecture

Although hardware manufacturers keep increasing the cores in CPU chips, the number of cores cannot be increased limitlessly due to physical limitations. To meet the urgent need for powerful computers, multiple CPU chips are integrated into a multi-socket multicore (MSMC) architecture, in which each CPU chip has multiple cores with a shared last-level cache and is plugged into a socket. MSMC architecture has already been widely adopted in emerging supercomputers and clusters.

Contemporary shared memory MSMC computers and large-scale supercomputing systems often employ a nonuniform memory access (NUMA)-based memory system, in which the whole main memory is divided into multiple memory nodes and each node is attached to the socket of a chip. The memory node attached to a socket is called its local memory node and those that are attached to other sockets are called remote memory nodes. The cores of a socket access its local memory node much faster than the remote memory nodes. For example, in an Intel-based machine, QuickPath Interconnect (QPI) is used to connect different sockets, while in an advanced micro devices (AMD)-based machine, HyperTransport is used to connect different sockets.

Figure 10.2 gives an example of MSMC computers that employ an NUMA-based memory system. As shown in Figure 10.2, different sockets are connected through interconnect (IC) modules. While a core c in CPU *S* accesses (either read or write) data from the memory node attached to another socket S_r, the data is transferred from S_r's memory node to core c through IC modules that connect socket *S* and socket S_r. MSMC architecture is developed on the basis of multicore architecture. The main difference between MSMC architecture and traditional multicore architecture is that cores have the same latency to access data from memory in traditional multicore architecture, while they have different latencies to access data from the local memory node and remote memory nodes in MSMC architecture.

10.1.3 Asymmetric Multicore Architecture

In asymmetric multicore (AMC) architectures, such as the Intel Quick-IA and ARM Big-Little architectures, different types of cores have different computational capacities. In

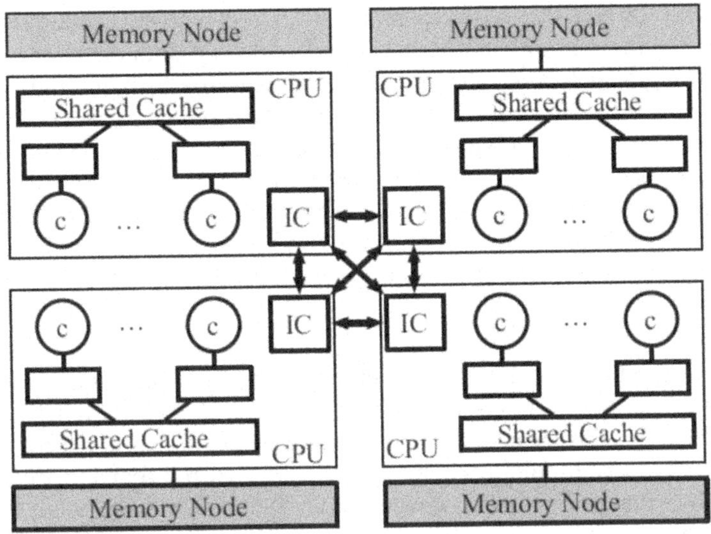

FIGURE 10.2
Multi-socket multicore architecture.

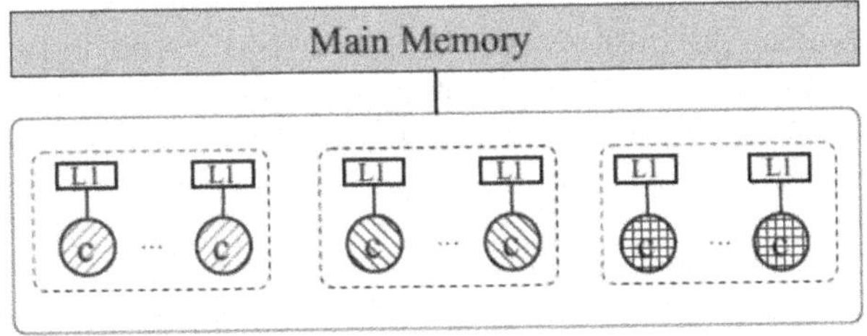

FIGURE 10.3
Asymmetric multicore architecture.

contrast, in traditional multicore architecture all the cores have the same computational capacities. Figure 10.3 presents an example of AMC architecture.

AMC is attractive because it has the potential to improve system performance, to reduce power consumption while closely observing Amdahl's law. Since an AMC architecture consists of a mix of fast cores and slow cores, it can better cater for applications with a heterogeneous mix of workloads. For example, fast and complex cores can be used to execute the serial code sections, while slow and simple cores can be used to crunch numbers in parallel—which is more power-efficient. For example, Nintendo WII and Nintendo DS use AMC processors. Also, many modern multicore chips offer dynamic voltage and frequency scaling (DVFS), which can dynamically adjust the operating frequency of each core and thus is able to turn a symmetric multicore chip into a performance-AMC chip.

10.2 Cache

The simplest form of a memory hierarchy is the use of a single cache between the processor and the main memory (one-level cache termed as L1 cache). The cache contains a subset of the data stored in the main memory, and a replacement strategy is used to bring new data from the main memory into the cache, replacing data elements that are no longer accessed. The goal is to keep those data elements in the cache that are currently most used. Today, two or three levels of cache are used for each processor, using a small and fast L1 cache and larger, but slower L2 and L3 caches. For multiprocessors with a shared address space, the top level of the memory hierarchy is the shared address space that can be accessed by each processor. The design of a memory hierarchy may have a large influence on the execution time of parallel programs, and memory accesses should be ordered such that a given memory hierarchy is used as efficiently as possible.

Caches are the building blocks of memory hierarchies and also have a significant influence on the memory consistency. For multiprocessor systems where each processor uses a separate local cache, there is the additional problem of keeping a consistent view on the shared address space for all processors. It must be ensured that a processor accessing a data element always accesses the most recently written data value (see Section 10.3).

A cache contains a copy of a subset of the data in the main memory; between the main memory and the cache, data is moved in blocks of data (containing a small number of words) called cache blocks or cache lines.

The size of the cache lines is fixed for a given architecture and cannot be changed during program execution. During program execution, as given by the load and store operations of the machine program, the processor specifies memory addresses to be read or to be written—independent of the organization of the memory system. After having received a memory access request from the processor, the cache controller checks whether the memory address specified

- Belongs to a cache line that is currently stored in the cache; in which case a cache hit occurs and the requested word is delivered to the processor from the cache.
- Does not belong to a cache line that is currently stored in the cache; in which case a cache miss occurs and the cache line is first copied from the main memory into the cache before the requested word is delivered to the processor. The corresponding delay time is also called a miss penalty. Since the access time to the main memory is significantly larger than the access time to the cache, a cache miss leads to a delay in operand delivery to the processor.

The number of cache misses may have a significant influence on the resulting runtime of a program. The memory access of a program can be characterized by the locality of memory accesses:

- *Spatial locality*: The memory accesses of a program are termed to have a high spatial locality, if the program often accesses memory locations with neighboring addresses at successive points in time during program execution. Thus, for programs with high spatial locality there is often the situation that after access to a memory location, one or more memory locations of the same cache line are also accessed shortly afterward before the cache block is replaced again, thus avoiding expensive cache misses.
- *Temporal locality*: The memory accesses of a program are termed to have a high temporal locality, if it often happens that the same memory location is accessed multiple times at successive points in time during program execution. Thus, for programs with a high temporal locality there is often the situation that after loading a cache block in the cache, the memory words of the cache block are accessed multiple times before the cache block is replaced again, thus avoiding expensive cache misses.

Since cache management is implemented in the hardware, the programmer cannot directly specify which data should reside in the cache at which point in the program execution. But the order of memory accesses in a program can have a large influence on the resulting runtime, and a reordering of the memory accesses may lead to a significant reduction in the program execution time.

10.2.1 Number of Caches

Most desktop processors have a three-level cache hierarchy, consisting of a first-level (L1) cache, a second-level (L2) cache, and a third-level (L3) cache. All these caches are integrated onto the chip area. For the L1 cache, split caches (i.e., an instruction cache to store instructions and a separate data cache to store data) are typically used; for the remaining levels, unified caches are standard.

The caches are hierarchically organized, and for three levels, the L1 cache contains a subset of the L2 cache, which contains a subset of the L3 cache, which contains a subset of the main memory. Typical access times are one or a few processor cycles for the L1 cache, between 15 and 25 cycles for the L2 cache, between 100 and 300 cycles for the main memory, and between 10 and 100 million cycles for the hard disk.

Split caches enable greater flexibility in the cache design, since the data and instruction caches can work independently of each other, and may have different size and associativity depending on the specific needs.

10.2.2 Cache Sizes

The size of caches is limited by the available chip area. Off-chip caches are rarely used to avoid the additional time penalty of off-chip accesses. Typical sizes for L1 caches lie between 8K and 128K memory words where a memory word is 4 or 8 bytes long, depending on the architecture. For the same technology, the access time of a cache increases slightly with the size of the cache because of the increased complexity of the addressing. However, using a larger cache leads to a smaller number of replacements as a smaller cache, since more cache blocks can be kept in the cache.

While designing a memory hierarchy, the points to be considered for fixing the size of the cache blocks are

- It is useful to use blocks with more than one memory word, since the transfer of a block with x memory words from the main memory into the cache takes less time than x transfers of a single memory word. This suggests the use of a larger cache block.
- Using larger blocks reduces the number of blocks that fit in the cache when using the same cache size. Consequently, cache blocks tend to be replaced earlier when using larger blocks compared to smaller blocks. This suggests the use of a cache block size as small as possible.

As a compromise, a medium block size is used. Typical sizes for L1 cache blocks are four or eight memory words.

10.2.3 Mapping of Memory Blocks to Cache Blocks

Data is transferred between the main memory and cache in blocks of a fixed length. Because the cache is significantly smaller than the main memory, not all memory blocks

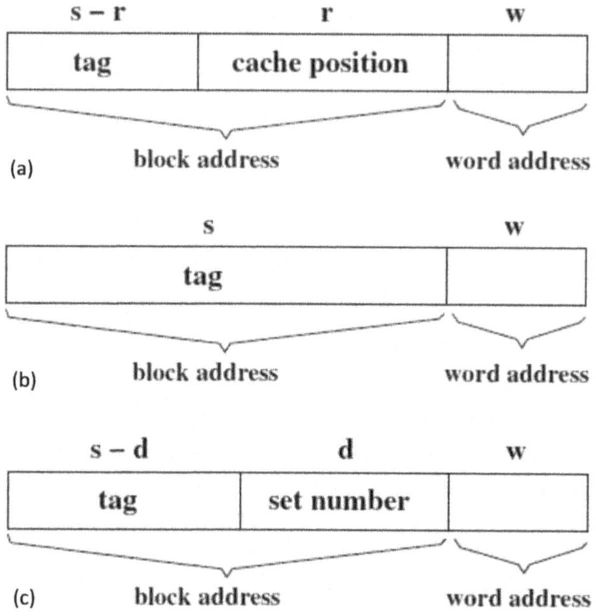

FIGURE 10.4
Memory address partitioning: (a) direct-mapped caches, (b) fully associative caches, and (c) set associative caches.

can be stored in the cache at the same time. Therefore, a mapping algorithm must be used to define at which position a memory block can be stored in the cache. The mapping algorithm used has a significant influence on the cache behavior and determines how a stored block is localized and retrieved from the cache.

The various methods for mapping the memory blocks to cache blocks are

- *Direct-mapped caches*: For a direct-mapped cache, the r rightmost bits of the block address of a memory location define at which of the $m=2^r$ cache positions the corresponding memory block must be stored if the block is loaded into the cache. The remaining $s-r$ bits can be interpreted as tag that specifies which of the 2^{s-r} possible memory blocks is currently stored at a specific cache position. This tag must be stored with the cache block. Thus, each memory address is partitioned as shown in Figure 10.4a.

  For each memory access specified by the processor, the cache position at which the requested memory block must be stored is identified by considering the r rightmost bits of the block address. Then, the tag stored for this cache position is compared with the $s-r$ leftmost bits of the block address. If both tags are identical, the referenced memory block is currently stored in the cache and the memory access can be done via the cache. A cache hit occurs. If the two tags are different, the requested memory block must first be loaded into the cache at the given cache position before the memory location specified can be accessed.

  Direct-mapped caches can be implemented in hardware without great effort, but they have the disadvantage that each memory block can be stored at only one cache position. Thus, it can happen that a program repeatedly specifies memory addresses in different memory blocks that are mapped to the same cache position. In this situation, the memory blocks will be continually loaded and replaced in the cache, leading to a large number of cache misses and therefore a large execution time. This phenomenon is also called thrashing.

- *Fully associative caches*: In a fully associative cache, each memory block can be placed in any cache position, thus overcoming the disadvantage of direct-mapped caches. A memory address can again be partitioned into a block address (s leftmost bits) and a word address (w rightmost bits). Since each cache block can contain any memory block, the entire block address must be used as a tag and must be stored with the cache block to allow the identification of the memory block stored. Thus, each memory address is partitioned as shown in Figure 10.4b. To check whether a given memory block is stored in the cache, all the entries in the cache must be searched, since the memory block can be stored at any cache position.

  The advantage of fully associative caches lies in the increased flexibility when loading memory blocks into the cache. The disadvantage is that the tags to be stored for each cache block are significantly larger as for direct-mapped caches. But the main disadvantage is that for each memory access, all cache positions must be considered to check whether the corresponding memory block is currently held in the cache. To make this search practical, it must be done in parallel using a separate comparator for each cache position, thereby significantly increasing the required hardware effort.

- *Set associative caches*: Set associative caches are a compromise between direct-mapped and fully associative caches. A memory address consists of a block address (s bits) and a word address (w bits). The $d = \log v$ rightmost bits of the block address determine the set to which the corresponding memory block is mapped. The leftmost $s–d$ bits of the block address are the tag that is used for the identification of the memory blocks stored in the individual cache blocks of a set. Thus, each memory address is partitioned as shown in Figure 10.4c.

  When a memory access occurs, the hardware first determines the set to which the memory block is assigned. Then, the tag of the memory block is compared with the tags of all cache blocks in the set. If there is a match, the memory access can be performed via the cache. Otherwise, the corresponding memory block must first be loaded into one of the cache blocks of the set.

When a cache miss occurs, a new memory block must be loaded into the cache. To do this for a fully occupied cache, one of the memory blocks in the cache must be replaced. For a direct-mapped cache, there is only one position at which the new memory block can be stored, and the memory block occupying that position must be replaced. For a fully associative or set associative cache, there are several positions at which the new memory block can be stored. The block to be replaced is selected using a replacement method. A popular replacement method is least recently used (LRU), which replaces the block in a set that has not been used for the longest time.

10.3 Write Policy

The write policy captures the exact replacement time and update method of the memory block in the main memory vis-à-vis the update of the cache block. Considering that a cache contains a subset of the memory blocks, when the processor issues a *write access* to a memory block that is currently stored in the cache, the referenced block is updated in the cache, since the next read access must return the most recent value. Correspondingly, the earliest possible update time for the main memory is immediately after the update in the cache, and the latest possible update time for the main memory is when the cache block is replaced by another block.

10.3.1 Write-Through Policy

Using write-through, a modification of a block in the cache using a write access is immediately transferred to the main memory, thus keeping the cache and the main memory consistent. This is also important for multicore systems, since after a write by one processor, all other processors always get the most recently written value when accessing the same block.

An advantage of this approach is that other devices such as input/output (IO) modules that have direct access to the main memory always get the newest value of a memory block. A disadvantage of write-through is that every write in the cache also causes a write to the main memory, which typically takes at least 100 processor cycles to complete. This could slow down the processor if it had to wait for completion. To avoid processor waiting, a write buffer can be used to store pending write operations into the main memory. After writing the data into the cache and into the write buffer, the processor can continue its execution without waiting for the completion of the write into the main memory.

10.3.2 Write-Back Policy

Using write-back, a write operation to a memory block that is currently held in the cache is performed only in the cache; the corresponding main memory entry is not updated immediately. Thus, the cache may contain newer values than the main memory. The modified memory block is written to the main memory when the cache block is replaced by another memory block. To check whether a write to the main memory is necessary when a cache block is replaced, a separate bit (dirty bit) is held for each cache block, which indicates whether the cache block has been modified or not:

- A dirty bit is initialized with 0 when a block is loaded into the cache.
- A dirty bit is set to 1 upon a write access to a cache block, indicating that a write to the main memory must be performed when the cache block is replaced.

An advantage of this approach is that it usually leads to fewer write operations to the main memory than write-through, since cache blocks can be written multiple times before they are written back to the main memory. The disadvantage of write-back is that the main memory may contain invalid entries, and hence I/O modules can only access the main memory through the cache.

10.4 Cache Coherency

The problem of keeping the different copies of a memory location consistent is also referred to as the *cache coherency problem*. Using a memory hierarchy with multiple levels of caches can help to bridge large access times to the main memory. But the use of caches introduces the effect that memory blocks can be held in multiple copies in caches and the main memory, and consequently subsequent to an update in the cache, other copies might become invalid, in particular if a write-back policy is used. This problem does not occur when the accessing device is a single processor. But for multiple accessing devices such as multicore processors, inconsistent copies can occur and should be avoided, and each execution core should always access the most recent value of a memory location.

In a single cache system, coherence between the memory and the cache is maintained using one of two policies, viz. write-through and write-back. When a task running on a processor P requests the data in memory location X, for example, the contents of X are copied to the cache, where it is passed on to P. When P updates the value of X in the cache, the other copy in the memory also needs to be updated in order to maintain consistency. In write-through, the memory is updated every time the cache is updated, while in write-back, the memory is updated only when the block in the cache is being replaced. Table 10.1a shows the write-through versus write-back policies for single processor systems.

In a multiprocessor system with different cores or processors, in which each processor has a separate local cache, the same memory block can be held as a copy in the local cache of multiple processors. If one or more of the processors updates a copy of a memory block in their local cache, the other copies become invalid and contain inconsistent values. Cache coherence protocols capture the behavior of a memory system for read and write accesses performed by different processors to the same memory location at the same time, by using the order of the memory accesses as a *relative* time measure, not the physical point in time at which the memory accesses are executed by the processors.

In a multiprocessing system, when a task running on processor P requests the data in global memory location X, for example, the contents of X are copied to processor P's local cache, where it is passed on to P. Now, suppose processor Q also accesses X. If Q wants to write a new value over the old value of X, the two fundamental cache coherence policies are

- Write-update maintains consistency by immediately updating all copies in all caches. All dirty bits are set during each write operation. When all copies have been updated, all dirty bits are cleared.

TABLE 10.1

Cache Policies for Single and Multiprocessor Systems

(a) Write-Through versus Write-Back Policies for Single Processor Systems

		Write-Through		Write-Back	
Serial	**Event**	**Memory**	**Cache**	**Memory**	**Cache**
1		X		X	
2	P reads X	X	X	X	X
3	P updates X	X′	X′	X	X′

(b) Write-Invalidate versus Write-Update Policies for Multiprocessor Systems

		Write-Update		Write-Invalidate	
Serial	**Event**	**P's Cache**	**Q's Cache**	**P's Cache**	**Q's Cache**
1	P reads X	X		X	
2	Q reads X	X	X	X	X
3	Q updates X	X′	X′	INV	X′
4	Q updates X′	X″	X″	INV	X″

- Write-invalidate maintains consistency by reading from local caches until a write occurs. When any processor updates the value of X through a write, posting a dirty bit for X invalidates all other copies. For example, processor Q invalidates all other copies of X when it writes a new value into its cache. This sets the dirty bit for X. Q can continue to change X without further notifications to other caches because Q has the only valid copy of X. However, when processor P wants to read X, it must wait until X is updated and the dirty bit is cleared.

Table 10.1b shows the write-invalidate versus write-update policies for multiprocessor systems.

For shared memory system coherence, the combinations to maintain coherence among all caches and global memory are

- Write-invalidate and write-through
- Write-invalidate and write-back
- Write-update and write-through
- Write-update and write-back

Cache coherence protocols are based on the approach to maintain information about the current modification state for each memory block while it is stored in a local cache. Depending on the coupling of the different components of a parallel system, there are two protocols:

- Snooping protocols
- Directory-based protocols

Snooping protocols are based on the existence of a shared medium (like a shared bus or shared cache) over which the memory accesses of the processor cores are transferred. For directory-based protocols, such a shared medium is not necessary.

10.4.1 Snooping Protocols

Snooping protocols can be used if all memory accesses are performed via a shared medium that can be observed by all processor cores. All memory accesses can be observed by the cache controller of each processors: when the cache controller observes a write into a memory location that is currently held in the local cache, it updates the value in the cache by copying the new value from the bus into the cache. Thus, the local caches always contain the most recently written values of memory locations. These protocols are also called *update-based* protocols, since the cache controllers directly perform an update. There are also *invalidation-based* protocols in which the cache block corresponding to a memory block is invalidated, so that the next read access must first perform an update from the main memory.

Snooping protocols are based on watching bus activities and carrying out the appropriate coherency commands when necessary. The global memory is moved in blocks, and each block has a state associated with it, which determines what happens to the entire contents of the block. The state of a block might change as a result of the operations read-miss, read-hit, write-miss, and write-hit. A cache miss means that the requested block is not in the cache or it is in the cache but has been invalidated. Snooping protocols differ in whether they update or invalidate shared copies in remote caches in case of a write operation. They also differ as to where to obtain the new data in the case of a cache miss.

The remaining part of this section discusses examples of snooping protocols that maintain cache coherence.

- Write-invalidate and write-through: In this simple protocol, the memory is always consistent with the most recently updated cache copy. Multiple processors can safely read block copies from the main memory until one processor updates its copy. At this time, all cache copies are invalidated and the memory is updated to remain consistent. The block states and protocol are summarized in Table 10.2a.
- Write-invalidate and write-back: In this protocol, a valid block can be owned by the memory and shared in multiple caches that can contain only the shared copies of the block. Multiple processors can safely read these blocks from their caches until one processor updates its copy. At this time, the writer becomes the only owner of the valid block and all other copies are invalidated. The block states and protocol are summarized in Table 10.2b.
- Write-update and write-through: This write-invalidate protocol uses a combination of write-through and write-back. Write-through is used the very first time a block is written. Subsequent writes are performed using write-back. The block states and protocol are summarized in Table 10.2c.
- Write-update and write-back: This protocol is similar to the previous one except that instead of writing through to the memory whenever a shared block is updated, memory updates are done only when the block is being replaced. The block states and protocol are summarized in Table 10.2d.

10.4.2 Directory-Based Protocols

An alternative to snooping protocols are directory-based protocols. These do not rely on a shared broadcast medium. Instead, a central directory is used to store the state of every memory block that may be held in a cache. Instead of observing a shared broadcast medium, a cache controller can get the state of a memory block by a lookup in the directory. The directory can be held shared, but it can also be distributed among different processors to avoid bottlenecks when the directory is accessed by many processors.

Directory protocols are typically used for distributed memory machines. For a parallel machine with a distributed memory, for each local memory a directory is maintained that specifies for each memory block of the local memory which caches of other processors currently store a copy of this memory block. Each directory is maintained by a directory controller that updates the directory entries according to the requests observed on the network. For a parallel machine with p processors, the directory can be implemented by maintaining:

- A bit vector with p presence bits. Each presence bit indicates whether a specific processor has a valid copy of this memory block in its local cache (value 1) or not (value 0).
- A number of state bits for each memory block. The additional dirty bit is used to indicate whether the local memory contains a valid copy of the memory block (value 0) or not (value 1).

TABLE 10.2

Snooping Protocol

(a) Write-Invalidate and Write-Through	
State	**Description**
Valid [VALID]	The copy is consistent with the global memory.
Invalid [INV]	The copy is inconsistent.
Event	**Actions**
Read-Hit	Use the local copy from the cache.
Read-Miss	Fetch a copy from the global memory. Set the state of this copy to Valid.
Write-Hit	Perform the write locally. Broadcast an Invalid command to all caches. Update the global memory.
Write-Miss	Get a copy from the global memory. Broadcast an invalid command to all caches. Update the global memory. Update the local copy and set its state to Valid.
Block replacement	Since memory is always consistent, no write-back is needed when a block is replaced.
(b) Write-Invalidate and Write-Back	
State	**Description**
Shared (Read-Only) [RO]	Data is valid and can be read safely. Multiple copies can be in this state.
Exclusive (Read-Write) [RW]	Only one valid cache copy exists and can be read from and written to safely. Copies in other caches are invalid.
Invalid [INV]	The copy is inconsistent.
Event	**Action**
Read-Hit	Use the local copy from the cache.
Read-Miss	If no Exclusive (Read-Write) copy exists, then supply a copy from the global memory. Set the state of this copy to Shared (Read-Only). If an Exclusive (Read-Write) copy exists, make a copy from the cache that set the state to Exclusive (Read-Write), update the global memory and local cache with the copy. Set the state to Shared (Read-Only) in both caches.
Write-Hit	If the copy is Exclusive (Read-Write), perform the write locally. If the state is Shared (Read-Only), then broadcast an Invalid to all caches. Set the state to Exclusive (Read-Write).
Write-Mass	Get a copy from either a cache with an Exclusive (Read-Write) copy, or from the global memory itself. Broadcast an Invalid command to all caches. Update the local copy and set its state to Exclusive (Read-Write).
Block replacement	If a copy is in an Exclusive (Read-Write) state, it has to be written back to the main memory if the block is being replaced. If the copy is in the Invalid or Shared (Read-Only) states, no write-back is needed when a block is replaced.
(c) Write-Update and Write-Through	
State	**Description**
Invalid [INV]	The copy is inconsistent.
Valid [VALID]	The copy is consistent with the global memory.
Reserved [RES]	Data has been written exactly once and the copy is consistent with the global memory. There is only one copy of the global memory block in one local cache.
Dirty [DIRTY]	Data has been updated more than once and there is only one copy in the local cache. When a copy is dirty, it must be written back to the global memory.
Event	**Actions**
Read-Hit	Use the local copy from the cache.
Read-Miss	If no dirty copy exists, then supply a copy from the global memory. Set the state of this copy to Valid. If a dirty copy exists, make a copy from the cache that set the state to Dirty, update the global memory and local cache with the copy. Set the state to Valid in both caches.

(*Continued*)

TABLE 10.2 (CONTINUED)

Snooping Protocol

Write-Hit	If the copy is Dirty or Reserved, perform the write locally, and set the state to Dirty. If the state is Valid, then broadcast an Invalid command to all caches. Update the global memory and set the state to Reserved.
Write-Mass	Get a copy from either a cache with a dirty copy or from the global memory itself. Broadcast an Invalid command to all caches. Update the local copy and set its state to Dirty.
Block replacement	If a copy is in a Dirty state, it has to be written back to the main memory if the block is being replaced. If the copy is in Valid, Reserved, or Invalid states, no write-back is needed when a block is replaced.
(d) Write-Update and Write-Back	
State	**Description**
Valid Exclusive [VAL-X]	This is the only cache copy and it is inconsistent with the global memory.
Shared Clean [SH-CLN]	Multiple cache copies are shared.
Shared Dirty [SH-DRT]	There are multiple shared cache copies. This is the last one being updated. (Ownership.)
Dirty [DIRTY]	This copy is not shared by other caches and has been updated. It is not consistent with the global memory. (Ownership.)
Event	**Action**
Read-Hit	Use the local copy from the cache. The state does not change.
Read-Miss	If no other cache copy exists, then supply a copy from the global memory. Set the state of this copy to Valid Exclusive. If a cache copy exists, make a copy from the cache. Set the state to Shared Clean. If the supplying cache copy was in a Valid Exclusion or Shared Clean, its new state becomes Shared Clean. If the supplying cache copy was in a Dirty or Shared Dirty state, its new state becomes Shared Dirty.
Write-Hit	If the state is Valid Exclusive or Dirty, perform the write locally and set the state to Dirty. If the state is Shared Clean or Shared Dirty, perform an update and change the state to Shared Dirty. Broadcast the updated block to all other caches. These caches snoop the bus and update their copies and set their state to Shared Clean.
Write-Miss	The block copy comes from either another cache or from the global memory. If the block comes from another cache, perform the update, set the state to Shared Dirty, and broadcast the updated block to all other caches. Other caches snoop the bus, update their copies, and change their state to Shared Clean. If the copy comes from the memory, perform the write and set the state to Dirty.
Block replacement	If a copy is in a Dirty or Shared Dirty state, it has to be written back to the main memory if the block is being replaced. If the copy is in Valid Exclusive, no write-back is needed when a block is replaced.

Each directory is maintained by a directory controller that updates the directory entries according to the requests observed on the network.

In the local caches, depending on their state the memory blocks are marked with

M (modified) indicating that the cache block contains the current value of the memory block and that all other copies of this memory block in other caches or in the main memory are invalid, that is, the block has been updated in the cache.

S (shared) indicating that the cache block has not been updated in this cache and that this cache contains the current value, as does the main memory and zero or more other caches.

I (invalid) indicating that the cache block does not contain the most recent value of the memory block.

When a read-miss or write-miss occurs at a processor i, the associated cache controller contacts the local directory controller to obtain information about the accessed memory block. If this memory block belongs to the local memory and the local memory contains a valid copy (dirty bit 0), the memory block can be loaded into the cache with local memory access. Otherwise, nonlocal (remote) access must be performed. A request is sent via the network to the directory controller at the processor owning the memory block (home node).

When a memory block with state M is to be replaced by another memory block in the cache of processor i, it must be written back into its home memory, since this is the only valid copy of this memory block. To achieve this, the cache controller of i sends the memory block to the directory controller of the home node, which writes the memory block back to the local memory and sets the dirty bit of the block and the presence bit of processor i to 0.

A cache block with state S can be replaced in a local cache without sending a notification to the responsible directory controller. Sending a notification avoids the responsible directory controller sending an unnecessary invalidation message to the replacing processor in case of a write-miss as previously described.

10.5 Memory Consistency

The concept of consistency models was introduced to describe the behavior of the memory system in multiprocessor environments. Using a consistency model, there is a clear definition of the allowable behavior of the memory system, which can be used by the programmer in the design of parallel programs.

A parallel program produces a variety of different results if different execution orders of the program statements by different processors are considered. The memory consistency model sets restrictions on the values that can be returned by a read operation in a shared address space. Intuitively, a read operation should always return the value that has been written last:

- In uniprocessors, the program order uniquely defines which value this is.
- In multiprocessors, different processors execute their programs concurrently and the memory accesses may take place in a different order depending on the relative progress of the processors.

10.5.1 Sequential Consistency

The sequential consistency model (SC model) is an intuitive extension of the uniprocessor model and places strong restrictions on the execution order of the memory accesses. A memory system is sequentially consistent if the memory accesses of each single processor are performed in the program order described by that processor's program and if the global result of all memory accesses of all processors appears to all processors in the same sequential order, which results from an arbitrary interleaving of the memory accesses of the different processors. Memory accesses must be performed as *atomic operations*, that is, the effect of each memory operation must become globally visible to all processors before the next memory operation of any processor is started.

For a memory system to be coherent, it is required that the write operations to the same memory location are sequentialized such that they appear to all processors in the same order. But there is no restriction on the order of write operations to different memory locations. On the other hand, sequential consistency requires that all write operations (to arbitrary memory locations) appear to all processors in the same order.

Sequential consistency provides an easy and intuitive model. But the model has a performance disadvantage, since all memory accesses must be atomic and since memory accesses must be performed one after another. Therefore, processors may have to wait for quite a long time before memory accesses that they have issued have been completed. To improve performance, consistency models with fewer restrictions have been proposed. However, different hardware manufacturers favor different relaxed consistency models.

10.6 Summary

A shared memory system is composed of multiple processors and memory modules that are connected via some interconnection network. Shared memory multiprocessors are usually bus based or switch based. In all cases, each processor has equal access to the global memory shared by all processors. Communication among processors is achieved by writing to and reading from the memory. Synchronization among processors is achieved using locks and barriers. The chapter discussed the main challenges of shared memory systems, namely, contention and cache coherence problems. Local caches are typically used to alleviate the bottleneck problem. However, scalability remains the main drawback of a shared memory system. The introduction of caches creates consistency problems among caches and between the memory and caches. Cache coherence schemes can be subdivided into snooping protocols and directory-based protocols.

11

Message-Passing Architecture

Message-passing systems provide alternative methods for communication and the movement of data among multiprocessors (compared to shared memory multiprocessor systems). A message-passing system typically combines local memory and the processor at each node of the interconnection network. There is no global memory so it is necessary to move data from one local memory to another by means of message passing. This is typically done by send/receive pairs of commands, which must be written into the application software by a programmer. Each processor has access to its own local memory and can communicate with other processors using the interconnection network. These systems eventually gave way to Internet-connected systems where the processor/memory nodes are cluster nodes, servers, clients, or nodes in a greater grid.

11.1 Message-Passing Paradigm

Large-scale clusters adopt distributed memory parallel architecture wherein different computer nodes often have their own private memory. When a core needs data stored in other nodes' memory, the data is transferred through networks.

11.1.1 Tightly Coupled Distributed Memory Architecture

Traditional clusters and emerging data centers adopt tightly coupled distributed memory architecture. In tightly coupled distributed memory architecture, the computer nodes are connected by a local high-speed inter-connect network using high-speed Ethernet and InfiniBand. These high-performance distributed memory platforms are used to house cloud computing or large-scale web applications.

Figure 11.1 shows the tightly coupled distributed memory architecture in terms of how clouds are built on top of data centers; nodes in a data center are often connected through a high-speed network. Users access cloud service through the Internet and the compute resource and data resource can be located on the same computer node.

11.1.2 Loosely Coupled Distributed Memory Architecture

In loosely coupled distributed memory architecture, computer nodes are normally connected with a conventional network interface, such as the Internet. Figure 11.2 shows the loosely coupled distributed memory architecture in terms of the grid computing architecture.

Grid computing is the representative example of loosely coupled distributed memory parallel architecture. Nodes in a grid tend to be more heterogeneous and geographically

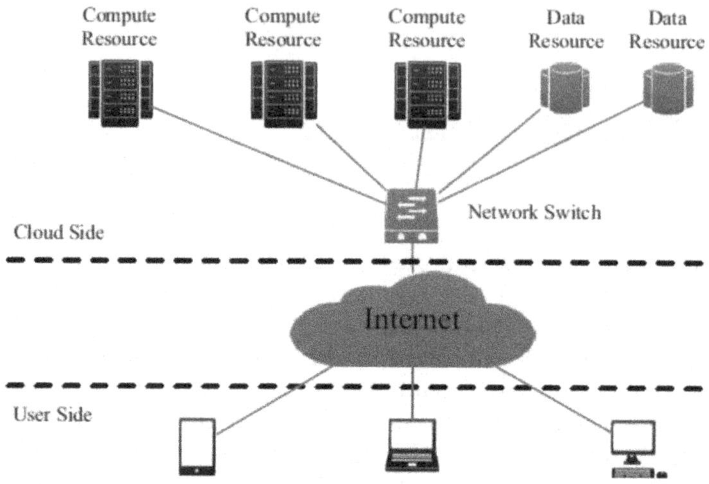

FIGURE 11.1
Tightly coupled distributed memory architecture.

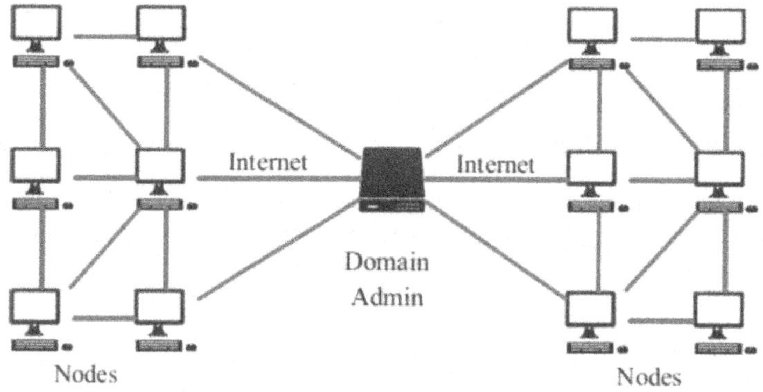

FIGURE 11.2
Loosely coupled distributed memory architecture.

dispersed (thus not physically coupled). Each grid domain has a domain admin that manages compute resource and data resource in the domain.

Grids were originally proposed for resource sharing between individual computer owners through the Internet. In the grid, the resource providers are also the resource consumers. The key objective of the grid is to organize and manage geographically dispersed nodes into dynamic virtualized resources, so that these nodes can work together on large-scale tasks.

11.2 Routing

Routing is defined as the techniques used for a message to select a path over the network channels. Direct and indirect interconnection networks provide the physical basis to send messages between processors. If two processors are not directly connected by a network link, a path in the network consisting of a sequence of nodes must be used for message transmission. This section describes how to select a suitable path in the network (routing) and the following section explains how messages are handled at intermediate nodes on the path (switching).

Routing techniques can be classified based on the method used to make the routing decision as centralized or distributed routing. In centralized routing, the routing decisions regarding the entire path are made before sending the message. Centralized routing requires complete knowledge of the status of the rest of the nodes in the network. In distributed routing, each node decides by itself which channel should be used to forward the incoming message. Distributed routing requires knowledge of only the status of the neighboring nodes.

11.2.1 Routing Algorithms for Broadcasting and Multicasting

There are two types of communication operations in message-passing systems:

- One-to-one (point-to-point or unicast) communication: In unicast, a node is allowed to communicate a message to only a single destination, which may be its immediate neighbors.
- Collective communication: Under collective communication, a number of routing operations are defined among which broadcast and multicast are the most widely used. In broadcast, also known as the one-to-all operation, one node sends the same message to all other nodes. In multicast, also known as the one-to-many operation, one node sends its messages to k distinct destinations.

A routing algorithm determines a path in a given network from a source node A to a destination node B. The path consists of a sequence of nodes, such that neighboring nodes in the sequence are connected by a physical netssswork link. The path starts at node A and ends at node B. A routing algorithm tries to select a path in the network connecting nodes A and B such that minimum costs result, thus leading to fast message transmission between A and B. A routing algorithm tries to reach an even load on the physical network links as well as avoid the occurrence of deadlocks. A set of messages is in a deadlock situation if each of the messages is supposed to be transmitted over a link that is currently being used by another message of the set. The resulting communication costs depend not only on the length but also on the load of the links on the path.

The path over the network channels is selected based on

- Network topology: The topology of the network determines which paths are available in the network to establish a connection between nodes A and B.
- Network contention: Contention occurs when two or more messages should be transmitted at the same time over the same network link, thus leading to a delay in message transmission.
- Network congestion: Congestion occurs when too many messages are assigned to a restricted resource (such as a network link or buffer) such that arriving messages have to be discarded since they cannot be stored anywhere. Thus, in contrast to contention, congestion leads to an overflow situation with message loss.

Routing algorithms can be of two types:

- Adaptive routing algorithms: A routing algorithm is said to be adaptive if, for a given source and destination pair, the path taken by the message depends on the network conditions, such as network congestion. Adaptive routing tries to avoid such contention by dynamically selecting the routing path based on load information. Between any pair of nodes, multiple paths are available. The path to be used is dynamically selected such that network traffic is spread evenly over the available links, thereby leading to an improvement in network utilization. Moreover, fault tolerance is also enabled to the extent that an alternative path can be used in case of a link failure.

Using the path length, adaptive routing algorithms can be further categorized into

- Minimal adaptive routing algorithms always select the shortest message transmission, which means that when using a link of the path selected, a message always gets closer to the target node. But this may lead to congestion situations.
- Nonminimal adaptive routing algorithms do not always use paths with minimum length if this is necessary to avoid congestion at intermediate nodes.

- Deterministic routing algorithms determine the path using only the source and destination, regardless of the network conditions. Although simple, deterministic routing algorithms make inefficient use of the bandwidth available between the source and destination. Moreover, deterministic routing can lead to an unbalanced network load. Path selection can be source oriented at the sending node or distributed during message transmission at intermediate nodes. An example of deterministic routing is dimension-order routing, which can be applied to network topologies that can be partitioned into several orthogonal dimensions as is the case for meshes, tori, and hypercube topologies. Using dimension-order routing, the routing path is determined based on the position of the source node and the target node by considering the dimensions in a fixed order and traversing a link in the dimension if necessary. This can lead to network contention because of the deterministic path selection.

11.2.2 Deadlocks and Routing Algorithms

Deadlock occurs when two messages, respectively, hold the resources required by the other in order to move; both messages will be blocked. It occurs whenever there exists cyclic dependency for resources. The management of resources in a network is the responsibility of the flow control mechanism used—resources must be allocated in a manner that avoids deadlock. A straightforward albeit inefficient way to solve the deadlock problem is to allow rerouting (possibly discarding) of the messages participating in a deadlock situation. Rerouting of messages gives rise to nonminimal routing, while discarding messages requires that messages be recovered at the source and retransmitted. This preemptive technique leads to long latency and, therefore, is not used by most message-passing networks.

A more common technique is to avoid the occurrence of deadlock. This can be achieved by ordering network resources and requiring that messages request use of these resources in a strict monotonic order. This restricted way of using network resources prevents the occurrence of circular wait, and hence prevents the occurrence of deadlock. The channel dependency graph (CDG) is a technique used to develop a deadlock-free routing algorithm. A CDG is a directed graph D=G(C, E), where the vertex set C consists of all the unidirectional channels in the network and the set of edges E includes all the pairs of connected channels, as defined by the routing algorithm. In other words $(c_i, c_j) \in$ E, then c_i and c_j are, respectively, an input channel and an output channel of a node and the routing algorithm may only route messages from c_i to c_j.

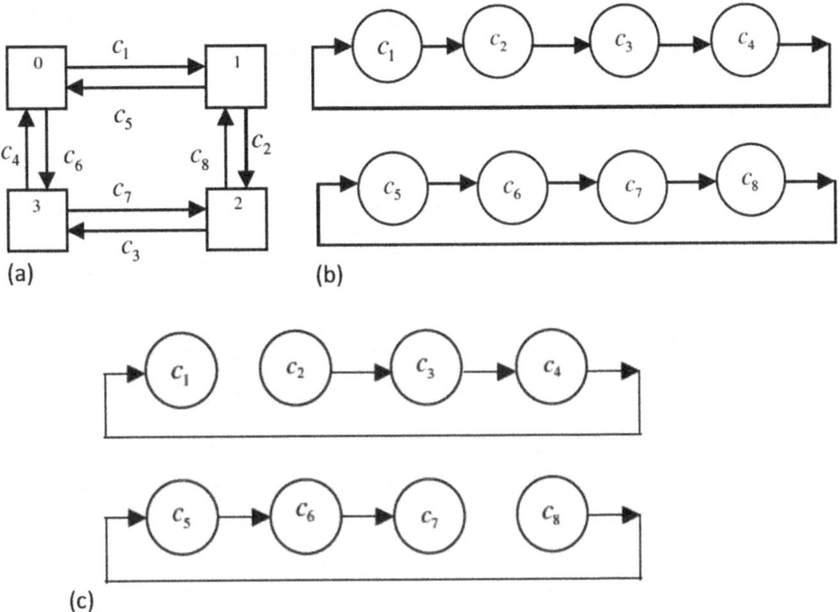

FIGURE 11.3
A four-node network and its CDGs: (a) a four-node network; (b) a channel dependency graph; and (c) a CDG for a deadlock-free version of the network.

A routing algorithm is deadlock free if there are no cycles in its CDG. Consider, for example, the four-node network shown in Figure 11.3a. The CDG of the network is shown in Figure 11.3b; with two cycles in the CDG, this network is subject to deadlock. Figure 11.3c shows the way to avoid the occurrence of deadlock by disallowing messages to be forwarded from channel c_1 to c_2 and from c_7 to c_8.

11.3 Switching

The switching strategy determines how a message is transmitted along a path that has been selected by the routing algorithm. The switching strategy may have a large influence on the message transmission time from a source to a destination.

The switching strategy determines

- Whether and how a message is split into pieces, which are called packets or flits (for flow control units).
- How the transmission path from the source node to the destination node is allocated.
- How messages or pieces of messages are forwarded from the input channel to the output channel of a switch or a router. The routing algorithm only determines which output channel should be used.

The time for message transmission is the actual transmission time over the physical link and the time needed for the software overhead of the protocol, both at the sender and the receiver side.

Performance measures used in this context are

- *Bandwidth* of a network link is defined as the maximum frequency at which data can be sent over the link. The bandwidth is measured in bits per second or bytes per second.
- *Throughput* of a network link is the effective bandwidth experienced by an application program.
- *Byte transfer time* is the time required to transmit a single byte over a network link. If the bandwidth is measured in bytes per second, the byte transfer time is the reciprocal of the bandwidth.
- *Time of flight*, also referred to as the channel propagation delay, is the time the first bit of a message needs to arrive at the receiver. This time mainly depends on the physical distance between the sender and the receiver.
- *Transmission time* is the time needed to transmit a message over a network link. The transmission time is the message size in bytes divided by the bandwidth of the network link, measured in bytes per second. The transmission time does not take conflicts with other messages into consideration.
- *Transport latency* is the total time that is needed to transfer a message over a network link. This is the sum of the transmission time and the time of flight, capturing the entire time interval from putting the first bit of the message onto the network link at the sender and receiving the last bit at the receiver.
- *Sender overhead*, also referred to as startup time, is the time that the sender needs for the preparation of message transmission. This includes the time for computing the checksum, appending the header, and executing the routing algorithm.
- *Receiver overhead* is the time that the receiver needs to process an incoming message, including checksum comparison and the generation of an acknowledgment if required by the specific protocol.

Using these performance measures, the total latency $T(m)$ of a message of size m is

$$T(m) = T_{\text{overhead}} + t_B \cdot m$$

where

byte transfer time $t_B = 1/B$, B is the bandwidth of the network link

T_{overhead} is the total sender and receiver overhead latency

When transmitting a message between two nodes that are not directly connected in the network, the message must be transmitted along a path between the two nodes. For transmission along a path, the switching techniques used are

- Circuit switching
- Packet switching with
  - Store-and-forward routing
  - Cut-through routing

11.3.1 Circuit Switching

In circuit switching, the entire path from the source node to the destination node is established exclusively for a message by suitably setting the switches or routers on the path and reserving them until the end of the message transmission (Figure 11.3a). Internally, the message can be split into pieces for transmission. These pieces can be so-called physical units (phits) denoting the amount of data that can be transmitted over a network link in one cycle. The size of the phits is determined by the number of bits that can be transmitted over a physical channel in parallel; typical phit sizes lie between 1 and 256 bits.

The transmission path for a message can be established using short probe messages along the path. The path can be released again by a message trailer or by an acknowledgment message from the receiver to the sender.

11.3.2 Packet Switching

For packet switching, the message to be transmitted is partitioned into a sequence of packets that are transferred independently from each other through the network from the sender to the receiver. Using an adaptive routing algorithm, the packets can be transmitted over different paths. Each packet consists of three parts:

- Header containing routing and control information
- Data containing a part of the original message
- Trailer that may contain an error control code

Each packet is sent separately to the destination according to the routing information contained in the packet. Figure 11.4 illustrates the partitioning of a message into packets. The network links and buffers are used by one packet at a time.

Packet switching can be implemented through

- Store-and-forward routing
- Cut-through routing

11.3.2.1 Store-and-Forward Routing

Packet switching with store-and-forward routing sends a packet along a path such that the entire packet is received by each switch on the path (store), before it is sent to the next switch on the path (forward). The connection between two switches A and B on the path is released for reuse by another packet as soon as the packet has been stored at B.

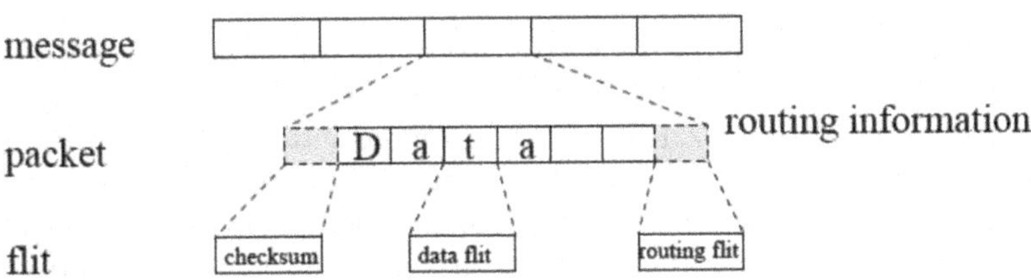

FIGURE 11.4
Partitioning of a message into packets and packets into flits (flow control units).

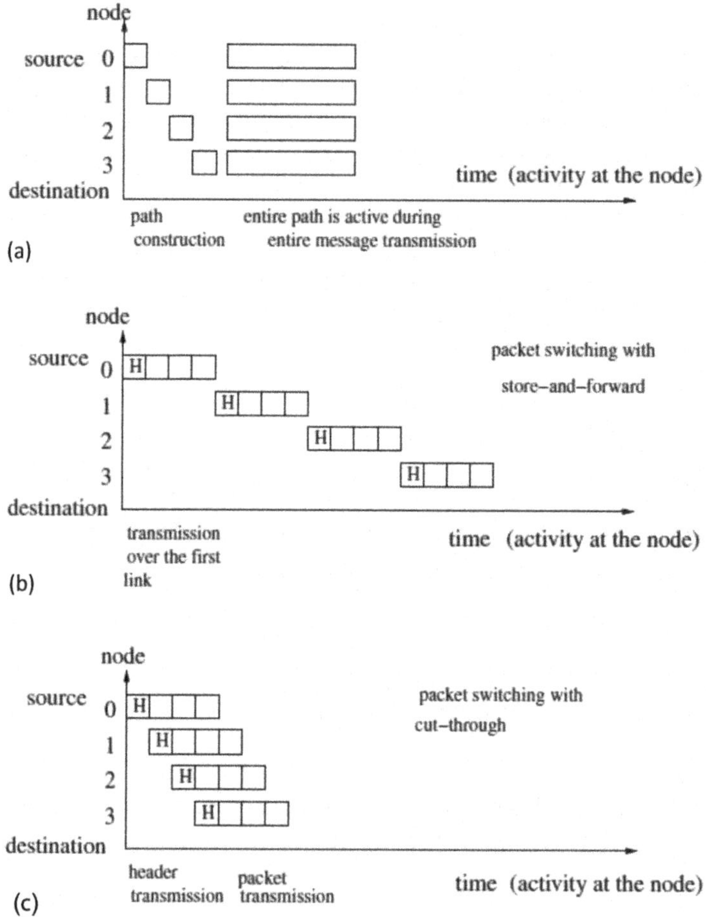

FIGURE 11.5
Latency of a point-to-point transmission along a path for: (a) circuit switching; (b) packet switching with store-and-forward routing; and (c) packet switching with cut-through routing.

Packet transmission with store-and-forward routing is illustrated in Figure 11.5b. The time for the transmission of an entire message, consisting of several packets, depends on the specific routing algorithm used. When using a deterministic routing algorithm, the message transmission time is the sum of the transmission time of all packets of the message, provided no network delays occur. For adaptive routing algorithms, the transmission of the individual packets can be overlapped, that is, pipelined, potentially leading to a smaller message transmission time.

The advantage of this strategy is that if the links connecting the switches on a path have different bandwidths, as is typically the case in wide area networks (WANs), store-and-forward routing allows the utilization of the full bandwidth for every link on the path. Another advantage is that a link on the path can be quickly released as soon as the packet has passed the links, thereby reducing the danger of deadlocks. The disadvantage of this strategy is that the packet transmission time increases with the number of switches that must be traversed from source to destination. Additionally, the entire packet must be stored at each switch on the path, thereby increasing the memory demands of the switches.

11.3.2.2 Cut-Through Routing

In cut-through routing, the idea of pipelining message packets can be extended by applying pipelining to individual packets. Using this approach, a message is again split into packets as required by the packet switching approach. The different packets of a message can take different paths through the network to reach their destination. Each individual packet is sent through the network in a pipelined way. To do so, each switch on the path inspects the first few phits (physical units) of the packet header, containing the routing information, and then determines over which output channel the packet is forwarded. Thus, the transmission path of a packet is established by the packet header and the rest of the packet is transmitted along this path in a pipelined way. A link on this path can be released as soon as all phits of the packet, including a possible trailer, have been transmitted over this link.

If multiple transmissions are performed concurrently, network contention may occur because of conflicting requests to the same links. This increases the communication time observed for the transmission. The switching strategy must react appropriately if contention happens on one of the links of a transmission path:

- Using store-and-forward routing, the packet can simply be buffered until the output channel is free again.
- Using cut-through routing, two popular options are available: virtual cut-through routing and wormhole routing.
  - Virtual cut-through routing: In the case of a blocked output channel at a switch, all phits of the packet in transmission are collected in a buffer at the switch until the output channel is free again. If this happens at every switch on the path, cut-through routing degrades to store-and-forward routing. However, by using partial cut-through routing, the transmission of the buffered phits of a packet can continue as soon as the output channel is free again, that is, not all phits of a packet need to be buffered.
  - Wormhole routing: This approach is based on the definition of flow control units (flits), which are usually at least as large as the packet header. The header flit establishes the path through the network. The rest of the flits of the packet follow in a pipelined way on the same path. In the case of a blocked output channel at a switch, only a few flits are stored at this switch, the rest are kept on the preceding switches of the path. Therefore, a blocked packet may occupy buffer space along an entire path or at least a part of the path. Thus, this approach has some similarities to circuit switching at the packet level. Storing the flits of a blocked message along the switches of a path may cause other packets to block, leading to network saturation. Moreover, deadlock may occur because of cyclic waiting. An advantage of the wormhole routing approach is that the buffers at the switches can be kept small, since they need to store only a small portion of a packet.

11.4 Summary

If scalability to larger and larger systems (as measured by the number of processing units) is required, systems have to use message-passing architectures. It is apparent that message-passing systems are the only way to efficiently increase the number of processors managed by a multiprocessor system. There are, however, a number of problems associated with message-passing systems. These include communication overhead and difficulty in programming. This chapter discussed the architecture and the network models of message-passing systems. It then shed some light on routing and network switching techniques.

12

Stream Processing Architecture

Many of today's performance-demanding applications come from the signal processing, image processing, graphics, and scientific computing domains. Applications in all of these domains exhibit high degrees of data parallelism, typically have structured control, and can exploit locality. The principles of the stream architecture are based on the key properties of many performance-demanding applications and the characteristics of modern very-large-scale integration (VLSI) technology. Stream processors (SPs) are designed for the strengths of modern VLSI technology with minimum execution overheads, providing efficiency on par with application-specific solutions such as Application-Specific Integrated Circuits (ASICs).

SPs embrace the principles of explicit locality and parallelism found in multicore architectures to achieve high performance with high efficiency for applications that use the stream programming model, rather than the traditional parallel extensions to the von Neumann execution model. SPs typically have a sustained performance that is a factor of 5–15 better than conventional architectures, while being 10–30 times more efficient in terms of performance per unit power. By allowing streaming software to take full advantage of the parallelism and locality inherent in the problem being solved, SP hardware is freed from many of the responsibilities required of processors when executing traditional programs.

The stream architecture focuses on the effective management of

- Locality (state)
- Bandwidth (communication)
- Optimizing throughput rather than latency

12.1 Dataflow Paradigm

The basic structure underlying all the architectures is the one proposed by von Neumann. Parallel and pipeline structures were used to enhance the system throughput and overcome the limitations of the von Neumann model. Von Neumann architectures are control driven and in them, data is passive and fetched only when an instruction needs it, that is, the operation of the machine is dictated by the instruction sequence (i.e., the program). In control flow architecture, the total control of the sequence of operations rests with the programmer. That is, a processor undergoes the fetch, decode, and execution phases for each instruction in the program. Data manipulation involves the transfer of data from one unit to another unit of the machine. Data is stored as variables (memory locations), taken to functional units, operated on as specified by the programmer, and the results are assigned to other variables.

Dataflow architectures, on the other hand, are data driven, since the readiness of data dictates the operation of the machine, that is, data is operated upon when it is available. In dataflow architecture, the sequence of operations is not specified, but depends on the need and the availability of data. There is no concept of passive data storage, instruction counter, variables, or addresses. The operation of the machine is entirely guided by data interdependencies and the availability of resources. The architecture is based on the concept that an instruction is executable as soon as all its operands are available—consequently, multiple operations can occur simultaneously.

This concept allows the employment of parallelism at the operator (i.e., the finest grain) level—all dataflow architectures employ instruction-level parallelism (ILP). Since the algorithms are represented at the finest-grain parallelism and at the maximum degree of concurrency possible, a very high throughput can be achieved by dataflow architectures. Therefore, dataflow architectures can be used advantageously for computation-intensive applications that exhibit a fine-grain parallelism.

A dataflow graph (DFG) is a directed graph whose nodes represent operators and arcs represent pointers for forwarding the results of operations to subsequent nodes. Figure 12.1 shows the three common types of operators in a DFG. The arithmetic and logical operators implement the usual binary operations. The array handling operator selects and outputs a particular element of the array based on the value of the selector input. Figure 12.2 shows the structure of two control operators (nodes). In the switch node, the control input selects the output arc to which the input token is transmitted. In the merge node, the control input selects one among the data inputs to be placed on the output.

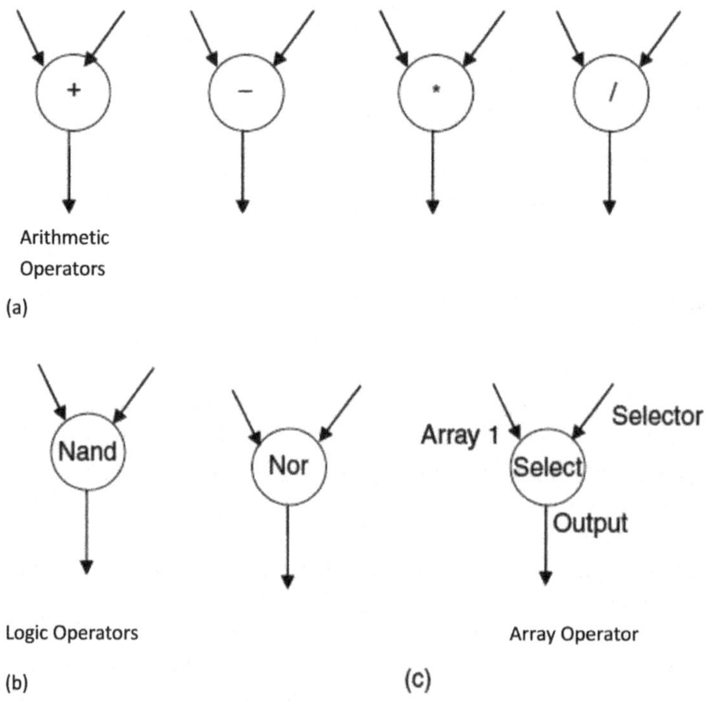

FIGURE 12.1
DFG operators.

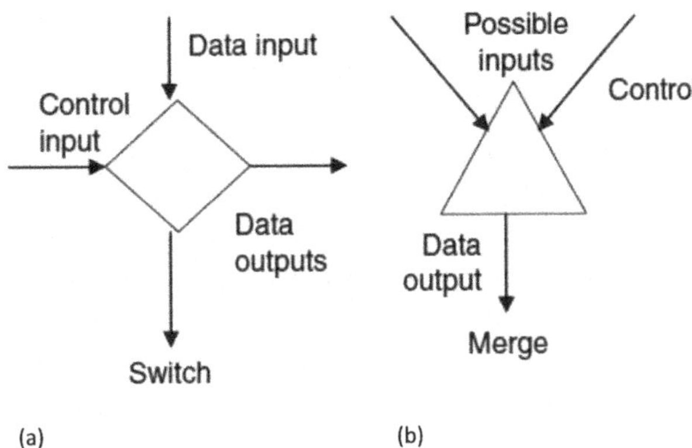

FIGURE 12.2
DFG control operators.

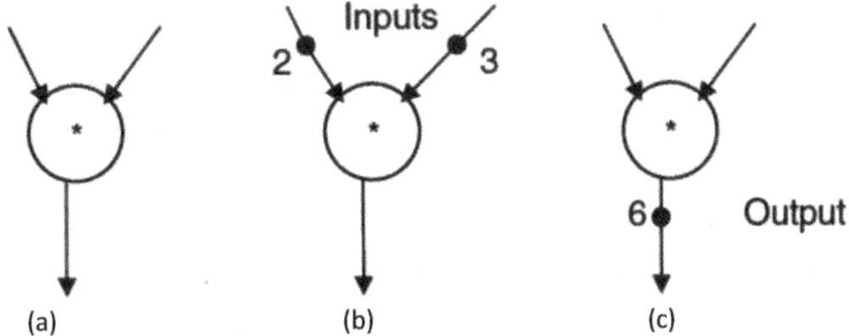

FIGURE 12.3
Node firing: (a) no inputs, (b) all inputs are in (c) output produced.

Consider the details of the firing of a (multiplier) node shown in Figure 12.3. Here, the availability of the data on an arc is indicated by the presence of a token on the arc. When a node has a data token on each of its input arcs, it fires and generates a data token on each of its output arcs. That is, when a node fires, the tokens on the input arcs are removed and each output arc gets a token.

In a DFG, the node firing semantics commonly employed are

- Static model

In the static model, a node fires only when each of its input arcs has a token and its output arcs are empty. Thus, an acknowledgment of the fact that a subsequent node has consumed its input token is needed before a node in a static DFG can fire.

Figure 12.4 shows a schematic view of a static dataflow machine. Each node receives as one of its input a control tag from the subsequent node indicating that the subsequent node has consumed the data on the output arc. The machine memory consists of a series of cells that have all the information needed for an operation to occur at an appropriate node in the DFG (Figure 12.4b). It consists of an operation code, number of input arcs (NI), number of output arcs (NO), NI input data slots, and NO output slots. Each data slot contains the data field and a flag that indicates whether the data value is ready or not. Each output slot points to a cell that receives the result of the operations of that cell. When all the input operands are ready, a cell is fireable.

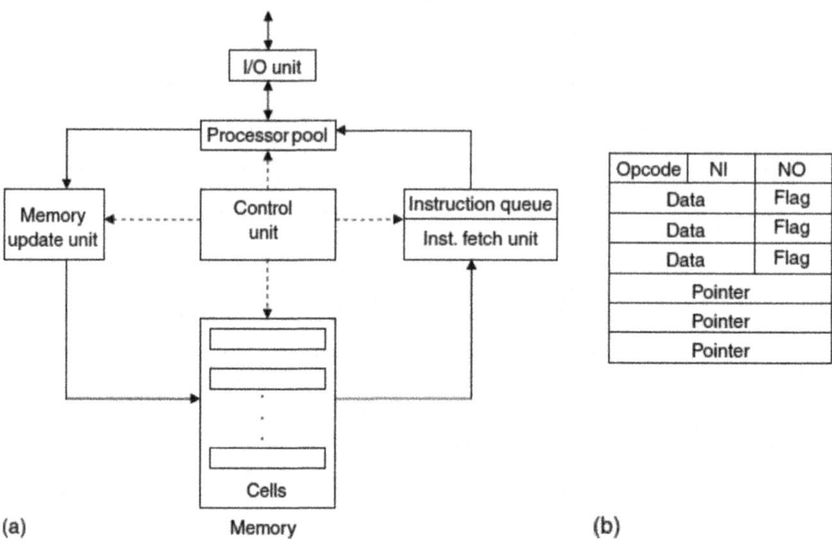

FIGURE 12.4
Static dataflow model: (a) structure and (b) cell.

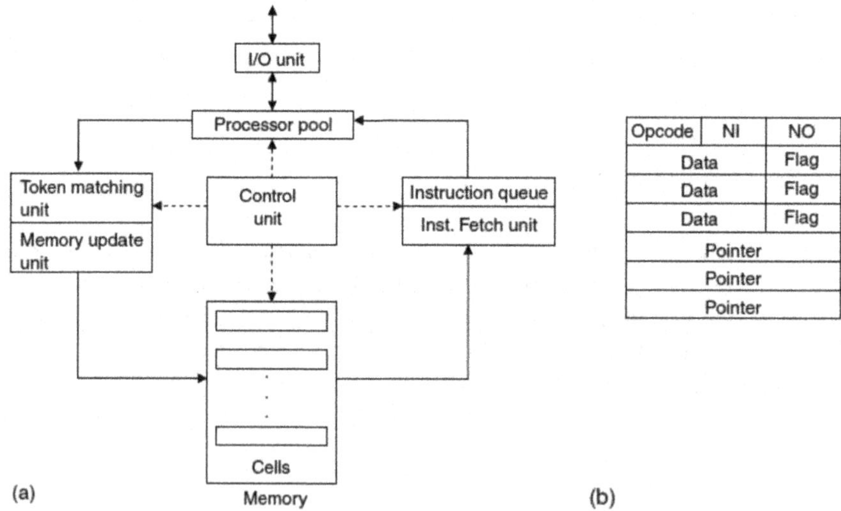

FIGURE 12.5
Dynamic dataflow model: (a) structure and (b) cell.

The instruction fetch unit consists of multiple fetch units operating in parallel, looking for fireable cells in the memory. They fetch fireable cells, convert them into instruction packets, and enter them into the instruction queue. When a processor becomes available, it executes an instruction from this queue and presents the output to the memory update unit, which in turn sends the results to appropriate memory cells based on the output pointers. This process continues until there are no fireable cells. The input/output (IO) unit manages the interaction with external devices and the control unit coordinates the activities of all the units.

- Dynamic model

In the dynamic model, a node fires when all its inputs have tokens and the absence of tokens on its outputs is not necessary. Thus, it is possible to have multiple tokens on an arc. A tagging scheme is employed in dynamic DFGs to associate tokens with the appropriate dataset. The tag carries the information as to when and how a token was generated and to which dataset it belongs.

Figure 12.5 shows a schematic of a dynamic dataflow machine. Here, the processors operate on the operands that have similar tags and the memory update unit uses the tags to update cells belonging to the same dataset.

12.2 Parallel Accelerators

Parallel accelerators, such as the Nvidia general-purpose graphics processing unit (GPGPU) and the Intel Xeon, are increasingly being proposed to speed up program execution. The Nvidia GPGPU executes an application in single instruction, multiple data (SIMD) pattern, and the Intel Xeon Phi executes an application in multiple instruction, multiple data (MIMD) pattern. Accelerators are often connected with the host machine through a PCIe bus.

Generally speaking, when a user decides to process a program on an accelerator, the program is processed in three steps:

- First the required data is transferred to the device memory (the memory of the accelerator)—before an accelerator is able to process a program.
- Then, using the data in the device memory, the accelerator executes the program.
- After the data is processed, the accelerator returns the result to the host central processing unit (CPU) through a PCIe bus.

A GPGPU is a type of many-core architecture processor that is vastly different from the CPU both in programming interface and performance characteristics. The CPU can synchronize with the graphics processing unit (GPU) via the driver, but this operation suffers from high overhead.

The GPU is famous for its parallel processing ability. If an algorithm requires little or no communication between threads or these communications have good space locality, the GPU can offer significant speedup compared with the CPU. The GPU is not good at executing programs with many branches and communications, some unoptimized algorithm may even be slower on a GPU than a CPU. The performance of the GPU varies for different sizes of workload. The GPU needs a large number of running threads to hide the latency of memory access. The number of running threads is related to the workload that the GPU receives. If the workload is too small, the GPU will not be able to reach its full performance potential.

Figure 12.6 shows a schematic of GPGPU architecture. A GPGPU consists of multiple stream multiprocessors (SMs) and a global device memory. Each SM is an SIMD processing element (PE). The old version of a GPGPU was only able to process a single kernel at a time. This constraint resulted in poor utilization of the GPGPU because the workload of a kernel was unable to fully utilize all the SMs. However, in the later GPGPU, such as the Nvidia K40, P100 etc., the GPGPU started to support concurrent kernel execution that allowed multiple kernels to run on a GPGPU concurrently.

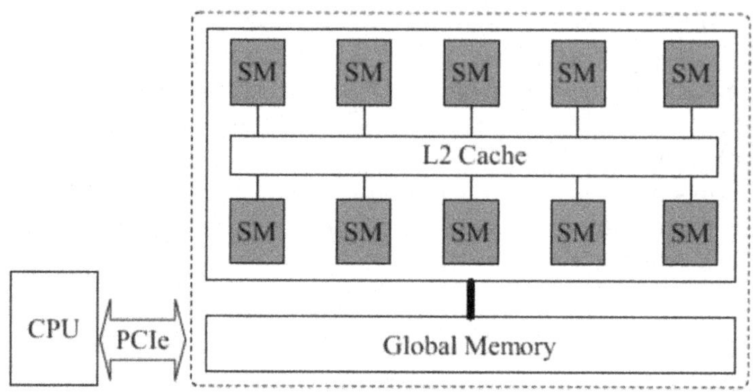

FIGURE 12.6
Schematic of GPGPU architecture.

A multithreading application developed for CPUs is not able to run directly on a GPGPU. A requirement of utilizing GPGPU to speed up the execution of a parallel application is that programmers need to first rewrite their programs using CUDA or OpenCL (see Chapter 16).

12.3 Stream Processors

SPs partition their functional units and storage into multiple PEs. However, in contrast to typical multicore architectures, which contain symmetric general-purpose cores and a cache hierarchy, SPs have a significantly leaner design. SPs are specifically designed for the stream execution model, in which applications have large amounts of explicit parallel computation, structured and predictable control, and memory accesses that can be performed at a coarse granularity. Applications in the streaming model are expressed in a *gather–compute–scatter* form, yielding programs with explicit control over transferring data *to and from* on-chip memory.

Stream architectures redefine the boundary between software and hardware responsibilities with the software bearing much of the complexity required to manage concurrency, locality, and latency tolerance. SPs have minimal control consisting of fetching medium- and coarse-grained instructions and executing them directly on the many arithmetic-logical units (ALUs).

Today's fabrication technology enables numerous execution resources, such as thousands of ALUs or hundreds of floating-point units (FPUs), to be integrated into a single chip, such that the execution resources are not the factor limiting the performance or the efficiency of processors. The challenge in efficiently and effectively providing the ALUs with data and instructions to sustain a high performance arises because of

- The bandwidth required to feed the ALUs must be maintained, which is perhaps the most difficult challenge. The cost of data transfer grows at least linearly with distance in terms of both the energy required and the available bandwidth.
- The resources devoted to controlling the ALUs must be restricted to a fraction of the resources of the ALUs themselves. In many modern general-purpose CPUs, in

contrast, the area and power devoted to the arithmetic units is a small fraction of the overall chip budget.

- The set of independent instructions must be identified in order for the ALUs to operate concurrently as well as for tolerating latencies (latencies can be hidden with concurrent useful work).

The principles of the stream architecture are based on the key properties of many performance-demanding applications and the characteristics of modern VLSI technology. The three key principles that work together to enable the high performance and efficiency of the stream architecture are

- Storage organized into a bandwidth hierarchy: This hierarchy ranges from high-bandwidth registers local to each ALU through on-chip static random-access memory (SRAM) to off-chip dynamic random-access memory (DRAM). Each level of the bandwidth can provide roughly ten times as much bandwidth at 1/10 the power requirement as the level above it, but it has a much smaller total capacity. This bandwidth hierarchy enables high-bandwidth data supply to the ALUs even with limited global and off-chip bandwidths.
- Exposed communication: This architectural feature allows the software to maximize its locality and be fully aware of the cost and importance of data movement and bandwidth usage. All communication and data movement in an SP is under explicit software control, including all allocation of state within the storage hierarchy as well as all transfers between levels. Even if data is not reused multiple times, exposing communication facilitates exploiting producer–consumer locality and enables the software to take on the task of hiding latency, relieving the hardware of this responsibility, and allowing for efficient throughput-oriented hardware design.
- Hierarchical control optimized for throughput and parallelism: SPs use a hierarchical control structure where a stream application is expressed using two levels of control:
  - At the higher level:
    - *Kernels* represent atomic bulk computations that are performed on an entire stream or block of data.
    - *Stream loads and stores* process asynchronous bulk data transfers that move entire streams between on-chip and off-chip storage. The system manages these coarse-grained bulk operations as atomic units with more efficient hardware mechanisms than if all the computations were managed at a word granularity.
  - At the lower level, parallel ALUs in different PEs are controlled by a single kernel microcode sequencer, amortizing instruction delivery overheads. Additionally, the stream memory system utilizes the asynchronous bulk semantics to optimize expensive and scarce off-chip bandwidth.

12.3.1 Stream Processor Architecture

This section presents how a stream application is executed on an SP and explains how the key principles of SPs—hierarchical control, bandwidth hierarchy, exposed communication, and throughput-oriented design—are manifested in the architecture. The explicit control given to streaming software enables a more predictable performance, increasing the effectiveness of programmer and compiler optimizations. The hardware architecture provides mechanisms for the software to take on the responsibilities for scheduling, allocation, and latency hiding, which gives it greater efficiency without sacrificing performance.

Effectively utilizing the many ALUs of an SP requires extensive use of parallelism:

- ALUs must be run concurrently on distinct data.
- ALUs must be provided with instructions.
- Small execution pipeline latencies must be tolerated.
- Long memory latencies must be overlapped with computation.

12.3.2 Execution Overview

An SP has a hierarchical control structure with the scalar unit at the top and the stream unit's compute clusters and stream load/store (SLS) unit at the bottom. A stream application consists of a high-level stream control program and a collection of kernel objects. The stream control program is executed on the scalar unit and is expressed in a conventional ISA with word-granularity load, store, arithmetic, logic, and control instructions augmented with coarse-grained stream memory and kernel instructions. When the scalar unit encounters a stream instruction, it does not execute it directly, but rather issues the stream instruction to the stream unit.

The major components of an SP are

- The scalar unit is a general-purpose processing core that is responsible for the overall execution and control of a stream application.
- The stream unit operates at a lower control hierarchy level and executes the computational kernels on the compute clusters and stream memory operations on the SLS units. The compute clusters are the stream unit's PEs and contain the large number of ALUs that are required to attain a high bandwidth, as well as an on-chip storage hierarchy. The address generators handle asynchronous bulk data transfers between off-chip and on-chip storage.
- The interconnect includes data and control paths.
- The memory and IO include DRAM, network, and I/O interfaces.

The bulk of a computation is contained within the coarse-grained stream instructions that are embedded as part of the scalar execution flow. The *stream controller* serves as the interface between the scalar and stream units, and coordinates the execution of stream memory operations, kernels, and their synchronization. The microcontroller and SLS operate at the granularity of individual word memory and arithmetic instructions, and through the stream controller, decouple this fine-grained execution from the control program. The clusters in an SP are controlled by a microcontroller that is responsible for sequencing the arithmetic instructions that were produced at the kernel scheduling step and represented as a binary. Stream loads and stores, which typically transfer hundreds or thousands of words from memory to on-chip storage, are similarly off-loaded from the scalar unit (which executes the stream control program) and executed by the SLS units.

The SP control hierarchy and its asynchronous bulk stream operations allow specialization of the hardware tuning the different control structures to work most effectively.

For example, sophisticated bulk memory transfers do not require a full hardware context or thread and are executed by dedicated and efficient SLS units.

Coarse-grained stream loads and stores in the stream control program initiate data transfer between the global memory and the on-chip storage. The stream control program uses a coarse-grained software pipeline to load more data into on-chip storage and save output streams to the main memory concurrent with kernel execution, hiding memory access latencies with useful computation. The memory system is optimized for throughput and can handle both strided loads and stores and indexed gathers and scatters in hardware. Kernel instructions in the stream control program cause the stream execution unit to start running a previously loaded kernel binary. Kernel execution is controlled by the microcontroller unit and proceeds in an SIMD manner with all clusters in the same node progressing in lock-step. Data transfers between various levels of the on-chip memory hierarchy are controlled from the microcode.

SPs offer a hierarchy of control and decoupled execution toward achieving its goals. The SP architecture focuses on efficient throughput-oriented design in terms of

- The arithmetic clusters that process kernel operations

  The microcontroller is responsible for issuing kernel instructions to the ALUs, and it relies on explicit software parallelism to maintain high-instruction bandwidth. SPs utilize data-level parallelism (DLP) across the clusters and the microcontroller issues a single instruction to all clusters in an SIMD fashion. Each of these kernel instructions, however, is a Very Long Instruction Word (VLIW) instruction that controls all ALUs within the cluster as well as the operation of the register files: local register file (LRF) and stream register file (SRF).

  The cluster has four major component types:

  - A number of arithmetic functional units (ALUs or FPUs)
  - Supporting units (SRF-in/out and communication)
  - The distributed LRF
  - The intra-cluster switch

  The microcontroller transmits a single VLIW instruction to all the clusters, and the VLIW independently controls all the units across all four cluster components. This cluster organization is enabled by the stream execution model, which decouples the unpredictable service time of off-chip memory requests from the execution pipeline. Because the clusters can only access the SRF, all latencies are known statically, and the compiler can optimize for ILP and DLP across the functional units and clusters.

  The static knowledge of latencies and abundant parallelism enables aggressive compilation and permits a spartan and efficient pipeline hardware design that does not require non-execution resources such as a branch predictor, a dynamic out-of-order scheduler, or even bypass networks (ample parallelism). Moreover, the cluster exposes all communication between functional units and does not rely on a central register file to provide connectivity. Significant area and energy saving is enabled by the partitioning of the register file into

  - Storage within the LRFs that are directly attached to the functional units.
  - Communication provided by the intra-cluster switch.

In addition to the LRF, switch, and arithmetic units, the cluster also contains supporting functional units:

- For accessing the SRF.
- For connecting the cluster to the inter-cluster switch.
- For providing explicit information exchange between all clusters without accessing the memory system.

- The memory system that executes stream loads and stores

  The memory system provides very deep buffers and performs memory access scheduling (MAS) because latency hiding is orchestrated by software in the coarse granularity of kernels and stream loads and stores. MAS is used to reorder the DRAM commands associated with pending memory accesses to enhance locality and optimize throughput. This technique maximizes memory bandwidth utilization over the expensive and power-hungry off-chip I/O interfaces and pins.

Stream memory systems are tuned for throughput in contrast to traditional memory systems that are often optimized for latency. Stream memory systems provide high throughput of multiple words per cycle using conventional DRAM technology by processing all requests in bulk asynchronous direct memory access (DMA)-style transfers. One or more address generators process bulk stream requests from the processor and issue them as potentially reordered fine-granularity word accesses to memory. This allows the memory system to support complex addressing modes including gathers, scatters, and atomic data-parallel read–modify–write (scatter-add).

12.3.3 Locality and Bandwidth Hierarchy

To support high sustained operand throughput, stream architectures are strongly partitioned into PEs, which are clusters of functional units with a hierarchy of storage. This is primarily because as VLSI technology scales and the distance an operand traverses from storage to functional unit grows, the operand bandwidth decreases.

The storage hierarchy directly forms the bandwidth hierarchy of an SP and provides the mechanisms required to support exposed communication software:

- LRF: Within each cluster, at the lowest level in the storage hierarchy, the LRF is directly connected to the functional units over short high-bandwidth wires. The LRF exploits kernel locality, which is a short-term producer–consumer within kernels. An efficient LRF structure can sustain the required operand bandwidth, and is able to provide over 90% of all operands in most applications by exploiting the kernel locality between instructions within a function or inner-loop body.
- SRF: At the second level in the storage hierarchy, the SRF is a fast local memory structure. The SRF has a larger capacity and is partitioned across the clusters (PEs). We refer to the portion of the SRF local to a cluster as an SRF *lane*. Being local to a cluster enables the SRF to supply data with high throughput on the chip. The SRF has a local address space in the processor that is separate from the global off-chip memory, and requires the software to *localize* data into the SRF before kernel computation begins.

Beyond the SRF is a global on-chip level of storage hierarchy composed of an interconnection network that handles direct communication between the clusters and connects them with the memory system.

Explicitly managing this distinct space in the software enables two critical functions:

- The SRF can reduce the pressure on the off-chip memory by providing an on-chip workspace and explicitly capturing the long-term producer–consumer locality between kernels.
- Explicit control allows the software to stage large granularity asynchronous bulk transfers in to and out of the SRF.

Thus, off-chip memory is accessed only with bulk asynchronous transfers, allowing for a throughput optimized memory system and shifting the responsibility of tolerating the ever-growing memory latencies from the hardware to the software. SPs rely on software-controlled bulk transfers to hide off-chip access latency and restrict cluster memory access to the local SRF address space. This results in predictable latencies within the execution pipeline, enabling static compiler scheduling optimizations.

12.4 Summary

This chapter discussed the architectural aspects of stream processing. The principles of the stream architecture are based on the key properties of many performance-demanding applications and the characteristics of modern VLSI technology. SPs are designed for the strengths of modern VLSI technology with minimum execution overheads, providing efficiency on par with application-specific solutions such as ASIC. The stream architecture focuses on the effective management of locality (state), bandwidth (communication), and throughput optimization rather than latency.

Section IV

Parallel Computing Programming

This section looks at parallel computing programming. Chapters 13 provides an overview of parallel programming APIs. Chapters 14 through 16 explain the primary categorical representatives of parallel computing APIs, namely, OpenMP, MPI, and CUDA.

Chapter 13 gives a thematic introduction to parallel computing programming APIs and programming languages. It introduces the three categories of parallel programming APIs, namely, shared memory, message passing, and stream processing programming.

Chapter 14 provides an introductory treatment to the essentials of OpenMP and explains how to program in parallel with it. OpenMP is among the most widely used parallel programming APIs. However, it is limited in scalability to hardware system architectures, providing near-uniform memory access (UMA) to shared memory.

Chapter 15 provides an introductory treatment to the essentials of MPI and explains how to program in parallel with it. Message passing is largely the model of choice on MIMD computers with physically distributed memory because the close relationship between the model and the hardware architecture allows the programmer to write code for the hardware in an optimal manner. In addition, message-passing libraries are available on virtually all parallel systems, making this paradigm appealing to those who desire portability across a variety of machines. Message passing is currently the only practical choice for use across clusters of machines.

Chapter 16 describes data streams–related data-parallel models where the execution of instructions in parallel is implicitly driven by the layout of the data structures in the memory. CUDA is both a parallel computing architecture and a programming model for high-performance computing; OpenCL (Open Computing Language) is an open-source standard for general-purpose parallel programming of heterogeneous computing systems, and OpenACC is similar to OpenMP, but targets acceleration devices such as GPUs.

13

Parallel Computing Programming Basics

This chapter gives a thematic introduction to parallel computing programming APIs and programming languages. It introduces the three categories of parallel programming APIs, namely, shared memory, message passing, and stream processing programming. OpenMP is an API for shared-memory-based parallel programming. 'An overarching goal of OpenMP is to enable programmers to incrementally parallelize existing serial applications written in C/C++ and Fortran. Haskell, the parallel language in this category, is usually considered the successor of the Miranda programming language, which was one of the most important lazy functional programming languages of the 1980s.

Message passing is usually the model of choice on MIMD computers with physically distributed memory because the close relationship between the model and the hardware architecture allows the programmer to write code for the hardware in an optimal manner. The programming model used by MPI is well suited for distributed memory systems such as clusters that are composed of computing nodes coupled with a fast interconnect. Erlang has a process-based model of concurrency. Concurrency is explicit and the user can precisely control which computations are performed sequentially and which are performed in parallel. The only method by which Erlang processes can exchange data is message passing.

In data streams–related data-parallel models, the execution of instructions in parallel is implicitly driven by the layout of the data structures in the memory. CUDA is both a parallel computing architecture and a programming model for high-performance computing; OpenCL is an open-source standard for general-purpose parallel programming of heterogeneous computing systems, and OpenACC is similar to OpenMP but targets acceleration devices such as GPUs. Scala is a new programming language developed by Martin Odersky and his team at the EPFL (École Polytechnique Fédérale de Lausanne, Lausanne, Switzerland) and is now supported by Typesafe. The name Scala is derived from Sca(lable) La(nguage). This is a multi-paradigm language, incorporating object-oriented approaches with functional programming. Appendix 13.A gives a description of functional programming.

13.1 Shared-Memory Programming

A shared-memory parallel computer is easy to program as it gives the user a uniform global address space. Scalability is, however, a problem. The number of PEs in a shared-memory computer using a shared bus is limited to around 16, due to the saturation of the bus. A-shared memory parallel computer using the interconnection network to connect PEs to memory alleviates this problem to some extent by providing multiple paths between PEs and memory. In this case it is not possible to increase the number of PEs beyond 64 due to the high cost of designing, high-bandwidth interconnection networks, and difficulties in maintaining cache coherence. This has led to the development of the distributed shared memory (DSM) parallel computer, in which a number of PEs with their own private memories (i.e., CEs) are interconnected. In this system, even though the memory is physically distributed, the programming model is a shared-memory model, which is easier to program. The system, however, allows a much larger number of CEs to be interconnected as a parallel computer at reasonable cost without severely degrading the performance. In other words, DSM parallel computers are scalable, while providing a logically shared-memory programming model.

In a DSM computer, the programmer assumes a single flat-memory address space and programs it using fork and join commands; each node is a full-fledged computer, i.e., it has a processor, cache, and memory. Each computer in the system is connected to an interconnection network through a Network Interface Unit (NIU) (also called by some authors "communication assist," as it often has processing capability of its own). Even though each CE has its own private memory and cache, the system comprises hardware and software assists to give the user the facility to program the machine as though it was a shared-memory parallel computer. In other words, a user can program assuming that there is a single global address space. From the structure of the machine it is clear that accessing data in the memory attached to a processor in a given node is much faster than accessing data in the memory belonging to a CE in another node connected to it via the interconnection network.

When each processor has its own cache memory, it is also necessary to maintain cache coherence between the individual processors. This is done by using a directory scheme similar to the method described in Subsection 10.4.2. Thus, currently, a more accurate nomenclature for DSM computers is cache coherent non-uniform memory access parallel computer (CC-NUMA)

13.1.1 Programming APIs

13.1.1.1 OpenMP

OpenMP is an API for shared-memory-based parallel programming. An overarching goal of OpenMP is to enable programmers to incrementally parallelize existing serial applications written in C/C++ and Fortran. OpenMP is an open-source standard. It provides a set of compiler directives (aka pragmas), a limited number of runtime functions, and environment variables for specifying shared-memory parallelism.

The pragmas and the runtime functions determine low-level details of how to partition a task and assign subtasks to threads. Pragmas are essentially parallelization instructions to the compiler.

A pragma may specify that a block of code is to be parallelized (e.g., #pragma omp parallel for).

An environment variable, for example OMP_NUM_THREADS, specifies the number of threads to run during the execution of an OpenMP program.

Another environment variable, OPM_SCHEDULE, defines the type of iteration schedule to use with the omp parallel for pragma.

Options for the iteration schedule are as follows:

- *Static option*: An *iteration block* corresponds to a subset of consecutive iterations through a *for loop*. The static option entails determining the mapping of iteration blocks to the execution threads in a round-robin fashion at compile time. Assume that you have two separate loops with the same number of iterations. Furthermore, suppose that each loop is executed with the same number of threads using the static schedule option. Then OpenMP runtime guarantees that each thread will receive exactly the same iteration block(s) in the execution of the two loops.

- *Dynamic* option: This lets each thread execute an iteration block first. Then any remaining iteration blocks are scheduled during the second round. This process will continue until all iteration blocks have been executed. The dynamic option results in better load balancing but entails a communication overhead.
- *Guided* option: This is similar to the dynamic option. Initially, the number of loop iterations (i.e., the iteration block size) assigned to a thread is proportional to the ratio of the number of loop iterations and the number of available threads. Subsequent allocation of loop iterations to a thread is proportional to the ratio of the number of loop iterations remaining and the number of available threads.
- *Runtime* option: This indicates that the scheduling decision is deferred until runtime.
- *Auto* option: This leaves the scheduling decision to the compiler and the runtime system.

13.1.1.2 Pthreads

POSIX is a standard for Unix-like operating systems—for example, Linux and Mac OS X. In particular, it specifies a API for multithreaded programming called POSIX Threads (Pthreads). The Pthreads API is only available on POSIX systems—Linux, Mac OS X, Solaris, HPUX, and so on.

Parallel execution on shared-memory multiprocessors is enabled by the Pthread library. If the number of threads is equal to the number of processors, the scheduler will execute each thread on a separate processor. Threads are used on single processors to allow a rapid response by interactive users. A time-consuming operation can be performed by one thread while a different thread interacts with the user. The scheduler runs the CPU-intensive thread while waiting for user interaction with the user interface. When the user interacts with the mouse or keyboard, the scheduler quickly suspends the compute-intensive task and resumes the interface task. This is mostly invisible to the user, and is particularly useful for programs using a graphic user interface. The user gets a nearly instantaneous response from one thread while computations by the other thread continue in the background.

The term "Pthreads" defines an API that allows the user to write multithreaded programs, in particular defining constants, types, and functions for:

- Thread creation and waiting for other threads (joining)
- Mutexes that allow implementation of mutually exclusive execution among threads,
- Condition variables that are useful when a thread might need to wait for a certain condition to be satisfied by another thread.

The first step in the parallelization of a program with Pthreads is to determine how the program computations will be divided among the threads. There are three general designs for partitioning calculations among threads:

- Functional decomposition
- Data decomposition
- Pipelining

The strategy for parallelizing a program depends on multiple factors, such as:

- Granularity
- Interthread dependencies
- Size of data sets
- Load balancing
- Memory contention

13.1.2 Programming Languages

13.1.2.1 Haskell

In a pure functional programming language such as Haskell, data is immutable and, generally, there are no side effects. Immutable data obviates the need for locking in developing thread-safe software. Haskell's pure functions have no side effects and this property makes writing code for parallel execution easier.

Most imperative languages do not encourage programming in the functional style. For example, many languages discourage or prohibit functions from being stored in data structures such as lists, from constructing intermediate structures such as a list of numbers, from taking functions as arguments or producing functions as results, or from being defined in terms of themselves. In contrast, Haskell imposes no such restrictions on how functions can be used, and provides a range of features to make programming with functions both simple and powerful.

Due to the high-level nature of the functional style, programs written in Haskell are often much more concise than in other languages, as illustrated by the example in the previous section. Moreover, the syntax of Haskell was designed with concise programs in mind, employing few keywords and allowing indentation to be used to indicate the structure of programs. Although it is difficult to make an objective comparison, Haskell programs are often between two and ten times shorter than programs written in other current languages.

Because programs in Haskell are pure functions, simple equational reasoning can be used to execute programs, to transform programs, to prove the properties of programs, and even to derive programs directly from specifications of their behaviour. Equational reasoning is particularly powerful when combined with the use of "induction" to reason about functions that are defined using recursion.

a) Introduction to Haskell

Haskell is usually considered the successor of the Miranda programming language, which was one of the most important lazy functional programming languages in the 1980s.

The structure of the Haskell program:

- At the topmost level, Haskell software is a set of modules. The modules allow the possibility to control all the code included and to reuse these modules in large and distributed software in the cloud.
- The top level of a model is compounded from a collection of declarations. Declarations are used to define things such as ordinary values, data types, type classes, and some fixed information.

- At a lower level are expressions. The way that expressions are defined in a software application written in Haskell is very important. Expressions denote values that have a static type and represent the heart of Haskell programming.
- The last level is that of lexical structure, which captures the concrete representation of a software in text files.

In Haskell, a piece of code consists of expressions, which are evaluated in a similar fashion to mathematical expressions. In an imperative language, methods consist of statements that change a global state. This is an important distinction because, in an imperative program, the same piece of code may have different results depending on its initial state when it's executed. It's important to notice here that elements outside of the program control (known as side effects), such as input and output, network communication, and randomness, are also part of this global state that may change between executions of the same function.

Expressions in Haskell cannot have side effects by default; these expressions are called "pure." The main benefits of purity are the improved ability to reason about the code and an easier approach to testing the code. The outcome of a pure function depends only on its parameters, and every run with the same inputs will give the same result. Pure functions are easier to compose because no interference arises in their execution. Actually, the evaluation of pure expressions is not dependent on the order in which it is done, so it opens the door to different execution strategies for the same piece of code. The Haskell libraries take advantage of this, providing parallel and concurrent execution.

Haskell uses an execution strategy called lazy evaluation. Under laziness, an expression is never evaluated until it is needed for the evaluation of a larger one. Once it has been evaluated, the result is saved for further computation, or it's discarded if it's not needed in any other running code. This has an obvious benefit because only the minimal amount of computation is performed during program execution, but it also has drawbacks because all the suspended expressions that have not yet been evaluated must be saved in the memory.

A *type system* is an abstraction that categorizes the values that could appear during execution, tagging them with a so-called "type." These types are normally used to restrict the possible set of actions that could be applied to a value. For example, it may allow concatenating two strings but forbid using the division operator between them. This tagging can be checked at two different times:

- At execution time (*dynamic* typing), which usually comes in languages with looser typing and allows implicit conversions between things such as integers and strings.
- At compilation time (*static* typing), in which case programs must be validated to be completely well typed in terms of the language rules before generating the target output code (usually machine code or bytecode) and being allowed to run.

b) Features of Haskell

- Powerful type system: Most modern programming languages include some form of type system to detect incompatibility errors, such as attempting to add a number and a character. Haskell has a type system that requires little type information from the programmer, but allows a large class of incompatibility errors in programs to be automatically detected prior to their execution, using a sophisticated process called "type inference." The Haskell type system is also more powerful than most current languages, and allows functions to be "polymorphic" and "overloaded".

- List comprehensions: One of the most common ways to structure and manipulate data in computing is using lists. To this end, Haskell provides lists as a basic concept in the language, together with a simple but powerful comprehension notation that constructs new lists by selecting and filtering elements from one or more existing lists. Using the comprehension notation allows many common functions on lists to be defined in a clear and concise manner, without the need for explicit recursion.
- Recursive functions: Most non-trivial programs involve some form of repetition or looping. In Haskell, the basic mechanism by which looping is achieved is the use of recursive functions that are defined in terms of themselves. Many computations have a simple and natural definition in terms of recursive functions, particularly when "pattern matching" and "guards" are used to separate different cases into different equations.
- Higher-order functions: Haskell is a higher-order functional language, which means that functions can freely take functions as arguments and produce functions as results. Using higher-order functions allows common programming patterns, such as composing two functions, to be defined as functions within the language itself. More generally, higher-order functions can be used to define "domain specific languages" within Haskell, that is for list processing, parsing, and interactive programming among others.
- Monadic effects: Functions in Haskell are pure functions that take all their input as arguments and produce all their output as results. However, many programs require some form of side effect that would appear to be at odds with purity, such as a reading input from the keyboard, or a writing output to the screen, while the program is running. Haskell provides a uniform framework for handling effects without compromising the purity of functions, based upon the mathematical notion of a monad.
- Lazy evaluation: Haskell programs are executed using a technique called "lazy evaluation," which is based upon the idea that no computation should be performed until its result is actually required. As well as avoiding unnecessary computation, lazy evaluation ensures that programs terminate whenever possible, encourages programming in a modular style using intermediate data structures, and even allows data structures with an infinite number of elements, such as an infinite list of numbers.

13.2 Message-Passing Programming

Message passing is the model of choice on MIMD computers with physically distributed memory because the close relationship between the model and the hardware architecture allows the programmer to write code in an optimal manner for the hardware. In addition, message-passing libraries are available on virtually all parallel systems, which makes this paradigm appealing to those who desire portability across a variety of machines. Message passing is currently the only practical choice for use across clusters of machines.

A message-passing computer is programmed using *send* and *receive* primitives. Message-passing models have a number of characteristics in common. The execution model allows for each task to operate separately, manage its own instruction stream, and control its private area of memory. Tasks are generally created at program startup or very shortly thereafter. Communication and synchronization between the tasks are accomplished through calls to library routines. The lower-level mechanism by which the message is sent is transparent to the application programmer.

Message-passing libraries usually perform a number of functions. These include operations to perform point-to-point communication, and collective operations such as broadcasts, global reductions, and gathering data from groups of tasks. Many of the collective functions could be written by the user employing the basic point-to-point operations, but they are generally supplied by the library for ease-of-use and for performance. As is the case with libraries for common mathematical functions, optimal versions of communication functions depend on the underlying hardware architecture and can often benefit from nontrivial algorithms. Thus, it is generally advantageous for the application programmer to use routines supplied by the library implementation.

Since message-passing models share the same basic structure, codes may be written so that the same source code is used with different message-passing libraries. Many of the applications described here do just that. Most often, this is accomplished by limiting the communication portions of a code to a relatively small set of routines. Versions of this small set of routines are written for each message-passing model desired. Another method utilizes preprocessors to modify the source code to use the desired message-passing system.

13.2.1 Programming APIs

13.2.1.1 PVM

PVM grew out of a research project at Oak Ridge National Laboratory to harness a group of heterogeneous computers into a single "virtual" machine, where there is a need for running across a heterogeneous group of processors, and capabilities such as fault tolerance and resource control are important.

PVM 3.0 was released in 1993; this version enabled PVM applications to run across a virtual machine composed of multiple large multiprocessors. In PVM, programs or tasks are initiated under the control of a daemon that spawns the program on the requested computer(s). The user may require multiple instances of a particular application, and the application itself may request tasks to be spawned; each task is assigned a unique identifier by which it is referred to in communication requests. Task creation and deletion is completely dynamic. The tasks composing the PVM application may be executing different programs.

PVM provides fault tolerance by allowing tasks to register for notification if one of the other tasks in the application terminates for some unexpected reason. This allows the notified task to take precautions so that it does not hang and can potentially generate new tasks if desired. This is particularly important in applications running across heterogeneous networks where the likelihood of a "node failure" may be high. PVM supplies mechanisms for resource control by allowing the user to add and delete systems from the virtual machine and to query the status of the systems.

PVM provides functions for point-to-point communications and for synchronization. It supplies collective functions for global reductions, broadcasts, and multicasts, and allows for the designation of groups that can be used in the collective functions and barriers. (Multicasts are similar to broadcasts with the exception that it is not necessary for all targets to attempt to receive the message.) The strength of PVM lies in its ability to run over heterogeneous networks. Because this includes the possibility that messages will be sent between machines with incompatible numeric formats, PVM performs translations of the data when messages are sent and received. Additionally, PVM provides for bypassing this translation when the application is running only on a homogeneous system. Messages are queued, which means that multiple messages may be sent from a task without blocking. Messages can be deleted from the queue.

PVM 3.4 introduced several new capabilities, including message context and a name service. The context allows PVM to distinguish between PVM messages sent by different components that make up the application, such as PVM-based libraries that may be utilized along with the main body of the application. A name service provides capability for multiple independent programs to query for information about one another.

PVM is sometimes criticized for providing a lower performance than other message-passing systems. This is certainly true on some machines. PVM was created to work over networks of computers, with portability and interoperability being the prime design considerations. For situations where performance is of the utmost importance, other message-passing systems should be considered.

13.2.1.2 MPI

The MPI-1 specification was approved by the MPI Forum in 1994. It became a recognized standard and the message-passing system of choice for most developers. This was as much due to its demonstrated performance as to its extensive collection of routines for the support of commonly occurring communication patterns.

Unlike PVM, MPI does not specify commands to the operating system for the creation of daemons. An MPI application may be initiated by a runtime command that includes an option to indicate how many tasks should be created. The tasks will be activated when the MPI_INIT call is encountered, if they were not already created at program initialization. All tasks continue executing until the MPI_Finalize call, unless a task has encountered an error situation, which may cause the MPI application to abort.

MPI-1 implementations do not generally provide the capability for different types of machines to talk to each other. For point-to-point communication, a wide variety of message-passing modes exists. The most commonly used modes are the standard send invoked by the MPI_send function and the asynchronous mode invoked with the MPI_isend function. For the standard mode, the message may or may not be buffered, depending on the implementation and on the size of the message. For cases where the message is not buffered, the sending task will not return from the call until the message has been sent and received. When the message is buffered, or if the MPI_isend function is used, the sender may return from the call before the message is sent out. This mode is commonly used where performance is important. The MPI-1 standard is not specific about how the actual message is transferred, in order to allow vendors leeway in implementing MPI in the most efficient way for their machines. Within MPI messages, it is possible to send scalar values or arrays of contiguous values for the MPI-defined data types. MPI also provides a method for the user to define noncontiguous patterns of data that may be passed to the MPI functions. These patterns are called derived types and may be built by a series of function calls to form virtually arbitrary patterns of data and combinations of data types.

MPI provides a comprehensive set of communication routines that are convenient for high-performance scalable programming. The communicator is passed to the collective functions to indicate which group of tasks is included in the operation. Collective functions are provided to perform global reductions, broadcasts, task synchronization, and a wide variety of gather-and-scatter operations. MPI also provides functions for defining a virtual Cartesian grid of processors that make it easier to program algorithms based on regular grid structures.

MPI allows a form of task groups called "communicators." A special communicator that includes all the tasks in an application, MPI_COMM_WORLD, is set up upon program initiation. Other communicators may be defined by the user to include any arbitrary set of processors. A task has a rank within each communicator, and this rank together with the communicator uniquely identifies that task within the application. Communicators are a convenient device by which the user can limit operations to a subset of tasks; they are a required input for most of the MPI functions.

13.2.1.3 MapReduce

As digital information began to increase over the past decade, organizations tried different approaches to solve these problems. At first, the focus was placed on providing individual machines more storage, processing power, and memory—only to quickly find that analytical techniques on single machines failed to scale. Over time, many realized the potential of distributed systems (distributing tasks over multiple machines), but data analytic solutions were often complicated, error-prone, or simply not fast enough. In 2002, while developing a project called Nutch (a search engine project focused on crawling, indexing, and searching Internet web pages), Doug Cutting and Mike Cafarella were struggling with a solution for processing a vast amount of information. To meet the storage and processing demands for Nutch, they realized that there was a need of a reliable distributed computing approach that would scale to the demand of the vast amount of website data that the tool would be collecting. A year later, Google published papers on GFS and MapReduce, an algorithm and distributed programming platform for processing large data sets; they utilized large numbers of commodity servers and built GFS and MapReduce in a way that assumed hardware failures would be commonplace—simply something that the software needed to deal with.

The MapReduce architecture and programming model pioneered by Google is an example of a modern systems architecture designed for processing and analyzing large data sets, and is being used successfully by Google in many applications to process massive amounts of raw web data. The MapReduce system runs on top of the Google File System, within which data is loaded and partitioned into chunks, before each chunk is replicated. Data processing is co-located with data storage: When a file needs to be processed, the job scheduler consults a storage metadata service to get the host node for each chunk and then schedules a map process on that node, so that data locality is exploited efficiently. Appendix 13.B gives a description of Hadoop MapReduce.

The MapReduce architecture allows programmers to use a functional programming style to create a map function that processes a key-value pair associated with the input data, in order to generate a set of intermediate key-value pairs and a reduce function that merges all intermediate values associated with the same intermediate key.

Users define a map and a reduce function as follows:

1. The map function processes a (key, value) pair and returns a list of intermediate (key, value) pairs:

   map (in_key, in_value) list → (out_key, intermediate_value).

2. The reduce function merges all intermediate values having the same intermediate key:

   reduce (out_key, list (intermediate_value)) → list(out_value).

The former processes an input key-value pair, producing a set of intermediate pairs. The latter is in charge of combining all the intermediate values related to a particular key, outputting a set of merged output values (usually just one). MapReduce is often explained illustrating a possible solution to the problem of counting the number of occurrences of each word in a large collection of documents. The following pseudocode refers to the functions that need to be implemented.

```
map(String input_key, String input_value):
//input_key: document name
//input_value: document contents
for each word w in input_value:
EmitIntermediate(w, "1");

reduce(String output_key,
Iterator intermediate_values):
//output_key: a word
//output_values: a list of counts
int result = 0;
for each v in intermediate_values:
result += ParseInt(v);
Emit(AsString(result));
```

The map function emits in output each word together with an associated count of occurrences (in this simple example, just one). The reduce function provides the required result by summing all the counts emitted for a specific word. MapReduce implementations (e.g., Google App Engine and Hadoop) then automatically parallelize and execute the program on a large cluster of commodity machines. The runtime system takes care of the details of partitioning the input data, scheduling the program's execution across a set of machines, handling machine failures, and managing required inter-machine communication.

The programming model for MapReduce architecture is a simple abstraction where the computation takes a set of input key-value pairs associated with the input data and produces a set of output key-value pairs. The overall model for this process is shown in Figure 13.1. In the Map phase, the input data is partitioned into input splits and assigned to Map tasks associated with processing nodes in the cluster. The Map task typically executes on the same node that contains its assigned partition of data in the cluster. These Map tasks perform user-specified computations on each input key-value pair from the partition of input data assigned to the task and generates a set of intermediate results for each key. The shuffle and sort phase then takes the intermediate data generated by each Map task, sorts it with intermediate data from other nodes, divides it into regions to be processed by the reduce tasks, and distributes it as needed to nodes where the Reduce tasks will execute. All Map tasks must complete prior to the shuffle and sort and reduce phases. The number of Reduce tasks does not need to be the same as the number of Map tasks. The Reduce tasks perform additional user-specified operations on the intermediate data, possibly merging values associated with a key to a smaller set of values to produce the output data. For more complex data processing procedures, multiple MapReduce calls may be linked together in sequence.

The MapReduce programs can be used to compute derived data from documents, such as inverted indexes, and the processing is automatically parallelized by the system that executes on large clusters of commodity-type machines, highly scalable to thousands of machines. Since the system automatically takes care of details such as partitioning the

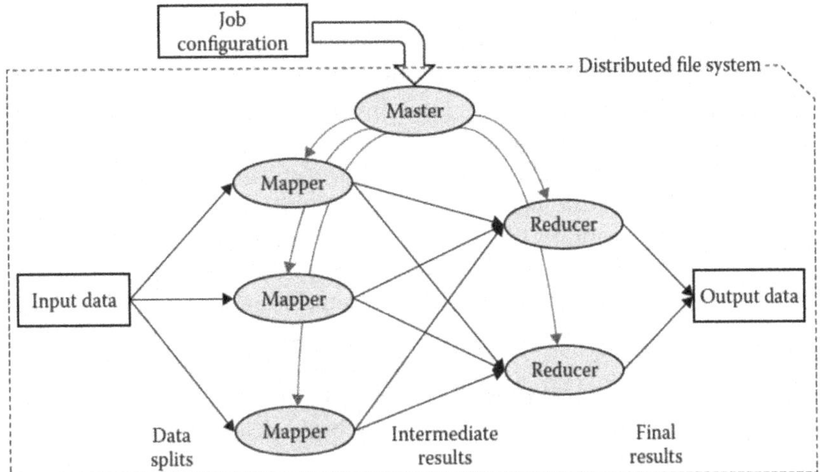

FIGURE 13.1
Execution phases in a generic MapReduce application.

input data, scheduling and executing tasks across a processing cluster, and managing the communications between nodes, programmers with no experience in parallel programming can easily use a large distributed processing environment.

13.2.2 Programming Languages

13.2.2.1 Erlang

Erlang is a declarative language for programming concurrent and distributed systems. It was developed by the authors at the Ericsson and Ellemtel Computer Science Laboratories.

Agner Krarup Erlang (1878–1929) was a Danish mathematician who developed a theory of stochastic processes in statistical equilibrium and whose theories are widely used in the telecommunications industry.

Erlang has a process-based model of concurrency. Concurrency is explicit and the user can precisely control which computations are performed sequentially and which are performed in parallel. Message passing between processes is asynchronous, that is, the sending process continues as soon as a message has been sent.

The only method by which Erlang processes can exchange data is message passing. This results in applications that can easily be distributed—an application written for a uniprocessor can easily be changed to run on a multiprocessor or network of uniprocessors. The language has built-in mechanisms for distributed programming, which makes it easy to write applications that can run either on a single computer, or on a network of computers.

a) Introduction to Erlang

Erlang was developed around 1986 by the Ericsson company as a programming language that supports concurrent programming, focusing on highly available programs in the area of telecommunications. Its main approach to increased availability is to strictly isolate the individual processes in a program, avoiding any means of shared memory. The processes are, however, allowed to communicate using message passing, both with processes on local cores and with processes on remote machines. An essential requirement for safe message passing is the usage of pure protocols, which do not employ any pointers or information that might be bound to a specific machine.

An Erlang program typically consists of thousands of processes, divided into worker and monitoring processes. Worker processes have links to monitoring processes, which form an error-propagation channel in case the worker process fails. This classification of process types as described in the Erlang Open Telecom Platform system suggests monitoring trees that hold a protocol which is initiated once a failure is detected. A failure of a working process is interpreted as the inability to perform a desired computation. Thus, a new (easier) approach for solving the problem is typically instantiated. In order to fork a process to run in parallel to the calling process, the spawn command must be used. This initiates a new process and reports its *process ID*, which can then be used as a communication address.

Programs are written entirely in terms of functions. Function selection is made by pattern matching, which leads to highly succinct programs. Variables in Erlang have the property of single assignment—once a value has been assigned to a variable, this value can never be changed. This property has important consequences when debugging or transforming a program. The Erlang system has an inbuilt notion of time—the programmer can specify how long a process should wait for a message before taking some form of action. This allows the programming of real-time applications. Erlang is suitable for most soft real-time applications where response times are in the order of milliseconds.

Many of the Erlang primitives provide solutions to problems that are commonly encountered when programming large concurrent real-time systems:

- Module system allows the structuring of very large programs into conceptually manageable units.
- Error detection mechanisms allow the construction of fault-tolerant software.
- Code loading primitives allow code in a running system to be changed without stopping the system.

Fault tolerance is further reached by allowing machines and processes to crash. Instead of trying to catch any possible exception in a process and reacting to it internally, an invalid process is left to crash. However, the crash of any process is communicated and detected by a monitoring process, which initiates actions upon the observation of such a failure. For this reason, the monitoring machine needs sufficient information to decide on the next steps. In particular, it needs information on the cause of the crash. Thus, fault tolerance is reached with replication and a safe-to-crash approach.

This approach was considered efficient back in the 1980s, especially due to the limited bandwidth and duplication of program state information (instead of using a shared memory). Nowadays, the main bottleneck in the execution of a program lies in missed cache hits in the case when illegal pointers are used. The approach of duplicating the program information for message passing fits the current trends of computer system architectures.

Error detection of remote or local processes is set up using a method called "link" (PID). This call links the current process to monitoring the behaviour of the process with process ID PID. In order to receive these out-of-band messages, the monitoring process is flagged as a system process using the command process_ flag (trap_exit, true). Upon an irregular termination of the monitored process, an error message is created containing the keyword Exit, the process ID of the broken process, and a reason, ('Exit', PID, Reason). This message is passed to the monitoring processes and evaluated there.

This simple approach enables the creation of large and complex applications. Message passing is used both between large components and within its constituent components. Any component of an application can be tested to ascertain whether it produces the expected results. Components producing unexpected or false results can be opened and tested recursively until the root of the failure is found.

b) Features of Erlang

  a. Declarative syntax. Erlang has a declarative syntax and is largely free from side effects.
  b. Concurrent. Erlang has a process-based model of concurrency with asynchronous message passing. The concurrency mechanisms in Erlang are lightweight, i.e., processes require little memory, and create or delete processes and message passing require little computational effort.
  c. Real-time. Erlang is intended for programming soft real-time systems where response times in the order of milliseconds are required.
  d. Continuous operation. Erlang has primitives that allow code to be replaced in a running system, and also allow old and new versions of code to execute at the same time. This is of great use in "non-stop" systems, telephone exchanges, air traffic control systems, etc., where the systems cannot be halted to make changes in the software.
  e. Robust. Safety is a crucial requirement in systems such as the above. There are three constructs in the language for detecting runtime errors. These can be used to program robust applications.
  f. Memory management. Erlang is a symbolic programming language with a real-time garbage collector. Memory is allocated automatically when required, and deallocated when no longer used. Typical programming errors associated with memory management cannot occur.
  g. Distribution. Erlang has no shared memory. All interaction between processes is by asynchronous message passing. Distributed systems can easily be built in Erlang. Applications written for a single processor can, without difficulty, be ported to run on networks of processors.
  h. Integration. Erlang can easily call or make use of programs written in other programming languages. These can be interfaced to the system in such a way that they appear to the programmer as if they were written in Erlang.

13.3 Stream Programming

In data-parallel models, the execution of instructions in parallel is implicitly driven by the layout of the data structures in the memory. The data structures are generally large arrays, and the operations on the elements are performed on the processor that owns the memory where a particular element resides. There is one thread of control, and parallelism is achieved when parallel constructs, such as DO-loops with independent iterations, are encountered. The programmer specifies the storage layout of data objects with compiler directives.

Data-parallel languages usually include several types of parallel constructs in order to allow the user mechanisms to control parallelism, in addition to DO-loops. Moreover, they typically supply intrinsic functions and library routines to perform common parallel operations. The first data-parallel languages were extensions to compilers, but the products currently available may be implemented either as compiler extensions or as source-to-source translators that analyze the code and substitute message-passing requests for the remote references. In the tter case, the resultant source is passed to the native compiler of the computer used.

13.3.1 Programming APIs

13.3.1.1 CUDA

CUDA is both a parallel computing architecture and a programming model for high-performance computing. It is a proprietary standard of Nvidia. CUDA is the computing engine in the graphics processing units (GPUs) of Nvidia. CUDA provides programmatic access to the native instruction set and memory of the parallel computational elements in the GPUs. GPUs have many cores and each core is capable of running thousands of threads simultaneously. They are called devices and operate in a host environment. The CPU and its memory comprise the host.

CUDA enables dramatic increases in computing performance by harnessing the power of GPUs. There are three ways to bring GPU-enabled acceleration to applications:

1. Replace or augment CPU-only libraries such as MKL BLAS, IPP, FFTW, and other widely used numerical libraries with GPU-accelerated libraries.
2. Use OpenACC directives for parallelizing loops in Fortran or C/C++ code.
3. Develop parallel algorithms and libraries using languages such as C, C++, Java, Fortran, Python, and C#.

Nvidia compiler (nvcc) is used for compiling CUDA programs. A typical CUDA program consists of both *serial* and *parallel* code. The serial (aka host) code targets the host and the parallel (aka device) code is run on the devices. The nvcc compiler first separates the code into serial/host and parallel/device components. The device code is processed by the nvcc compiler and the serial code is processed by standard host compilers such as the *gcc*.

Processing flow in the CUDA environment comprises the following steps:

1. Input data is copied from the host memory to the GPU memory.
2. Devices execute parallel code and cache data on the chip for performance.
3. Results are copied from the GPU memory to the CPU memory.

13.3.1.2 OpenCL

OpenCL (Open Computing Language) is an open-source standard for general-purpose parallel programming of heterogeneous computing systems. The latter can be a diverse mix of multi-core CPUs from AMD, GPUs from Nvidia, Cell Broadband Engine from IBM, and other parallel processors such as DSPs, including Sony's PlayStations.

An OpenCL application can leverage both types of parallelism:

- Data-level parallelism: Each device executes the same code but operates on different sets of data.
- Task-level parallelism: Each task executes on a different device in parallel and the code for each task is different.

Nvidia and AMD provide free and popular OpenCL SDKs. The latter contains libraries and tools for developing OpenCL applications. The OpenCL SDK is pre-installed on recent versions of Mac OS X. OpenCL provides a standard set of primitive data types. They are similar to their C/C++ counterparts. For example, the OpenCL data type cl_uint corresponds to the unsigned int of C/C++. The OpenCL standard defines a set of data types, data structures, and functions that augment C and C++. OpenCL programs can be compiled to run on any OpenCL-compliant hardware.

Though vector instructions are vendor-specific, when you compile an OpenCL application for a specific hardware, the OpenCL compiler for the hardware will generate vector instructions that match the underlying hardware architecture. Portability, standardized vector processing, and parallel programming are distinctive features of OpenCL.

13.3.1.3 OpenACC

OpenACC is similar to OpenMP but targets acceleration devices such as GPUs. It is maintained by an industry consortium. The OpenACC specification, like that of OpenMP, includes compiler directives, runtime routines, and environment variables. Currently, OpenACC adoption is not widespread due to a lack of OpenACC compilers. Though commercial solutions are available from the Portland Group and CAPS, OpenACC support is not available for the GCC and Clang compilers.

OpenMP uses #pragma parallel for parallelizing a loop for a multithreaded CPU. OpenACC uses #pragma acc kernels to turn parallelizable loops into kernel functions, which are executed on the GPUs. Much of the complexity of this task is managed by the programmer in the case of CUDA and OpenCL, but it is transparent to the programmer in OpenACC. Unlike for OpenCL, there is no need for two separate compilation units (one targeting the CPU/host, and the other for GPUs).

13.3.2 Programming Languages

13.3.2.1 Scala

Scala is a new programming language developed by Martin Odersky and his team at EPFL and now supported by Typesafe. The name Scala is derived from Sca(lable) La(nguage) and is a multi paradigm language, incorporating Object Oriented approaches with Functional Programming. Like any other object-oriented language (such as Java, C#, or C++), Scala can exploit inheritance, polymorphism, and abstraction and encapsulation techniques. However, you can also develop solutions using purely functional programming principles in a similar manner to languages such as Haskell or Clojure; in such an approach, programs are written purely in terms of functions that take inputs and generate outputs without any side effects. Thus, it is possible to combine the best of both worlds when creating a software system: Object-oriented principles can be exploited to structure a solution, integrating functional aspects when appropriate.

One of the design goals of the Scala development team was to create a scalable language suitable for the construction of component-based software within highly concurrent environments. This means that it has several features integrated into it that support large software developments. For example, the Actor model of concurrency greatly simplifies the development of concurrent applications. In addition, the syntax reduces the amount of code that must be written by a developer (at least compared with Java).

Scala can be compiled to Java Byte Codes. This means that a Scala system can run on any environment that supports the Java Virtual Machine (or JVM). There are already several languages that compile to Java Byte codes, including Ada, JavaScript, Python, Ruby, Tcl and Prolog, etc. However, the additional advantage of using Scala is that it can be integrated with any existing Java code base in a project. This also allows Scala to exploit the huge library of Java projects available both for free and for commercial use.

Characteristics of Scala:

- Provides object-oriented concepts including classes, objects, inheritance, and
- abstraction.
- Extends these (at least with reference to Java) to include traits that represent
- data and behaviour that can be mixed into classes and objects.
- Includes functional concepts, such as functions as first-class entities in the language,
- as well as concepts such as partially applied functions and currying, which allow new functions to be constructed from existing functions.
- Has interoperability (mostly) with Java.
- Uses statically typed variables and constants with type inference whenever possible in order to avoid unnecessary repetition.
    1. Scala Advantages

The characteristics of Scala—strong type system, preference for immutability, functional capabilities, and parallelism abstractions—make it easy to write reliable programs and minimize the risk of unexpected behavior.

- Interoperability with Java: Scala runs on the Java virtual machine; the Scala compiler compiles programs to Java byte code. Thus, Scala developers have access to Java libraries natively. Given the phenomenal number of applications written in Java, both open source and as part of the legacy code in organizations, the interoperability of Scala and Java helps explain the rapid popularity of Scala.
- Parallelism: Parallel programming is difficult because we, as programmers, tend to think sequentially. Reasoning about the order in which different events can happen in a concurrent program is very challenging.

Scala provides several abstractions that greatly facilitate the writing of parallel code. These abstractions work by imposing constraints on the way parallelism is achieved. For instance, parallel collections force the user to phrase the computation as a sequence of operations (such as map, reduce, and filter) on collections. Actor systems require the developer to think in terms of actors that encapsulate the application state and communicate by passing messages.

- Static typing and type inference: Scala's static typing system is very versatile. A lot of information as to the program's behavior can be encoded in types, allowing the compiler to guarantee a certain level of correctness. This is particularly useful for code paths that are rarely used. A dynamic language cannot catch errors until a particular branch of execution runs, so a bug can persist for a long time until the program runs into it. In a statically typed language, any bug that can be caught by the compiler will be caught at compile time, before the program has even started running.

- Immutability: Having immutable objects removes a common source of bugs. Knowing that some objects cannot be changed once instantiated reduces the number of places bugs can creep in. Instead of considering the lifetime of the object, we can narrow in on the constructor.

Scala encourages the use of immutable objects. In Scala, it is very easy to define an attribute as immutable:

```
val amountExpnd = 200
The default collections are immutable:
val rolIds = List("123", "456")//List is immutable
rollIds(1) = "589"              //Flag Compile-time error
```

- Scala and functional programs: Scala encourages functional code. A lot of Scala code consists of using higher-order functions to transform collections. The developer does not have to deal with the details of iterating over the collection.

Consider the problem of locating the position of occurrence of an identified element in a list. In Scala, we first declare a new list, collection.rollWithIndex, whose elements are pairs of the collection's elements and their indexes i.e., (collection(0), 0), (collection(1), 1), and so on.

We subsequently tell Scala that we want to iterate over this collection, binding the currentElem variable to the current element and index to the index. We apply a filter on the iteration, selecting only those elements for which currentElem == elem. We then tell Scala to just return the index variable.

A sample occurrencesOf function would be:

```
def occurrencesOf[A](elem:A, collection:List[A]):List[Int] = {
for {
(currentElem, index) <- collection.rollWithIndex
if (currentElem == elem)
} yield index
}
```

There is no need to deal with the details of the iteration process in Scala. The syntax is very declarative: we tell the compiler that we want the index of every element equal to elem in collection and let the compiler worry about how to iterate over the collection.

- Null pointer uncertainty: Scala, like other functional languages, introduces the Option[T] type to represent an attribute that might be absent. We might then write the following:

```
class User {
...
val email:Option[Email]
...
}
```

Thus, Scala achieves a higher degree of provable correctness. Never using null, we know that we will never run into null pointer exceptions. Achieving the same level of correctness in languages without Option[T] requires writing unit tests on the client code to verify that it behaves correctly when the e-mail attribute is null.

Scala introduces many concepts such as implicits, type classes, and composition using traits that might not be familiar to programmers coming from the object-oriented world. Its type system is very expressive, but getting to know it well enough to use its full power takes time and requires adjusting to this new programming paradigm.

2. Scala Benefits
   - Increased productivity: Having a compiler that performs a lot of type checking and works as a personal assistant is, in our opinion, a significant advantage over languages that check types dynamically at runtime, and the fact that Java is a statically typed language is probably one of the main reasons that made it so popular in the first place. The Scala compiler belongs to this category as well and goes even further by finding out many of the types automatically, often relieving the programmer from specifying these types explicitly in the code. Moreover, the compiler in the IDE (Integrated Development Environment) gives instant feedback, and therefore, increases productivity.
   - Natural evolution from Java: Scala integrates seamlessly with Java, which is a very attractive feature, to avoid reinventing the wheel. Users can start running Scala today in a production environment. Large corporations such as Twitter, LinkedIn, and Foursquare (to name a few) have been doing that on large-scale deployments for many years now, followed recently by other big players such as Intel and Amazon. Scala compiles to Java bytecode, which means that performance will be comparable. Most of the code that users are running while executing Scala programs is probably Java code, the major differences being what programmers see and the advanced type checking while compiling code.
   - Better fit for asynchronous and concurrent code: To achieve better performance and handle more load, modern Java frameworks and libraries for web development are now tackling difficult problems that are tied to multi-core architectures and the integration with unpredictable external systems. Scala's incentive to use immutable data structures and functional programming constructs as well as its support for parallel collections has a better chance to succeed in writing concurrent code that will behave correctly. Moreover, Scala's superior type system and macro support enable DSLs for trivially safe asynchronous constructs, for example, composable futures and asynchronous language extensions.

Scala is the only language that is statically typed, runs on the JVM and is totally Java compatible, is both object-oriented and functional, and is not verbose, thus leading to better productivity, less maintenance, and therefore more fun.

13.4 Summary

This chapter gave thematic introduction to parallel computing programming APIs and programming languages. It introduced the three categories of parallel programming APIs, namely, shared memory, message passing, and stream processing programming.

OpenMP is an API for shared-memory-based parallel programming. An overarching goal of OpenMP is to enable programmers to incrementally parallelize existing serial applications written in C/C++ and Fortran. Message passing is largely the model of choice on MIMD computers with physically distributed memory because the close relationship between the model and the hardware architecture allows the programmer to write code in an optimal manner for the hardware. The programming model used by MPI is well suited for distributed memory systems such as clusters that are composed of computing nodes coupled with a fast interconnect. Data stream-related data-parallel models describe models where the execution of instructions in parallel is implicitly driven by the layout of the data structures in memory. CUDA is both a parallel computing architecture and a programming model for high-performance computing; OpenCL is an open-source standard for general-purpose parallel programming of heterogeneous computing systems, and OpenACC is similar to OpenMP but targets acceleration devices such as GPUs.

Amongst the parallel programming languages, Haskell is usually considered the successor of Miranda, which was one of the most important lazy functional programming languages in the 1980s. Erlang has a process-based model of concurrency. Concurrency is explicit and the user can precisely control which computations are performed sequentially and which are performed in parallel. The only method by which Erlang processes can exchange data is message passing. Scala is a new programming language developed by Martin Odersky and his team at the EPFL and is now supported by Typesafe. The name Scala is derived from Sca(lable) La(nguage) This is a multi-paradigm language, incorporating object-oriented approaches with functional programming (Figures 13B.1 and 13B.2).

Appendix 13.A: Functional Programming

Functional programming has its roots in the lambda calculus, originally developed in the 1930s, to explore computability. Many functional programming languages can thus be considered as elaborations on this lambda calculus. There have been numerous pure functional programming languages including Common Lisp, Clojure, and Haskell. Scala allows you to write in a purely functional programming style or to combine functions with objects. When doing this, care needs to be taken that the principles of functional programming, and thus the corresponding advantages of functional programming, are not undermined. However, when used judiciously, functional programming can be a huge benefit for, and an enhancement to, the purely object-oriented world.

Programming paradigms can be of two fundamental types:

- Imperative programming is currently perceived as traditional programming; it is the style of programming used in languages such as C, C++, Java, C#, and so on. In these languages, a programmer tells the computer what to do, for example, $x = y + z$ and so on. It is thus oriented around control statements, looping constructs, and assignments.
- Functional programming aims to describe the solution. Functional programming is defined as a programming paradigm including a style of building the structure and elements of computer programs that treats computation as the evaluation of

mathematical functions and avoids state and mutable data. The functions produce results based on input data and computations to generate a new output; they do not rely on any side effects and they also do not depend on the current state of the program.

13.A.1 Characteristics of Functional Programming

- Functional programming aims to avoid side effects: functions disallow any hidden side effects; the only observable output allowed is the return value; the only output dependency allowed are the arguments that are fully determined before any output is generated. Lack of hidden side effects evidently makes it easier to understand what the program is doing and also makes comprehension, development, and maintenance easier.
- Functional programming avoids concepts such as state. If some operation is dependent upon the state of the program or some element of a program, then its behavior may differ depending upon that state; this may make it harder to comprehend, implement, test, and debug. As all of these impact on the stability and probably the reliability of a system, state-based operations may result in less reliable software being developed. As functions do not rely on any given state but only on the data they are given, their results are easier to understand, implement, test, and debug.
- Functional programming promotes declarative programming (it is, in fact, a subtype of declarative programming), which means that programming is oriented around expressions that describe the solution rather than focusing on the imperative approach of most procedural programming languages. These languages emphasize aspects of how the solution is derived.

  For example, an imperative approach to looping through some container and printing out each result in turn would look like

  ```
  int sizeOfCarton = carton.length
  for (int I = 1 to sizeOfcarton) do
  element = carton.get(i)
  print(element)
  enddo
  ```

  Whereas a functional programming approach would look like

  ```
  carton.foreach(print)
  ```

- Functional programming promotes immutable data. Immutability indicates that once created, data cannot be changed. In Scala, strings are immutable. Once you create a new string you cannot modify it. Any functions that apply to a string that would conceptually alter the contents of the string, result in a new string being generated. Scala takes this further by having a presumption of immutability, which means that by default all data-holding types are immutable. This ensures that functions cannot have hidden side effects, thereby simplifying programming in general.

The Akka Actor model builds on this approach to provide a very clean model for multiple interacting concurrent systems.

- Functional programming promotes recursion as a natural control structure. Functional languages tend to emphasize recursion as a way of processing structures that would use some form of looping constructs in an imperative language. While recursion is very expressive and is a great way for a programmer to write a solution to a problem, it is not as efficient at runtime as looping. However, any expression that can be written as a recursive routine can also be written using looping constructs. Functional programming languages often incorporate tail-end recursive optimizations to convert recursive routines into iterative ones at runtime, that is, if the last thing a routine does before it returns is to call another routine, rather than actually invoking the routine and having to set up the context for that routine, it should be possible to reuse the current context and to treat it in an iterative manner as a loop around that routine. This means that both the programmer benefits of an expressive recursive construct and the runtime benefits of an iterative solution can be achieved using the same source code. This option is typically not available in imperative languages.

13.A.2 Advantages of Functional Programming

- Good for prototyping solutions: Solutions can be created very quickly for algorithmic or behavior problems in a functional language, thereby allowing ideas and concepts to be explored in a rapid application development style.
- Modular functionality: Functional programming is modular in terms of functionality (where object-oriented languages are modular in the dimension of components). It is thus well suited to situations where it is natural to want to reuse or componentize the behavior of a system.
- The avoidance of state-based behavior: As functions only rely on their inputs and outputs (and avoid accessing any other stored state), they exhibit a cleaner and simpler style of programming. This avoidance of state-based behavior makes many difficult or challenging areas of programming simpler (such as those used in concurrency applications).
- Additional control structures: A strong emphasis on additional control structures such as pattern matching, managing variable scope, and tail recursion optimizations.
- Concurrency and immutable data: As functional programming systems advocate immutable data structures, it is simpler to construct concurrent systems. This is because the data being exchanged and accessed is immutable. Therefore, multiple executing threads or processes cannot adversely affect each other.
- Partial evaluation: Since functions do not have side effects, it also becomes practical to bind one or more parameters to a function at compile time and to reuse these functions with bound values as new functions that take fewer parameters.

13.A.3 Disadvantages of Functional Programming

- Input–output is harder in a purely functional language. Input–output flows naturally align with stream-style processing, which does not neatly fit into the "data in, results out" nature of functional systems.
- Interactive applications are harder to develop. An interactive application is constructed via "request response" cycles initiated by a user action. Again, these do not sit naturally within the purely functional paradigm.
- Not data oriented. A pure functional language does not really align with the needs of the primarily data-oriented nature of many of today's systems. Many commercial systems are oriented around the need to retrieve data from a database, manipulate it in some way, and store that data back into a database: such data can be naturally (and better) represented via objects in an object-oriented language.
- Continuously running programs such as services or controllers may be more difficult to develop, as they are naturally based upon the idea of a continuous loop that does not sit naturally within the purely functional paradigm.
- Functional programming languages have tended to be less efficient on current hardware platforms. This is partly because current hardware platforms are not designed with functional programming in mind and also because many of the systems previously available were focused on the academic community for whom performance was not the primary focus per se. However, this has changed to a large extent with Scala and the functional language Heskell.

For many reasons, functional programming is not as prevalent as imperative programming:

- Programmers are less familiar with functional programming concepts and thus find it harder to pick up function-oriented languages.
- Functional programming idioms are often less intuitive to programmers than imperative programming idioms (such as lazy evaluations), which can make debugging and maintenance harder.
- Many functional programming languages have been viewed as exotic languages that are only relevant to academics. While this has been true of some of the older functional languages, the situation is changing with the advent of languages such as Scala.

Appendix 13.B: Hadoop MapReduce

Hadoop was modeled after two papers produced by Google, one of the many companies to have these kinds of data-intensive processing problems. The first paper, presented in 2003, describes a pragmatic, scalable, distributed file system optimized for storing enormous datasets, called the Google File System (GFS). In addition to simple storage, GFS was built to support large-scale, data-intensive, distributed processing applications. In 2004, the second paper titled "Map-Reduce: Simplified Data Processing on Large Clusters," was presented, defining a programming model and accompanying framework that provided automatic parallelization, fault tolerance, and the scale to process hundreds of terabytes of data in a single job over thousands of machines. When paired, these two systems could be used to build large data processing clusters on relatively inexpensive commodity machines. These papers directly inspired the development of the Hadoop Distributed File System (HDFS) and Hadoop MapReduce, respectively.

Hadoop's MapReduce computing platform consists of two components: JobTracker, which acts as a master in the Hadoop cluster, and TaskTracker. A typical activity flow in Hadoop is as follows:

- A server, called JobTracker, accepts jobs (MapReduce programs) from clients. A job is associated with a mapper method, a reducer method, and a set of input files and output files.
- The JobTracker contacts the Name node to get the location of the input files. The JobTracker applies the appropriate scheduling algorithm to assign tasks to a set of computing nodes, called TaskTrackers. The scheduling algorithm takes data locality into account to optimize data movements.
- The JobTracker distributes the mapper and reducer methods among the scheduled TaskTrackers. In addition to the mapper and reducer methods, the JobTracker also distributes the job configuration so that the mapper and reducer methods run based on the provided configuration.
- The TaskTracker performs the assigned mapper task. The TaskTracker reads input from data nodes and applies the given method on the input.
- The map task creates and writes intermediate key-value pairs to a file on the local file system of the TaskTracker.
- The partitioner reads the results from the map task and finds an appropriate TaskTracker to run reduce task. The intermediate results emitted by map tasks are then propagated to reduce tasks.
- The TaskTrackers that are scheduled to run reduce tasks apply operations programmed in reduce function on the data elements streamed from map tasks and emit key-value pairs as output. The output data elements are then written to the HDFS.

It is important to highlight that the tasks come down to data location to perform designated operations. If no computing resources are available at the machine where the data is located, the computation is carried out by the machine nearest to the data. In the MapReduce context, such behavior is called data locality. Data locality improves the distributed computations by reducing the data movements in the network within the cluster.

Figure 13B.1 presents the Hadoop MapReduce architecture.

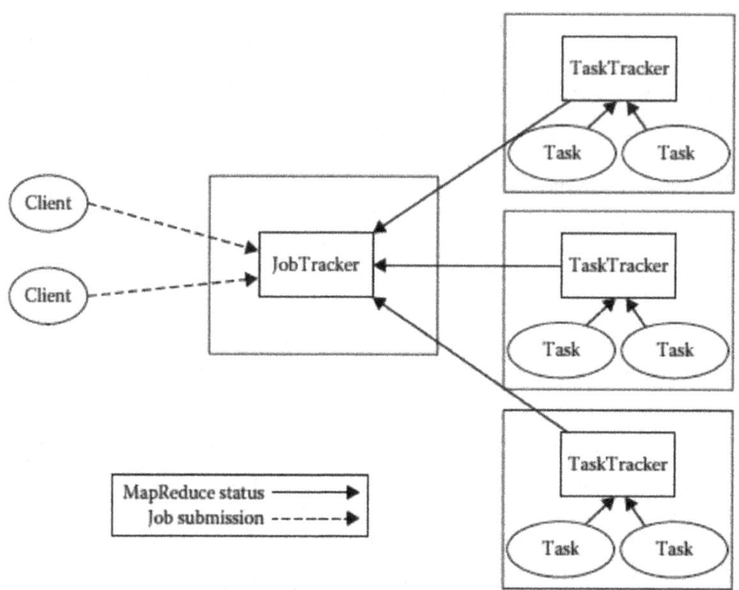

FIGURE 13.B.1
Hadoop MapReduce architecture.

13.B.1 MapReduce Processing

13.B.1.1 JobTracker

JobTracker is a server that implement necessary user interfaces needed to submit and run a map reduce job. Once a map reduce job is submitted to a Hadoop cluster, the JobTracker of the Hadoop cluster engineers a scheme to run the submitted job. The scheme involves identifying TaskTrackers in the cluster to perform map operations, triggering the mappers on TaskTrackers, and monitoring the task while it is running. JobTracker runs in listening mode to take requests from clients. When a client submits a job, the JobTracker communicates with the Name node to obtain a list of machines that carry the input data for the job. The list is used in an optimization algorithm, and the JobTracker comes up with an optimized scheme to run the job on TaskTrackers.

The scheme attempts to reduce network bandwidth utilization within the cluster by adopting the data locality feature. By data locality, the preference in decreasing the priority to run a task on a data chunk is

- The machine where the data is located.
- The rack where the data is located.
- A computing machine in the cluster.

It is not always possible to find a node for a map task to run on local data; therefore, the next best possibility is to find a node in the same rack. If no node is available in the same rack to take the task, then any machine in the cluster that can handle the task, even if not optimally, performs the task. One of the reasons a TaskTracker may not be available to take a task is that the TaskTracker may have been running the tasks up to its maximum capacity. Whenever the JobTracker identifies a TaskTracker to run a task, it monitors the task until it terminates. If a task fails on a TaskTracker, the JobTracker finds another optimal TaskTracker to handle the task. By restarting a task on another TaskTracker, the JobTracker ensures that the job does not terminate even if a single task has failed even once. A job cannot be deemed to have been completed unless all the tasks of the job complete without errors.

The responsibilities of a JobTracker can be summarized as follows:

- Manage TaskTrackers and their resources as jobs are being submitted.
- Schedule tasks among available resources.
- Monitor the tasks of jobs and restart the failed tasks for the configured number of attempts.

JobTracker is the heart of the MapReduce computing platform as it is the entry and exit points for clients to submit a job. However, as only one JobTracker process runs on a Hadoop cluster, the JobTracker poses a single point of failure for the Hadoop MapReduce service because there is no alternate when the only running JobTracker shuts down. When the JobTracker fails, all the jobs running on the cluster are deemed to have been halted for the client.

13.B.1.2 TaskTracker

TaskTracker is a daemon running on the computing nodes of a Hadoop cluster. The TaskTracker receives instructions to perform map and/or reduce tasks from the JobTracker. The TaskTracker posts the available resources in the node and a heartbeat message at every specific interval of time to the JobTracker. The JobTracker performs bookkeeping of the TaskTracker and the corresponding resource, and exploits the information in job

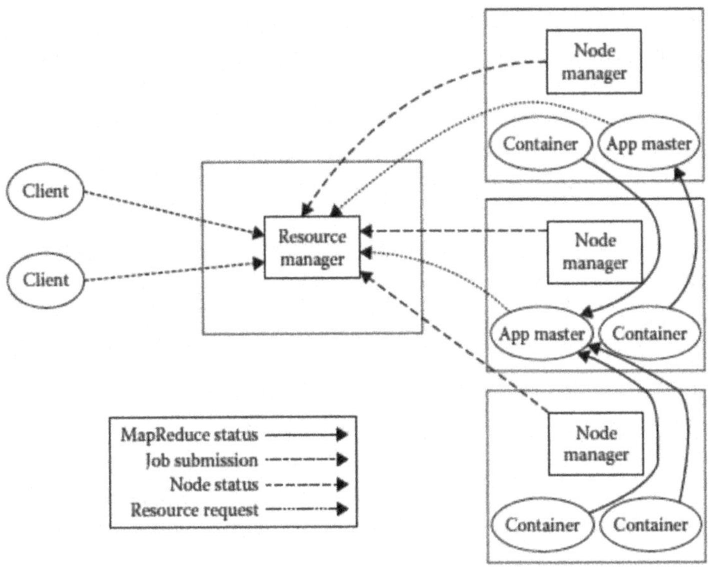

FIGURE 13.B.2
YARN architecture.

scheduling. The TaskTracker performs the assigned tasks (map, reduce) on the given data. The JobTracker tracks the TaskTrackers for the tasks that are running and instructs the TaskTrackers where to send the output data.

A TaskTracker performs a mapper method or a reduce method.

13.B.2 MapReduce Enhancements and Extensions

While the basic implementation of MapReduce is very useful for handling data processing and data loading in a heterogeneous system with many different storage systems, this basic architecture suffers from some limitations. In this section, we present an overview of some of these limitations and also the workarounds, enhancements, and extensions to MapReduce that have been devised to address these limitations.

13.B.2.1 Supporting Iterative Processing

Many data analysis techniques (e.g., PageRank algorithm, recursive relational queries, and social network analysis) require iterative computations. These techniques have a common requirement, which is that data is processed iteratively until the computation satisfies a convergence or stopping condition. The basic MapReduce framework does not directly support these iterative data analysis applications. Instead, programmers must implement iterative programs by manually issuing multiple MapReduce jobs and orchestrating their execution using a driver program. In practice, there are two key problems with manually orchestrating an iterative program in MapReduce:

- Even though much of the data may be unchanged from iteration to iteration, the data must be reloaded and reprocessed at each iteration, wasting input/output (I/O), network bandwidth, and central processing unit (CPU) resources.
- The termination condition may involve the detection of when a fixpoint has been reached. This condition may itself require an extra MapReduce job on each iteration, again incurring overhead in terms of scheduling extra tasks, reading extra data from disk, and moving data across the network.

To accommodate the requirements of iterative data analysis applications, HaLoop has incorporated the following changes to the basic Hadoop MapReduce framework:

- It exposes a new application programming interface to users that simplifies the expression of iterative MapReduce programs.
- It's master node contains a new loop control module that repeatedly starts new map-reduce steps that compose the loop body until a user-specified stopping condition is met.
- It uses a new task scheduler that leverages data locality.
- It caches and indices application data on slave nodes. In principle, the TaskTracker manages not only task execution but also caches and indices on the slave node and redirects each task's cache and index accesses to the local file system.

The HaLoop system achieves this by extending the basic MapReduce framework with two main functionalities:

- Caching the invariant data in the first iteration and then reusing it in later iterations.
- Caching the reducer outputs, which makes checking for a fixpoint more efficient, without an extra MapReduce job.

HaLoop relies on the same file system and has the same task queue structure as Hadoop, but the task scheduler and TaskTracker modules are modified, and the loop control, caching, and indexing modules are newly introduced to the architecture. The TaskTracker manages not only task execution but also caches and indices on the slave node, and redirects each task's cache and index accesses to the local file system.

In the MapReduce framework, each map or reduce task contains its portion of the input data and the task runs by performing the map/reduce function on its input data records where the life cycle of the task ends when the processing of all the input data records has been completed.

The iMapReduce framework supports the feature of iterative processing by keeping alive each map and reduce task during the entire iterative process. In particular, when all the input data of a persistent task are parsed and processed, the task becomes dormant, waiting for the new updated input data:

- For a map task, it waits for the results from the reduce tasks and is activated to work on the new input records when the required data from the reduce tasks arrives.
- For the reduce tasks, they wait for the map tasks' output and are activated synchronously as in MapReduce.

The iMapReduce runtime system carries out a termination check after each iteration. To terminate the iterations by a fixed number of iterations, the persistent map/reduce task records its iteration number and terminates itself when the number exceeds a threshold. To bound the distance between the output from two consecutive iterations, the reduce tasks can save the output from two consecutive iterations and compute the distance. If the termination condition is satisfied, the master will notify all the map and reduce tasks to terminate their execution. Jobs can terminate their iterative process in one of two ways:

- Defining a fixed number of iterations: The iterative algorithm stops after it iterates n times.
- Bounding the distance between two consecutive iterations: The iterative algorithm stops when the distance is less than a threshold.

13.B.2.1.1 Join Operations

One main limitation of the MapReduce framework is that it does not support the joining of multiple datasets in one task. However, this can still be achieved with additional MapReduce steps:

- Standard repartition join: The two input relations are dynamically partitioned on the join key and the corresponding pairs of partitions are joined using the standard partitioned sort-merge join approach.
- Improved repartition join: One potential problem with the standard repartition join is that all the records for a given join key from both input relations have to be buffered. Therefore, when the key cardinality is small or when the data is highly skewed, all the records for a given join key may not fit in the memory. The improved repartition join strategy fixes the buffering problem by introducing the following key changes:
    - In the map function, the output key is changed to a composite of the join key and the table tag. The table tags are generated in a way that ensures records from one input relation will be sorted ahead of those from the other input relation on a given join key.
    - The partitioning function is customized so that the hashcode is computed from just the join key part of the composite key. In this way, records with the same join key are still assigned to the same reduce task.
    - As records from the smaller input are guaranteed to be ahead of those from larger input for a given join key, only the records from the smaller input are buffered and the records from the larger input are streamed to generate the join output.
- Broadcast join: Instead of moving both input relations across the network as in the repartition-based joins, the broadcast join approach moves only the smaller input relation so that it avoids the preprocessing sorting requirement of both input relations and, more importantly, it avoids the network overhead for moving the larger relation.
- Semijoin: This join approach tries to avoid the problem of the broadcast join approach where it is possible to send many records of the smaller input relation across the network while they may not actually be referenced by any records in the other relation. It achieves this goal at the cost of an extra scan of the smaller input relation where it determines the set of unique join keys in the smaller relation, sends them to the other relation to specify the list of actual referenced join keys, and then sends only these records across the network for the real execution of the join operation.
- Per-split semijoin: This join approach tries to improve the semijoin approach with a further step to address the fact that not every record in the filtered version of the smaller relation will join with a particular split of the larger relation. Therefore, an extra process step is executed to determine the target split(s) of each filtered join key.

Based on statistics, such as the relative data size and the fraction of the join key referenced, the trade-offs of the join strategies can be summarized as follows:

- If data is not preprocessed, the right join strategy depends on the size of the data transferred via the network. If the network cost of broadcasting an input relation R to every node is less expensive than transferring both R and projected L, then the broadcast join algorithm should be used.
- When preprocessing is allowed, semijoin, per-split semijoin, and directed join with sufficient partitions are the best choices. Semijoin and per-split semijoin offer

further flexibility since their preprocessing steps are insensitive to how the log table is organized and thus suitable for any number of reference tables. In addition, the preprocessing steps of these two algorithms are cheaper since there is no shuffling of the log data.

13.B.2.1.2 Data Indices

One of the main limitations of the original implementation of the MapReduce framework is that it is designed such that the jobs can only scan the input data in a sequential-oriented fashion. Hence, the query-processing performance of the MapReduce framework is unable to match the performance of a well-configured parallel database management system (DBMS). The Hadoop++ system aims to boost the query performance of the Hadoop system without changing any of the system internals, by injecting their changes through user-defined functions (UDFs), which only affect the Hadoop system from inside without any external effect:

- Trojan index: The original Hadoop implementation does not provide index access due to the lack of a priori knowledge of schema and the MapReduce jobs being executed; the Hadoop++ system is based on the assumption that if the schema and the anticipated MapReduce jobs are known, then appropriate indices for the Hadoop tasks can be created. These indices are created during the data-loading time and thus have no penalty at query time.
- Each Trojan index provides an optional index access path, which can be used for selective MapReduce jobs. These indices are created by injecting appropriate UDFs inside the Hadoop implementation.

The main features of Trojan indices can be summarized as follows:

- Optional access path: They provide an optional index access path that can be used for selective MapReduce jobs. However, the scan access path can still be used for other MapReduce jobs.
  - Seamless splitting: Data indexing adds an index overhead for each data split. Therefore, the logical split includes the data as well as the index, as it automatically splits the indexed data at logical split boundaries.
  - Partial index: A Trojan index need not be built on the entire split. However, it can also be built on any contiguous subset of the split.
  - Multiple indices: Several Trojan indices can be built on the same split. However, only one of them can be the primary index. During query processing, an appropriate index can be chosen for data access based on the logical query plan and the cost model.
  - Noninvasive: They do not change the existing Hadoop framework. The index structure is implemented by providing the right UDFs.
  - No external library or engine: Trojan indices integrate indexing capability natively into the Hadoop framework without imposing a distributed structured query language (SQL) query engine on top of it.
- Trojan join: The Hadoop++ system assumes that if the schema and the expected workload are known, then the input data can be co-partitioned during the loading

time. In particular, given any two input relations, they apply the same partitioning function on the join attributes of both the relations at data loading time and place the co-group pairs, having the same join key from the two relations, on the same split and, hence, on the same node. As a result, join operations can then be processed locally within each node at query time. Implementing the Trojan joins does not require any changes to be made to the existing implementation of the Hadoop framework. The only changes are made on the internal management of the data splitting process. In addition, Trojan indices can be freely combined with Trojan joins.

13.B.2.2 Column Storage

Column storage is related to the design and implementation of a column-oriented and binary back-end storage format for Hadoop. In general, a straightforward way to implement a column-oriented storage format for Hadoop is to store each column of the input dataset in a separate file. However, this raises two main challenges:

- It requires generating roughly equal-sized splits so that a job can be effectively parallelized over the cluster.
- It needs to ensure that the corresponding values from different columns in the dataset are colocated on the same node running the map task.

The first challenge can be tackled by horizontally partitioning the dataset and storing each partition in a separate subdirectory. The second challenge is harder to tackle because of the default three-way block-level replication strategy of the HDFS that provides fault tolerance on commodity servers but does not provide any colocation guarantees. However, this can be addressed by implementing a modified HDFS block placement policy that guarantees that the files corresponding to the different columns of a split are always colocated across replicas. Hence, when reading a dataset, the column input format can actually assign one or more split directories to a single split, the column files of a split directory are then scanned sequentially, and the records are reassembled using values from corresponding positions in the files. A lazy record construction technique is used to mitigate the deserialization overhead in Hadoop, as well as eliminate unnecessary disk I/O. The basic idea behind lazy record construction is to deserialize only those columns of a record that are actually accessed in a map function.

Each column of the input dataset can be compressed using one of the following compression schemes:

- Compressed blocks: This scheme uses a standard compression algorithm to compress a block of contiguous column values. Multiple compressed blocks may fit into a single HDFS block. A header indicates the number of records in a compressed block and the block's size. This allows the block to be skipped if no values are accessed in it. However, when a value in a block is accessed, the entire block needs to be decompressed.
- Dictionary compressed skip list: This scheme is tailored for map-typed columns. It takes advantage of the fact that the keys used in maps are often strings that are drawn from a limited universe. Such strings are well suited for dictionary compression. A dictionary is built of keys for each block of map values and stores the

compressed keys in a map using a skip-list format. The main advantage of this scheme is that a value can be accessed without having to decompress an entire block of values.

One advantage of this approach is that adding a column to a dataset is not an expensive operation. It can be done by simply placing an additional file for the new column in each of the split directories. However, a potential disadvantage of this approach is that the available parallelism may be limited for smaller datasets. Maximum parallelism is achieved for a MapReduce job when the number of splits is at least equal to the number of map tasks.

SAP HANA is an in-memory database that is delivered as an appliance and is tightly integrated with SAP BW. This data is stored in both columnar- and row-wise tables, making it capable of working efficiently with both types of workload. SAP HANA stores data in a compressed format, thereby increasing the amount of data that can be stored in the database. The data loading is done through incremental updates only when the data is changed. Data can be partitioned to increase the performance and parallel capabilities. One advantage of the system that excels is that a single data store can be used for both transactional and analytical applications. There are use cases in the current organizations where the analytical decision is integrated with normal applications such as recommendation engines or personalized news feeds.

13.B.3 YARN

The fundamental idea of Yet Another Resource Negotiator (YARN) is to split the two major responsibilities of the JobTracker—resource management and job scheduling/monitoring—into separate daemons:

- A global Resource Manager
- A per-application Application Master (AM)

The Resource Manager and per-node slave, the NodeManager (NM), form the new, and generic, operating system for managing applications in a distributed manner. The Resource Manager is the ultimate authority that arbitrates division of resources among all the applications in the system. The per-application Application Master is a framework-speci_c entity and is tasked with negotiating for resources from the Resource Manager and working with the NodeManager(s) to execute and monitor the component tasks.

The per-application ApplicationMaster is responsible for negotiating appropriate resource containers from the Scheduler, tracking their status, and monitoring their progress. From the system perspective, the ApplicationMaster runs as a normal container.

A container is a resource lease that has the privilege of using CPU and memory on a specific worker node. Containers are allocated to the NodeManagers for running distributed processes on the DataNodes. There is flexibility where storage and networking may be added in the future. A container is a logical definition of resources (for example, 4GB of RAM, 1 CPU core) for a specific worker node. A job may run multiple containers spread across the worker nodes in the cluster.

Application Masters can work with Node Managers to launch containers that are written in C, Java, Python, Scala, and so on. A container will have information, such as the command line to start the process or JVM in the container, defined environmental variables, security tokens, jars, libraries, data files, or any additional objects required to run the code in the container. Following is an example for determining how many containers per node can be allocated:

```
# of containers = min (2*CORES, 1.8*DISKS, [Total available RAM] /
MIN_CONTAINER_SIZE)
```

where, MIN_CONTAINER_SIZE is minimum container size in GB (RAM).

The Resource Manager has a pluggable scheduler component, which is responsible for allocating resources to the various running applications subject to the familiar constraints of capacity, queues, and other factors. The Scheduler is a pure scheduler in the sense that it performs no monitoring or tracking of status for the application, offering no guarantees on restarting tasks that are not carried out due to either application failure or hardware failure. The scheduler performs its scheduling function based on the resource requirements of an application by using the abstract notion of a resource container, which incorporates resource dimensions such as memory, CPU, disk, and network.

The NodeManager is the per-machine slave, which is responsible for launching the applications' containers, monitoring their resource usage (CPU, memory, disk, network), and reporting the same to the Resource Manager.

14

Shared-memory Parallel Programming with OpenMP

This chapter provides an introductory treatment to the essentials of OpenMP and how to program in parallel with it. OpenMP is among the most widely used parallel programming API. However, it is limited in scalability to hardware system architectures providing UMA to shared memory.

14.1 OpenMP

OpenMP stands for *open multiprocessing*. It greatly simplifies the development of multiple-threaded parallel programming compared to, for example, low-level operating system (OS) support services for threads and shared memory. It gives easy access to the resources of the general class of symmetric multiprocessor (SMP) computers for parallel applications. OpenMP is an API that supports the shared-memory multiple-thread form of parallel application development. Moreover, it incorporates separate sets of bindings for the sequential programming languages Fortran, C, and C++.

OpenMP provides extensions to C in the form of compiler directives, environment variables, and runtime library routines to expose and execute parallel threads in the context of shared memory. A principle of its design philosophy is to permit incremental changes to sequential C code for ease of use and natural migration from initial C-based applications to parallel programs. In so doing it provides a practical and powerful means of parallel computing, admittedly within the scalability limits of the SMP class of parallel computers.

Shared-memory parallel architectures were first developed in the 1980s and a number of APIs were devised to assist in programming these. The OpenMP specification standard process began in 1997 based on this prior work and an early draft of the interface, ANSI X3H5, was released in 1994. OpenMP evolution is overseen by the OpenMP Architecture Review Board, consisting of industry and government partners. The first C-based specification, C/C++ 1.0, was released in 1998, followed by C/C++ 2.0 in 2002. C and Fortran specifications were released together in 2005, with OpenMP 2.5, 3.0, and 3.1 released in 2005, 2008, and 2011, respectively. The most recent version, 4.5, was released in 2015.

The extensions to API are primarily driven towards increasing thread count that can be supported by shared-memory architectures, including multi-core systems, the wider use of accelerators along with general-purpose CPUs, and the broad adoption of parallelism in hardware—from laptops all the way to supercomputers. In all these endeavours, there is an essential tension between, on the one hand, the desire to maintain a relatively simple, high-level programming interface, and, on the other hand, the need to satisfy the expression of a broad variety of parallel computations, and to facilitate their exploitation on a variety of platforms.

14.2 Overview of Features

OpenMP was designed to facilitate the creation of programs able to exploit the features of parallel computers where the memory is shared by the individual processor cores. OpenMP is intended to facilitate the construction of portable parallel programs by enabling the application developer to specify the parallelism in a code at a high level, via an approach that, moreover, permits the incremental insertion of its constructs. However, it also permits a low-level programming style, where the programmer explicitly assigns work to individual threads.

OpenMP provides a particularly straightforward method of converting a sequential program written in C, C++, or Fortran for execution on a system with multiple cores, several processors, or both. Mostly, all the application developer needs to do is insert a few directives (or pragmas) into a preexisting source code and select the appropriate compiler option. The compiler will then "recognize" these directives and use the information they contain to translate the program for multithreaded execution. If the corresponding compiler option is not specified at translation time, then the directives will be ignored and a single-threaded, sequential code will be generated. Hence, if a few rules are observed, the same application code can be both sequential and parallel: This can be particularly useful for development and testing purposes.

The advantage of such an approach is that the application developer does not have to explicitly create the code that will run on the different cores, or processors. This is the job of the OpenMP implementation. As a result, it can be one of the easiest, and fastest, means of converting existing applications for use on multi-core platforms.

It is possible to convert parts of a program for multithreaded execution and leave the rest of the code in sequential form. If almost all of the work of a program is in one loop, for instance, it might make sense to parallelize that loop using OpenMP's features and to leave the rest of the program untouched.

OpenMP is also an explicit (not automatic) programming model, which gives programmers full control over parallelization. It allows the programmer to *incrementally* parallelize the application without major restructuring. It also allows easy extension of sequential applications such as those written in C or Fortran, so that the execution of selected regions within the code is performed in parallel. This programming model distinguishes regions executed in parallel separated by parts of the code executed sequentially—such as those for data aggregation and subsequent partitioning for parallel processing.

OpenMP uses the fork-join, multithreading, shared address model of parallel execution and the central entity in an OpenMP program is a thread rather than a process. An OpenMP program typically creates multiple cooperating threads that run on multiple processors or cores. The execution of the program begins with a single thread called the *"master thread"*, which executes the program sequentially until it encounters the first *parallel* construct. At the parallel construct the master thread creates a *team* of threads consisting of a certain number of new threads called "slaves," and the master itself. Note that the fork operation is implicit. The program code inside the parallel construct is called *"parallel region"* and is executed in parallel, typically using the SPMD mode by the team of threads. Threads communicate by sharing variables.

The OpenMP API comprises of:

- A collection of directives for expressing the parallelism that is to be exploited in a computation.

- A small number of library routines that may be used to access or influence execution parameters.
- Some environment variables for setting default values.

Programs that rely primarily on directives for the specification of parallelism have a different flavor from those that mainly use the library routines to express the parallelism. Typically, both directives and library routines are needed to create an OpenMP program. Directives may have several attributes and arguments that specify how parallelization within particular regions is performed.

Parallelism in OpenMP is controlled by compiler directives. In C/C++, these are specified by #pragma omp string (called sentinel). The syntax of the most important compiler directive, parallel construct, is as follows:

```
#pragma omp parallel [clause [clause] ...]
{ structured block }
```

The OpenMP "parallel for" directive ("#pragma omp parallel for") creates a team of threads to execute the following structured block, which must be a for loop. The loop is parallelized by dividing the iterations of the loop among the threads, that is, the iterations of the loop are assigned to the threads of the parallel region and are executed in parallel.

It is possible to incrementally parallelize a sequential program that has many for loops by successively using the OpenMP *parallel for* directive for each of the loops. However, this directive has the following restrictions:

1. The total number of iterations is known in advance.
2. The iterations of the for loop must be independent of each other.

The variables that are declared in the main function (in this program, noOfThreads, threadId, THREAD_COUNT) or those declared before the parallel directive are shared by all the threads in the team started by the parallel directive. Thus, they have shared scope, while the variables declared inside the structured block (for example, local variables in functions) have private scope. In this program, the scope for the variable threadId is changed from shared to private using the private clause so that each thread, having its own private copy of threadId, can be uniquely identified in the team. OpenMP provides:

- Private(list-of-variables) clauses to declare variables in their list to be private to each thread.
- Shared(list-of-variables) shared among all the threads in the team.

There can be dependences among the statements within a single iteration of the loop but not dependences across iterations, because OpenMP compilers do not check for dependences among iterations, with *parallel for* directive. It is the responsibility of the programmers to identify loop-carried dependences (by looking for variables that are read/written in one iteration and written in another iteration) in *for* loop and eliminate them by restructuring the loop body. If it is impossible to eliminate them, then the loop is not amenable to parallelization. OpenMP does not parallelize *while* loops and *do-while* loops, and it is the responsibility of the programmers to convert them into equivalent *for* loops for possible parallelization.

OpenMP *for* directive, unlike the *parallel for* directive, does not create a team of threads. It partitions the iterations in *for* loop among the threads in an existing team.

OpenMP for construct shares iterations of a loop across the team representing "data parallelism". The OpenMP *sections* construct, which breaks work into separate independent sections that can be executed in parallel by different threads, can be used to implement "task or functional parallelism".

OpenMP supports different scheduling strategies, specified by the schedule parameters, for distribution or mapping of loop iterations to threads. It should be noted that a good mapping of iterations to threads can have a very significant effect on the performance. The simplest possible is static scheduling, specified by *schedule(static, chunk_size)*, which assigns blocks of size *chunk_size* in a round-robin fashion to the threads. If the amount of work (computation) per loop iteration is not constant (for example, Thread 0 gets a vastly different workload), static scheduling leads to load imbalance.

A possible solution to this problem is to use dynamic scheduling, specified by *schedule(dynamic, chunk_size)*, which assigns a new block of size *chunk_size* to a thread as soon as the thread has completed the computation of the previously assigned block. However, there is an overhead (bookkeeping in order to know which thread is to compute the next block/chunk) associated with dynamic scheduling. Guided scheduling, specified by *schedule(guided, chunk_size)*, is similar to dynamic scheduling, but the chunk_size is relative to the number of iterations left. The *chunk_size* is approximately the number of iterations left divided by the number of threads. Another scheduling strategy supported by the OpenMP is *schedule(auto)*, where the mapping decision is delegated to the compiler and/or runtime system.

At the end of the parallel region there is an implicit barrier synchronization (join operation), and only the master thread continues to execute further. OpenMP offers several synchronization constructs for the coordination of threads within a parallel region. It also offers several high-level (such as critical, atomic, and barrier) and low-level (such as locks and flush) synchronization constructs to protect critical sections or avoid race conditions, as multiple threads in a parallel region access the same shared data.

The *critical* construct guarantees that the structured block (critical section) is executed by only one thread at a time.

```
#pragma omp critical
{ structured block }
```

The *atomic* construct ensures that a single line of code (only one statement, for example x = x + 1) is executed by only one thread at a time. While the critical construct protects all the elements of an array variable, the atomic construct can be used to enforce exclusive access to one element of the array.

```
#pragma omp atomic
statement_expression
```

The *barrier* construct is used to synchronize the threads at a specific point of execution. That is, every thread waits until all the other threads arrive at the barrier.

```
#pragma omp barrier
```

The *nowait* eliminates the implicit synchronization that occurs by default at the end of a parallel section.

```
#pragma omp parallel for nowait
```

OpenMP provides several lock library functions for ensuring mutual exclusion between threads in critical sections. For example, the following functions:

- omp_init_lock() initialize a lock variable;
- omp_set_lock() set the lock, unset;
- omp_unset_lock() release the lock respectively.

Different threads can have different values for the same shared variable (for example, value in register). To produce a consistent view of memory, flush construct updates (writes back to memory at this synchronization point) all variables given in the list, so that the other threads see the most recent values. If no list is specified, then all thread visible variables are updated. OpenMP uses a relaxed memory consistency model.

```
#pragma omp flush [(list)]
```

Reduction (operator: list) reduces a list of variables to one variable, using the operator. It provides a neat way to combine private copies of a variable into a single result at the end of a parallel region.

1. Without changing any code and by adding one simple line, the sequential code fragment shown below gets parallelized:

Sequential code fragment:	Parellelized code fragment:

`int A[MAX], I, sum = 0;`
`double average;`
`for (I = 0; I < MAX; i++) {`
` sum = sum + A[i];`
`}`
`average = sum/MAX;`
	`int average, A[MAX], i, sum = 0;`
	`double average;`
	`#pragma omp parallel for`
	` reduction(+:sum)`
	`for (i = 0; < MAX; i++) {`
	` sum = sum + A[i]`
	`}`
	`average = sum/MAX;`

2. With the reduction clause, a private copy for the variable sum is created for each thread and initialized, and at the end all the private copies are reduced into one using the addition operator.
3. No synchronization construct such as critical construct is required to combine the private copies of the variable sum.

OpenMP provides several environment variables that can be used to control the parallel execution environment, including:

- OMP_SCHEDULE: It alters the behaviour of the schedule clause (mapping of iterations to threads) when schedule(runtime) clause is specified in for or parallel for directive.
- OMP_NUM_THREADS: It sets the maximum number of threads to use in a parallel region during execution.
- OMP_DYNAMIC: It specifies whether the runtime can adjust the number of threads in a parallel region.
- OMP_STACKSIZE: It controls the size of the stack for slaves (non-master threads).

A master thread spawns a team of threads as required. As parallelism is added incrementally until the performance goals are realized, the sequential program evolves into a parallel program.

14.3 Additional Feature Details

14.3.1 OpenMP Directives

OpenMP is directive based. Most parallelism is specified through the use of compiler directives that are embedded in C/C++ or FORTRAN. A directive in C/C++ has the following format:

```
#pragma omp <directive-name> [clause,...]
Example
#pragma omp parallel num threads(4)
```

14.3.1.1 Parallel Region Construct

The directive to create threads is as follows:

```
#pragma omp parallel [clause [, ]clause] ...]
```

where clause is one of the following:

```
if(scalar-expression)
num_threads(integer-expression)
default(shared| none)
private(list)
firstprivate(list)
shared(list)
copyin(list)
reduction(operator: list )
```

14.3.1.2 Work-sharing Constructs

A work-sharing construct distributes the execution of the associated region among the threads encountering it. However, it does not launch new threads by itself. It should be used within the parallel region or combined with the parallel region constructs.

The directive for the loop construct is as follows:

```
#pragma omp for [clause[[,] clause] ...]
```

where the clause is one of the following:

```
private(list)
firstprivate(list)
lasstprivate(list)
reduction(operator: list )
schedule(kind[, chunck_size ])
collapse(n)
ordered
nowait
```

14.3.1.3 Directive Clauses

The private clause declares variables in its list to be private to each thread. For a private variable, a new object of the same type is declared once for each thread in the team, and all references to the original object are replaced with references to the new object. Hence, variables declared private should be assumed to be uninitialized for each thread.

The firstprivate clause has the same behavior of the private clause, but it automatically initializes the variables in its list according to their original values.

The lastprivate `clause` does what the private clause does and copies the variable from the last loop iteration to the original variable object.

The shared clause declares variables in its list to be shared among all threads.

The default clause allows the user to specify a default scope for all variables within a parallel region to be either shared or not.

The copyin clause provides a means for assigning the same value to threadprivate variables for all threads in the team.

The reduction clause performs a reduction on the variables that appear in its list. A private copy for each list variable is created for each thread. At the end of the reduction, the reduction variable is applied to all private copies of the shared variable, and the final result is written to the global shared variable.

14.3.2 Synchronization

`Critical`

The critical directive specifies a region of code that must be executed by only one thread at a time. An optional name may be used to identify the critical construct. All critical constructs without a name are considered to have the same unspecified name. Thus, if two or more independent blocks of critical procedure exist in the same parallel region, it is important to assign different names to them so that these blocks can be executed in parallel.

```
#pragma omp critical [name ]
  Structured_block
```

`Atomic`

The atomic directive ensures that a specific storage location is updated atomically, rather than exposing it to the possibility of multiple, simultaneous writings (race condition). The atomic directive applies only to the statement immediately following it, and only the variable being updated is protected by this directive. The difference between atomic and critical directives is that atomic operations can be executed in parallel when updating different elements, while critical blocks are guaranteed to be serial.

```
#pragma omp atomic
  Statement_expression
```

`Barrier`

The barrier directive synchronizes all threads in the team. When a barrier directive is reached, a thread will wait at that point until all other threads have reached that barrier. All threads then resume executing in parallel the code that follows the barrier.

```
#pragma omp barrier
```

`flush`

The flush directive identifies a synchronization point at which the implementation must provide a consistent view of memory. Thread-visible variables are written back to memory at this point.

`#pragma omp flush` (*list*)

14.3.3 Runtime Library Routines

The OpenMP standard defines an API for library calls that perform a variety of functions:

- Query the number of threads/processors.
- Set the number of threads to use.
- General purpose locking routines (semaphores).
- Portable wall clock timing routines.
- Set execution environment functions: Nested parallelism and dynamic adjustment of threads. For C/C++, it may be necessary to specify the include file "omp.h".

14.3.3.1 Execution Environment Routines

`Omp _ set _ num _ threads`

This sets the number of threads that will be used in the next parallel region. It must be a positive integer.

void omp_set_num_threads(int num_threads).

`Omp _ get _ num _threads`

returns the number of threads that are currently in the team executing the parallel region from which it is called.

int omp_get_num_threads(void).

`Omp _ get _ max _threads`

This returns the maximum value that can be returned by a call to the OMP GET NUM THREADS function.

int omp get max threads(void).

`Omp _ get _ thread _num`

returns the thread number of the thread, within the team, making this call. This number will be between 0 and OMP GET NUM THREADS –1. The master thread of the team is thread 0.

`int omp _ get _ thread _num(void).`

`Omp _ in _parallel`

To determine whether the section code that is executing is parallel or not.

`int omp _ in _parallel(void).`

14.3.3.2 Lock Routines

The OpenMP runtime library includes a set of general-purpose lock routines that can be used for synchronization. These general-purpose lock routines operate on OpenMP locks that are represented by OpenMP lock variables. An OpenMP lock variable must be accessed only through the routines described in this section; programs that access OpenMP lock variables otherwise are non-conforming.

The OpenMP lock routines access a lock variable in such a way that they always read and update the most current value of the lock variable. The lock routines include a flush with no list; the read and update to the lock variable must be implemented as if they were atomic with the flush. Therefore, it is not necessary for an OpenMP program to include explicit flush directives to ensure that the lock variable's value is consistent among different tasks.

`Omp _ init _lock`

This subroutine initializes a lock associated with the lock variable.

`void omp _ init _ lock(omp _ lock _t *lock).`

`Omp _ destroy _lock`

This subroutine disassociates the given lock variable from any locks.

`void omp _ destroy _ lock(omp _ lock _t *lock).`

`Omp _ set _lock`

This subroutine forces the executing thread to wait until the specified lock is available. A thread is granted ownership of a lock when it becomes available.

`void omp _ set _ lock(omp _ lock _t *lock).`

`Omp _ unset _lock`

This subroutine releases the lock from the executing subroutine.

`void omp _ unset _ lock(omp _ lock _t *lock).`

`Omp _ test _lock`

This subroutine attempts to set a lock, but does not block if the lock is unavailable.

`int omp _ test _ lock(omp _ lock _t *lock).`

14.3.3.3 Timing routines

`Omp _ get _wtime`

This routine returns elapsed wall clock time in seconds.

`double omp _ get _wtime(void).`

`Omp _ get _wtick`

This routine returns the precision of the timer used by omp get wtime.

`double omp _ get _ wtick(void).`

14.4 Summary

This chapter provided an introductory treatment to the essential features of OpenMP and explained how to program in parallel with it. OpenMP is among the most widely used parallel programming APIs. However, it is limited in scalability to hardware system architectures providing UMA to shared memory. OpenMP stands for *open multiprocessing*. It greatly simplifies the development of multiple-threaded parallel programming compared to, for example, low-level OS support services for threads and shared memory. It gives easy access to the resources of the general class of SMP computers for parallel applications. OpenMP is an API that supports the shared-memory multiple-thread form of parallel application development. OpenMP incorporates separate sets of bindings for the sequential programming languages Fortran, C, and C++.

15

Message Passing Parallel Programming with MPI

This chapter provides an introductory treatment to the essential features of MPI and explains how to program in parallel with it. Message passing is the model of choice on MIMD computers with physically distributed memory, because the close relationship between the model and the hardware architecture allows the programmer to write code in an optimal manner for the hardware. In addition, message-passing libraries are available on virtually all parallel systems, which makes this paradigm appealing to those who desire portability across a variety of machines. Message passing is currently the only practical choice for use across clusters of machines.

15.1 Introduction to MPI

The programming model used by MPI is well suited for distributed memory systems such as clusters that are composed of computing nodes coupled with a fast interconnect. A standard MPI application consists of processes that perform computations and interact with each other by sending messages. Each process of the application is identified with a so-called rank, unique within a group of processes in an MPI_COMM_WORLD MPI communicator.

The basic component of an MPI application is a process. A process executes an algorithm expressed in the code making use of resources such as memory, caches, disk, etc., and communicates with other processes in order to send and receive data, and to synchronize. The characteristics of MPI processes within an application are as follows:

1. Each process within a group is identified by a so-called rank, which is a unique integer number within this group.
2. Processes communicate with one another within a communicator. The default communicator for the group of processes started in the application is MPI_COMM_WORLD. There are two types of communicators: intracommunicators for communication within a group, and intercommunicators for communication between groups.
3. The MPI specification allows the use of threads within MPI processes, with the level of support for invoking MPI functions depending on a particular MPI implementation.

In MPI, communication routines can be characterized in terms of:

1. Working modes that define how many processes are involved.

2. The way synchronization is performed: Communication routines can be characterized depending on how synchronization is performed, from the point of view of the calling process.
   - Blocking—the function blocks the execution of the process until the function has been executed (such as message received), or progressed until a certain step (such as copied to a final/additional buffer for a send operation such that the input buffer can be modified).
   - Non-blocking—the function returns immediately to the calling process, and the execution of the call may progress in the background. In this case, such a function can be thought of as a request for execution. There is a handle MPI_Request identified with the request, which needs to be passed to additional functions to check the status of a call or to terminate the call in a blocking way.
3. Execution of communication is performed: MPI processes can send and receive messages in one of two modes:
   - Point-to-point—there are two processes involved in a communication routine. A process sends/receives a message to/from another process. When sending a message, a destination rank needs to be specified. When receiving a message, it is possible to specify a particular rank of the destination process or allow receiving from any process.
   - Collective/group—several processes are involved in communication and exchange of data. Processes in a communicator all take part in a group exchange of data, or synchronization. Special hardware solutions can be used in the implementation of such routines, rather than implementing them by using point-to-point communication routines.

15.2 Basic Point-to-point Communication Routines

1. MPI_Send for sending a message to a destination process identified by a specific rank. MPI_Send is a blocking function. Specifically, following the MPI specification, the send operation will return when it is safe to modify data in the send buffer. An implementation may have copied data to a final destination or an intermediate buffer. The specification of the call is the following:

   int MPI_Send(const void *buffer,int count,

   MPI_Datatype datatype,int destination,int tag,

   MPI_Comm comm)

   with the following parameters:
   - buffer—a pointer to a buffer that contains the message to be sent, which can contain either a certain number of elements of a given simple data type or elements of several data types;
   - count—the number of elements of the given data type;
   - datatype—data type for elements used in the message. It is also possible to use a data type that encapsulates a complex structure containing several simple data types;

- destination—the rank of the destination process;
- tag—a label associated with the given message; usually tags are used in order to denote types of messages used in the application, e.g., tag DATA_DISTRIBUTION for data distribution, tag DATA_MERGING for collection of data, etc. (It is a good practice to use #define in order to define tags used throughout the application.);
- comm—denotes the communicator within which communication is performed and the process identified.

2. MPI_Recv for a blocking receive of a message from a source process:

   int MPI_Recv(void *buffer,int count,

   MPI_Datatype datatype,int source,int tag,

   MPI_Comm comm,MPI_Status *status)

   with the following parameters:

   - buffer—a pointer to a buffer for storing the incoming message; the buffer should have been allocated before;
   - count—the number of elements of the given data type;
   - datatype—data type for elements used in the message;
   - source—the rank of a sender process, instead of a specific rank, MPI_ANY_SOURCE can be used for receiving from any process;
   - tag—a label associated with the given message, instead of a specific tag, MPI_ANY_TAG can be used for receiving a message with any tag;
   - comm—denotes the communicator within which communication is performed and the process identified;
   - status—contains information related to the message such as the rank of the sender and the message tag.

15.3 Basic MPI Collective Communication Routines

While communication among several processes can be implemented using point-to-point communication functions, this may be suboptimal and introduce unnecessary complexity into the code. Several collective communication calls that are useful in a variety of applications are available. In MPI, in contrast to the point-to-point mode, all processes involved in a collective call invoke the same function. The meaning of some arguments may be different depending on the rank of a process. MPI functions from this group include:

1. Barrier—a group of processes is synchronized, i.e., a process from the group is allowed to pass the barrier only after each of the other processes from the group has reached the barrier. The function is invoked by processes in the comm communicator:

```
int MPI_Barrier(MPI_Comm comm)
```

2. Scatter—one or more processes distribute data to a group of processes. In the standard MPI_Scatter, one selected process sends chunks of data to a group of processes:

```
int MPI_Scatter(const void *sendbuffer,int sendcount,
MPI_Datatype senddatatype,void *receivebuffer,
int receivecount,MPI_Datatype receivedatatype,
int root,MPI_Comm comm)
```

with the following parameters:

- sendbuffer—a pointer to data that needs to be sent to processes, this value will be used only in the root process;
- sendcount—how many elements should be sent to each process;
- senddatatype—what data type is used for elements;
- receivebuffer—a pointer to a preallocated space for the data to be received from the root process;
- receivecount—the number of elements in receivebuffer;
- receivedatatype—data type used for the data in receivebuffer;
- root—the rank of the process distributing data;
- comm—communicator for the group of processes involved in communication.

Additionally, there are other versions of this basic scatter routine:

```
int MPI_Scatterv(const void *sendbuffer,
const int *sendcounts,const int *displacements,
MPI_Datatype senddatatype,void *receivebuf,
int receivecount,MPI_Datatype receivedatatype,
int root,MPI_Comm comm)
```

which allow sending data of various lengths to various processes. Additional parameters include:

- sendcounts—an array that specifies how many elements to send to each of the processes;
- displacements—an array with displacements for data to be sent to processes.

3. Gather—an operation opposite to scatter. In the basic MPI_Gather, one selected root process gathers chunks of data from a group of processes. This particular call:

```
MPI_Gather(const void *sendbuffer,int sendcount,
MPI_Datatype senddatatype,void *receivebuffer,
int receivecount,MPI_Datatype receivedatatype,
int root,MPI_Comm comm)
```

has the following parameters:

- sendbuffer—a pointer to a buffer with the data to be sent;
- sendcount—the number of elements to be sent;

- senddatatype—the data type for elements to be sent;
- receivebuffer—a pointer to a buffer that will collect data gathered from the processes involved in communication;
- receivecount—the number of elements received from each process only valid for the root process;
- receivedatatype—data type for elements received in the receive buffer by the root process;
- root—the rank of the receiving process;
- comm—communicator for the group of processes involved in communication.

Additionally, there is also a version of MPI_Gather that allows receiving various data sizes from various processes:

```
int MPI_Gatherv(const void *sendbuffer,int sendcount,
MPI_Datatype senddatatype,void *receivebuffer,
const int *receivecounts,const int *displacements,
MPI_Datatype recvtype,int root,MPI_Comm comm)
```

with the following additional parameters:

- receivecounts—an array of integers that specify the numbers of elements received from the processes;
- displacements—an array of integers that specify displacements for data chunks to be received by the root process, i.e., where to put the received data counting from the beginning of receivebuffer.

Additionally, the gather functions also include a version that allows all processes to receive data, not only the root process. This is possible by invoking the following function:

```
int MPI_Allgather(const void *sendbuffer,int sendcount,
MPI_Datatype senddatatype,void *receivebuffer,
int receivecount,MPI_Datatype receivedatatype,
MPI_Comm comm)
```

which allows each process to receive data chunks from each process in such a way that the data chunk from the process with rank i is put into the i-th part of receivebuffer.

Similarly, MPI_Allgatherv allows receiving data chunks of various lengths:

```
int MPI_Allgatherv(const void *sendbuffer,int sendcount,
MPI_Datatype senddatatype,void *receivebuffer,
const int *receivecounts,const int *displacements,
MPI_Datatype receivetype,MPI_Comm comm)
```

4. Broadcast—in this case, one process broadcasts data to all the processes in the communicator:

```
int MPI_Bcast(void *buffer,int count,
MPI_Datatype datatype,int root,MPI_Comm comm)
```

with the following parameters:

- buffer—data to be sent out by the root process;
- count—the number of elements to send from buffer;
- datatype—data type for the elements in buffer;
- root—the rank of the process that sends the data;
- comm—communicator for the group of processes involved in the communication.

5. Reduce—in some cases it is preferable to perform operations on data that is gathered from processes involved in communication. MPI_Reduce allows communication and a given operation on data:

```
int MPI_Reduce(const void *sendbuffer,void *receivebuffer,
int count,MPI_Datatype datatype,MPI_Op op,
int root,MPI_Comm comm)
```

Specifically, each of the processes in the communicator provides a value or multiple values as input. Corresponding values from the processes are gathered and operation op is performed on them. This results in an output value that is put into the receivebuffer of the process with rank root. In case each process provides more than one value, operations are performed for corresponding values provided by processes. The meaning of the parameters is as follows:

sendbuffer—contains a value or values provided by each process involved in the operation;

receivebuffer—space provided for results in the process with rank root;

count—the number of values each process provides to the operation;

datatype—data type of the elements for which the values are provided;

op—the operation performed on the values. MPI provides several predefined operations including:

- MPI_MAX—maximum of values,
- MPI_MIN—minimum of values,
- MPI_PROD—product of values,
- MPI_SUM—sum of values,
- MPI_LXOR—a logical xor of values, etc.

It should also be noted that it is possible to create a new operation using the following function:

```
int MPI_Op_create(MPI_User_function *user_function,
int iscommutative,MPI_Op *op)
```

6. All-to-all communication. In this case, all processes send data to all other processes. This communication mode implemented by function MPI_Alltoall can be thought of as an extension of MPI_Allgather. In this particular case, each process sends various data to various receiving processes. Specifically, the process with rank i sends the j-th chunk of data to the process with rank j. The process with rank j receives this data chunk to the i-th chunk location. Details of this function are as follows:

```
int MPI_Alltoall(const void *sendbuffer,int sendcount,
MPI_Datatype senddatatype,void *receivingbuffer,
int receivecount,MPI_Datatype receivedatatype,
MPI_Comm comm)
```

with the same meaning of parameters such as for MPI_Allgather.

Additionally, MPI specifies MPI_Alltoallv, which allows sending data chunks of various sizes between processes. Otherwise, the way of placement of received data is analogous to MPI_Alltoall. However, specific placement of data chunks is provided with displacements:

```
int MPI_Alltoallv(const void *sendbuffer,
const int *sendcounts,const int *senddisplacements,
MPI_Datatype sendtype,void *receivebuffer,
const int *receivecounts,const int *receivedisplacements,
MPI_Datatype receivedatatype,MPI_Comm comm)
```

Compared to the previous functions, additional parameters include:

- sendcounts—an array of integers that specify how many elements should be sent to each process.
- senddisplacements —an array that specifies displacements for data to be sent to particular processes, i.e., senddisplacements[i] specifies the displacement for data to be sent to process i counting from the pointer sendbuffer.
- receivedisplacements—an array that specifies displacements for data to be received from particular processes, i.e., receivedisplace ments[i] specifies the displacement for data to be received from process i counting from the pointer receivebuffer.

15.4 Environment Management Routines

Several of the more commonly used MPI environment management routines are described below:

MPI Init

MPI Init initializes the MPI execution environment. This function must be called in every MPI program, before any other MPI functions, and must be called only once in an MPI program. For C programs, MPI Init may be used to pass the command line arguments to all processes, although this is not required by the standard and is implementation dependent.

```
MPI Init(*argc,*argv)
MPI INIT(ierr)
```

MPI_Comm_size

This determines the number of processes in the group associated with a communicator. It is generally used within the communicator MPI_COMM WORLD to determine the number of processes being used by the application.

```
MPI_Comm_size(comm,*size)
MPI_COMM_SIZE(comm,size,ierr)
```

MPI_Comm_rank
MPI_Comm_rank determines the rank of the calling process within the communicator. Initially, each process will be assigned a unique integer rank between 0 and P–1, within the communicator MPI_COMM_WORLD. This rank is often referred to as a "task ID." If a process becomes associated with other communicators, it will have a unique rank within each of these as well.

```
MPI_Comm_rank(comm,*rank)
MPI_COMM_RANK(comm,rank,ierr)
```

MPI_Abort
This function terminates all MPI processes associated with a communicator. In most MPI implementations, it terminates all processes regardless of the communicator specified.

```
MPI_Abort(comm,errorcode)
MPI_ABORT(comm,errorcode,ierr)
```

MPI_Get_processor_name
This gets the name of the processor on which the command is executed. It also returns the length of the name. The buffer for the name must be at least MPI_MAX_PROCESSOR_NAME characters in size. What is returned into the name is implementation dependent—it may not be the same as the output of the hostname or host shell commands.

```
MPI_Get_processor_name(*name,*resultlength)
MPI_GET_PROCESSOR_NAME(name, resultlength, ierr)
```

MPI_Initialized
MPI Initialized indicates whether MPI Init has been called and returns a flag as either true (1) or false (0). MPI requires that MPI Init be called once and only once by each process. This may pose a problem for modules that want to use MPI and are prepared to call MPI_Init if necessary. MPI Initialized solves this issue.

```
MPI_Initialized(*flag)
MPI_INITIALIZED(flag,ierr)
```

MPI_Wtime
This returns an elapsed wall clock time in seconds (double precision) on the calling processor.

```
MPI_Wtime()
MPI_WTIME()
```

```
MPI_Wtick
```

This returns the resolution in seconds (double precision) of MPI_Wtime.

```
MPI_Wtick()
MPI_WTICK()\
```

MPI_Finalize
terminates the MPI execution environment. This function should be the last MPI routine called in every MPI program; no other MPI routines may be called after it.

```
MPI_Finalize()
MPI_FINALIZE(ierr)
```

15.5 Point-to-point Communication Routines

15.5.1 Blocking Message Passing Routines

MPI_Send

As a basic blocking send operation, this routine returns only after the application buffer in the sending task is free for reuse. Note that this routine may be implemented differently on different systems. The MPI standard permits the use of a system buffer but does not require it. Some implementations may actually use a synchronous send (discussed below) to implement the basic blocking send.

```
MPI_Send(*buf,count,datatype,dest,tag,comm)
MPI_SEND(buf, count, data type, dest, tag, comm, ierr)
```

Buffer: This is the program (application) address space that references the data that is to be sent or received. In most cases, this is simply the variable name that is being sent/received. For C programs, this argument is passed by reference and usually must be prepended with an ampersand (&var1).

Data Count: Indicates the number of data elements of a particular type to be sent.

Data Type: For reasons of portability, MPI predefines its data types.

Programmers may also create their own data types (derived types).

MPI types MPI_BYTE and MPI_PACKED do not correspond to standard C or FORTRAN types. Table 15.1 lists the MPI data types for both C and FORTRAN.

Destination: This is an argument to send routines which indicates the process where a message should be delivered. It is specified as the rank of the receiving process.

Source: For MPI_Recv, there is an argument source corresponding to a destination in MPI_Send. This is an argument to receive routines which indicates the originating process of the message. Specified as the rank of the sending process, it may be set to the wild card MPI_ANY_SOURCE to receive a message from any task.

Tag: An arbitrary, non-negative integer assigned by the programmer to uniquely identify a message. Send and receive operations should match message tags. For a receive operation, the wild card ANY TAG can be used to receive any message regardless of its tag. The MPI standard guarantees that integers from the range [0, 32767] can be used as tags, but most implementations allow a much larger range.

Communicator: Indicates the communication context, or set of processes for which the source or destination fields are valid. Unless the programmer is explicitly creating new communicators, the predefined communicator MPI_COMM_WORLD is usually employed.

Status: For a receive operation, this indicates the source of the message and the tag of the message. In C, this argument is a pointer to a predefined structure MPI_Status (ex. stat.MPI_SOURCE stat.MPI_TAG).

In FORTRAN, it is an integer array of size MPI_STATUS_SIZE (ex.stat(MPI_SOURCE) stat(MPI_TAG)). Additionally, the actual number of bytes received is obtainable from the status via the MPI_Get_count_routine.

TABLE 15.1
MPI Data Types

MPI C data types		MPI FORTRAN data types	
MPI_CHAR	signed char	MPI_CHARACTER	character(1)
MPI_SHORT	signed chort int		
MPI_INT	signed int	MPI_INTEGER	integer
MPI_LONG	signed long int		
MPI_UNSIGNED_CHAR	unsigned char		
MPI_UNSIGNED_SHORT	unsigned short int		
MPI_UNSIGNED	unsigned int		
MPI_UNSIGNED_LONG	unsigned int		
MPI_FLOAT	float	MPI_REAL	real
MPI_DOUBLE	double	MPI_DOUBLE_ PRECISION	double precision
MPI_LONG_DOUBLE	long double		
		MPI_COMPLEX	complex
		MPI_LOGICAL	logical
MPI_BYTE	8 binary digits data packed or unpacked with MPI_Pack()/ MPI_Unpack	MPI_BYTE	8 binary digits data packed or unpacked with MPI_Pack()/MPI_Unpack
MPI_PACKED		MPI_PACKED	

Request: This is used by non-blocking send and receive operations. Since non-blocking operations may return before the requested system buffer space is obtained, the system issues a unique "request number." The programmer uses this system-assigned "handle" later (in a WAIT type routine) to determine the completion of the non-blocking operation. In C, this argument is a pointer to a predefined-structure MPI_Request. In FORTRAN, it is an integer.

MPI_Recv

Receives a message and blocks until the requested data is available in the application buffer in the receiving task.

```
MPI_Recv(*buf,count,datatype,source,tag,comm,*status)
MPI_RECV(buf,count,datatype,source,tag,comm,status,ierr)
```

MPI_Ssend

Synchronous blocking send: Sends a message and blocks until the application buffer in the sending task is free for reuse and the destination process has started to receive the message.

```
MPI_Ssend(*buf,count,datatype,dest,tag,comm,ierr)
MPI_SSEND(buf,count,datatype,dest,tag,comm,ierr)
```

MPI_Bsend

Buffered blocking send: Permits the programmer to allocate the required amount of buffer space into which data can be copied until it is delivered. It insulates against the problems associated with insufficient system buffer space. Routine returns after the data has been copied from application buffer space to the allocated send buffer. This must be used with the MPI_Buffer_attach routine.

```
MPI_Bsend(*buf,count,datatype,dest,tag,comm)
MPI_BSEND(buf,count,datatype,dest,tag,comm,ierr)
```

MPI_Buffer attach, MPI_Buffer detach

This is used by the programmer to allocate/deallocate message buffer space to be used by the MPI_Bsend routine. The size argument is specified in actual data bytes—not a count of data elements. Only one buffer can be attached to a process at a time. Note that the IBM implementation uses MPI_BSEND_OVERHEAD bytes of the allocated buffer for overhead.

```
MPI_Buffer attach(*buffer,size)
MPI_Buffer detach(*buffer,size)
MPI_BUFFER ATTACH(buffer,size,ierr)
MPI_BUFFER DETACH(buffer,size,ierr)
```

MPI_Rsend

A blocking ready send should only be used if the programmer is certain that the matching receive has already been posted.

```
MPI_Rsend(*buf,count,datatype,dest,tag,comm)
MPI_RSEND(buf,count,datatype,dest,tag,comm,ierr)
```

MPI_Sendrecv

sends a message and posts a receive before blocking. This will block until the sending application buffer is free for reuse and until the receiving application buffer contains the received message.

```
MPI_Sendrecv(*sendbuf,sendcount,sendtype,dest,sendtag,
*recv buf,recvcount,recvtype,source,recvtag,comm,*status)
MPI_SENDRECV(sendbuf,sendcount,sendtype,dest,sendtag,
recvbuf,recvcount,recvtype,source,recvtag,comm,status,ierr)
```

MPI_Probe

performs a blocking test for a message. The "wild cards" MPI_ANY SOURCE and MPI_ ANY TAG may be used to test for a message from any source or with any tag. For the C routine, the actual source and tag will be returned in the status structure as status. MPI_SOURCE and status.MPI_TAG.

For the FORTRAN routine, they will be returned in the integer array status(MPI_ SOURCE) and status(MPI_TAG).

```
MPI_Probe(source,tag,comm,*status)
MPI_PROBE(source,tag,comm,status,ierr)
```

15.5.2 Non-blocking Message Passing Routines

The more commonly used MPI non-blocking message passing routines are described below.

MPI_Isend

This identifies an area in the memory that will serve as a send buffer. Processing continues immediately, without waiting for the message to be copied out from the application buffer. A communication request handle is returned for handling the pending message status. The program should not modify the application buffer until subsequent calls to MPI_Wait or MPI_Test indicate that the non-blocking send has completed.

```
MPI_Isend(*buf,count,datatype,dest,tag,comm,*request)
MPI_ISEND(buf,count,datatype,dest,tag,comm,request,ierr)
```

MPI_Irecv

This identifies an area in the memory that will serve as a receive buffer. Processing continues immediately, without actually waiting for the message to be received and copied into the application buffer. A communication request handle is returned for handling the pending message status. The program must use calls to MPI_Wait or MPI_Test to determine when the non-blocking receive operation completes and the requested message is available in the application buffer.

```
MPI_Irecv(*buf,count,datatype,source,tag,comm,*request)
MPI_IRECV(buf,count,datatype,source,tag,comm,request,ierr)
```

MPI_Issend

Non-blocking synchronous send. Similar to MPI_Isend(), except MPI Wait() or MPI_Test() indicates when the destination process has received the message.

```
MPI_Issend(*buf,count,datatype,dest,tag,comm,*request)
MPI_ISSEND(buf,count,datatype,dest,tag,comm,request,ierr)
```

MPI_Ibsend

A non-blocking buffered send that is similar to MPI_Bsend() except MPI_Wait() or MPI_Test() indicates when the destination process has received the message. It must be used with the MPI_Buffer attach routine.

```
MPI_Ibsend(*buf,count,datatype,dest,tag,comm,*request)
MPI_IBSEND(buf,count,datatype,dest,tag,comm,request,ierr)
```

MPI_Irsend

Non-blocking ready send is similar to MPI_Rsend() except MPI_Wait() or MPI_Test() indicates when the destination process has received the message. This function should only be used if the programmer is certain that the matching receive has already been posted.

```
MPI_Irsend(*buf,count,datatype,dest,tag,comm,*request)
MPI_IRSEND(buf,count,datatype,dest,tag,comm,request,ierr)
```

MPI_Test, MPI_Testany, MPI_Testall, MPI_Testsome

MPI_Test checks the status of a specified non-blocking send or receive operation. The "flag" parameter is returned as logical true (1) if the operation has completed, and as logical false (0) if not. For multiple non-blocking operations, the programmer can specify any, all, or some completions.

```
MPI_Test(*request,*flag,*status)
MPI_Testany(count,*array_of_requests,*index,*flag,*status)
MPI_Testall(count,*array_of_requests,*flag, *array_of_statuses)
MPI_Testsome(incount,*array_of_requests,*outcount, *array_of_offsets,
*array_of_statuses)
MPI_TEST(request,flag,status,ierr)
MPI_TESTANY(count,array_of_requests,index,flag,status,ierr)
MPI_TESTALL(count,array_of_requests,flag,array_of_statuses, ierr)
MPI_TESTSOME(incount,array_of_requests,outcount, Array_of_offsets,
array_of_statuses,ierr)
MPI_Wait, MPI_Waitany, MPI_Waitall, MPI_Waitsome
```

MPI_Wait blocks until a specified non-blocking send or receive operation has completed. For multiple non-blocking operations, the programmer can specify any, all, or some completions.

```
MPI_Wait(*request,*status)
MPI_Waitany(count,*array_of_requests,*index,*status)
MPI_Waitall(count,*array_of_requests,*array_of_statuses)
MPI_Waitsome(incount,*array_of_requests,*outcount,
*array_of_offsets,*array_of_statuses)
MPI_WAIT(request,status,ierr)
MPI_WAITANY(count,array_of_requests,index,status,ierr)
tt MPI_WAITALL(count,array_of_requests,array_of_statuses,ierr)
MPI_WAITSOME(incount,array_of_requests,outcount, Array_of_offsets,
array_of_statuses,ierr)
MPI_Iprobe
```

performs a non-blocking test for a message. The "wildcards" MPI_ANY_SOURCE and MPI_ANY_TAG may be used to test for a message from any source or with any tag. The integer "flag" parameter is returned as logical true (1) if a message has arrived, and as logical false (0) if not.

For the C routine, the actual source and tag will be returned in the status structure as status.MPI_SOURCE and status.MPI_TAG.

For the FORTRAN routine, they will be returned in the integer array status(MPI_SOURCE) and status(MPI_TAG).

```
MPI_Iprobe(source,tag,comm,*flag,*status)
MPI_IPROBE(source,tag,comm,flag,status,ierr)
```

15.6 Collective Communication Routines

Collective communication involves all processes in the scope of the communicator. All processes are, by default, members in the communicator MPI_COMM_WORLD.

There are three types of collective operations:

1. Synchronization: Processes wait until all members of the group have reached the synchronization point.
2. Data movement: Broadcast, scatter/gather, all to all.
3. Collective computation (reductions): One member of the group collects data from the other members and performs an operation (min, max, add, multiply, etc.) on that data.

Collective operations are blocking. Collective communication routines do not take message tag arguments. Collective operations within subsets of processes are accomplished by first partitioning the subsets into new groups and then attaching the new groups to new communicators. Finally, users should work with MPI defined datatypes—not with derived types.

15.6.1 Synchronization

MPI_Barrier

Creates a barrier synchronization in a group. Each task, when reaching the MPI_Barrier call, blocks until all tasks in the group reach the same MPI_Barrier call.

```
MPI_Barrier(comm)
MPI_BARRIER(comm,ierr)
```

15.6.2 Data Movement

MPI_Bcast

broadcasts (sends) a message from the process with rank "root" to all other processes in the group.

```
MPI_Bcast(*buffer,count,datatype,root,comm)
MPI_BCAST(buffer,count,datatype,root,comm,ierr)
```

MPI_Scatter

distributes distinct messages from a single source task to each task in the group.

```
MPI_Scatter(*sendbuf,sendcnt,sendtype,*recvbuf,ecvcnt, recvtype,root,comm)
MPI_SCATTER(sendbuf,sendcnt,sendtype,recvbuf,recvcnt, recvtype,root,
comm,ierr)
```

MPI_Gather

gathers distinct messages from each task in the group to a single destination task. This routine is the reverse operation of MPI_Scatter.

TABLE 15.2
The Predefined MPI Reduction Operations

MPI reduction operation		C data types	FORTRAN data types
MPI_MAX	maximum	integer, float	integer, real, complex
MPI_MIN	minimum	integer, float	integer, real, complex
MPI_SUM	sum	integer, float	integer, real, complex
MPI_PROD	product	integer, float	integer, real, complex
MPI_LAND	logical AND	integer	logical
MPI_BAND	bit-wise AND	integer, MPI_BYTE	integer, MPI_BYTE
MPI_LOR	logical OR	integer	logical
MPI_BOR	bit-wise OR	integer, MPI_BYTE	integer, MPI_BYTE
MPI_LXOR	logical XOR	integer	logical
MPI_BXOR	bit-wise XOR	integer, MPI_BYTE	integer, MPI_BYTE
MPI_MAXLOC	max value and location	float, double, long double	real, complex, double precision
MPI_MINILOC	min value and location	float, double, long double	real, complex, double precision

```
MPI_Gather(*sendbuf,sendcnt,sendtype,recvbuf,recvcount,
recvtype,root,comm)
MPI_GATHER(sendbuf,sendcnt,sendtype,recvbuf,recvcount,
recvtype,root,comm,ierr)
```

MPI_Allgather
Concatenation of data to all tasks in a group. Each task in the group, in effect, performs a one-to-all broadcasting operation within the group.

```
MPI_Allgather(*sendbuf,sendcount,sendtype,recvbuf,
recvcount,recvtype,comm)
MPI_ALLGATHER(sendbuf,sendcount,sendtype,recvbuf,
recvcount,recvtype,comm,info)
```

MPI_Reduce
applies a reduction operation on all tasks in the group and places the result in one task. See Table 15.2.
Users can also define their own reduction functions by using the MPI Op create route.

```
MPI_Reduce(*sendbuf,*recvbuf,count,datatype,op,root,comm)
MPI_REDUCE(sendbuf,recvbuf,count,datatype,op,root,comm,ierr)
```

MPI_reduction operations:

MPI_Allreduce
applies a reduction operation and places the result in all tasks in the group. This is equivalent to an MPI_Reduce followed by an MPI_Bcast.

```
MPI_Allreduce(*sendbuf,*recvbuf,count,datatype,op,comm)
MPI_ALLREDUCE(sendbuf,recvbuf,count,datatype,op,comm,ierr)
```

MPI_Reduce_scatter
first does an element-wise reduction on a vector across all tasks in the group. Next, the result vector is split into disjoint segments and distributed across the tasks. This is equivalent to an MPI_Reduce followed by an MPI_Scatter operation.

```
MPI_Reduce scatter(*sendbuf,*recvbuf,recvcount,datatype,op,comm)
MPI_REDUCE SCATTER(sendbuf,recvbuf,recvcount,datatype,op,comm,ierr)
```

MPI_Alltoall
Each task in a group performs a scatter operation, sending a distinct message to all the tasks in the group in order by index.

```
MPI_Alltoall(*sendbuf,sendcount,sendtype,*recvbuf,recvcnt,recvtype,comm)
MPI_ALLTOALL(sendbuf,sendcount,sendtype,recvbuf,recvcnt,recvtype,comm,
ierr)
```

MPI_Scan
performs a scan operation with respect to a reduction operation across a task group.

```
MPI_Scan(*sendbuf,*recvbuf,count,datatype,op,comm)
MPI_SCAN(sendbuf,recvbuf,count,datatype,op,comm,ierr)
```

15.7 Summary

This chapter introduced MPI. Message passing is largely the model of choice on MIMD computers with physically distributed memory because the close relationship between the model and the hardware architecture allows the programmer to write code in an optimal manner for the hardware. In addition, message-passing libraries are available on virtually all parallel systems, which makes this paradigm appealing to those who desire portability across a variety of machines. Message passing is currently the only practical choice for use across clusters of machines.

16

Stream Processing Programming with CUDA, OpenCL, and OpenACC

This chapter shows that while CUDA and OpenCL allow for (comparably) lower-level programming with management of computing devices, and explicit management of streams and queues respectively, OpenACC uses directives to point out sections of code that may include parallelism or point out specific constructs such as loops that may be parallelized.

In data streams–related data-parallel models, the execution of instructions in parallel is implicitly driven by the layout of the data structures in the memory. CUDA is both a parallel computing architecture and a programming model for high-performance computing; OpenCL is an open-source standard for general-purpose parallel programming of heterogeneous computing systems, and OpenACC is similar to OpenMP but targets acceleration devices such as GPUs.

16.1 CUDA

CUDA, a parallel programming model and software environment developed by Nvidia, enables programmers to write scalable parallel programs using a straightforward extension of C/C++ and FORTRAN languages for Nvidia's GPUs. A GPU consists of an array of streaming multi-processors (SMs). Each SM further consists of a number of streaming processors (SPs). The threads of a parallel program run on different SPs, and each SP has a local memory associated with it. Also, all the SPs in an SM communicate via a common shared memory provided by the SM. Different SMs access and share data among them by means of GPU DRAM, different from the CPU DRAM, which functions as the GPU main memory, called the global memory.

CPU (which has a smaller number of very powerful cores, aimed at minimizing the latency or the time taken to complete a task/thread) and GPU (which has thousands of less powerful cores, aimed at maximizing the throughput, that is, the number of parallel tasks/threads performed per unit time) are two separate processors with separate memories.

In CUDA terminology, CPU is called the host and GPU, where the parallel computation of tasks is done by a set of threads running in parallel, the device. A CUDA program consists of code that is executed on the host as well as code that is executed in the device, thus enabling heterogeneous computing (a mixed usage of both CPU and GPU computing).

The execution of a CUDA device program (parallel code or "kernel") involves the following steps:

1. (Device) global memory for the data required by the device is allocated.
2. Input data required by the program is copied from the host memory to the device memory.
3. The program is then loaded and executed on the device.

4. The results produced by the device are copied from the device memory to the host memory.
5. The memory on the device is deallocated.

The parts of the program that can be executed in parallel are defined using special functions called kernels, which are invoked by the CPU and run on the GPU. A kernel launches a large number of threads that execute the same code on different SPs, thus exploiting data parallelism.

The maximum number of threads that can be assigned to an SM is 1,536. The set of all threads launched by a kernel is called a grid. The kernel grid is divided into thread blocks with all thread blocks having an equal number of threads. There is a maximum number of threads that each thread block can support: Newer GPUs support 1,024 threads per block, while the older ones can only support 512. A maximum of 8 thread blocks can be executed simultaneously on an SM. A thread is the smallest execution unit of a program.

Each SM can execute one or more thread blocks; however, a thread block cannot run on multiple SMs. The grid is a set of loosely coupled thread blocks (expressing coarse-grained data parallelism), and a thread block is a set of tightly coupled threads (expressing fine-grained data/thread parallelism).

The hierarchical grouping of threads into thread blocks that form a grid has many advantages.

- Different thread blocks operate independently of each other. Hence, thread blocks can be scheduled in any order relative to each other (in serial or in parallel) on the SM cores. This makes CUDA architecture scalable across multiple GPUs that have different numbers of cores.
- Threads belonging to the same thread block are scheduled on the same SM concurrently. These threads can communicate with each other by means of the shared memory of the SM. Thus, only the threads belonging to the same thread block need to synchronize at the barrier. Different thread blocks execute independently and hence no synchronization is needed between them.

Once the execution of one kernel is completed, the CPU invokes another kernel for execution on the GPU. In newer GPUs (for example, Kepler), multiple kernels can be executed simultaneously (expressing task parallelism).

CUDA supports three special keywords for function declaration. These keywords are added before the normal function declaration and differentiate normal functions from kernel functions. They include:

__global__ keyword indicates that the function being declared is a kernel function which is to be called only from the host and is executed on the device.

__device__ keyword indicates that the function being declared is to be executed on the device and can only be called from a device.

__host__ keyword indicates that the function being declared is to be executed on the host.

Whenever a kernel is launched, the number of threads to be generated by the kernel is specified by means of its execution configuration parameters, including:

- *grid dimension,* defined as the number of thread blocks in the grid launched by the kernel, and
- *block dimension,* defined as the number of threads in each thread block.

Their values are stored in the predefined variables gridDim and blockDim respectively. They are initialized by the execution configuration parameters of the kernel functions. These parameters are specified in the function call between <<< and >>> after the function name and before the function arguments.

CUDA has certain built-in variables with pre-initialized values. These can be accessed directly in the kernel functions. Two such variables are threadIdx and blockIdx, representing the thread index in a block and the block index in a grid respectively. These keywords are used to identify and distinguish threads from one another. This is necessary since all the threads launched by a kernel need to operate on different data. Thus, by associating a unique thread identifier with each thread, the thread-specific data is fetched. gridDim and blockDim are also the pre-initialized CUDA variables.

The threads in a thread block are grouped into warps. The reason for grouping the threads into warps is to reduce the idle time a device spends waiting for memory access operations to get completed. For instance, if a memory read/write instruction is executed by a warp, the device, instead of waiting, immediately selects some other warp for execution. The overhead involved in switching from one warp to another is very minimal in GPUs and this is referred to as *zero-overhead thread scheduling.* The number of threads present in a warp depends upon the device. In CUDA devices, this is 32. All the threads in a warp are scheduled to be executed at the same time. These threads follow the SIMD execution model. The warps consist of threads with consecutive increasing ID values; for example, threads with threadIdx.x value between 0 and 31 will form one warp, threads between 32 and 63 will form a second warp, and so on.

A basic way to coordinate threads is by means of the barrier synchronization function, __syncthreads(). The threads of a block wait at the point in the program where __syncthreads() is used, and their execution is stalled till other threads reach the same point. Once all the block threads reach the barrier, they continue their execution. Note that __syncthreads() provides coordination among the threads belonging to the same block. As mentioned earlier, different thread blocks execute independently of each other and in random order, hence no synchronization is required between them.

16.2 OpenCL

OpenCL is a new, open standard for programming heterogeneous systems consisting of devices such as CPUs, GPUs, DSPs (digital signal processors), and FPGAs (field-programmable gate arrays), unlike CUDA which is proprietary to Nvidia GPUs. The standard, maintained by an industry consortium called Khronos Group (https://www.khronos.org/opencl/), enables programmers to write their application programs in C/C++ languages that execute on a wide variety of devices produced by different vendors, thereby achieving application code portability. It supports both data-parallel and task-parallel models of computing.

An OpenCL program has two parts:

1. Compute kernels, which are executed by one or more devices, and
2. A host program, which is executed by one CPU to coordinate the execution of these kernels.

Work-item, work-group, and NDRange in OpenCL correspond to thread, thread block, and grid in CUDA, respectively. The smallest unit of execution on a device is called *work-item*. A set of work-items that are executed simultaneously constitutes a *work-group*. The set of all work-groups that are invoked by the host constitutes an index space called NDRange (ndimensional range).

Synchronization among work-items belonging to the same work-group is realized by means of barriers that are equivalent to __syncthreads() in CUDA. NDRange and work-group sizes are specified as an array of type size_t and they can be specified.

The following are the typical steps in the host code to execute an OpenCL kernel:

1. Discover and select the OpenCL computing/target devices.
2. Create "context" (this defines the OpenCL environment in which work-items execute, which includes devices, their memories, and "command queues") and create "command queues" (in OpenCL, the host submits work, such as kernel execution and memory copy, to a device through a command queue).
3. Compile the OpenCL kernel program.
4. Create/allocate OpenCL device memory buffers.
5. Copy the host memory buffer to the device buffer.
6. Execute the OpenCL kernel.
7. Copy the results back to host memory.
8. Free memory on devices.

In OpenCL terminology, there is a distinction between hosts and devices. A host is any traditional CPU-based computer, and devices refer to an assortment of processors including CPU-based computers, GPGPUs, and the processors found on gaming devices. An OpenCL application consists of two types of code. The first is the normal C/C++ code that runs on a host computer—host application. The second type is referred to as a kernel, which is a specially coded function that is intended for execution on any OpenCL-compliant devices. Kernels are sent to their intended target devices by the host applications.

As a first step in developing OpenCL applications, users need to understand six fundamental *data structures*: *platform*, *device*, *context*, *program*, *kernel*, and *command queue*.

- Platform—defines the environment in which computations will take place. Specifically, a host may have one or more compute devices installed.
- Device—refers to a particular computing component on which computations will be executed. Each compute device consists of compute units, which in turn include processing elements. Compared to the CUDA terminology, compute device corresponds to device in CUDA; compute unit to streaming multi-processor, and processing element to streaming processor in CUDA.
- Context—defines a space in which kernels can be executed, and where it is possible to manage data and synchronize processing. It includes and refers to one or more devices.
- Program—an object representing a program that can be defined using source code. A program is created within a specified context.
- Kernel—defines a function code that can be executed in parallel by work items. The function is defined within a program that must have been created earlier.

- Command queue—represents a component that allows the submission of operations to a particular device for which the command queue is created. By default, commands submitted to a given queue will be performed in order. However, it is possible to specify out-of-order execution of commands. Commands submitted to a queue include launching a kernel (processing), writing and reading memory objects (such as for initialization of input data before processing on a device and fetching results), as well as synchronization of operations.
- Memory object—typically, in the context of GPGPU, buffers will be used for representation of data (either input, intermediate, or output) on which kernel functions will operate.
- Event—can be used for synchronization of invocations of OpenCL functions.

A parallel application in OpenCL has a structure similar to that found in Nvidia CUDA, but with different names of particular components. Specifically, the application grid is called "NDRange," and consists of blocks called "work groups," which in turn include "work items." Index spaces used for the arrangement of components of lower levels may be defined in one, two, or three dimensions. Each work item can be identified using a local ID within its work group and a global ID within NDRange. ID dimensions correspond to dimensions defined for a work group and for an NDRange respectively.

In terms of memory types defined within OpenCL, the following can be distinguished:

- Global memory—all work items can read and write locations of this memory. It can also be accessed by a host thread.
- Constant memory—visibility is as for the global memory. However, while this memory can be written to by a host, it can only be read from by work items.
- Local memory—accessible only to work items executing a kernel; space allocated within local memory can be shared by work items of one work group.
- Private memory—visibility such as local memory in CUDA.

A typical sequence of operations that are executed for parallel computations on a device in OpenCL includes:

1. Fetch a platform using a call to clGetPlatformIDs(…).
2. Find out devices (either all or devices of certain types, such as CPUs or GPUs, within a platform using a call to clGetDeviceIDs(…).
3. Create a context for a device(s) using clCreateContext(…).
4. Create a command queue on a device within a context using clCreateCommand QueueWithProperties(…).
5. Create a program within a context from sources given as input using clCreate ProgramWithSource(…).
6. Compile the program using clBuildProgram(…).
7. Allocate space for input/output data that will be used by a kernel—in case of buffers this can be done using calls to clCreateBuffer(…) within a context.
8. Select a kernel(s) within a program using clCreateKernel(…).
9. Set arguments to a kernel using function clSetKernelArg(…).

10. Write input data to input buffers (if necessary) using function clEnqueueWriteBuffer(...)—the function queues transfer into a command queue.
11. Queue the start of a kernel to a command queue using function clEnqueueNDRangeKernel(...).
12. Read output data from buffers using function clEnqueueReadBuffer(...)—the function queues transfer from a given buffer.
13. Finish computations with clFinish(...) on a command queue that blocks until the completion of the commands submitted to the queue.

For each data structure, two types of functions are provided. The functions in the first type are used to create the above data structures, and the ones in the second kind are used to retrieve information about the data structures.

a) Using clGetPlatformIDs() and the cl_platform_id data structure, you can query the number of OpenCL platforms available on a computing system and choose one or more of them to execute the OpenCL application. clGetPlatformInfo() describes the capabilities of the OpenCL version supported by the platform.

The following functions return a variable of type cl_int—a value equal to CL_SUCCESS in case of a successful call.

Function

```
cl_int clGetPlatformIDs(cl_uint numberofplatformentries,
cl_platform_id *platforms,
cl_uint *numberofplatformsreturned)
```

returns available platforms—the number of platforms can be limited to numberofplatformentries, which describes the maximum number of platforms that can be stored in platforms. The number of returned platforms is stored in a variable pointed at by numberofplatformsreturned.

Function:

```
cl_int clGetPlatformInfo(cl_platform_id platform,
cl_platform_info parametername,
size_t sizeofparametervalueinbytes,
void *pointertoparametervalue,
size_t *returnedsizeofparametervalueinbytes)
```

returns information about a platform—in particular involving a name (the parameter name should be CL_PLATFORM_NAME), version (the parameter name should be CL_PLATFORM_VERSION), or vendor (the parameter name should be CL_PLATFORM_VENDOR). In these cases, strings are returned. The actual meaning of the parameters is as follows:

- platform—the platform about which the call queries;
- parameternamethe name of a parameter as mentioned above;
- pointertoparametervalue—points to a space where a given value will be stored;
- sizeofparametervalueinbytes—the size of the space available, pointed by pointertoparametervalue;

- returnedsizeofparametervalueinbytes—the returned (actual) size of the value.

b) Given a platform ID, clGetDeviceIDs() is used to retrieve the devices available in the platform. The context data structure enables managing devices as a group. All the devices in a context must be provided by the same platform. However, a host application can manage devices using more than one context. Moreover, a host application can create multiple contexts from devices in a single platform.

function:

```
cl_int clGetDeviceIDs(cl_platform_id platform,
cl_device_type typeofdevice,
cl_uint numberofdeviceentries,
cl_device_id *devices,
cl_uint *numberofdevicesreturned)
```

where information about typeofdevice device types is queried on the given platform. Numberofdeviceentries denotes how many device IDs can be stored in devices. The number of returned devices is stored in a variable pointed at by numberofdevicesreturned.

Device types typically searched for include: all (CL_DEVICE_TYPE_ALL), CPUs (CL_DEVICE_TYPE_CPU), GPUs (CL_DEVICE_TYPE_GPU), and accelerators (CL_DEVICE_TYPE_ACCELERATOR).

function:

```
cl_int clGetDeviceInfo (cl_device_id device,
cl_device_info parametername,
size_t sizeofparametervalueinbytes,
void *pointertoparametervalue,
size_t *returnedsizeofparametervalueinbytes)
```

with the following parameters:

- device—the platform about which the call queries;
- parametername—the name of a parameter referring to a particular feature of the device;
- pointertoparametervalue—points to a space where a given value will be stored;
- sizeofparametervalueinbytes—the size of the space available, pointed to by pointerto parametervalue;
- returnedsizeofparametervalueinbytes— the returned (actual) size of the value.

c) The program data structure holds the source program, which is targeted for execution on the devices. The OpenCL function clBuildProgram() compiles the source program. The compiled program needs further preparation before dispatching to the devices (e.g., specifying arguments to kernel functions). The kernel data structure is used to specify the arguments. Finally, the command queue enables queuing and scheduling of OpenCL kernel code for execution on the devices. Command queue is a means for the host to convey to the devices what to compute. When a kernel is enqueued to a command queue, the device(s) will execute the kernel function.

Preparation of an application will typically involve specification of source code by stringcount strings, each with stringlengths characters (stringlengths[i] can be 0, which requires a corresponding "\0" terminated string), including kernel(s) with function:

```
cl_program
clCreateProgramWithSource(cl_context context,
cl_uint stringcount,
const char **strings,
const size_t *stringlengths,
cl_int *returnederrorcode)
```

compiling and linking program for numberofdevices listed in listofdevices (also can be NULL which builds for all devices associated with the sources) can be done in one step with function:

```
cl_int clBuildProgram(cl_program program,
cl_uint numberofdevices,
const cl_device_id *listofdevices,
const char *options,
void (CL_CALLBACK *functionpointertonotificationfunction)(
cl_program program,
void *notificationfunctiondata),
void *notificationfunctiondata)
```

The call is blocking when functionpointertonotificationfunction is NULL; otherwise it is asynchronous. Notificationfunctiondata is given as input to the callback function.

The creation of the kernelname kernel can be performed using the following function for the given program:

```
cl_kernel clCreateKernel(cl_program program,
const char *kernel_name,
cl_int *errcode_ret)
```

and subsequent allocation of buffersizeinbytes memory for a buffer:

```
cl_mem clCreateBuffer(cl_context context,
cl_mem_flags bufferflags,
size_t buffersizeinbytes,
void *hostbufferpointer,
cl_int *returnederrorcode)
```

with bufferflags specifying, in particular, access mode (read-write from the point of view of the kernel by default) to the buffer, such as

```
CL_MEM_WRITE_ONLY (write only from the point of view of the kernel),
CL_MEM_READ_ONLY (read only from the point of view of the kernel).
```

Setting kernel arguments can be done using one or more calls to function:

```
cl_int clSetKernelArg(cl_kernel kernel,
cl_uint argumentindex,
size_t argumentsize,
const void *argumentpointer)
```

where kernel identifies the kernel, argumentindex is the index of a given argument starting with 0, argumentsize denotes the size of the argument (such as the size of the buffer), and argumentpointer points at the input data that should be used for the argument (such as a pointer to a buffer).

An OpenCL program uses several qualifiers that denote the corresponding elements of a program:

- __kernel for annotating a kernel function;
- __global to denote a pointer to an element or an array in the global memory;
- __constant for annotating the constant memory;
- __local for denoting data in the local memory—can be used for a pointer in a kernel argument or within a kernel code at the function scope;
- __private denotes data in each work item scope— by default, variables without qualifiers in functions or function arguments are of this scope.

Pointers in kernel arguments must refer to data in local, global, or constant memory scopes.

There are several functions that allow to release previously allocated objects, returning CL_SUCCESS if they are finished without an error. Specifically, functions for releasing a kernel, a program, a memory object, a command queue, and a context actually decrease a counter referring to particular objects. If a respective counter reaches 0, then a given object is freed. The relevant functions include:

```
cl_int clReleaseKernel(cl_kernel kernel)
cl_int clReleaseProgram(cl_program program)
cl_int clReleaseMemObject(cl_mem memoryobject)
cl_int clReleaseCommandQueue(cl_command_queue commandqueue)
cl_int clReleaseContext(cl_context context)
```

16.2.1 Synchronization functions

In OpenCL, work items of a work group can synchronize using the following barrier function:

```
void barrier(cl_mem_fence_flags flags)
```

A barrier must be executed by all the work items of a work group. It is possible to specify synchronization of variables/memory fence on local or global memory if work items wish to use memory values after the barrier. This can be done using flags equal to CLK_LOCAL_MEM_FENCE or CLK_GLOBAL_MEM_FENCE respectively.

Synchronization in OpenCL is possible through events. Specifically, an event is associated with function calls that submit commands to command queues. The latter return an event object. Possible states of such commands include CL_QUEUED, CL_RUNNING, CL_COMPLETE, or a negative integer value in case of an error.

Specifically, the following synchronization functions are available:

1. The earlier-mentioned functions allowing the submission of operations to a command queue with optional synchronization—waiting for operations associated with events.

2. Waiting on the host side for events corresponding to certain commands to complete, using function:

```
cl_int clWaitForEvents(cl_uint numberofevents,
const cl_event *eventlist)
```

3. Submission of a marker command to a given queue—the function does not block processing, but waiting for the returned event allows waiting later (e.g., using clWaitForEvents(…)) for the specified events to finalize or, if no events have been specified, to wait for all the operations that have been submitted to the given queue so far.

```
clEnqueueMarkerWithWaitList(cl_command_queue commandqueue,
cl_uint numberofeventsinwaitlist,
const cl_event *eventwaitlist,
cl_event *event)
```

This function returns CL_SUCCESS in case of successful execution.

4. Submission of a barrier command to a given queue—commands submitted after this command will execute only after it has completed. Waiting for the returned event allows waiting later for the specified events to finalize or, if no events have been specified, waiting for all operations that have been submitted to the given queue. The function itself does not block the host.

```
cl_int
clEnqueueBarrierWithWaitList(cl_command_queue commandqueue,
cl_uint numberofeventsinwaitlist,
const cl_event *eventwaitlist,
cl_event *event)
```

This function returns CL_SUCCESS in case of successful execution.

5. cl_int clFinish(cl_command_queue commandqueue) —waits (blocks the host) until all commands submitted to a command queue have been finalized. The function returns CL_SUCCESS in case of successful execution.

16.3 OpenACC

At the level of API, OpenACC is similar to OpenMP, because it primarily uses directives to describe potential parallelism in a standard program. While CUDA and OpenCL allow for a (comparably) lower-level programming with management of computing devices and explicit management of streams and queues respectively, OpenACC uses directives to point out sections of code that may include parallelism or point out specific constructs, such as loops that may be parallelized. The OpenACC API specifies ways of expressing parallelism in C and Fortran codes, so that some computations can be offloaded to accelerators such as GPUs.

OpenACC allows three levels of parallelism through consideration and incorporation of:

- Gangs—a certain number of gangs
- Workers—each gang may run one or more workers.
- Vector lanes—each worker will have one or more vector lanes.

16.3.1 Common Directives

Typical constructs used to express parallelism within a C program with OpenACC are as follows:

a) Launching computations in parallel on an accelerator:

```
#pragma acc parallel
<block>
```

One or more gangs start the execution of the code within the block, with one worker per gang starting the execution. Similarly to OpenMP, iterations of loops within a parallel block can be processed in parallel.

Following the parallel keyword, several clauses can be specified. The most important clauses are as follows:

- private(varlist)—specifies that a private copy of each variable is created for every gang;
- firstprivate(varlist) —as in private, but additionally each variable on the list is initialized to the value of the thread before the construct;
- reduction(operator:varlist) —similarly to OpenMP, private copies for each gang are created and their results are merged into a final result. The latter can be used after the construct has been terminated;
- if(condition) —if the condition is true then the following block will be executed on a device, otherwise it will be executed by the original thread.

Furthermore, the configuration can be controlled using optional clauses such as:

- num_gangs(number) —specifies the number of gangs that are requested to execute the block (in reality, it may be lower).
- num_workers(number)—specifies the number of workers within a gang when multiple workers are used for execution (such as loop parallelization among workers).
- vector_length(number) —specifies the number of vector lanes used when parallelizing loops such that loops are assigned to vector lanes first (see below).

b) Marking a code region that may contain code which can be run as a sequence of kernels:

```
#pragma acc kernels
<block>
```

Parallelization of configurations (number of gangs, workers, and vectors) for kernels might differ. Clauses num_gangs(number), num_workers (number), and vector_length(number) can be used similarly as in the case of the parallel construct.

c) Marking a for loop for which parallel execution might be applied:

```
#pragma acc loop<loop>
```

The gang parameter specifies distribution of loop iterations for parallel execution among gangs.

The static:<sizeofchunk> keyword specifies a chunk size and round robin assignment of loop iterations.

The runtime system may select the chunk size if * to be used for the chunk size.

Furthermore, the worker keyword instructs the distribution of loop iterations among workers in a gang.

The vector keyword instructs the distribution of loop iterations among vector lanes.

The tile keyword instructs the conversion of a loop in a loop nest to two loops to exploit locality during computations.

The private(varlist) of a loop construct makes the specified variables private at the used parallelization level for the loop.

reduction(operator:varlist) will create private copies of the specified variables and merge values into a final value using the given operator.

16.3.2 Data Management

OpenACC considers two reference counts: structured incremented when entering a region and decremented upon exit, and, dynamic incremented for enter data and decremented for exit data clauses as described next.

There are several clauses referring to data management that may be used with kernels or parallel constructs:

- create(varlist) —allocates memory on a device if it does not exist; a reference count is increased. When exiting a region, the reference count is decreased;
- copy(varlist) —allocates memory on a device if it does not exist; a reference count is increased; and data is copied to the device. When exiting a region, the reference count is decreased. If both reference counts are equal to 0, then data is copied from the device to the host, and space on the device is freed;
- copyin(varlist) —similar to copy, but the data is not sent back to the host upon exiting a region;
- copyout(varlist) —similar to copy, but the data is not sent to the device when entering a region;
- present(varlist) —specifies that the data is present on a device; the reference count is incremented when entering a region and decremented upon exiting.

It is possible to use the following constructs:

a) Data construct that defines data management within a following block with the following syntax:

   #pragma acc data <clause>

   <block>

   where, in particular, the following clauses are allowed with the meaning described above: create, copy, copyin, copyout, and present.

b) Enter data for definition of data on a device until exit data is stated or a program exits. Specifically, the syntax is as follows:

   #pragma acc enter data <clause>

   where a clause can be, in particular, create, copyin, if.

Similarly, the following can be used at exit:

```
#pragma acc exit data <clause>
```

where a clause can be, in particular, copyout, delete, if.

OpenACC allows the expression of operations to be atomic in order to avoid issues resulting from races. Specifically, the syntax is as follows:

```
#pragma acc atomic <clause>
```

<expression>

where a clause can be one of the following referring to a variable being accessed: read, write, update (increments, decrements, binary operations), capture (update with a read).

16.3.3 Asynchronous Processing and Synchronization

OpenACC allows the use of an async clause, especially in the parallel and kernels constructs but also, in particular, in enter data and exit data constructs. Without it, the execution of corresponding blocks would block the initiating thread until the execution finishes.

With async(intargument), a block would be able to execute asynchronously with respect to the initiating thread. The argument is used to identify a queue on a device to which execution will be submitted, if the device supports multiple queues.

Correspondingly, a wait clause can be used in the parallel and kernels constructs, but also, in particular, in enter data and exit data constructs. By default, the execution of corresponding blocks starts the execution at once. The wait clause with an argument such as that used in async clauses can be used to force waiting with execution until corresponding computations (identified by the argument) are completed.

16.3.4 Device Management

An OpenACC runtime library allows the management and use of several devices.

Among many functions of the library, the following ones can be employed for this purpose:

To set the type of a device to be used

- void acc_set_device_type(acc_device_t devicetype)

To set the active device (number) of the given type

- void acc_set_device_num(int devicenumber,
- acc_device_t devicetype)

To obtain the number of available devices of the given type

- int acc_get_num_devices(acc_device_t devicetype)

16.4 Summary

This chapter described data streams–related data-parallel models where the execution of instructions in parallel is implicitly driven by the layout of the data structures in the memory. CUDA is both a parallel computing architecture and a programming model for high-performance computing; OpenCL is an open-source standard for general-purpose parallel programming of heterogeneous computing systems; and OpenACC is similar to OpenMP but targets acceleration devices such as GPUs.

This chapter showed that while CUDA and OpenCL allow for (comparably) lower-level programming with management of computing devices, and explicit management of streams and queues respectively, OpenACC uses directives to point out sections of code that may include parallelism or point out specific constructs such as loops that may be parallelized.

Section V

Internet of Things Big Data Stream Processing

This section covers the components of an IoT (Internet of Things) big data stream processing system. Chapters 17 through 20 explain the corresponding technologies of IoT, sensor data processing, big data computing, and stream processing.

Chapter 17 introduces IoT, enabled primarily by the availability of cloud and big data technologies. Subsequenly, it describes radio frequency identification (RFID), a wireless automatic identification technology whereby an object with an attached RFID tag is identified by an RFID reader. Following this, the main concept is introduced: Wireless sensor network technology enabled by the availability of smaller, cheaper, and intelligent sensors that have important applications, such as remote environmental monitoring.

Chapter 18 starts with a discussion of sensor data-gathering and data-dissemination mechanisms. The main purpose of a sensor database system is to facilitate the data-collection process. Data fusion can be performed with different objectives such as inference, estimation, feature maps, aggregation, abstract sensors, classification, and compression. Techniques, methods, and algorithms used to fuse data can be classified based on several criteria, such as data abstraction level, parameters, mathematical foundation, purpose, and type of data.

Chapter 19 describes the characteristic features of big data systems, including volume, velocity, variety, and veracity of big data. This chapter explores the challenges of big data computing: Managing and processing exponentially growing data volumes, significantly reducing associated data analysis cycles to support practical, timely applications, and developing new algorithms that can scale to search and process massive amounts of data. The chapter ends by describing an overview of major classes of Not only SQL (NoSQL) databases, namely, column-oriented stores, key-value stores, documented-oriented databases, and graph-databases.

Chapter 20 provides an overview of several stream processing system implementations. It describes academic or research prototype systems such as

TelegraphCQ, STREAM, Aurora, Borealis, IBM SYSTEM S and IBM SPADE. It describes open-source systems such as Apache Storm, Yahoo! S4, Apache Samza, and Apache Streaming. In addition, it describes commercial systems such as Streambase, IBM InfoSphere Streams, TIBCO BusinessEvents, and Oracle CEP.

17

Internet of Things (IoT) Technologies

A single smart device (e.g., in a refrigerator) will communicate to a router installed in the house or with a cellular tower, and the same thing will happen for similar devices installed in other equipment and places. But in places where a large number of these devices are used, an aggregation point might be required to collect the data and then send it to a remote server. Examples of such deployment can be industrial process control, monitoring of utilities supply lines—such as oil pipelines or water sewage lines, and product supply chain in a warehouse or in a secured area.

IoT refers to a network of inter-connected things, objects, or devices on a massive scale connected to the Internet. These objects, being smart, sense their surroundings, and gather and exchange data with other objects. Based on the gathered data, the objects make intelligent decisions, such as triggering an action or sending data to a server over the Internet, then waiting for its decision. The most common nodes in IoT are:

- Sensors used in many areas from industrial process control.
- Sensors used inside ovens and refrigerators.
- RFID chips used as tags in many products of everyday use.

Almost all of these smart devices have a short communication range and require very little power to operate. Bluetooth and IEEE ZigBee are the most common communication technologies used in this regard.

Just like the Internet and Web connect humans, IoT is a revolutionary way of architecting and implementing systems and services based on evolutionary changes. The Internet as we know it is transforming radically, from being an academic network in the 1980s and early 1990s to a mass-market, consumer-oriented network. Now, it is set to become fully pervasive, connected, interactive, and intelligent. Real-time communication is possible not only for humans but also for things at any time and from anywhere.

It is quite likely that sooner or later most items connected to the Internet will not be humans, but things. IoT will primarily expand communication from the 7 billion people around the world to the estimated 50–70 billion machines. This would result in a world where everything is connected and can be accessed from anywhere—it has the potential to connect the 100 trillion things that are deemed to exist on Earth. With the advent of IoT, the physical world itself will become a connected information system. In the world of IoT, sensors and actuators embedded in physical objects are linked through the wired and wireless networks that connect the Internet. These information systems churn out huge volumes of data that flow to computers for analysis. When objects can both sense the environment and communicate, they become tools for understanding the complexity of the real world and responding to it swiftly.

The increasing volume, variety, velocity, and veracity of the data produced by IoT will continue to fuel the explosion of data for the foreseeable future. With estimates ranging from 16 to 50 billion Internet-connected devices by 2020, the hardest challenge for large-scale, context-aware applications and smart environments is to tap into disparate and ever-growing data streams originating from everyday devices, and to extract hidden but relevant and meaningful information and hard-to-detect behavioral patterns out of them. To reap the full benefits, any successful solution to build context-aware data-intensive applications and services must be able to make this valuable or important information transparent and available at a much higher frequency, in order to substantially improve the decision making and prediction capabilities of the applications and services.

17.1 Introduction to IoT

IoT was originally introduced by the Auto-ID research centre at the MIT (Massachusetts Institute), where an important effort was made on the unique identification of products named EPC (electronic product code). This was then commercialized by EPCglobal, which was created to follow the AutoID objectives in the industry, with EAN.UCC (European Article Numbering—Uniform Code Council), now called GS1, as a partner to commercialize Auto-ID research, mainly the electronic product code.

IoT aims to integrate, collect information from, and offer services to, a very diverse spectrum of physical things used in different domains. "Things" are everyday objects for which IoT offers a virtual presence on the Internet, allocates a specific identity and virtual address, and adds capabilities to self-organize and communicate with other things without human intervention. To ensure high-quality services, additional capabilities can be included, such as context awareness, autonomy, and reactivity.

Very simple things, like books, can have RFID tags that help tracking them without human intervention. For example, in an electronic commerce system, a RFID sensor network can detect when a thing left the warehouse and trigger specific actions, such as inventory updates or customer rewarding for buying a high-end product. RFIDs enable the automatic identification or things, the capture of their context (for example the location), and the execution of corresponding actions if necessary. Sensors and actuators are used to transform real things into virtual objects with digital identities. In this way, things may communicate, interfere, and collaborate with each other over the Internet.

Adding part of application logic to things transforms them into smart objects, which have additional capabilities in order to sense, log, and understand the events occurring in the physical environment, autonomously react to context changes, and intercommunicate with other things and people. A tool endowed with such capabilities is able to register when and how the workers used it and produce a financial cost figure. Similarly, smart objects used in the e-health domain could continuously monitor the status of a patient and adapt the therapy according to the needs. Smart objects also include general-purpose portable devices such as smart phones and tablets, which have processing and storage capabilities, and are endowed with different types of sensors for time, position, temperature, etc. Both specialized and general-purpose smart objects have the capability to interact with people.

IoT includes a hardware, software, and services infrastructure for things networking. IoT infrastructure is event-driven and real-time, supporting the context sensing, processing, and exchange with other things and the environment. The infrastructure is very complex due to the huge number (50–100 trillion) of heterogeneous, (possibly) mobile things that dynamically join and leave IoT, and generate and consume billions of parallel and simultaneous events geographically distributed all over the world. The complexity is augmented by the difficulty to represent, interpret, process, and predict the diversity of possible contexts. The infrastructure must have important characteristics such as reliability, safety, survivability, security, and fault tolerance. Also, it must manage communication, storage, and compute resources.

The main function of the IoT infrastructure is to support communication among things (and other entities such as people, applications, etc.) This function must be flexible and adapted to a large variety of things, from simple sensors to sophisticated smart objects. More specifically, things need a communication infrastructure that is low-data-rate, low-power, and low-complexity. Actual solutions are based on short-range radio frequency (RF) transmissions in ad-hoc wireless personal area networks (WPANs). A main concern for IoT infrastructure developers is supporting heterogeneous things by adopting appropriate standards for the physical and media access control (MAC) layers, and for communication protocols. The protocol and compatible inter-connection for the simple wireless connectivity with relaxed throughput (2–250 kb/s), low range (up to 100 m), moderate latency (10–50 ms) requirements, and low cost, adapted to devices previously not connected to the Internet, were defined in IEEE 802.15.4. The main scope of IoT specialists is the world-wide network of inter-connected virtual objects uniquely addressable and communicating through standard protocols. The challenge here is coping with a huge number of (heterogeneous) virtual objects.

Table 17.1 presents a comparison of conventional Internet with IoT.

The characteristics of successful IoT deployments are:

- Distributivity: IoT will likely evolve in a highly distributed environment. In fact, data might be gathered from different sources and processed by several entities in a distributed manner.
- Interoperability: Devices from different vendors will have to cooperate in order to achieve common goals. In addition, systems and protocols will have to be

TABLE 17.1

Comparison of Conventional Internet and IoT

	Internet	IoT
1	In the Internet, end-nodes are full computers ranging from workstations to smart phones, with regular access to public power-supply networks.	In IoT, end-nodes are very small electronic devices with low energy consumption. Compared to Internet computers, their functionality is limited and they cannot interact directly with humans.
2	In the Internet, the number of connected devices is envisaged to be in billions.	In IoT, the number of connected devices is envisaged to be in trillions.
3	In the Internet, not only the long-distance connection but also the last-mile connection has become very fast (in the range of megabits/sec).	In IoT, the speed of the last mile to an RFID tag is quite slow (in the range of kilobits/sec).
4	In the Internet, there are globally accepted identification and address schemes (e.g., IP and MAC addresses).	In IoT, such standards cannot be employed by devices because they require too much energy. Many vendor-specific solutions exist, but they prevent objects from being globally identified and addressed.
5	In the Internet, the major share of functionality is addressed to human users such as the WorldWideWeb (www), e-mail, chat, and e-commerce.	In IoT, devices usually interact directly, not via human intervention.
6	Internet enabled a breakthrough in human communication and interaction.	IoT enabled a breakthrough in sensing the physical environment; sensing enables measurement, which in turn enables management.

designed in a way that allows objects (devices) from different manufacturers to exchange data and work in an interoperable way.

- Scalability: In IoT, billions of objects are expected to be part of the network. Thus, systems and applications that run on top of them will have to manage this unprecedented amount of generated data.
- Resources scarcity: Both power and computation resources will be highly scarce.
- Security: Users' feelings of helplessness and being under some unknown external control could seriously hinder IoT's deployment.

17.1.1 IoT Building Blocks

The IoT architecture supports the integration of physical things in the Internet and the complex interaction flow of services triggered by the occurrence of events. The main concepts involved in the basis for the development of independent cooperative services and applications are:

1. Sensing technologies: RFID and Wireless Sensor Networks (WSNs) are the two main building blocks of sensing and communication technologies for IoT. However, these technologies suffer from different constraints (e.g., energy limitation, reliability of wireless medium, security and privacy, etc.) In particular, the scarcity of energy resources available in the embedded devices is a sensitive issue. Consequently, to increase energy efficiency, a number of solutions have been introduced in the literature. For instance, lightweight MAC protocols, energy-efficient routing protocols, and tailored security protocols have been proposed to mitigate the impact of the scarcity of resources on sensing technologies. Nevertheless, their limited autonomy remains a considerable obstacle to their widespread deployment into our daily lives.

   i) Radio-frequency identification (RFID): RFID is a tiny microchip (e.g., 0.4 mm×0.4 mm×0.15 mm) attached to an antenna (called "tags"), which is used for both receiving the reader signal and transmitting the tag identity, which can be appended to an object of our daily life. Like an electronic barcode, the data stored in these tags can automatically be used to identify and extract useful information about the object. RFID devices are classified into two categories: passive and active. The passive RFID tags are not battery-powered; they use the power of the readers' interrogation signal to communicate their data. They are also used in bank cards and road toll tags as a means to control access; and in many retail, supply-chain management, and transportation applications.

   ii) Wireless Sensor Networks (WSNs): WSN, along with RFID, systems enable to better track the status of things (e.g., their location, temperature, movements, etc.) Sensor networks consist of a large number of sensing nodes communicating in a wireless multi-hop fashion, reporting their sensing results into a small number of special nodes called "sinks" (or basestations).

   The main areas of concern are as follows:

   - Energy efficiency (which is a limited resource in WSNs).
   - Scalability (the number of nodes can rise significantly).
   - Reliability (the system might be involved in critical applications).
   - Robustness (the nodes might be subject to failure).

iii) Integration: Integration of heterogeneous technologies, like sensing technologies into passive RFID tags, would bring completely new applications into the context of IoT. Sensing RFID systems will allow to build RFID sensor networks, which consist of small RFID-based sensing and computing devices. RFID readers would constitute the sinks of data generated by sensing RFID tags. Moreover, they would provide the power for the different network operations. Efficiently networking tag readers with RFID sensors would allow real-time queries on the physical world leading to better forecasts, new business models, and improved management techniques.

2. Compute technologies: The middleware is a software interface between the physical layer (i.e., hardware) and the application layer. It provides the required abstraction to hide the heterogeneity and the complexity of the underlying technologies involved in the lower layers. Indeed, the middleware is essential to spare both users and developers from the exact knowledge of the heterogeneous set of technologies adopted by the lower layers. The service-based approaches lying on a cloud infrastructure open the door to highly flexible and adaptive middleware for IoT.

   Decoupling the application logic from the embedded devices, and moving it to the cloud, will allow developers to provide applications for the heterogeneous devices that will compose the future IoT environment. It is possible to create a set of sensor services to be exploited in different applications for different users through the cloud. A sensor-cloud infrastructure provides to the end user service instances based on virtual sensors in an automatic way.

3. Actuate technologies: IoT enhances the passive objects around us with communication and processing capabilities to transform into pervasive objects. However, this can only be realised with corresponding physical support. Cloud-robotics abstracts robotic functionalities and provides a means for utilizing them. Various types of equipment and devices, such as individual robots, sensors, and smart phones, which can measure the world or interact with people in both the physical and digital worlds, are treated uniformly. These robots are logically gathered to form a cloud of robots by networking.

Single-board computers (SBCs) are the main IoT hardware components for acquiring and presenting indoor information from its surroundings by sensors, either embedded in them/or connected to them. They consist of a single-circuit board memory and a processor. Most SBCs have I/O interfaces where different kinds of sensors can be plugged in: These computers usually do not have extension slots like regular PCs, and the processors used in them are usually of low cost. The size of these devices ranges from a matchbox to a playing card. Some of them have USB and memory card interfaces. SBCs can run versions of embedded Linux and even Windows, while some only have programmable microprocessors that provide output to their proprietary workbench. There are more than 20 different types of SBCs, including:

- Arduino Development Boards
- BeagleBoard
- Raspberry Pi
- Orange Pi

17.1.2 IoT Architecture

IoT connects a large number of "smart" objects, each of them possessing a unique address. This creates a huge amount of traffic and therefore the demand for large volumes of computational power and huge data storage capabilities. Additional challenges arise in the areas of scalability, interoperability, security, and quality of service (QoS).

Figure 17.1 shows the IoT architecture.

The envisaged architecture consists of what follows:

1. The perception layer is the lowest layer in the IoT architecture, and its purpose is to perceive the data from the environment and identify objects or things.

   This layer consists of the physical objects and all the sensor devices. These devices can be RFID, barcodes, infrared sensors, embedded sensors, and actuator nodes. In this layer, the information is gathered and categorized. Firstly, the physical properties of each object (such as location, orientation, temperature, motion, etc.) are perceived. However, in order to successfully perceive the desired properties, most objects need to have appropriate microchips installed in them that sense the desired information and perform preliminary processing to convert it into corresponding digital signals. These are used by the next layer for network transmission.
2. The network layer is like the network and transport layers of the OSI model. It collects the data from the perception layer and sends it to the Internet. The network layer may only include a gateway, having one interface connected to the sensor network and another to the Internet. In some scenarios, it may include a network management centre or information processing centre.

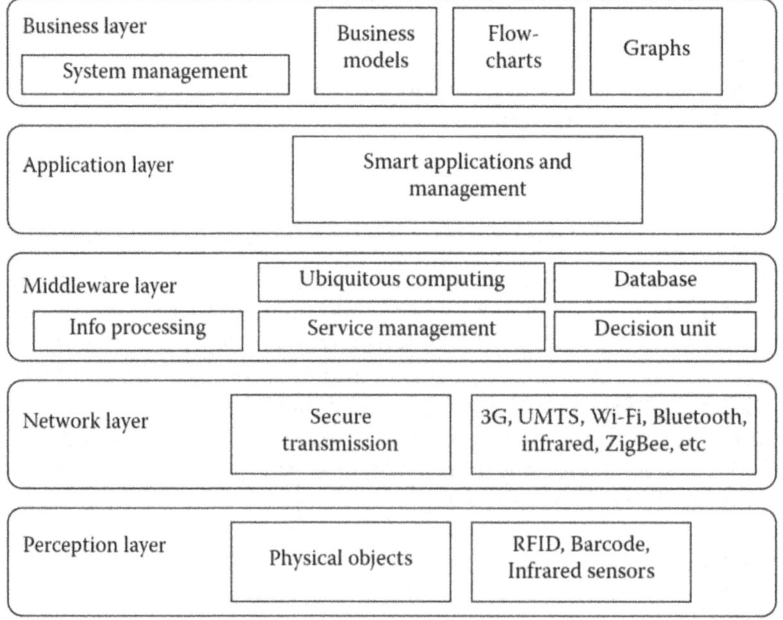

FIGURE 17.1
IoT architecture.

The main role of this layer is to securely transfer the information gathered by the sensor devices to the processing centre of the system. The transmission is possible through all the common mediums, such as the wireless network, the cable network, and even LANs (local area networks). The different communication technologies and protocols enabling this transfer include 3G/4G cellular networks as well as Wi-Fi (Wireless Fidelity), Bluetooth, ZigBee, Infrared, etc. This layer also includes several protocols such as IPv6 (Internet Protocol version 6), whose responsibility is the proper IP addressing of the objects.

3. The middleware layer receives data from the network layer. Its purpose is service management, storing data, performing information processing, and taking decisions based on the results automatically. It then passes the output to the next layer—the application layer.

   The middleware layer or "processing" layer is considered as the core layer of the IoT system. Initially, all the information received from the network layer is stored in the system's database. Furthermore, the information is analyzed and processed, and, based on the results, appropriate automated decisions are taken. This layer is also responsible for the service management of the devices. Since each IoT device implements specific types of services, this layer helps in the management of all the different services of the system, by deciding which devices should connect and communicate in order to provide the optimum requested service results.

4. The application layer performs the final presentation of data. This layer receives information from the middleware layer and provides global management of the application presenting that information, based on the information processed by the middleware layer. According to the needs of the user, the application layer presents the data in the form of: smart city, smart home, smart transportation, vehicle tracking, smart farming, smart health, and many other kinds of applications.

   The role of this layer is very important since it practically supports the applications envisaged by different industries. The applications implemented by IoT cover a huge area of technology fields, such as healthcare, intelligent transportation, smart home, smart cities, supply chains, and logistics management.

5. The business layer is all about making money from the service being provided. Data received at the application layer is molded into a meaningful service and then further services are created from the existing services. Based on the analysis of the results of the above, users can determine their business strategies and future actions.

   The business layer is responsible for managing the higher level of the IoT system, mainly the applications and their services to the users. Unless IoT can provide efficient and effective business models to the users, its long-term use and development won't be feasible. Finally, another task of this layer is managing the issues related to users' privacy and security of .

17.1.3 Widened Address Space with IPv6

Like the uniform resource locators (URLs) used by Web applications and HTTP, network layer protocols, such as IP, use network layer addresses such as IP addresses (for example, 124.65.120.43.) For a network node to forward packets to their destinations, it is necessary that both source and destination computers have unique addresses. In the Internet, these addresses are known as IP addresses or the Internet addresses. The Internet Corporation for Assigning Names and Numbers (ICANN) and numerous private companies/organizations that are authorized by ICANN manage IP addresses and domain names. IP addresses are assigned typically in groups when the domain names are registered. In IPv4, the source and destination IP addresses are indicated in a packet by a 4-byte (32-bit) field each. The IP address example shown above is called *dotted decimal notation*, where a decimal number corresponding to each byte, rather than a binary number, is shown for human use only. Based on the so-called "classful addressing scheme," ICANN assigns the IP addresses in "classes," varying the size of the address pool, depending on the size of the organization. This is an inefficient and wasteful assignment, which results in a shortage of IP addresses to be assigned to new entrants into the network.

IPv6 uses a 128-bit (16-byte) field, allowing an extremely large number (2^{128}) of IP addresses to be assigned. IPv6 does not use dotted decimal notation; instead, it relies on a hexadecimal colon notation to make the addresses more readable. An IPv6 address consists of 32 hexadecimal digits grouped into four and separated by a colon. The following is an example of an IPv6 address:

F45A:B2C4:04C5:0043:ADB0:0000:0039:FFEF

Figure 17.2 shows formats of IPv4 and IPv6 messages. Table 17.2 shows a comparison between IPv4 and IPv6.

Once an organization obtains a range of IP addresses, it is its responsibility to assign specific IP addresses to its computers within its private network. Various techniques,

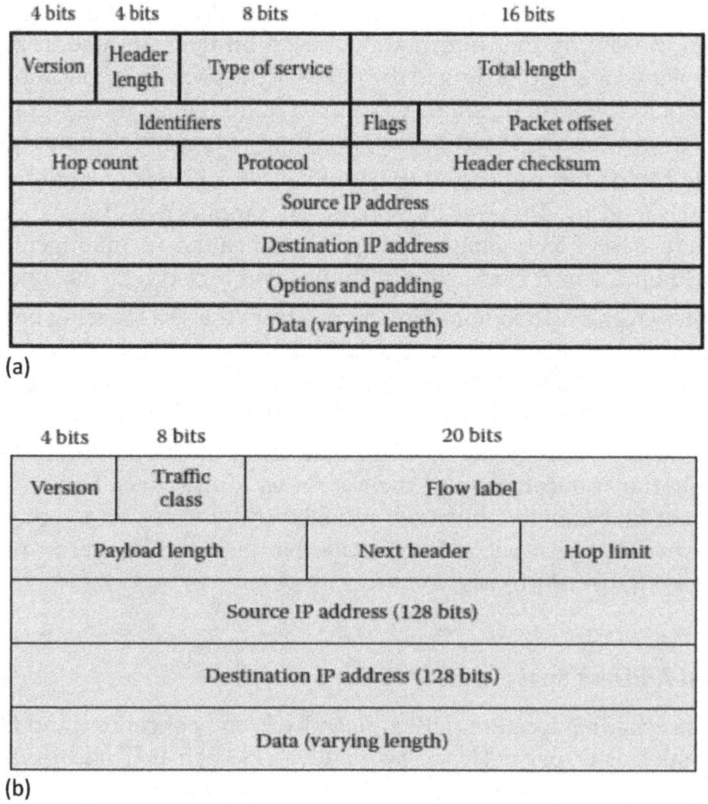

4 bits 4 bits 8 bits 16 bits
Version
Header length
Type of service
Total length
Identifiers
Flags
Packet offset
Hop count
Protocol
Header checksum
Source IP address
Destination IP address
Options and padding
Data (varying length)
(a)

4 bits 8 bits 20 bits
Version
Traffic class
Flow label
Payload length
Next header
Hop limit
Source IP address (128 bits)
Destination IP address (128 bits)
Data (varying length)
(b)

FIGURE 17.2
(a) Format of IPv4 messages (b) Format of IPv6.

TABLE 17.2

Comparison of IPv4 and IPv6

Feature	IPv4	IPv6
Packet header	Variable size (40+ bytes), complex	Fixed size (32 bytes), simple
Address field	32 bits (4 bytes) resulting in over 109 possible addresses	128 bits (16 octets) resulting in 1,038 possible addresses
Address allocation	Classful: Network classes A, B, C CIDR: Stopgap measure to deal with address space limitation	Hierarchical by registry, provider, subscriber, and subnet Hierarchical by geographic region IPv4 compatibility
Address notation (numeric)	Dotted decimal notation	Hexadecimal with colons and abbreviations IPv4 addresses a special case
Quality of service	Defined but not generally used consistently	Support for real-time data and multimedia distribution Flow labeling Priority
Security	No IP-level authentication or encryption	Authentication (validation of packet origin) Encryption (privacy of contents)
	Relies on other protocols	Requires administration of "security associations" to handle key distribution, etc.

including manual, centralized, automated, or a combination of them, may be used for this purpose. The most common technique is called subnetting. A group of computers on a LAN may be given a group of IP addresses with the same prefix, which is called "subnet address." Subnet addresses make it easier to separate the subnet part of the address from the host part. By applying a corresponding subnet mask, a router/gateway can easily determine whether the packets stay in the same subnet or go outside of the subnet.

The assignment of an IP address to an individual computer can be permanent or temporary. Typically, the computers providing server functions have permanent IP addresses. Also, ISPs assign IP addresses permanently to broadband modems. However, almost all client computers in an enterprise lack permanent IP addresses. Once a range of IP addresses is allocated to a subnet, the assignment of individual IP addresses to individual computers is usually performed dynamically via a Dynamic Host Control Protocol (DHCP) server. This eliminates the tedious task of assigning addresses manually to every client computer in the network. When a computer connected to the subnet is turned on, it communicates with a DHCP server requesting an IP address (along with the subnet mask and gateway address). The server, from the existing pool, determines an available IP address and assigns it to this computer. When the computer is turned off, the IP address is returned to the pool and may be assigned to some other computers. There is no guarantee that the same IP will be assigned to the same computer the following time.

As discussed above, the application layer protocols typically use application layer addresses involving domain names. But the network layer operates on the IP addresses. Therefore, a mechanism is needed to translate between the domain name–based application layer addresses and the IP addresses. This is called "address resolution" and is performed via the Domain Name System (DNS). DNS is a set of distributed and hierarchical directories that contain the mappings of the IP addresses to the domain names. ICANN maintains the root DNS directories for root domains such as .com and .org. Then, each individual organization maintains at least one DNS directory for their domains and subdomains. Smaller organizations rely on their ISPs to provide this service. Furthermore, each computer maintains a local directory to keep track of the IP addresses used and the corresponding application layer addresses, so that the next time the user tries to exchange information with an application, the computer can easily determine the corresponding IP address by looking it up in its local directory without polling an external DNS server.

Appendix 17.A gives a description of Internet of Things (IoT) in 5G mobile technologies.

17.2 RFID (Radio Frequency Identification)

RFID, also known as radio frequency identification, is a form of auto ID (automatic identification), i.e., the "identification of an object with minimal human interaction". Barcodes identify items through the encoding of data in various sized bars using a variety of symbologies, or coding methodologies. The most familiar type of barcode is the universal product code (UPC), which provides manufacturer and product identification. While barcodes have proven to be very useful, and indeed, have become an accepted part of product usage and identity, there are limitations with the technology. Barcode scanners must have line of sight in order to read barcode labels. Label information can be easily compromised by dirt, dust, or rips. Barcodes take up a considerable footprint on product labels. Even the newer barcode symbologies, such as 2D, or two-dimensional, which can store a significant amount of data in a very small space, remain problematic.

The limitations of barcodes are overcome through the use of RFID labeling to identify objects. While using RFID, since the data is exchanged using radio waves, it is not necessary to have line of sight between a reader and a tag. This permits a great deal more flexibility in the use of RFID. RFID was first employed commercially in the 1960s by companies that developed security-related devices called "electronic article surveillance (EAS) equipment." Although EAS could only present the detection or absence of a tag, the tags were low cost and provided valuable deterrents to theft.

The mining industry was an early adopter of RFID technology. In mining, RFID tags were used to validate the correct movement of haulage vehicles. These vehicles have read-only tags permanently attached to their dump beds. As a vehicle approaches a dump area, a reader validates the fact that it is approaching the correct dump bed. Information concerning the transaction, including the vehicle number, the weight of the vehicle before and after the dump, and the time, are recorded automatically. Using RFID obviates the need for human interaction between the scales operator and the vehicle driver.

The radio frequency transmissions in RFID travel between the two primary components:

- An RFID reader can be mobile or stationary, consists of an antenna and a transceiver, is supplied with power, and generates and transmits a signal from its antenna to the tag, then reads the information reflected from the tag. The antenna is used to send and receive signals; the transceiver is used to control and interpret the signals sent and received.
- An RFID tag, a transponder, consists of three components: antenna, silicon chip, and substrate or encapsulation material. The antenna is used for receiving and transmitting radio frequency waves to and from the reader. The chip contains information

pertaining to the item tagged, such as part number and manufacturer. Chips can be either read-only or read-write; the costs are higher for the read-write chips. There is a crucial difference between read-only chips and read-write chips. Read-only chips are essentially electronic barcodes. Once the data has been encoded onto the chip, it cannot be modified and, therefore, cannot transmit information about the product as it moves through a sequence of events. The tag is affixed to the object being identified, such as an automobile, a shipping pallet, or a tagged marine mammal.

The portion of the electromagnetic spectrum used by radio frequency identification includes LF (low frequency), HF (high frequency), and UHF (ultra-high frequency), which are all portions of the radio wave frequency bands, hence the term "radio frequency identification." An advantage of radio waves over visible light is that they can penetrate many substances that would block visible light. Radio waves range from 300 kHz to 3 GHz.

Electromagnetic waves are comprised of a continuum of emanations, including visible light waves, and invisible frequencies such as television and radio waves, which are lower frequency than light, and X-rays and gamma rays, which are higher frequency than light.

The range over which devices using radio waves can consistently communicate is affected by the following factors:

- Power contained in the wave transmitted
- Sensitivity of the receiving equipment
- Environment through which the wave travels
- Presence of interference

17.3 Sensor Networks

17.3.1 Wireless Networks

The main characteristics of wireless networks are as follows:

- Access for anybody, from anywhere, at any time—mobility
- On-line/real-time access
- Relative high communication speed
- Shared access to files, data/knowledge bases
- Exchange of picture, voice—multimedia applications.

Table 17.3 shows the characteristics of several wireless networks.

Wireless networks can be categorized into five groups based on their coverage range:

a) Satellite communication (SC):

The handheld satellite telephones provide voice, fax, Internet access, short messaging, and remote location determination services (via Global Positioning System GPS) in the covered area. All of this is provided through geosynchronous satellites,

TABLE 17.3

Characteristics of Several Wireless Networks

Wireless network type	Operation frequency	Data rate	Operation range	Characteristics
Satellite	2,170–2,200 MHz	Different (9.6 kbps–2 Mbps)	Satellite coverage	Relative high cost, availability
WWAN				
GSM (2–2.5 G)	824–1,880 MHz	9.6–384kbps (EDGE)	Cellular coverage	Reach, quality, low cost
3G/UMTS	1,755–2,200 MHz	2.4 Mbps	Cellular coverage	Speed, big attachments
iMode (3G/ FOMA)	800 MHz	64–384 kpbs	Cellular coverage	Always on, easy to use
FLASH-OFDM	450 MHZ	Max. 3 Mbps	Cellular coverage	High speed, respond time less than 50 milliseconds
WMAN				
IEEE 802.16	2–11 GHz	Max. 70 Mbps	3–10 (max. 45) km	Speed, high operation range
WWLAN				
IEEE 802.11A	5 GHz	54 Mbps	30m	Speed, limited range
IEEE 802.11b	2.4 GHz	11 Mbps	100 m	Medium data range
IEEE 802.11g	2.4 GHz	54 Mbps	100–150 m	Speed, flexibility
WPAN				
BLUETOOTH	2.4 GHz	720 kpbs	10 m	Cost, convenience
UWB	1.5–4 GHz	50–100 Mbps	100–150 m	Low cost, low power
ZigBee	2.4 GHz, 915–868 Mhz	250 Kbps	1–75 m	Reliable, low power, cost effective
Infrared	300 GHz	9.6 kbps–4Mbps	0.2–2 m	Non-interfering, low cost
RFID	30–500 KHz 850–950 MHz 2.4–2.5 GHz	linked to bandwidth, max. 2 Mbps	0.02 m–30 m	High reading speeds, responding in less than 100 milliseconds

but when satellite coverage is not necessary, the handset can also access the GSM cellular network. Fax and digital data is transmitted at 9,600 bps throughputs, but when users need high-speed Internet access, in special cases, a 2 Mbps data transmission rate can be achieved. A satellite phone can fulfill all the requirements regarding mobile communications in many application fields.

b) Wireless Wide Area Networks (WWANs):

   i) Mobile phone: This device offered everyone the possibility to make contact with others from anywhere, at any time.

      Different mobile systems/network protocols are:

      - CDMA (Code Division Multiple Access—2G): CDMA networks incorporate spread-spectrum technology to gracefully allocate data over available cells.
      - CDPD (Cellular Digital Packet Data—2G): CDPD is a protocol built exclusively for sending wireless data over cellular networks. CDPD is built on TCP/IP standards.
      - GSM (Global System for Mobile Communications—2G): GSM networks, mainly popular in Europe.

- GPRS (General Packet Radio Service—2.5 G): GPRS technology offers significant speed improvements over existing 2G technology.
- iMode (from DoCoMo—2.5G): iMode was developed by DoCoMo and is the standard wireless data service for Japan. iMode is known for its custom markup language enabling multimedia applications to run on phones.
- 3G: 3G networks promise speeds rivalling wired connections. Both in Europe and North America, carriers have aggressively bid for a 3G spectrum, but no standard has yet emerged.

The introduction of Wireless Application Protocol (WAP) was a big step forward for the mobile communication, as this protocol made it possible to connect mobile devices to the Internet. By enabling WAP applications, a full range of wireless devices, including mobile phones, smart phones, PDAs, and handheld PCs, gain a common method for accessing Internet information. The spread of WAP became even more intensive as the mobile phone industry actively supported it by installing it into the new devices. Nowadays, WAP applications enable users to view a variety of WEB content, manage e-mail from a handset, and gain better access to network operators' enhanced services. Beyond these information services, content providers have developed different mobile solutions, such as mobile e-commerce (mCommerce).

ii) FLASH-OFDM (Fast, Low-latency Access with Seamless Handoff—Orthogonal Frequency Division Multiplexing) is a cellular, IP-based broadband technology for data services on the 450 MHz band. It has full cellular mobility, 3.2 Mbps peak data rates, 384 kbps at the edge of the cell and less than 20 milliseconds of latency. The FLASH-OFDM system consists of an airlink, an integrated physical and media access control layer, and IP-based layers above the network layer (layer 3). The IP-based layers support applications using standard IP protocols.

FLASH-OFDM is a wide-area technology that enables full mobility to speeds of up to 250 km/h (critical to vehicle and rail commuters). Its ability to support a large number of users over a large area, and nationwide buildouts (via wireless carriers), will do for data what the cellular networks did for voice. The IP interfaces in Flash-OFDM enable operators to offer their enterprise customers access to their LANs, and users the benefits of the mobile Internet. FLASH-OFDM support voice-packet switched voice, not circuit-switched voice, Radio routers, and IP routers with radio adjuncts handle packet traffic, and serve as the equivalent of cellular base stations. Consumers connect with Flash-OFDM networks via PC cards in their notebooks and via flash-memory cards in handheld devices.

c) Wireless Metropolitan Area Networks (WMANs):

WiMAX (Worldwide Interoperability for Microwave Access) is considered the next step beyond Wi-Fi because it is optimized for broadband operation, fixed and later mobile, in the wide area network. It already includes numerous advances that are slated for introduction into the 802.11 standard, such as quality of service, enhanced security, higher data rates, and mesh and smart antenna technology, allowing better utilization of the spectrum.

The term WiMAX has become synonymous with the IEEE 802.16 Metropolitan Area Network (MAN) air interface standard. Metropolitan area networks or MANs are large computer networks usually spanning a campus or a city. They typically use optical fiber connections to link their sites. In its original release (early in 2002), the 802.16 standard addressed applications in licensed bands in the 10 to 66 GHz frequency range. It requires line-of-sight towers called fixed wireless. Here, a backbone of base stations is connected to a public network, and each base station supports hundreds of fixed subscriber stations, which can be both public Wi-Fi "hot spots" and enterprise networks with firewalls.

d) Wireless Local Area Networks (WLANs):

Local area wireless networking, generally called Wi-Fi, or wireless fidelity, enables computers to send and receive data anywhere within the range of a base station with a speed that is several times faster than the fastest cable modem connection. Wi-Fi connects the user to others and to the Internet without the restriction of wires, cables, or fixed connections. Wi-Fi gives the user freedom to change locations (mobility)—and to have full access to files, office, and network connections wherever she or he is. In addition, Wi-Fi will easily extend an established wired network.

Wi-Fi networks use radio technologies called IEEE 802.11b or 802.11a standards to provide secure, reliable, and fast wireless connectivity. A Wi-Fi network can be used to connect computers to each other, to the Internet, and to wired networks (which use IEEE 802.3 or Ethernet). Wi-Fi networks operate in the 2.4 (802.11b) and 5 GHz (802.11a) radio bands, with an 11 Mbps (802.11b) or 54 Mbps (802.11a) data rate or with products that contain both bands (dual band), so they can provide real-world performance similar to the basic 10BaseT wired Ethernet networks used in many offices. 802.11b has a range of approximately 100 meters. Products based on the 802.11a standard were first introduced in late 2001.

Wi-Fi networks can work well both for home (connecting a family's computers together to share such hardware and software resources as printers and the Internet) and for small businesses (providing connectivity between mobile salespeople, floor staff, and "behind-the-scenes" departments). Because small businesses are dynamic, the built-in flexibility of a Wi-Fi network makes it easy and affordable for them to change and grow. Large companies and universities use enterprise-level Wi-Fi technology to extend standard wired Ethernet networks to public areas such as meeting rooms, training classrooms, and large auditoriums, and also to connect buildings. Many corporations also provide wireless networks to their off-site and telecommuting workers to use at home or in remote offices.

e) Wireless Personal Area (or Pico) Network (WPAN)

WPAN represents wireless personal area network technologies such as ultra-wideband (UWB), ZigBee, Bluetooth, and RFID. Designed for data and voice transmission, low-data rate standards include ZigBee and Bluetooth (IEEE 802.15.1), and enable wireless personal area networks to communicate over short distances, generating a new way of interacting with our personal and business environment.

1. Bluetooth is a short-range radio device that replaces cables with low-power radio waves to connect electronic devices, whether they are portable or fixed. It is a WPAN specified in IEEE 802.15, working group for wireless personal area networks. Named after Harald Bluetooth, the 10th-century Viking king, this is a consortium of companies (3Com, Ericsson, Intel, IBM, Lucent Technologies, Motorola, Nokia, and Toshiba) bonded together to form a wireless standard.

A Bluetooth device also uses frequency hopping to ensure a secure, high-quality link, and it employs ad hoc networks, meaning that it connects peer-to-peer. When devices are communicating with one another, they are known as piconets, and each device is designated as master unit or slave unit, usually depending on who initiates the connection. However, both devices have the potential to be either a master or a slave. The Bluetooth user has the choice of point-to-point or point-to-multipoint links, whereby communication can be held between two devices, or up to eight.

2. RFID

   The main purpose of the RFID technology is the automated identification of objects with electromagnetic fields. An RFID system has three basic components: transponders (tags), readers (scanners), and application systems for further processing of the acquired data. There is a large variety of different RFID systems; they can use low, high, or ultrahigh frequencies. Tags may emanate only a fixed identifier or have significant memory and processing capabilities. Transponders can contain effective security protocols or no security features at all. Most of the tags are passive powered by the radio field emitted by the reader, but there are also *active* tags with a separate power supply.

   RFID systems can be distinguished according to their frequency ranges. Low-frequency (30 KHz to 500 KHz) systems have short reading ranges and lower system costs. They are usually used in, for example, security access and animal identification applications. High-frequency (850 MHz to 950 MHz and 2.4 GHz to 2.5 GHz) systems, offering long reading ranges (greater than 25 meters) and high reading speeds, are used for such applications as railroad car tracking and automated toll collection. However, the higher performance of high-frequency RFID systems generates higher system costs.

17.3.2 Sensor

The objective of the sensor is to measure a physical quantity from the environment and transform it into a signal (either analog or digital) that drives outputs/actuators or feeds a data analysis tool (see Figure 17.2). The choice of a sensor in a WSN is application-dependent and strictly related to the physical phenomenon object of the monitoring action. The wide and heterogeneous range of possible physical phenomena to be monitored is well reflected by the complexity and the heterogeneity of the sensors that have been designed and developed to acquire data from them. Examples of possible applications, physical phenomena to be monitored, and the corresponding sensors of interest are summarized in Table 17.4 and Table 17.5.

Figure 17.3 shows the measurement chain of sensors.

Table 17.4 presents examples of possible applications, physical phenomena to be monitored, and the corresponding sensors: Table 17.5 presents types of sensors for various measurement objectives.

The measurement of a physical quantity and the subsequent conversion into signals are performed by sensors through a *measurement chain* that is generally composed of three different stages:

- The transducer stage transforms one form of energy into another, here converting the monitored physical quantity into an electric signal.
- The conditioning circuit stage conditions the signal provided by the transducer to reduce the effect of noise, amplify the sensitivity of the sensor, and adapt the electrical properties of the signal to the needs of the next stage.

TABLE 17.4

Examples of Possible Applications, Physical Phenomena to Be Monitored, and the Corresponding Sensors

Applications	Physical phenomenon	Sensors
Environmental monitoring	Temperature	Thermometers, thermocouples, thermistor
	Light	Photodiodes/phototransistor, CCD cameras
	Humidity	Humidity sensors
	Pressure	Switches, strain gauges
Visual and audio processing	Visual	CCD and other cameras
	Audio	Microphones
Motion/acceleration analysis	Motion/acceleration	Accelerometers, motion detectors, magnetic fields, angular sensors
Location	Indoor	Tags, badges
	Outdoor	GPS, GSM cells
Biological and chemical analysis	Biological	ECG, heart rate sensors, blood pressure sensors, pulse oximetry, skin resistance, DNA analyzer
	Chemical	Contaminant sensors, solid/liquid/gas sensors, electrochemical cells

- The output formatting stage aims at transforming the conditioned signal into a signal ready to be used to drive outputs or actuators and to be processed by the data analysis tool.

The measurement chain of sensors is characterized by:

1. Functional attributes specifying the functional behaviour. Functional attributes refer to specific functions or behaviors the sensor must exhibit. Examples are the measurement range (i.e., the range of measurements the sensor can acquire), the duty-cycle sampling rates (i.e., the range of sampling rates the sensor can support), and the condition stage parameters (e.g., the filter parameters).
2. Nonfunctional attributes specifying the requirements/properties of the sensor itself. Nonfunctional attributes refer to properties characterizing how the sensor is providing its functionalities. Examples are the size/weight of the sensor, the accuracy and the precision of the measurement chain, and the power consumption.

The term "sensor" does not necessarily refer only to physical hardware devices, but also to every source of data providing information of interest. Hence, in addition to physical hardware sensors (which is, however, the most frequently considered source of information in WSNs), virtual and logical sensors are often employed. Virtual sensors refer to nonphysical sources of information; for example, the location of a person can be determined by means of tracking systems through GPS location (physical devices) as well as by looking at electronic calendars or analyzing travel bookings or e-mails (nonphysical sources of information). Electronic calendars, travel bookings, and e-mails do not require a real measurement of the person position and are referred to as "virtual sensors." Logical sensors rely on two or more sources of information to provide high-level data; for example, a logical sensor could aggregate data coming from both a physical sensor and a virtual sensor as well as information coming from a database system.

TABLE 17.5

Types of Sensors for Various Measurement Objectives

Sensor	Features
Linear/rotational sensor	
Linear/rotational variable differential transducer (LVDT/RVDT) optical encoder	High resolution with wide-range capability. Very stable in static and quasi-static applications Simple, reliable, and low-cost solution. Good for both absolute and incremental measurements
Electrical tachometer Hall effect sensor capacitive transducer	Resolution depends on type such as generator or magnetic pickups. High accuracy over a small to medium range. Very high resolution with high sensitivity. Low power requirements
Strain gauge elements	Very high accuracy in small ranges. Provides high resolution at low noise levels.
Interferometer	Laster systems provide extremely high resolution in large ranges. Very reliable and expensive. Output is sinusoidal
Magnetic pickup Gyroscope Inductosyn	Very high resolution over small ranges
Acceleration sensors	
Seismic and Piezoelectric accelerometers	Good for measuring frequenices up to 40% of its natural frequency. High sensitivity, compact, and rugged. Very high natural frequency (100 kHz typical)
Force, torque, and pressure sensor	
Strain gauge, dynamometers/load cells, piezoelectric load celss, tactile sensor, and ultrasonic stress sensor	Good for both static and dynamic measurements. They are also available as micro-and nanosensors. Good for high precision dynamic force measurements. Compact, has wide dynamic range. Good for small force measurements.
Proximity sensors	
Inductance, eddy current, hall effect, photoelectric, capacitance, etc.	Robust noncontact switching action. The digital outputs are often directly fed to the digital controller
Light sensors	
Photo resistors, photodiodes, photo transistors, photo conductors, etc. Charge-coupled diode.	Measure light intensity with high sensitivity. Inexpensive, reliable, and noncontact sensor. Compares digital image of a field of vision
Temperature sensors	
Thermocouples	This is the cheapest and the most versatile sensor. Applicable over wide temperature ranges (–200 to 1,200oc typical)
Thermostats	Very high sensitivity in medium ranges (up to 100 c typical). Compact but nonlinear in nature
Thermo diodes, and thermo transistors	Ideally suited for chip temperature measurements. Minimized self-heating.
RTD-resistance temperature detector	More stable over a long period for time compared to thermocouple. Linear over a wide range
Infrared type and infrared thermograph	Noncontact point sensor with resolution limited by wavelength. Measures whole-field temperature distribution
Flow sensors	
Pitot tube, orifice plate, flow nozzle, and venture tubes	Widely used as a flow rate sensor to determine speed in aircrafts. Least expensive with limited range. Accurate on wide range of flow. More complex and expensive
Rotameter	Good for upstream flow measurements. Used in conjunction with variable inductance sensor
Ultrasonic type	Good for very high flow rates. Can be used for upstream and downstream flow measurements

(Continued)

TABLE 17.5 (CONTINUED)

Types of Sensors for Various Measurement Objectives

Sensor	Features
Turbine flow meter	Not suited for fluids containing abrasive particles. Relationship between flow rate and angular velocity is linear
Electromagnetic flow meter	Least intrusive as it is noncontact type. Can be used with fluids that are corrosive, contaminated, etc.. The fluid has to be electrically conductive
Smart material sensors	
Optical fiber as strain sensor, as level sensor, as force sensor, and as temperature sensor	Alternate to strain pages with very high accuracy and bandwidth. Sensitive to the reflecting surface's orientation and status. Reliable and accurate. High resolution in wide ranges. High resolution and range (up to 2,000 oc)
Piezoelectric as strain sensor, as force sensor, and as accelerometer	Distributed sensing with high resolution and bandwidth. Most suitable for dynamic applications. Least hysteresis and good set point accuracy
Magnetostrictive as force sensor and as torque sensor	Compact force sensor with high resolution and bandwidth. Good for distributed and noncontact sensing applications. Accurate, high bandwidth, and noncontract sensor
Micro- and nano-sensors	
Micro CCD image sensor, fiberscope micro-ultrasonic sensor, micro-tactile sensor	Small size, full field image sensor, Small (0.2 mm diameter) field vision scope using SMA coil actuators. Detects flaws in small pipes. Detects proximity between the end of catheter and blood vessels.

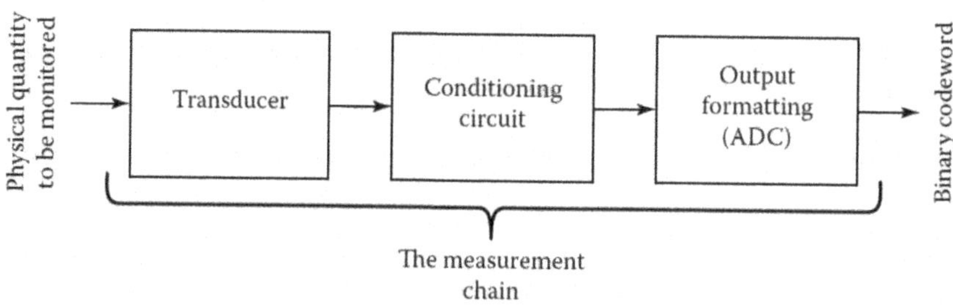

FIGURE 17.3
The measurement chain of sensors.

Regardless of the kind of sensor (physical, virtual, or logical) or the object of the sensing activities (places, people, or object), sensing activity has four essential characteristics:

- *Identity* refers to the ability to univocally identify the entity which is the object of the sensing, e.g., by assigning unique identifiers in the namespace used by the application.
- *Location* encompasses all the aspects related to the position of the sensed entity. It could include not only a position in space but also orientation, elevation, and proximity to relevant locations.
- *Status* refers to the physical quantity (or the virtual/logical quantity) object of the sensing. In case of a temperature sensor, the status refers to the temperature value measured at a specific time instant.

- *Time* indicates temporal information associated with the sensed measurements. The temporal information often refers to a timestamp specifying the exact time instant at which the measurement has been acquired. A wide range of time coarseness could be considered (e.g., from nanoseconds to decades), depending on the application needs.

17.3.3 WSNs

WSNs have been widely considered as one of the most important technologies for the twenty-first century. Enabled by recent advances in microelectronic mechanical systems (MEMS) and wireless communication technologies, tiny, cheap, and smart sensors deployed in a physical area and networked through wireless links and the Internet provide unprecedented opportunities for a variety of applications, such as environmental monitoring and industry process control. In contrast with traditional wireless communication networks such as cellular systems and mobile ad hoc networks (MANETs), the development and application of WSNs present many challenges because of many have unique characteristics like denser level of node deployment, higher unreliability of sensor nodes, and severe energy, computation, and storage constraints.

A sensor network consists of a large number of sensor nodes that are densely deployed in a sensing region and collaborate to accomplish a sensing task. It requires a suite of network protocols to implement various network control and management functions, for example, synchronization, self-configuration, medium access control, routing, data aggregation, node localization, and network security. However, existing network protocols for traditional wireless networks, for example, cellular systems and MANETs, cannot be applied directly to sensor networks because they do not consider the energy, computation, and storage constraints in sensor nodes. On the other hand, most sensor networks are application specific and have different application requirements. For these reasons, a new suite of network protocols is required, which takes into account not only the resource constraints in sensor nodes, but also the requirements of different network applications. For this reason, it is important to define a protocol stack to facilitate the protocol design for WSNs.

As discussed in Section 17.1.1 earlier, the WSN hardware platforms are composed of:

- The sensing module, which contains one or more sensors, each of which is devoted to measure a physical quantity of interest and generate the associated codeword (i.e., the digital data).
- The processing module, which is generally equipped with a small memory/storage unit, manages the unit, and carries out the processing tasks according to the application needs.
- The transmission module, which provides the mechanisms to communicate with the other units of the WSN or to a remote control room.

Hardware platforms for WSNs are presented in Table 17.6.

OSs represent the intermediate layer between the hardware of the WSN unit and WSN applications. They aim to control the hardware resources and provide services and functionalities to the application software (e.g., hardware abstraction, scheduling of tasks, memory management, and file system). Simplified versions of desktop/mainframe OSs could be considered only in high-performance hardware platforms (e.g., the StarGate platform is able to run a simplified version of Linux). The constraints on hardware and energy

TABLE 17.6
Hardware Platforms for WSN

	Processor					Radio		
Platform	**Type**	**Frequency**	**RAM (byte) int./ext.**	**Flash (byte) int./ ext.**	**Power consumption (mW) sleep/run**	**Type**	**TX power (dB)**	**Sensors type**
MICaz	ATMegal28	8 MHz	4K/n.a.	128K/n.a.	0.036/60	CC2420	Up to 0	n.a.
BTnode	ATMegal28	7.38 MHz	4K/n.a.	128K/n.a.	0.036/60	CC1000	Up to +10	n.a.
Mulle	M16C/62P	Up to 24 MHz	20K/n.a.	128K/n.a.	0.015/75	Bluetooth	Up to +4	Temperature
Shimmer	MSP430	8 MHz	10K/n.a.	48K/uSD	0.006/4	CC2420	Up to 0	MEMS
TelosB	MSP430	8 MHz	10K/n.a.	48K/1Mb	0.006/4	CC2420	Up to 0	Temperature, humidity, light
Imote2	PXA271	13–416 MHz	256K/32Mb	32Mb/n.a.	0.39/up to 992	CC2420	Up to 0	n.a.
StarGate	PXA255	400 MHz	64K/64Mb	32Mb/ext.	15/1455	n.a.	n.a.	n.a.
NetBrick	STM32F103	8–72 MHz	64K/1Mb	512 Kb/128Mb	0.083/226	JN5148	Up to +20	Temperature, humidity, MEMS

n.a. not available, ext. external

TABLE 17.7
Operating Systems for WSN

	Architecture	Preemption	Multithreading	Remote reprogramming	Language
TinyOS	Monolithic	No	Partial	No	NesC
Contiki	Modular	Yes	Yes	Yes	C
MANTIS	Layered	Yes	Yes	Yes	C

of WSN units (as pointed out in Table 17.5) led to the development of OSs specifically devoted to networked embedded systems. Examples of OSs for WSNs are TinyOS, Contiki, and MANTIS (see Table 17.7).

TinyOS is an open-source, flexible, and component-based OS for WSN units. It is characterized by a very small footprint (400 bytes), which makes it particularly suitable for low-power hardware platforms (such as the MICAz). TinyOS relies on a monolithic architecture where software components (including those providing hardware abstraction) are connected together through interfaces. It supports a non-preemptive first-in-first-out scheduling activity (which makes it unsuitable for computational-intensive or real-time applications). TinyOS applications must be written in NesC (which is a dialect of the C language) and cannot be updated/modified at runtime (applications are compiled together with the OS kernel as a single image).

Contiki is an open-source OS for networked embedded systems. It is built around a modular architecture composed of an event-driven-based microkernel, OS libraries, a program loader, and application processes. Interestingly, Contiki supports preemptive multithreading and remote reprogramming (through the program loader). The memory occupation is 2 KB of RAM and 4 KB of read-only memory (ROM). Both the OS and the applications are written in C.

MANTIS is a multithreaded OS for WSNs that is based on a traditional layered architecture. Each layer provides services to upper layers from the hardware to the application threads. MANTIS supports cross-platform design by preserving the programming interface across different platforms. The scheduling activity is based on a preemptive priority-based scheduler, while remote reprogramming is supported by the dynamic loading of threads. Even in this case, both the OS and the application threads are written in C.

17.3.3.1 WSN Characteristics

A WSN typically consists of a large number of low-cost, low-power, and multi-functional sensor nodes that are deployed in a region of interest. These sensor nodes are small in size, but are equipped with sensors, embedded microprocessors, and radio transceivers, and therefore have not only sensing capability, but also data processing and communicating capabilities. They communicate over a short distance via a wireless medium and collaborate to accomplish a common task.

1. Application specific. Sensor networks are application specific. A network is usually designed and deployed for a specific application. The design requirements of a network change with its application.
2. No global identification. Due to the large number of sensor nodes, it is usually not possible to build a global addressing scheme for a sensor network because it would introduce a high overhead for the identification maintenance.

3. Dense node deployment. Sensor nodes are usually densely deployed in a field of interest. The number of sensor nodes in a sensor network can be several orders of magnitude higher than that in a MANET.
4. Frequent topology change. Network topology changes frequently due to node failure, damage, addition, energy depletion, or channel fading.
5. Many-to-one traffic pattern. In most sensor network applications, the data sensed by sensor nodes flows from multiple source sensor nodes to a particular sink, exhibiting a many-to-one traffic pattern.
6. Battery-powered sensor nodes. Sensor nodes are usually powered by battery. In most situations, they are deployed in a harsh or hostile environment, where it is very difficult or even impossible to change or recharge the batteries.
7. Severe energy, computation, and storage constraints. Sensor nodes are highly limited in energy, computation, and storage capacities.
8. Self-configurable. Sensor nodes are usually randomly deployed without careful planning and engineering. Once deployed, sensor nodes have to autonomously configure themselves into a communication network.
9. Unreliable sensor nodes. Sensor nodes are usually deployed in harsh or hostile environments and operate without attendance. They are prone to physical damages or failures.
10. Data Redundancy. In most sensor network applications, sensor nodes are densely deployed in a region of interest and collaborate to accomplish a common sensing task. Thus, the data sensed by multiple sensor nodes typically has a certain level of correlation or redundancy.

Appendix 17.B gives a description of edge and fog computing.

17.4 Summary

IoT refers to a network of inter-connected things, objects, or devices on a massive scale connected to the Internet. These objects, being smart, sense their surroundings, and gather and exchange data with other objects. Based on the gathered data, the objects make intelligent decisions, triggering an action or sending the data to a server over the Internet, then waiting for its decision. IoT aims to integrate, collect information from, and offer services to a very diverse spectrum of physical things used in different domains. "Things" are everyday objects for which IoT offers a virtual presence on the Internet, allocates a specific identity and virtual address, and adds capabilities to self-organize and communicate with other things without human intervention. To ensure high-quality services, additional capabilities can be included such as context awareness, autonomy, and reactivity.

This chapter began with an introduction to IoT. Subsequently, it described RFID, a wireless automatic identification technology whereby an object with an attached RFID tag is identified by an RFID reader. Following this, the concept of wireless sensor network technology was introduced. This is enabled by the availability of smaller, cheaper and intelligent sensors and has important applications such as remote environmental monitoring.

Appendix 17.A: Internet of Things (IoT) in 5G Mobile Technologies

The fifth-generation (5G) networks are promising to meet the demands of various individual applications with a significant increase in size, content, and rate. The 5G evolution is being fueled by a number of factors such as the explosion of mobile data traffic, the increasing demand for high data rates, and the growth in connected and searchable devices for low-cost, energy-saving, and environmentally friendly wireless communications. The applications of 5G cellular networks will spread across smart city infrastructure with high capacity storage, intelligent transportation, and smart communication systems.

Beyond the current 4G systems with long-term evolution advanced (LTE-A) standards, the 5G wireless systems have been proposed to be the next telecommunications standards aiming to provide a higher capacity, higher reliability, and higher density of mobile broadband users. In order to address the high traffic growth and increasing demand for high-bandwidth connectivity, the development of 5G networks becomes crucial to support a massive number of connected devices with real-time services and high-reliability communications in critical applications (Figure 17A.1). By providing wireless connectivity for a diversity of applications from wearable devices, smartphones, tablets, and laptops to utilities within smart homes, transportation, and industry, the 5G networks are promising to provide ubiquitous connectivity for any kind of device, enabling and accelerating the development of the IoT.

Apart from improving the maximum throughput, the 5G systems are expected to provide lower power consumption dealing with battery issues, concurrent data transfer paths, lower outage, and better coverage for cell-edge and high-mobility users. Moreover, the 5G systems are required to be more secure and have better cognitive functionality via software-defined radio (SDR), and artificial intelligence (AI) capabilities. With the employment of the SDR, a lower infrastructure cost could be favorably achieved, which might help reduce traffic fees while users can experience high-quality multimedia beyond 4G speeds. The evolution of mobile technologies from 1G to 5G is illustrated in Figure 17A.2.

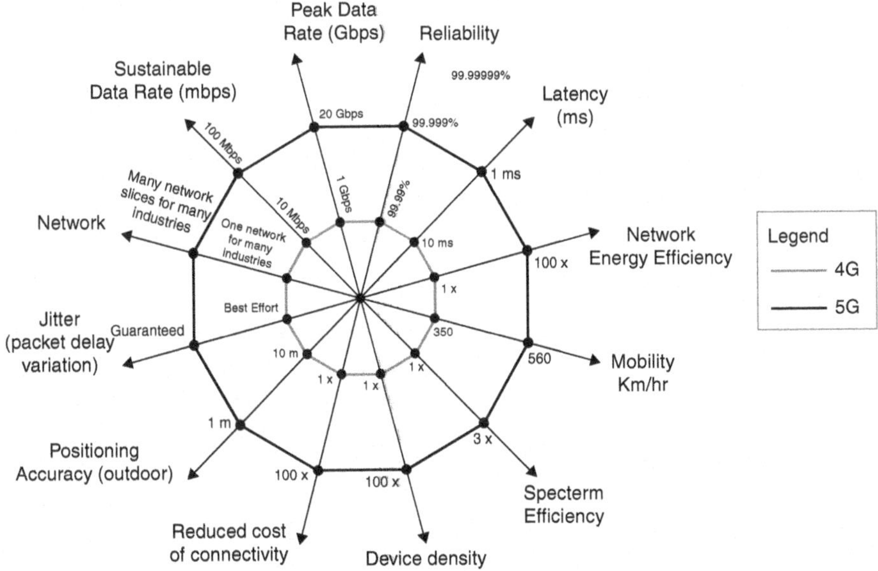

FIGURE 17.A.1
Comparison of 5G with 4G systems.

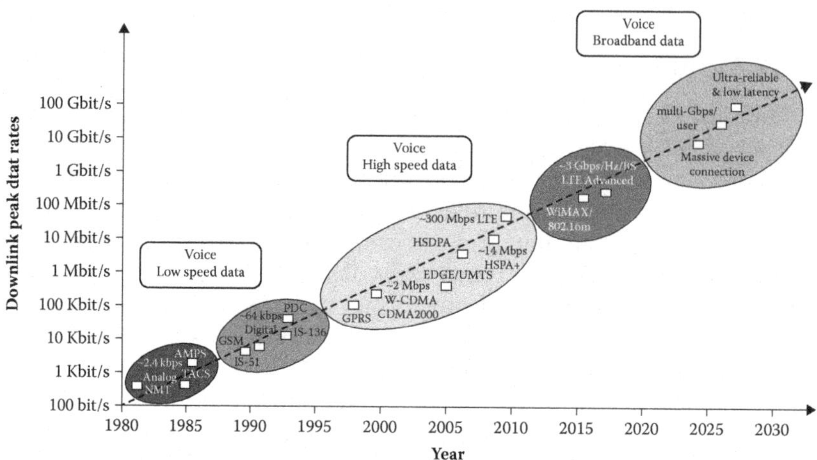

FIGURE 17.A.2
Evolution of mobile technologies.

17.A.1 5G Trends

As one of the key new services in the 5G networks, the IoT will influence the number of connected devices that will enter the marketplace. Additionally, the IoT will have a significant impact on 5G traffic patterns as well as their quality of service (QoS) requirements, all of which will also affect backhaul requirements and specifications. The aggregate data demand of the IoT should be very different from that of smartphone-oriented experiences. Capacity demands will grow and more base stations (BSs) will have to be deployed to achieve the required QoS, which are absolutely necessary for the IoT to be successful.

As the IoT expands, there are five key trends of the underlying 5G networks:

- More capacity per device: In order to meet the requirements of ultrahigh capacity per end device, either more spectrums for improved spectrum efficiency or enhanced technologies are required.
- More devices of different types: The average number of devices per person is anticipated to rapidly increase in both quantity and diversity with a variety of device types for different services such as smartphones and tablets, and wearable devices such as smart watches and glasses. The 5G systems are therefore required to overhaul such exponential augmentation of devices.
- Higher capacity for denser networks: With the increased number of devices, the 5G systems aim to increase the site capacity by up to 1000 times the current networks. Although such a task sounds feasible given numerous evolved technologies, several challenges need to be addressed. For instance, the current wireless backhaul links need to support a data rate of 10 Gigabits per second (Gbps) or higher and are also required to cover denser networks.
- Enhanced backhaul capability for critical applications: Many new service types are developing in mission-critical networks for government, transportation, public safety, healthcare systems, and military services. For these critical applications, coverage, ultralow latency, and strict security are required of the wireless backhaul infrastructure in the 5G systems to lessen the risks of communication failure.

- Diverse virtual and cloud-based services: Cloud technology promises savings on capital expenditure and operating expenses along with the opening of potential markets for a variety of virtual and cloud-based services. The 5G wireless systems therefore provide operators and researchers with the opportunity to review and adapt the current technologies to the cloud platform.

17.A.2 5G Requirements

5G is intended to be the major component of the networked or IoT/machine-to-machine (M2M)-oriented society, and will help to realize the IoT vision toward unlimited access to information and sharing of pervasive data (anywhere and anytime) for anyone (human-centric approach) and anything (device/things-oriented approach). The aim of 5G is not only mobile connectivity for people, but also mobile and ubiquitous connectivity for any kind of computing device and application that may benefit from being connected to the Internet (IoT) and also to the Web (WoT—Web of Things).

Consequently, 5G networks need to meet the following requirements:

- User experiences should be consistently and ubiquitously delivered in the 5G systems at a high data rate and low latency with optional mobility support for specific user demands of certain services.

  The 5G data rates requirements are

  - 10 Gbps in specific scenarios such as indoor and dense outdoor environments.
  - 100 Mbps should be generally achievable in urban and suburban environments.
  - At least 10 Mbps should be achievable essentially everywhere, including sparsely populated rural areas.
- Devices/terminals need to be smarter, allowing operator control capabilities with programmability and configurability, supporting multiple frequency bands, increasing battery life, and improving resource and signaling efficiency.
- Networks/systems need to support massive connected devices with high traffic density, high spectrum efficiency, and high coverage.
- Network deployment, operation, and management are needed to provide the new enhanced services at a low cost and low-energy consumption to ensure the sustainability of the 5G and beyond networks, and also to facilitate future upgrades and innovation, ensuring flexibility and scalability.
- Services to provide connectivity transparency with seamless, ubiquitous, and high-reliability communications for mobile users are indispensable, improving localization with additional three-dimensional space attributes, protecting users' data from possible cybersecurity attacks, and ensuring the availability and resilience of mission-critical services.

17.A.3 5G Objectives

Consequently, the 5G networks need to meet the following objectives:

- Enhanced user experiences: The 5G systems will not simply be the evolution of enhanced 4G systems, but they will aim to bring new network and service capabilities given limited bandwidth and power resources. With the novel design of the 5G networks, user experiences will be enriched, guaranteeing that users can continuously access mobile broadband networks, especially in critical circumstances, for instance, high-mobility trains, airplanes, and dense areas.
- Platform for the IoT: The 5G systems will be driven toward providing a platform for the IoT. A massive number of smart sensors will be connected to deliver various kinds of service in our daily life given the inevitable fact that they have severely limited power and a short lifetime.
- Sustainable and scalable network: The 5G systems will be particularly focused on energy consumption reduction and energy harvesting, targeting at compensating the radical increase in energy usage. With automation integration and hardware optimization, the operational cost is expected to considerably reduce for a sustainable and scalable network model.
- Ecosystem for innovation: The 5G systems will be a means to involve vertical markets in different sectors and areas, such as energy, transportation, manufacturing, agriculture, health care, education, government, and so on. This will be an excellent opportunity to encourage start-ups and innovations in these diverse trading businesses.
- Improved mission-critical services: The 5G systems will be destined for mission-critical services, such as public safety, health care, disaster, and emergency services, which require high-reliability communications with low latency and high coverage.
- Incorporated market for operators: The 5G systems will be directed to enable operators to collaborate over a digital or virtual market by taking advantage of cloud computing. Such a market will make room for further development of the 5G networks.

17.A.4 5G-enabling Technologies

5G-enabling technologies are

- Massive multiple-input multiple-output (MIMO) (also known as large-scale MIMO or large-scale antenna systems) is an emerging technology in the next-generation mobile system, that is, 5G and beyond, which has been upgraded from the conventional multiuser MIMO (MU-MIMO) technology. The massive MIMO exploits the spatial multiplexing gain to increase the capacity almost 10 times and the energy efficiency 100 times compared with the MU-MIMO systems. In the massive MIMO, large arrays of antennas that contain a few hundred antenna elements are deployed at BSs to simultaneously serve several terminals using the same time–frequency resources.
- All mmWave Massive MIMO current mobile systems are allocated in the microwave frequency bands of which most operate in the bands below 3 GHz and share

the scarce spectrum resources of 600 MHz divided among operators. In contrast, mmWave frequency bands ranging from 3 to 300 GHz can offer multi-GHz of unlicensed bandwidth.

mmWave massive MIMO has the potential to provide ultra-large bandwidth and high spectrum efficiency that may significantly improve the overall system throughput in future 5G cellular networks. However, due to the special propagation features and hardware requirements of the mmWave systems, there are several challenges when deploying the mmWave massive MIMO at the physical and upper layers. In particular, the network architecture and protocols must be considered carefully in the network design to adapt signaling and resource allocation, as well as to cope with severe channel attenuation, directionality, and blockage.

- To cope with the rapid growth of wireless traffic demands in 5G communications, the deployment of a large number of small cells (femtocell, picocell, and microcell) has been shown to be a feasible solution to achieve high capacity, leading to a heterogeneous network (HetNet). The HetNet is typically a multitier network architecture consisting of multiple types of infrastructure elements including macro-BSs, micro-BSs, pico-BSs, and femto-BSs with different transmission powers and coverage sizes. The range of a microcell or picocell is about a few hundred meters, whereas femtocells are used to provide indoor coverage within the range of a few meters.

  By deploying a variety of cells of different sizes, the HetNet architecture is highly probable to increase the radio capacity, improve throughput, and serve several types of users with different QoS requirements in the next-generation cellular networks. In addition, the deployment of low-power, small-cell BSs in dense areas is one of the key solutions to enhance coverage and provide more capacity by covering a smaller area than macro-BSs as well as improve the spectral efficiency of cellular networks. Moreover, the small cell integrated with macrocells provides a potential opportunity to decouple the control plane and user plane in which low-power, small-cell BSs handle the control plane, while the overall control signaling to all users and cell-specific reference signals of small-cell BSs can be delivered to powerful high-power macro-BSs. Therefore, HetNets have the advantages of serving hotspot customers with high data rates and bursty traffic.

  Along with a number of advantages, the HetNet is facing a critical issue when too dense, low-power, small-cell BSs underlaid with macro-BSs reusing the same spectral resources could incur severe inter-tier interferences. Hence, advanced signal-processing techniques are vital to fully obtain the potential gains of HetNets. Specifically, advanced coordinated multipoint (CoMP) transmission and reception techniques have been proposed to suppress both intra-tier and inter-tier interference and improve the cell-edge user throughput. Another technique for enhancing the performance of the HetNet is co-locating a massive MIMO BS and low-power, small-cell access in which the massive MIMO ensures outdoor mobile coverage whereas small-cell access equipped with cognitive and cooperative functionalities enables the HetNet to provide high capacity indoor and outdoor coverage for low-mobility users.

- Another approach in dealing with dense networks is the employment of a distributed antenna system (DAS). The DAS has shown high potential in providing more uniform coverage, especially in shadowed and indoor areas, as well as enhancing the transmit capability of a BS by adding multiple remote antenna units (RAUs) geographically distributed in a macrocell.

- The security of mobile devices access in ultradense heterogeneous networks is largely based on the specific features and architecture of the network system. We may find that vulnerabilities in ultradense heterogeneous networks can occur in some cases, such as Internet protocol (IP) spoofing, interference management attack, handover management attack, unauthorized cell identification, and radio-frequency identification (RFID) tags.

5G networks need to tackle several challenges in order to meet the requirements as stated in subsection 17A.2. As one of the critical issues in the existing technologies, energy performance needs to be improved with appropriate resource allocation. The resources should be optimized to facilitate better utilization in a dynamic and adaptable manner. Additionally, given the scarcity of spectrum resources, an efficient spectrum usage is crucial in the 5G systems to support massive connected devices of different kinds.

The 5G systems need to cope with higher coverage with a higher density of mobile broadband users. Indeed, the 5G systems will need to manage a very dense heterogeneous network. Radio resource management will become of paramount problem to handle the dense deployment of small cells in coordination with existing macrocells and billions of connected devices.

Appendix 17.B: Edge Computing and Fog Computing

The Internet of Things (IoT) is experiencing explosive growth and is virtually transforming all aspects of modern life. Cisco has predicted that 50 billion devices will be linked to the IoT by 2020. As these new technologies enter the everyday lives of consumers, new challenges arise that cannot be safely addressed through a centralized cloud computing structure, including stringent latency, capacity constraints, useful resource-confined devices, uninterrupted services with intermittent connectivity, improved security, and latency needs. Because the records increase each day on the network, the performance of the machines continues to be affected. This appendix discusses basic information about the IoT, the associated challenges, and statistics reduction techniques for edge computing to reduce data and latency time.

As the IoT grows, the data in the network is also increasing. To reduce this data, the technology of edge computing may be used. Edge computing allows devices to perform computations at the edge of the network:

- On downstream data on behalf of cloud services.
- On upstream data on behalf of IoT services.

Here, "edge" refers to any computing and network resources that are between the data sources and the cloud data centers; the "things" are data consumers and data producers. For example, a smartphone is the edge between an individual and the cloud, a gateway in a smart home is the edge between the house and the cloud, and a micro data center and a cloudlet are the edge between a mobile device and the cloud. The edge can perform computing offloading, data storage, caching and processing, request distributions, and distribution accommodations from the cloud to the user. The edge has quality of service (QoS) requirements such as reliability, security, and privacy firewalls.

IoT applications generate enormous amounts of data by IoT sensors. The big data is subsequently analyzed to determine reactions to events or to extract analytics or statistics. However, sending all of this data to the cloud would require a prohibitively high network bandwidth. In edge computing, the massive data generated by different kinds of IoT devices can be processed at the network edge instead of transmitting the data to a centralized cloud infrastructure due to bandwidth and energy consumption concerns:

- Edge computing can provide services with a faster response and better quality than cloud computing.

  Push from cloud services: Putting all computing tasks on the cloud is an efficient way to process data because the cloud's computing power outclasses the capability of the things at the edge. However, compared with the fast-developing speed of data processing, the bandwidth of the network has reduced to almost a crawl. For instance, for an autonomous vehicle, 1 GB of data is generated by a car every second, and it requires real-time processing for the vehicle to make correct decisions. If all the data needed to be sent to the cloud for processing, the response time would be too long. Furthermore, it would be challenging for the current network bandwidth and reliability to support many vehicles in one area. In this case, the data needs to be processed at the edge for shorter response times, more efficient processing, and reduced network pressure.
- Edge computing is suitable for integration with the IoT to provide efficient and secure services for many end users.

  Pull from the IoT: Many kinds of electrical devices will become part of the IoT. These devices will play the roles of both data producers and data consumers, such as air quality sensors, light-emitting diode (LED) bars, streetlights, and Internet-connected microwave ovens. The raw data produced by almost 1 billion devices will be enormous, with conventional cloud computing being too inefficient to handle this data. Thus, most of the data produced by the IoT will never be transmitted to the cloud. Instead, it needs to be consumed at the edge of the network itself.

In conventional cloud computing, data producers generate raw data and transfer it to the cloud, and data consumers send a request for consuming data to the cloud. However, this structure is not sufficient for the IoT because

- Data quantity at the edge is too large, which will lead to unnecessary bandwidth computing resource usage.
- Privacy protection requirements will pose an obstacle to cloud computing in the IoT.

Most of the end nodes in the IoT are energy-constrained things, whereas the wireless communication module is usually very energy hungry. Thus, offloading some computing tasks to the edge could be more energy efficient.

17.B.1 Implementation of Edge Computing

17.B.1.1 Data Reduction Techniques

The three data reduction techniques that can reduce data collection and transmission process times are

- Data sampling either reduces the amount of sensory data to be processed further, paying special attention to extracting the most representative points of the dataset, or chooses a subset of sensors that contribute sensory data among all the IoT sensors. An adaptive sampling approach, in which only a few sensor nodes are first activated to sample—leverages spatial correlations. Higher correlations (i.e., IoT sensors are closer to each other) require fewer active sensors to sample the data. The data is then sent to a data fusion center, which derives valuable information regarding the environment and the phenomenon under observation, activating more nodes if needed.
- Compression minimized datasets are easier to use in terms of processing and inside the network movement for large storage. Compression-based techniques are useful and appropriate for data reduction in edge computing. Compression can be applied to already-sensed data.
- Data aggregation consists of considering diverse sources of data and gathering them together to build an accurate representation of the phenomena under observation. These sources differ in that each of them is responsible for a specific sensing task. In the IoT and wireless sensor networks, data aggregation techniques include operations such as solving the maximum, minimum, sum, average, median, and count. Aggregation methods can be divided into
  - Centralized methods requiring continuous communication among network entities. Hence, the communication overhead incurs additional costs; consequently, such methods are not suitable for sensor networks.
  - Distributed methods such as clustering, multipath, and aggregate trees are commonly employed.

Based on when data is sensed, two main categories of approaches can be used for IoT data reduction at the network edge:

- Time series compression approaches: Time series compression and aggregation techniques are based on the sampling, summarization, approximation approach. For example,
  - Fast time sequence indexing for arbitrary Lp norms is based on piecewise approximation and the replacement of every n point with its arithmetic means.
  - Selecting only the "perceptually important points" (PIPs) of the time series, which measures importance based on their distance from other PIPs and on local minima and maxima, respectively.

Such solutions are not designed to act upon streams (i.e., per incoming data item), but rather on already collected datasets (posteriori).

- Event- or policy-based engines: Data handling solutions that use event- or policy-based engines often (implicitly) have a similar final goal as time series compression approaches—namely data reduction, although they usually rely on domain-specific rules rather than on time series characteristics. For example,
    - Internet protocol (IP) multimedia subsystems policies in order to perform (among others) a kind of data aggregation on network-edge (gateway) devices in machine-to-machine (M2M) systems.

These approaches stop at designing policy engines and policy languages for data reduction, without developing or providing actual data reduction techniques. Thus, they practically require the network edge developer to implement the data reduction logic from scratch. This approach also includes experiments showing how different data reduction techniques (mainly compression and visualization-based data reduction) perform when applied at the network edge.

17B.1.2 Fog Computing

Fog computing is one of the technologies essential for the implementation of edge computing. The OpenFog consortium was founded to drive industry and academic leadership in fog computing architecture, test bed development, and a variety of interoperability and composability deliverables that seamlessly leverage cloud and edge architectures to enable end-to-end IoT scenarios. The OpenFog consortium defines fog computing as "a system-level horizontal architecture that distributes resources and services of computing, storage, control and networking anywhere along the continuum from Cloud to Things" (https://www.openfogconsortium.org).

Edge architecture places servers, applications, and small clouds at the edge. Fog computing differs from edge computing by providing tools for distributing, orchestrating, managing, and securing resources and services across networks and between devices that reside at the edge. Fog computing jointly works with the cloud, whereas edge is defined by its exclusion of the cloud.

18

Sensor Data Processing

The node distribution, communication, and dissemination strategies as well as the cooperative processing capabilities of hundreds or even thousands of small devices are critical aspects to assure the actual performance and reliability of a planned application. The chapter starts with a discussion of sensor data-gathering and data-dissemination mechanisms. The main purpose of a sensor database system is to facilitate the data-collection process. Once data is gathered by multiple sources (e.g., sensors in the vicinity of the event of interest), it are forwarded perhaps through multiple hops to a single destination (sink). The information gathered by neighboring sensors is often redundant and highly correlated, and the energy is much more constrained (because once deployed, most sensor networks operate in the unattended mode), hence there is a need for data fusion.

Data fusion can be performed with different objectives such as inference, estimation, feature maps, aggregation, abstract sensors, classification, and compression. Techniques, methods, and algorithms used to fuse data can be classified based on several criteria, such as the data abstraction level, parameters, mathematical foundation, purpose, and type of data. Many architectures and models have been introduced to serve as guidelines to design data fusion systems.

18.1 Sensor Data-Gathering and Data-Dissemination Mechanisms

Two major factors that determine the system architecture and design methodology are:

1. The number of sources and sinks within the sensor network: Sensor network applications can be classified into three categories:
    - One-sink–multiple-sources
    - One-source–multiple-sinks
    - Multiple-sinks–multiple-sources.

   An application wherein the interaction between the sensor network and the subscribers is typically through a single gateway (sink) node falls in the multiple-sources-one-sink category. On the other hand, a traffic-reporting system that disseminates the traffic condition (e.g., an accident) at a certain location to many drivers (sinks) falls in the one-source–multiple-sinks category.
2. The trade-offs between energy, bandwidth, latency, and information accuracy: An approach cannot usually optimize its performance in all aspects. Instead, based on the relative importance of its requirements, an application usually trades less important criteria for optimizing the performance of the most important attribute. For instance, for mission-critical applications, the end-to-end latency is perhaps

the most important attribute and needs to be kept below a certain threshold, even at the expense of additional energy consumption.

Data-gathering and data-dissemination mechanisms are based on the following three factors:

- Storage location
- Direction of diffusion
- Structure of devices.

18.1.1 Mechanisms Based on Storage Location

In order to process historical queries, data collected at different sensors has to be properly stored in a database system for future query processing. Placing storage at different locations presents three scenarios:

a) External Storage (ES): All the data collected at sensors in a sensor network is relayed to the sink and stored in its storage for further processing. For a sensor network with n sensor nodes, the cost of transmitting data to the external storage is $O(\sqrt{n})$. There is no cost for external queries, while a query within the network incurs a cost of $O(\sqrt{n})$.

b) Local Storage (LS): Data is stored at each sensor's local storage and thus no communication cost for data storage is incurred. However, each sensor needs to process all queries and a query is flooded to all sensors. The cost of flooding a query is $O(\sqrt{n})$.

c) Data-centric Storage (DCS): DCS stores the data at a sensor (or a location) in the sensor network based on the content of the data. Data storage in a DCS system consists of two steps: First, the sensor maps an event it detects to a label via a consensus hash function, and then it routes the data to a node according to the label. The label can be a location and the sensor can route the data via geographic routing. We will introduce two of the representative approaches relying on geographic information, namely, Geographic Hash Table (GHT) and Distributed index for multi-dimensional (DIM) data. Both data and query communication costs are $O(\sqrt{n})$.

18.1.1.1 Database with Geographic Information

One of the most common hash functions in sensor database systems maps the data to a location and then sends the data via geographic routing to the sensor node that is closest to the mapped location for storage. If all of the sensors have the same hash function, a query with a specific content can be converted to a location where the data was stored for future retrieval.

Adopting greedy perimeter stateless routing (GPSR) as the underlying routing protocol, two differing hash functions can be employed:

a) GHT: In this, the input to the hash function is a reading of a single attribute or a specific type of event, and the hash result is a point in the two-dimensional space. If no sensor node is located at the precise coordinates of the hash result, the data is stored at the node closest to the hash result. With the use of the perimeter mode of

GPSR, the data packet traverses the entire perimeter enclosing the location of the hash result, and the closest location can be identified.

b) DIM: This function is designed especially for multidimensional range queries. DIM maps a vector of readings with multiple attributes to a two-dimensional geographic zone. Assuming that the sensors are static and are aware of their own locations and field boundaries, the entire field is divided recursively into zones. The sequence of divisions is vertical, horizontal, and so on. Each zone is encoded with a unique code based on (say) the following rule: For a vertical division (the ith division where i is an odd number), the ith bit code of the zone is encoded as "1" if it is in the right region, and as "0" otherwise. Similarly, the even bit of the code word is determined by whether the zone is above ("1") or below ("0") the divided line.

Due to the fact that sensors may not be uniformly deployed in an area, every zone just defined may not contain a sensor. In other words, a sensor needs to determine the zone(s) it owns where no other sensors reside. This can be easily achieved when a node is aware of its neighbors' locations. With the encoding rules for both zones and events, the next task is to route the event to the node that owns the zone (code word) of the event.

18.1.2 Classification of Data-Gathering Mechanisms Based on the Direction of Diffusion

The data-gathering process usually consists of two steps: Query and reply. A sink (or user) sends a query to a sensor network, and sensors that detect events matching the query send replies to the sink. Applications with different requirements opt for different communication paradigms.

1. One-phase pull diffusion: The overheads of flooding of both queries and replies are high in cases when:
   a. There exist a large number of sinks or sources.
   b. The rate of queries for different events is high.

   One-phase pull diffusion skips the flooding process of data diffusion. Instead, replies are sent back to neighbors that first send the matching queries. In other words, the reverse path is the route with the least latency. One-phase pull diffusion is well suited for scenarios in which a large number of disparate events are being queried.
2. Two-phase pull diffusion: The most representative approach in this category is directed diffusion. Both the queries for events of interest and the replies are initially disseminated via flooding, and multiple routes may be established from a source to the sink. In the second pull phase, the sink reinforces the best route (usually with the lowest latency) by increasing its data rate (i.e., gradient). Data is then sent to the sink along this route. Two-phase pull diffusion is especially well suited for applications with many sources and only a few sinks.
3. Push diffusion: In the push-diffusion mechanism, a source actively floods the information collected when it detects an event and sinks subscribe to events of interest via positive enforcements. Push diffusion is well suited for:
   a. Applications with many sinks and only a few sources, and sources generate data only occasionally.

b. Target-tracking applications in which data sources constantly change with time, and hence data routes cannot be established effectively via reinforcement. The sensor protocol for information via negotiation (SPIN) can be classified as a protocol built upon the push-diffusion mechanism.

With the knowledge of geographic scooping of either sources or sinks, users can apply the energy- and location-aware routing protocols to further reduce the flooding region, hence saving more energy.

18.1.2.1 Directed Diffusion

Directed diffusion is a two-phase pull routing mechanism in which data consumers (sinks) search for the data sources matching their interests, and the sources find the best routes to route their data back to the subscribers. Directed diffusion consists of three phases: interest propagation, data propagation, and reinforcement (Figure 18.1). Sinks first broadcast interest packets to their neighbors. When a node receives an interest packet, the packet is cached and rebroadcast to other neighbors if it is new to this node. Propagation of interest packets also sets up the gradient in the network to facilitate data delivery to the sink. A gradient specifies both a data rate and a direction to relay data. The initial data rate of the gradient is set to be a small value and will be increased if the gradient along the path is enforced.

When a node matches an interest (e.g., it is in the vicinity of the event in the target-tracking application), it generates a data packet with the data rate specified in the gradient. The data packet is unicast individually to the neighbors from which the interest packet is received. When a node receives a data packet matching a query in its interest cache, the data packet is relayed to the next hop toward the sink. Both interest and data propagation are exploratory, but the initial data rate is low.

When a sink receives data packets from some neighbors, it reinforces one of the neighbors by increasing the data rate in the interest packet. Usually, this neighbor is the one on the least-delay path. If a node receives an interest packet with a higher data rate, it also reinforces the path in the interest cache. Since the entries in the interest cache are kept as soft state, eventually only one path remains while other paths are torn down.

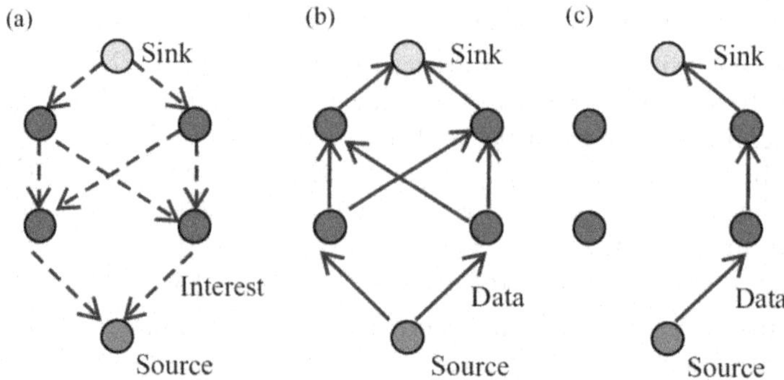

FIGURE 18.1
Three phases in directed diffusion (a) Interest propagation; (b) Data propagation; (c) Data delivery along a reinforced path.

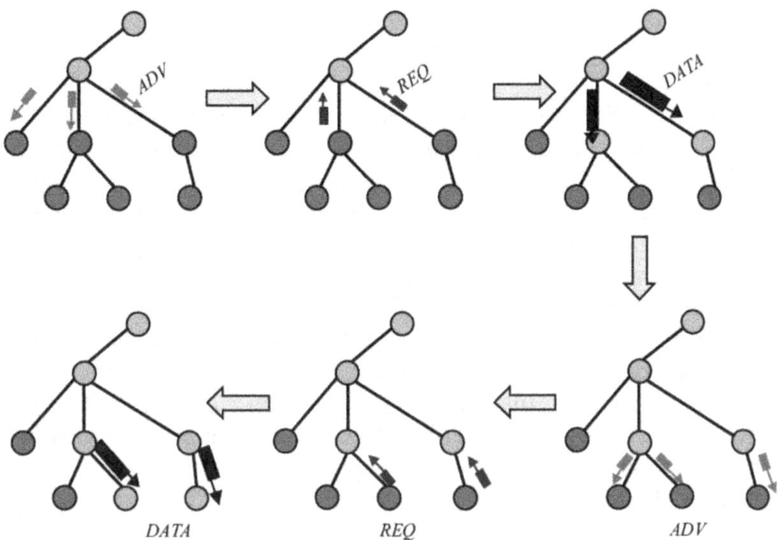

FIGURE 18.2
Three-phase handshaking protocols in SPIN.

18.1.2.2 SPIN

Sensor Protocol for Information via Negotiation (SPIN) is a push-diffusion mechanism in which data sources initiate the data-sending activities. SPIN consists of three-stage handshaking operations (Figure 18.2), including ADV (advertisement), REQ (request for data), and DATA (data message). Instead of directly flooding new data, its metadata is exchanged in the first two advertisement–subscription phases to reduce message overhead. If a node receives an advertisement with new information that is of interest to it, it replies with a request packet. The real data is then transmitted in the third phase upon receipt of such a request. Propagation of new information is executed hop-by-hop throughout the entire network.

18.1.3 Mechanisms Based on the Structure of Dissemination

The number of sources and sinks in sensor network applications not only determines the direction of diffusion but also plays a crucial role in laying the structure of dissemination in the system, especially when it is considered in conjunction with data fusion.

1. Tree

One of the most common dissemination structures used in sensor networks is a tree that is rooted at the sink and spans the set of sources from which the sink will receive information. It is usually constructed in the reverse multicast fashion. TAG (tiny aggregation) and TinyDB use sink trees for data dissemination. On the other extreme, in the scenario of a single source and multiple sinks, a tree is rooted at a source and constructed in the usual multicast fashion. The sinks broadcast their interest packets for certain events. Upon receipt of an interest packet, each sensor updates its distance to the sink and forwards the packet if it is new to the sensor. Each of the interest packets that record a minimum distance from some sink will be used by the source to construct the shortest path tree. The tree grows from the root and follows the reverse paths to reach sinks. A sensor node with a new stimulus joins the tree at the on-tree sensor that is closest to it, thus creating a new branch of the tree.

In the scalable energy-efficient asynchronous dissemination (SEAD) protocol, a dissemination tree is built to deliver data from a source (root) to multiple mobile sinks (leaves). The tree is built upon an underlying geographical routing protocol. When a mobile sink wishes to receive data from a source, it connects to the dissemination tree through one of its neighboring sensors, called an "access node." Similarly to the home agent in Mobile IP (Internet protocol), the access node acts as an anchor node to relay data to the sink. When the sink moves out of the transmission range of its access node, it informs its access node of its new whereabouts by sending a PathSetup message. The latter will then forward all the data packets that are of interest to the node.

When the distance to the original access node exceeds a predetermined threshold, the mobile sink joins a new access node. In order to reduce the number of messages transmitted over the tree, a source node duplicates its data at several replicas. The criterion for placing a replica on the tree is to minimize the extra cost of constructing a branch for a new join request.

2. Cluster

When data fusion is integrated with data dissemination, data generated by sensors is first processed locally to produce a concise digest, which is then delivered to a sink. A hierarchical cluster structure is better suited for this purpose. The low-energy adaptation clustering hierarchy (LEACH), which aims to balance the load of sensors with achievement of energy efficiency, is a two-level clustering mechanism in which sensors are partitioned into clusters. Each sensor volunteers to become a clusterhead (CH) with a certain probability, so that the task of being a CH is evenly distributed and rotated among all sensors. Once a sensor elects itself as the CH, it broadcasts a message to notify other nearby sensor nodes of the fact that it is willing to be a CH. The remaining sensors then select a minimum transmission power to join their closest CHs. Within the cluster, a CH uses time-division multiple access (TDMA) to allocate time slots to cluster members (so that the latter can relay their readings to the CH), compresses received data, and transmits a digested report directly to the base station (sink).

3. Grid

Similar to SEAD, two-tier data dissemination (TTDD) is designed for scenarios with a single source and multiple mobile sinks; however, unlike SEAD, a grid structure is adopted as the dissemination structure in TTDD. In the higher tier, a source that detects an event proactively constructs a grid structure where sensors close to the grid points are elected as dissemination nodes. In the lower tier, a mobile sink sends a query to, and receives data from, its nearest grid point on the local grid. When a sink moves to another grid, it can quickly connect to the grid structure, and the information access delay thus incurred is reduced. One of the applications for which TTDD is particularly well suited is target tracking in the battlefield.

4. Chain

If the energy efficiency and bandwidth usage requirement is more important than the latency requirement, the chain structure that allows aggregation of data along a path ending at a sink is a competitive solution. The power-efficient gathering in sensor information system

(PEGASIS) is designed to aggregate data collected by all sensors in the entire network. Only one leader is elected each time, and the leadership is rotated among all the sensors. Under the assumption that the network topology is a complete graph, the leader is able to connect all the sensors with the chain structure. Starting from the sensor at one end of the chain, data is propagated and aggregated along the chain toward the leader. Then the data dissemination and aggregation processes continue from the other end. The aggregations from both ends arrive at the leader, which directly transmits the aggregation result to the sink.

Appendix 18.A gives a brief on Wireless Sensor Network (WSN) anomalies.

18.2 Time Windows

Time windows are a commonly used approach to solve queries in open-ended data streams. Instead of computing an answer over the whole data stream, the query (or operator) is computed, eventually several times, over a finite subset of tuples. In this model, a time stamp is associated with each tuple. The time stamp defines when a specific tuple is valid (e.g., inside the window) or not. Queries run over the tuples inside the window. However, when joining multiple streams, the semantics of time stamps is much less clear, e.g., the time stamp of an output tuple.

a) Landmark windows id entify relevant points (the landmarks) in the data stream and the aggregate operator uses all record seen so far after the landmark (Figure 18.3a). Successive windows share some initial points and are of growing size. In some applications, the landmarks have a natural semantic. For example, in daily basis aggregates, the beginning of the day is a landmark.
b) Sliding windows: Most of the time, we are not interested in computing statistics over all the past but only in the recent past. The simplest solution is *sliding windows* of fixed size (Figure 18.3b). These types of windows are similar to *first in, first out* data structures. Whenever an element j is observed and inserted in the window, another element j – w, where w represents the window size, is forgotten.
c) Tilted windows: Previous windows models use a catastrophic forget; that is, any past observation is either in the window or not inside the window. In tilted

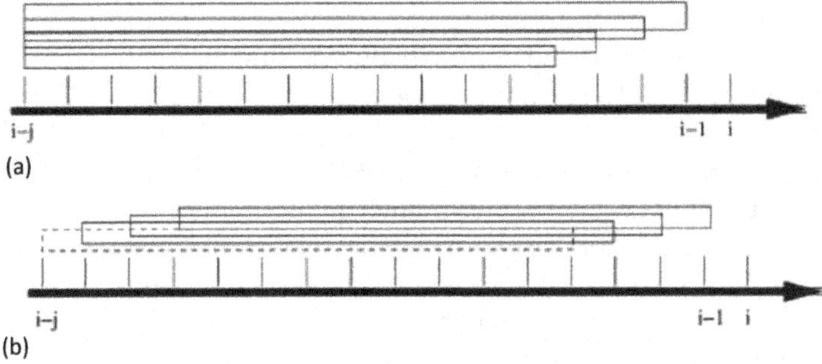

FIGURE 18.3
(a) Landmark window; (b) Sliding window.

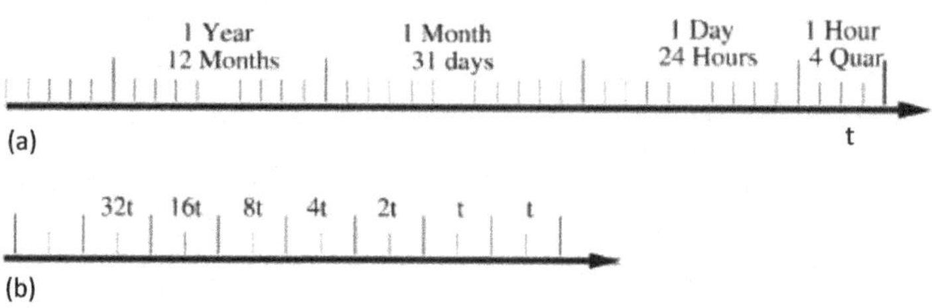

FIGURE 18.4
(a) Natural tilted window; (b) Logarithmic tilted window.

windows, the time scale is compressed. The most recent data is stored inside the window at the finest detail (granularity). Oldest information is stored at a coarser detail, in an aggregated way. The level of granularity depends on the application. This window model is designated a *tilted time window.*

Tilted time windows can be designed in several ways:

1. In *natural titled windows*, data is stored with granularity according to a natural time taxonomy: Last hour at a granularity of 15 minutes (4 points), last day in hours (24 points), last month in days (32 points), and last year in months (12 points) (Figure 18.4a).
2. In *logarithmic tilted windows*, given a maximum granularity with periods of t, the granularity decreases logarithmically as data gets older. As time goes by, the window stores the last time period t, the one before that, and consecutive aggregates of less granularity (two periods, four periods, eight periods, etc.) (Figure 18.4b.)

18.3 Sensor Database

The main purpose of a sensor database system is to facilitate the data-collection process. Users specify their interests via simple, declarative structured query language (SQL). Upon receipt of a request, the sensor database system efficiently collects and processes data within the sensor network, and disseminates the result to users. A query-processing layer between the application layer and the network layer provides an interface for users to interact with the sensor network. The layer should also be responsible for managing the resources (especially the available power).

Sensor networks can be envisioned as a distributed database for users to query the physical world. In most sensor network applications, sensors extract useful information from the environment, and either respond to queries made by users or take an active role to disseminate the information to one or more sinks. The information is then exploited by subscribers and/or users for their decision making.

Consider an environment monitoring and alert system that uses several types of sensors, including rainfall sensors, water-level sensors, weather sensors, and chemical sensors, to record the precipitation and water level regularly, to report the current weather conditions, and to issue flood or chemical pollution warnings.

A complete hierarchical architecture (four-tier) of sensor database systems for such a monitoring application is shown in Figure 18.5a. The lowest level is a group of sensor nodes that perform sensing, computing, and in-network processing in a field. The data

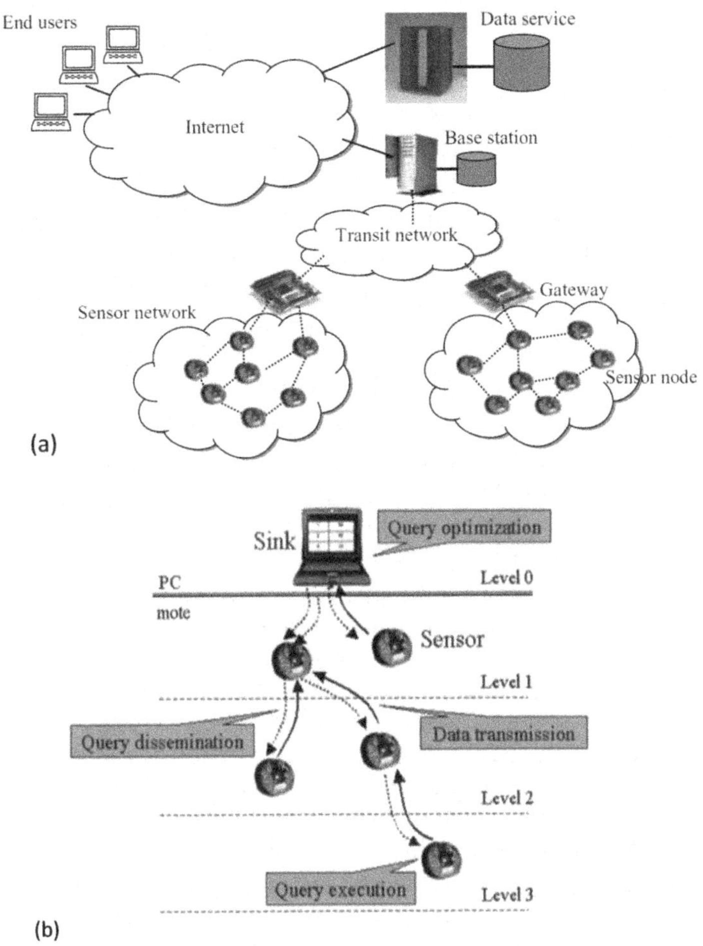

FIGURE 18.5
(a) Sensor database system architecture; (b) Procedures for query and data extraction in TinyDB.

collected within the sensor network is first propagated to its gateway node (second level). Next, the gateway node relays the data through a transit network to a remote base station (third level). Finally, the base station connects to a database replica across the Internet. Among the four tiers, the resource within the sensor networks is the most constrained. In most of the applications, the sensor network is composed of sensors and a gateway node (sink), as shown in Figure 18.5b, although the number of sinks or sources might vary from application to application.

TinyDB evolved from TAG, and is built on top of the TinyOS operating system. The sink and sensors are connected in a routing tree, shown in Figure 18.5b. A sensor chooses its parent node, which is one hop closer to the root (sink). The sink accepts queries from users outside the sensor network. Query processing can be performed in four steps:

a) Query optimization
b) Query dissemination
c) Query execution
d) Data dissemination.

For the monitoring application under consideration, there are five types of queries that users typically make:

1. Historical queries. These queries are concerned with aggregate, historical information gathered over time and stored in a database system, for example, "What was the average level of rainfall of Thane District in May 2010?"
2. Snapshot queries. These queries are concerned with the information gathered from the network at a specific (current or future) time point, for example, "Retrieve the current readings of temperature sensors in Thane District."
3. Long-running queries. These queries ask for information over a period of time, for example, "Retrieve every 30 minutes the highest temperature sensor reading in Thane District from 6 p.m. to 10 p.m. tonight."
4. Event-triggered queries. These queries prespecify the conditions that trigger queries, for example, "If the water level exceeds 10 meters in Thane District, query the rain-fall sensors about the amount of precipitation during the past hour. If the amount of precipitation exceeds 100 mm, send an emergency message to the base station to issue a flood warning."
5. Multidimensional range queries. These queries involve more than one attribute of sensor data and specify the desired search range as well, for example, "In Thane District, list the positions of all sensors that detect water level between 5 to 8 meters and have temperatures between 50 and 60 °F."

TinyDB provides a declarative SQL-like query interface for users to specify the data to be extracted. Similarly to SQL, the acquisitional query language used in TinyDB, TinySQL, consists of a select-from-where clause that supports selection, join, projection, and aggregation. The data within sensor networks can be considered as virtually a table, each column of which corresponds to an attribute and each row of which corresponds to a sample measured at a specific location and time. The query language in the sensor database differs from SQL mainly in that its queries are continuous and periodic.

Upon reception of a query, the sink performs query optimization to reduce the energy incurred in the pending query process:

- Ordering of sampling operations: Since the energy consumption incurred in retrieving readings from different types of sensors is different, the sampling operations should be reduced for sensors that consume high energy.
- Query aggregation: By combining multiple queries for the same event into a single query, only one query needs to be sent.

One distinct characteristic of query execution in TinyDB is that sensors sleep during every epoch and are synchronized to wake up, receive, transmit, and process the data in the same time period.

After a query is optimized at the sink, it is broadcast by the sink and disseminated to the sensor network. When a sensor receives a query, it has to decide whether to process the query locally and/or rebroadcasts it to its children. A sensor only needs to forward the query to those child nodes that may have the matched result. To this end, a sensor has to maintain information on its children's attribute values. In TinyDB, a semantic routing tree (SRT) containing the range of the attributes of its children is constructed at each sensor. The attributes can be static information (e.g., location) or dynamic information (e.g., light readings). For attributes that are highly correlated among neighbors in the tree, SRT can reduce the number of disseminated queries.

18.4 Data-Fusion Mechanisms

In most of the sensor network applications, sensors are deployed over a region to extract environmental data. Once data is gathered by multiple sources (e.g., sensors in the vicinity of the event of interest), it is forwarded (perhaps through multiple hops) to a single destination (sink). This, coupled with the facts that the information gathered by neighboring sensors is often redundant and highly correlated, and that the energy is much more constrained (because once deployed, most sensor networks operate in the unattended mode), necessitates data fusion. Instead of transmitting all the data to a centralized node for processing, data is processed locally and a concise digest is forwarded (perhaps through multiple hops) to sinks. Data fusion reduces the number of packets to be transmitted among sensors, and thus the usage of bandwidth and energy. Its benefits become manifest especially in a large-scale network: for a network with n sensors, the centralized approach takes $O(\sqrt{n^{3/2}})$ bit-hops, while data fusion takes only $O(\sqrt{n})$ bit-hops to transmit data.

When data fusion is considered in conjunction with data gathering and dissemination, the conventional address-centric routing, which finds the shortest routes from sources to the sink, is no longer optimal. Instead, data-centric routing, which considers in-network aggregation along the routes from multiple sources to a sink, achieves better energy and bandwidth efficiency, especially when the number of sources is large, and/or when the sources are located closely to one another and far from the sink. Figure 18.6 gives a simple illustration of data-centric routing versus address-centric routing. Source 1 chooses node A as the relaying node in address-centric routing, but node C as the relaying and data aggregation node in data-centric routing. As a result, a smaller number of packets is transmitted in data-centric routing.

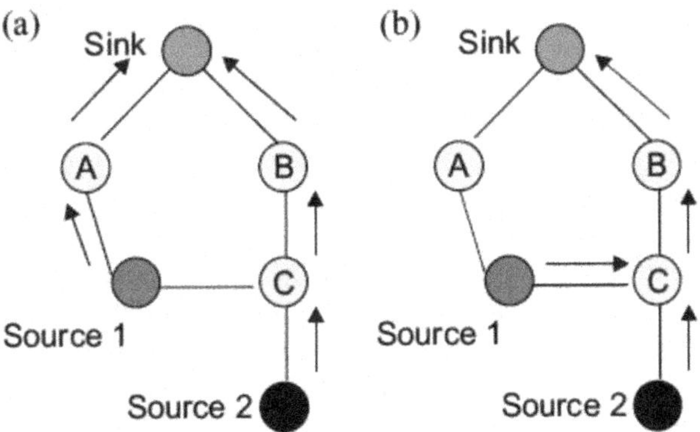

FIGURE 18.6
Address-centric routing versus data-centric routing.

18.4.1 Classification of Data-fusion Mechanisms Based on Functions

The major purpose of incorporating data fusion into the data-gathering and dissemination process is to reduce the number of packets to be transmitted, and hence the energy consumption incurred in transmission. There are two types of data aggregation: "Snapshot aggregation" is data fusion for a single event, such as tracking a target, while "periodic aggregation" periodically executes the data-fusion function, such as monitoring an environment parameter periodically.

Depending on the application requirements, three types of data-fusion functions can be used:

1. Basic operations. The most basic operations for data fusion include: COUNT, MIN, MAX, SUM, and AVERAGE.
2. Redundancy suppression. Data fusion, in this case, is equivalent to data compression. Due to the fact that correlation exists in sensor data both in spatial and temporal domains, one of the most important data-fusion functions is to eliminate data redundancy, or in more concrete terms, to exploit the correlation structure that exists in sensor data via distributed source coding.
3. Estimation of a system parameter. Based on the observations from several pieces of sensor data, the data-fusion function aims to solve an optimization problem to minimize the estimation error of a system parameter. An example of such an optimization problem is to average all the temperature readings of sensors within a room to estimate its temperature. The estimation is optimal with respect to the minimum square error (MSE) criterion. Another example is to track targets to minimize the estimation error of the target's location.

18.4.2 System Architectures of Data Fusion

Besides the sources and sinks, a sensor network that considers data fusion has an additional component—the data aggregator. There are many ways to determine the location of the data aggregator.

Data funneling is intrinsically an energy-efficient routing protocol integrated with data aggregation and compression techniques. The basic idea of data funneling is to build a cost field with the funnel shape to pull the data from sources to the sink. The sink initials directional flooding to send an interest packet toward a target region. During the process of forwarding interest packets, a forwarder computes its (energy) cost for communicating back to the sink and updates the cost field in the interest packet.

When a node within the target region receives an interest packet from the nodes outside the region, it designates itself a border node. The cost required to reach the sink (i.e., the cost in the interest packet) is recorded, and a field that is used to keep track of the cost to reach the border node is also included. Since there could be multiple "entries" (border nodes) to the target region, a node within the target region might receive multiple interest packets from border nodes. Instead of requesting all the nodes to send individual reports back to the sink, one of the border nodes is responsible for the task of collecting and aggregating all reports in the region and sending a single packet to the sink. All the sensors within the region share a common schedule of which border node is going to be the data aggregator during each round of reporting. The schedule is determined by a deterministic function of the costs to reach the sink from all border nodes. Sensors with a longer distance to the designated aggregator send their reports earlier and the readings are concatenated in a single packet to eliminate redundant headers. After receiving reports from all the sensors within the region, the designated border node further compresses the data by applying a coding technique based on ordering.

18.4.3 Trade-offs of Resources

Depending on the resource constraints in a sensor network, the following trade-offs apply: energy vs. estimation accuracy, energy vs. aggregation latency, and bandwidth vs. aggregation latency.

1. Trade-off between energy and accuracy

   The requirement of higher accuracy demands more message exchanges and leads to higher energy consumption. A distributed periodic aggregation approach, used to estimate the maximum value of sensor data in a field, entails the fact that the maximum value of sensor data is modeled to be Gaussian-distributed. Compared with multiple "snapshot aggregations," the proposed approach exploits the energy–accuracy trade-off, and provides users with a system-level knob to control the desired accuracy and energy consumption. The distributed optimization approach shows that $O(\varepsilon^{-2})$ iterations of aggregation are required to achieve the desired accuracy ε.

2. Trade-off between energy and latency

   This deals with the trade-off between energy consumption and propagation latency from data sources to a sink. Energy is saved via directly turning off the radio circuitry when a sensor is not transmitting or receiving data. While the lowduty cycle reduces power consumption, it increases the propagation latency from a data source to the sink. The protocol, sparse topology and energy management (STEM), is proposed to deal with the problem. STEM utilizes dual bands for data transmission and wake-up signaling. The channel for wake-up signaling is operated in a low-duty cycle. Each node periodically turns on the radio circuitry for the wake-up channel to hear whether any other node has attempted to communicate with it. Once a node detects such an activity in the wake-up signaling channel, it turns on its radio circuitry for the data channel. The increased latency due to the sleep state is thus bounded by the sleep–listen period in the wake-up channel. STEM is especially well suited for applications with most operations in the monitoring state. For instance, in a fire alarm system, the network only senses the environment in an energy-efficient way and the system stays in the monitoring state most of the time. Once an event takes place, the system quickly changes to the transfer state and reports the event to the data sink in a timely manner.

18.5 Data-fusion Techniques, Methods, and Algorithms

Data fusion can be performed with different objectives such as inference, estimation, feature maps, aggregation, abstract sensors, classification, and compression. Techniques, methods, and algorithms used to fuse data can be classified based on several criteria, such as the data abstraction level, parameters, mathematical foundation, purpose, and type of data.

18.5.1 Inference

Decisions are typically taken based on the knowledge of the perceived situation; fusions for making decisions are based on inference methods. Inference refers to the transition from one likely true proposition to another—whose truthfulness is believed to result from the truthfulness of the previous one. Classical inference methods are based on the Bayesian inference and the Dempster-Shafer belief accumulation theory.

1. Bayesian inference: Data fusion based on Bayesian inference provides a formalism to merge evidence according to rules of probability theory. The uncertainty is represented in terms of conditional probabilities describing the belief, and it can assume values in the [0, 1] interval, where 0 is the absolute disbelief and 1 is the absolute belief. Within the WSN domain, Bayesian inference has been used to solve the localization problem. For instance, as an alternative to finding a unique point for each node location, data from a mobile beacon can be processed by using Bayesian inference to determine the most likely geographical location of each node.
2. Dempster-Shafer inference: This is based on the Dempster-Shafer belief accumulation, which is a mathematical theory that generalizes the Bayesian theory. It deals with beliefs or mass functions just as Bayes' rule does with probabilities. The Dempster-Shafer theory introduced a formalism that can be used for incomplete knowledge representation and evidence combination. For instance, by using a WSN composed of unmanned aerial vehicles (UAVs) as sensor nodes, Dempster-Shafer inference can be used to build dynamic operational pictures of battlefields for situation evaluation.
3. Neural networks: These represent an alternative to Bayesian and Dempster-Shafer theories, being used by classification and recognition tasks in the data-fusion domain. A key feature of neural networks is the capability of learning from examples of input/output pairs in a supervised fashion. For that reason, neural networks can be used in learning systems while fuzzy logic is used to control the learning rate. For instance, neural networks have been applied to data fusion mainly for automatic target recognition using multiple complementary sensors.
4. Fuzzy logic: This generalizes probability and, therefore, is able to deal with approximate reasoning to draw conclusions from imprecise premises. Each quantitative input is fuzzyfied by a membership function. The fuzzy rules of an inference system generate fuzzy outputs which, in turn, are defuzzyfied by a set of output rules. This structure has been successfully used in real-world situations that defy exact modeling, from rice cookers to complex control systems. For instance, fuzzy reasoning can be used for deciding the best CHs in a WSN.
5. Semantic data fusion: In this method, raw sensor data is processed so that nodes exchange only the resulting semantic interpretations. The semantic abstraction allows a WSN to optimize its resource utilization when storing, collecting, and processing data. Semantic data fusion usually comprises of two phases: pattern matching and knowledge-base construction. For instance, the concept of semantic data fusion, which was applied for target classification.

18.5.2 Estimates

The estimation method was inherited from control theory and used the laws of probability to compute a process state vector from a measurement vector or a sequence of measurement vectors.

1. Least squares: A mathematical optimization technique that searches for a function that best fits a set of input measurements. This is accomplished by minimizing the sum of the square error between points generated by the function and the input measurements. The least squares method is suitable when the parameter to be estimated is considered fixed. It does not assume any prior probability.
2. Maximum likelihood (ML): Estimation methods based on likelihood are suitable when the state being estimated is not the outcome of a random variable. A distributed and localized ML can be proposed that is robust to the unreliable communication links of WSN; every node computes a local unbiased estimate that converges towards the global ML solution. This can be further extended to support asynchronous and timely delivered measurements, i.e., measurements taken at different time steps that happen asynchronously in the network. Other distributed implementations of ML for WSN include the decentralized expectation maximization (DEM) algorithm and the local ML estimator, which relaxes the requirement of sharing all the data.
3. Moving average (MV) filter: This filter is broadly adopted in DSP solutions; it computes the arithmetic mean of a number of input measurements to produce each point of the output signal. The MV filter is optimal for reducing random white noise while retaining a sharp step response. This is the reason that makes the MV the major filter for processing encoded signals in the time domain. For instance, the MV filter is used on target locations to reduce errors of tracking applications in WSN.
4. Kalman filter: This filter is used to fuse low-level redundant data. If a linear model can describe the system and the error can be modeled as Gaussian noise, the Kalman filter recursively retrieves statistically optimal estimates. However, in order to deal with non-linear dynamics and non-linear measurement models, other methods should be adopted. In WSN, schemes can be found to approximate distributed Kalman filters, in which the solution is computed based on reaching an average consensus among sensor nodes.
5. Particle filter: This filter is a recursive implementation of a statistical signal processing known as sequential Monte Carlo methods. The particles are propagated over time, sequentially combining, sampling, and resampling steps. At each time step, the resampling is used to discard some particles, increasing the relevance of regions with high posterior probability. Target tracking is currently the principal research problem wherein particle filters have been used. Although Kalman filter is a classical approach for state estimation, particle filters represent an alternative for applications with non-Gaussian noise, especially when computational power is rather cheap and the sampling rate is slow.

18.6 Data-fusion Architectures and Models

Many architectures and models have been introduced to serve as guidelines to design data-fusion systems. These models are useful for guiding the specification, proposal, and usage of data fusion in WSN. Some of these models, such as the Intelligent Cycle and the Boyd Control Loop, provide a task view of data fusion. whereas others, such as the JDL and Frankel-Bedworth, provide a systemic view of data fusion.

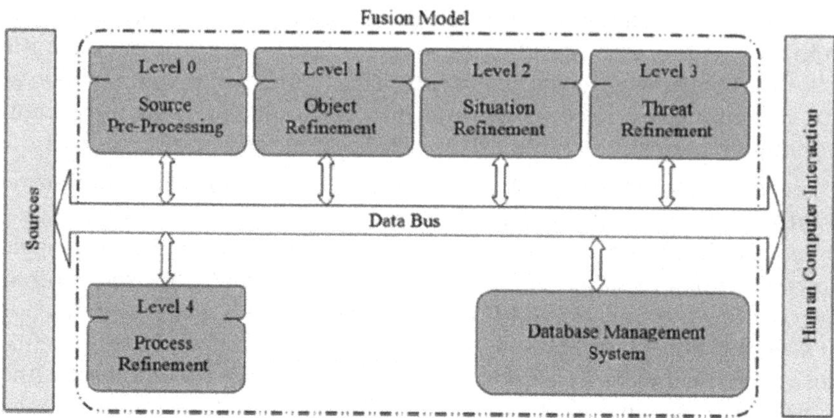

FIGURE 18.7
The JDL model.

18.6.1 Data-based Models

This section introduces the models that specify their stages based on the abstraction levels of data manipulated by the fusion system.

a) JDL model: JDL is a well-known model in the fusion research area. It was originally proposed by the U.S. Joint Directors of Laboratories (JDL) and the U.S. Department of Defense (DoD). The model consists of five processing levels as described below (Figure 18.7):
   - Level 0 (source preprocessing): Also referred to as process alignment, this level aims to reduce the processing load by allocating data to appropriate processes and selecting appropriate sources.
   - Level 1 (object refinement): It converts the data into a consistent structure. Source localization, and, therefore, all tracking algorithms are in level 1, since they transform different types of data, such as images, angles, and acoustic data, into a target location.
   - Level 2 (situation refinement): It attempts to provide a contextual description of the relationship between objects and observed events. It uses a prior knowledge and environmental data to identify a situation.
   - Level 3 (threat refinement): It estimates the current situation, projecting it into the future to identify possible threats, vulnerabilities, and opportunities for operations. This is a difficult task because it deals with computation complexities and enemies' intent assessment.
   - Level 4 (process refinement): It is responsible for monitoring the system performance and allocating the sources according to the specified goals. This function may be outside the domain of specific data-fusion functions.

b) Dasarathy model: The Dasarathy model is a fine-grained data-centered model in which the elements of data fusion are specified based on their inputs and outputs. It is also known as Data-Feature-Decision (DFD) (Figure 18.8). In contrast to the JDL model, the DFD model does not provide a systemic view; instead it provides a

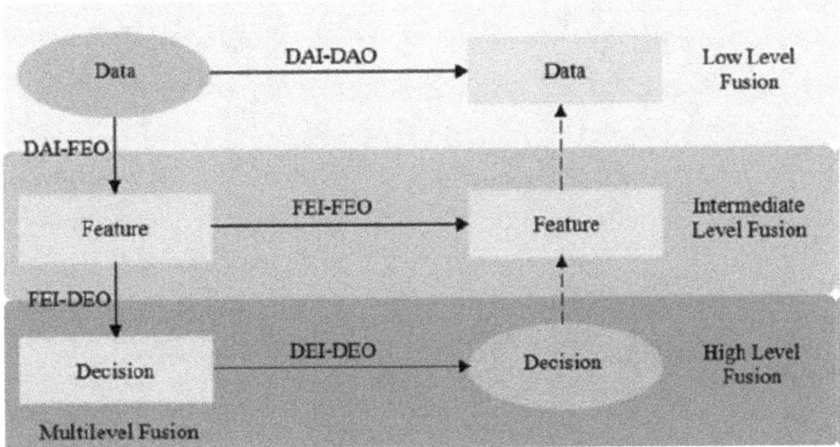

FIGURE 18.8
The DFD model.

fine-grained way to specify fusion tasks by means of the expected input and output data. The DFD model is useful for specifying and designing fusion algorithms in WSNs with different purposes, such as ambient noise estimation.

Data fusion processes are categorized based on the level of abstraction of the input and output data:

- Data in–data out (DAI-DAO): In this class, data fusion deals with raw data and the result is also raw data, possibly more accurate or reliable.
- Data in–feature out (DAI-FEO): Data fusion uses raw data from sources to extract features or attributes that describe an entity. Entity here means any object, situation, or world abstraction.
- Feature in–feature out (FEI-FEO): It works on a set of features to improve/refine a feature, or extract new ones.
- Feature in–decision out (FEI-DEO): Data fusion takes a set of features of an entity generating a symbolic representation or a decision.
- Decision in–decision out (DEI-DEO): Decisions can be fused in order to obtain new decisions or give emphasis to previous ones.

18.6.2 Activity-based Models

Some models are specified based on the activities that must be performed by the data-fusion system. The activities and their correct sequence of execution, in such models, are explicitly specified.

1) Boyd control loop: This is a cyclic model composed of four stages. It is known also as the observe, orient, decide, act (OODA) loop (Figure 18.9a). This model is a representation of the classic decision-support mechanism of military data systems, and because such systems are strongly coupled with fusion systems, the OODA loop has been used to design data-fusion systems.

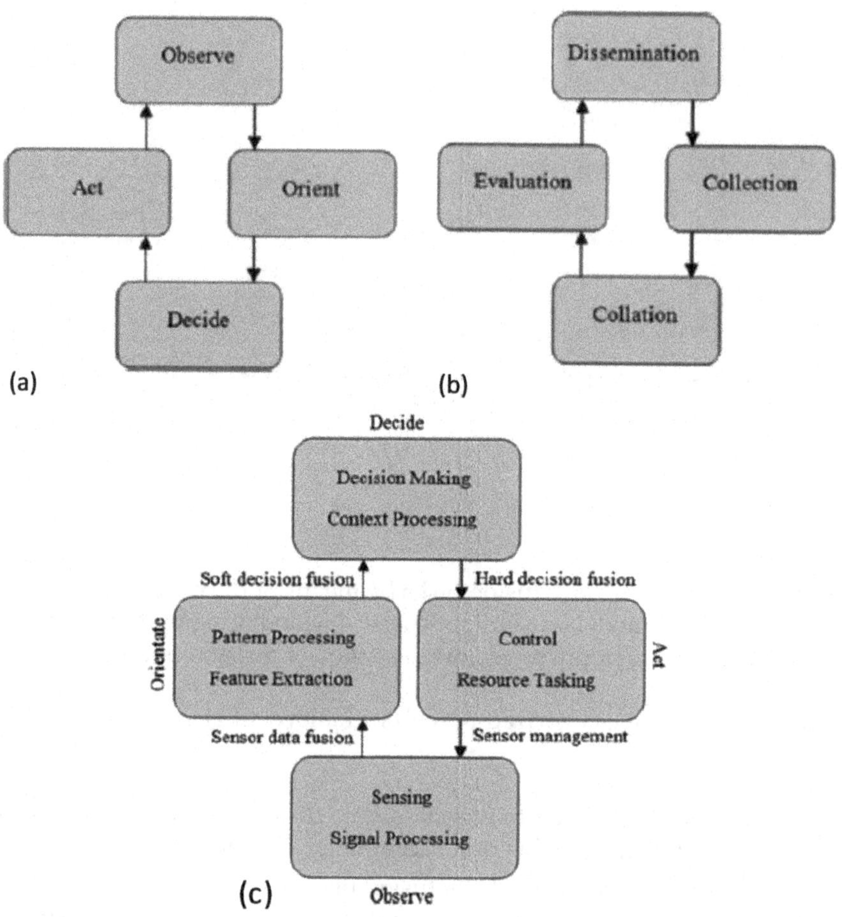

FIGURE 18.9
(a) OODA loop (b) Intelligent cycle; (c) Omnibus model.

The stages of the OODA loop define the major activities related to the fusion process:

- Observe: Data gathering from the available sources. It corresponds to level 0 of the JDL model.
- Orient: Gathered data is fused to obtain an interpretation of the current situation. It encompasses levels 1, 2, and 3 of the JDL model.
- Decide: Specify an action plan in response to the understanding of the situation. It matches level 4 of JDL model.
- Act: The plan is executed. It is not dealt with by the JDL model.

2) Intelligence cycle: The intelligence process is a four-stage cycle called "intelligence cycle" (Figure 18.9b). The activities constituting this cycle are:

- Collection: Raw data is collected from the environment. It matches level 0 of the JDL model.
- Collation: Collected data is compared, analyzed, and correlated. Irrelevant and unreliable data is discarded. It includes level 1 of the JDL model.

- Evaluation: Collated data is fused and analyzed. It comprises levels 2 and 3 of the JDL model.
- Dissemination: Fusion results are delivered to users who utilize the fused data to produce decisions and actions in response to the detected situation. It corresponds to level 4 of the JDL model.

3) Omnibus model: This model organizes the stages of a data-fusion system in a cyclic sequence, just as the intelligence cycle and the OODA loop do. The omnibus model should be applied during the design phase of a data-fusion system. Initially, it should be used to model the framework providing a general perception of the system. Then, the model can be employed to design the subtasks, providing a fine-grained understanding of the system. Figure 18.9c shows the omnibus model, which is suitable for data systems that deal with any kind of sources, including sensors.

18.6.3 Role-based Models

The role-based model represents a change of focus on how data-fusion systems can be modeled and designednThese systems are specified based on the fusion roles and the relationships among them, providing a more fine-grained model for the fusion system. Like the JDL model, the role-based model provides a systemic view of data fusion. It provides a set of roles and specifies the relationships among them, but it does not specify fusion tasks or activities.

1) Object-oriented model: This model (Figure 18.10a) consist of four roles:
   - Actor: It is responsible for the interaction with the world, collecting data, and acting on the environment.
   - Perceiver: After data is gathered, the perceiver assesses such data providing a contextualized analysis to the director.
   - Director: The director builds an action plan specifying the system's goals, based on the analysis provided by the perceiver.
   - Manager: It controls the actors to execute the plans formulated by the director.

2) Frankel-Bedworth architecture:

This architecture introduces the notion of a global process separated from the local process. The global control process rules the local process by monitoring its performance and controlling its goals. Moreover, the local process is supposed to perform and implement fusion methods and algorithms to accomplish the system's objectives. This architecture expands the previous models, which were concerned only with the local process aspects. In WSN, the global control process will most likely be performed by human beings who feed the network with operation guidelines, whereas the local estimation process should be implemented within the computational system.

The Frankel-Bedworth architecture is composed by two self-regulatory processes (Figure 18.10b):

1) Local: The local estimation process manages the execution of the current activities based on goals and timetables provided by the global process. It tries to achieve the specified goals and maintain the specified standards. This process has the role

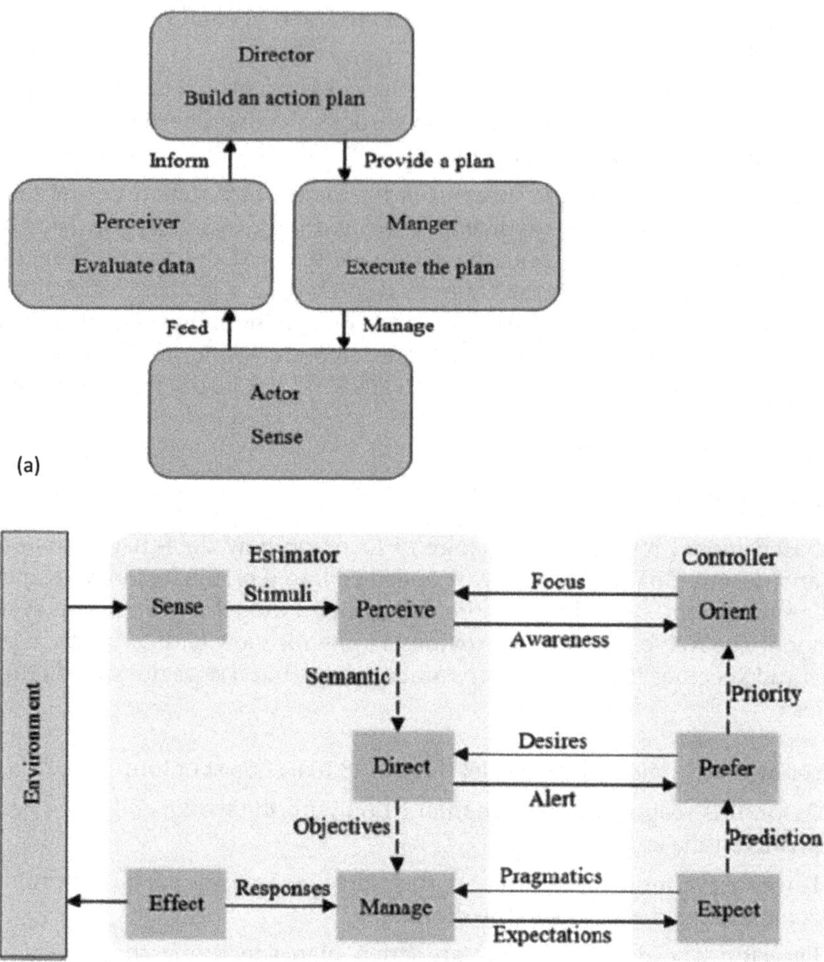

FIGURE 18.10
(a) Object-oriented model; (b) Frankel-Bedworth architecture.

of estimator, which is similar to the previous fusion models and includes the following tasks:

- Sense: Data is gathered by the data sources.
- Perceive: Stimuli retrieved by sensing are dealt with according to their relevance (focus), and the controller is informed of which stimuli are being used (awareness).
- Direct: Based on the comprehension of the perception (semantics), the estimator can provide feedback (alert) to the controller. The disparity between the current situation and the desired situation is evaluated. Then, the estimator is fed forward with desires that specify new goals and timetables.
- Manage: Based on the objectives, the controller is activated to define what is practical (pragmatics) so the estimator can provide an appropriate response.

Then, the estimator provides a feedback to the controller by reporting the expectations about the provided decision (sensitivity).

- Effect-selected decisions (responses) are applied and the control loop is closed by sensing the changes in the environment.

2) Global: The global process updates the goals and timetables according to the feedback provided by the local process. It manages the goals of the system during the execution of the local process and has the role of controller; this means it is responsible for controlling and managing the estimator role, and includes the following tasks:

   - Orient: The relevance of sensed stimuli is configured.
   - Prefer: Priority is given to the aspects that are most relevant to the goal-achieving behavior, detailing the local goals.
   - Expect: A prediction is made and the intentional objective is filtered, determining what is practical to the estimator pragmatics.

18.7 Summary

The node distribution, communication, and dissemination strategies as well as the cooperative processing capabilities of hundreds or even thousands of small devices are critical aspects to ensure the actual performance and reliability of the planned application. The chapter started with a discussion on sensor data-gathering and data-dissemination mechanisms. The main purpose of a sensor database system is to facilitate the data-collection process.

Once data is gathered by multiple sources (e.g., sensors in the vicinity of the event of interest), it is forwarded (perhaps through multiple hops) to a single destination (sink). This, coupled with the facts that the information gathered by neighboring sensors is often redundant and highly correlated, and that the energy is much more constrained (because once deployed, most sensor networks operate in the unattended mode), creates the need for data fusion.

Data fusion can be performed with different objectives such as inference, estimation, feature maps, aggregation, abstract sensors, classification, and compression. Techniques, methods, and algorithms used to fuse data can be classified based on several criteria, such as data abstraction level, parameters, mathematical foundation, purpose, and type of data. Many architectures and models have been introduced to serve as guidelines to design data-fusion systems.

Appendix 18.A: Wireless Sensor Networks Anomalies

Wireless sensor networks (WSNs) can experience unexpected problems during deployment, due to hardware, software, or environmental anomalies especially since they rely on resource-constrained embedded devices for communicating, processing, and sensing. This appendix examines WSN anomalies from a systems perspective, covering anomalies that arise at the network, node, and data levels. WSNs and other networks used in extreme conditions (e.g., in space) are more likely than conventional networks to experience anomalies related to connectivity or hardware failures.

One of the main challenges for WSN anomaly detection is determining where to embed the intelligence for detecting and localizing anomalies. From a WSN user or operator perspective, it is crucial that a network management tool embeds the required intelligence to detect all possible anomaly types, as the network is perceived holistically as an intelligent data delivery system. While centralized approaches rely on more comprehensive network state information available at the back-end and are thus simpler to implement, distributed approaches provide more scalable and responsive anomaly detection, as nodes can immediately detect network problems in their vicinity. A challenge for distributed anomaly detection is its implementation complexity and the limited state information available at resource-constrained sensor nodes.

Anomalies can range from faults, such as complete hardware failure, to unexpected system performance, such as gradual degradation. The conditions that signal an anomaly relate to the user policy for a particular application. For instance, an operator sets the frequency and time-out period for data delivery by the sensor nodes. These determine the thresholds for detecting and reporting anomalies to operators. The frequency, urgency, and level of detail within the notification can also be user defined.

WSN anomalies fall into three broad categories:

- Network anomalies: Network anomalies are communication-related problems that arise in WSNs. Their typical symptoms are an unexpected increase or decrease in the amount of packets traversing the network loss.
  - Loss of connectivity can occur at a group of nodes, or indeed at all network nodes. The detection of connectivity losses follows a simple process: any network entity can keep track of incoming packets from other nodes. The lack of reception of packets from a group of nodes for a certain duration, defined by the time-out period set in the operator policy, signals partial or full loss of connectivity with these nodes. Alternatively, operators can set a threshold for the number of missed packets to signal loss of connectivity.
  - Intermittent connectivity is a related network anomaly. Intermittent connectivity occurs when the frequency of the data reception from certain nodes is highly variable relative to an operator-set link stability threshold. This anomaly also varies in scope and can cover few or all nodes.
  - Routing loops occur when a packet is relayed across several nodes and arrives back at the originating node. Because such packets may never make it to the base node, detecting this anomaly requires either:
    - Injection of diagnostic packets by the base into the network to determine that the routing loops exist and the software problem that is causing them.
    - Maintenance of the full network topology at the base node.
    - Use of source routing protocols to allow nodes to detect their own ID in the path to the destination, and to generate problem reports.

    Since routing loops inherently involve several nodes, all of the foregoing methods involve large communication overhead to maintain node IDs in packets or to generate global topology information at the base, so they do not scale well with network size.

- Broadcast storms. Nodes that lose connectivity with their routing parents may decide to continuously broadcast packets to discover alternate paths to the base station. Trickle timers are used for maintaining a consistent state within WSNs. As long as there are no changes to the local state, a node doubles its Trickle timer, effectively doubling the beaconing period. However, when a node detects a change in its local state, it resets its Trickle timer to the lowest possible value (commonly in the range of milliseconds). When multiple nodes simultaneously follow this behavior, the local channel becomes heavily congested. If a certain number of duplicate broadcast packets arrive from more than one node, then a broadcast storm has started. A common root cause of broadcast storms is loss of routing connectivity, which causes nodes to probe neighbors in the hope of regaining connectivity.

- Node anomalies:
  - Node-level anomalies are rooted in hardware or software problems at a single node and are not related to communications with neighboring nodes. Because they arise in single nodes, distributed detection of node anomalies can be highly effective. A common node-level symptom is when a node stops transmitting data. The most likely cause of this node anomaly is the failure/degradation of solar panels or battery issues that lead to onboard power drops.
  - Node failure. The node memory, central processing unit (CPU), or radio may also enter a locked state or fail during a deployment. This situation may arise due to poor or defective hardware components, or poor software integration of the components. Detecting this anomaly is challenging, as the problem with a specific component may not exhibit any detectable symptoms by neighbors or at the base node. In this case, only proactive checking of node integrity can detect the problem's existence.

Malicious entities may attempt to gain control of sensor nodes and alter their operation. If the attack specifically alters data readings, this may be detectable by statistical methods.

- Data anomalies:

  Data anomaly detection depends on statistical irregularities in the data. These irregularities may be caused by
  - Miscalibrated or faulty sensor hardware: Sensor hardware problems are data anomalies rather than node anomalies because they manifest themselves in erroneous data values rather than the failure or degraded performance of the node. Faulty sensors typically report extreme or unrealistic values that are easily distinguishable.
  - Environmental variations: Environmental variation causes sensor data values to change rapidly, but the sensor readings remain within reasonable ranges.

One can distinguish data anomalies by spatial or temporal comparison between several sensors since it is unlikely that many sensors will exhibit a calibration skew or failure at the same time. Security breaches can also lead to anomalous data values from sensor nodes.

There are three broad categories of data anomalies:

- *Temporal anomaly* at a single node location due to changes in data values over time. The detection of temporal data anomalies can take place locally at each node, which requires the node to store historical data, or at a central point.
    - Temporal anomalies exhibit one of several symptoms:
        - High variability in subsequent sensor readings at the same node could signify major changes or events in the sensed environment, or they could arise from sensor voltage fluctuations.
        - Lack of change in sensor readings may indicate a locked state or that the sensor has failed to obtain new samples.
        - Gradual reading skews could indicate a need for sensor recalibration.
        - Out-of-bound readings represent sensor values that are physically not possible, which points toward a major malfunction of the sensor.
- *Spatial anomaly* at a single node location due to comparison with neighboring nodes. For example, if the measurement of air temperature on one node differs from the measurements of all the surrounding nodes, then it is highly likely that the data is spatially anomalous, and is due to a calibration error in the sensor. This applies to some types of data, such as temperature and humidity, which typically have low spatial variation, but not to data such as audio and video, which differs dramatically at neighboring nodes, depending on the angle and location of signal capture.
- *Spatiotemporal anomaly* detected through a number of node locations due to changes in data value over time and space. Spatiotemporal data anomalies combine both spatial and temporal variations, inherently involving more than one node. For example, changes in the chemical content of a waterway represent a spatiotemporal anomaly. This will affect nodes along the waterway at different times. Diagnosing this anomaly should account for data throughout the network over a certain period of time. Temporal anomalies can be detected locally at each node, while spatial and spatiotemporal anomalies require more involved inter-node interaction to establish the existence of the anomaly.

18.A.1 Architectural Design Guidelines

The architectural choices for various anomaly types are

- For network anomalies, centralized detection is useful when diagnostic network data can be piggybacked in packets, providing the centralized anomaly detector with a comprehensive view of the network state. More complex network anomalies, such as routing loops, are best detected with distributed or hybrid detection, where nodes can snoop on packets that they forward to detect a loop, or link quality changes, where a node is in the best position to determine the quality of its own links.

- For node anomalies, centralized, hybrid, and distributed approaches are all suitable for detection and localization using the source node ID. However, finding the root cause of the node anomaly is more challenging in centralized detection, as the strategy can only hypothesize on the cause on the basis of the data at the back-end. A distributed approach provides more responsive node anomaly detection.
- For data anomalies, centralized detection is slow relative to distributed detection, which can rely on threshold, spatial, or temporal comparisons run locally at each node. For computationally challenging anomalies, a hybrid approach that locally detects problems then triggers more involved analysis centrally is most suitable.

19

Big Data Computing

The rapid growth of the Internet and World Wide Web has led to vast amounts of information becoming available online. In addition, business and government organizations create large amounts of both structured and unstructured information, which needs to be processed, analyzed, and linked. The amount of information stored in digital form in 2007 is estimated at 281 exabytes, and the overall compound growth rate at 57%, with information in organizations growing at an even faster rate. It is also estimated that 95% of all current information exists in unstructured form, which has increased data processing requirements compared to structured information. The storing, managing, accessing, and processing of this vast amount of data represents a fundamental need, and it will be an immense challenge to satisfy all requirements to search, analyze, mine, and visualize this data as information.

The web is believed to have well over a trillion web pages, at least 50 billion of which have been catalogued and indexed by search engines such as Google, which made them searchable by all of us. This massive web content spans well over 100 million domains (i.e., locations where we point our browsers, such as <http://www.wikipedia.org>). These are themselves growing at a rate of more than 20,000 net domain additions daily. Facebook and Twitter have over 900 million users each, who generate over 300 million posts a day (roughly 250 million tweets and over 60 million Facebook updates). Added to this are over 10,000 credit-card payments made per second, well over 30 billion point-of-sale transactions per year (via dial-up POS devices), and finally over 6 billion mobile phones, of which almost 1 billion are smart phones. Many of these are GPS-enabled, with access the Internet for e-commerce, tweets, and to post updates on Facebook. Finally, and last but not least, there are the images and videos on YouTube and other sites, which by themselves outstrip all these put together in terms of the sheer volume of data they represent.

Big Data batch computing is a model of storing and then computing, such as the MapReduce framework open-sourced by the Hadoop implementation. Big data stream computing (BDSC) is a model of straight-through computing, such as Storm and S4, which does for stream computing what Hadoop does for batch computing (see Chapter 20).

For applications such as sensor networks, network monitoring, microblogging, web exploring, social networking, and so on, a big data input stream has the characteristics of high speed, real time, and large volume. These data sources often take the form of continuous data streams, and timely analysis of such a data stream is very important as the life cycle of most of this data is very short. The volume of data is so high that there is not enough space for storage, and not all data needs to be stored. Thus, the "storing and then computing" batch computing model does not suit such requirements at all. Increasingly, data in big data environments has been acquiring the features of streams, and BDSC has emerged as a panacea for computing data online within real-time constraints.

Stream computing is a computing paradigm that reads data from collections of software or hardware sensors in stream form and computes such continuous data streams, where the output results are also in the form of a real-time data stream. Thus,

1. Data stream is a sequence of data sets.
2. Continuous stream is an infinite sequence of data sets.
3. Parallel streams have more than one stream to be processed at the same time.

Stream computing is an effective way to support big data by providing extremely low-latency velocities with massively parallel processing (MPP) architectures and is becoming the fastest and most efficient way to obtain useful knowledge from big data, allowing organizations to react quickly when problems appear or to predict new trends in the near future.

19.1 Introduction to Big Data

This deluge of data, along with emerging techniques and technologies used to handle it, is commonly referred to as "big data." Such big data is both valuable and challenging, because of its sheer volume. So much so that the volume of data created in the five years from 2010 to 2015 will exceed all the data generated in human history by far. The web, where all this data is being produced and resides, consists of millions of servers, with data storage soon to be measured in zettabytes.

Cloud computing provides the opportunity for organizations with limited internal resources to implement large-scale big data computing applications in a cost-effective manner. The fundamental challenges of big data computing are managing and processing exponentially growing data volumes, significantly reducing associated data analysis cycles to support practical, timely applications, and developing new algorithms that can scale to search and process massive amounts of data. The answer to these challenges is the use of scalable, integrated computer systems' hardware and software architecture designed for parallel processing of big data computing applications. This chapter explores the challenges of big data computing.

19.1.1 What Is Big Data?

Big data can be defined as volumes of data available in varying degrees of complexity, generated at different velocities and varying degrees of ambiguity that cannot be processed using traditional technologies, processing methods, algorithms, or any commercial off-the-shelf solutions. Data defined as big data includes weather, geospatial, and geographic information system (GIS) data; consumer-driven data from social media; enterprise-generated data from legal, sales, marketing, procurement, finance, and human-resources departments; and device-generated data from sensor networks, nuclear plants, X-ray and scanning devices, and airplane engines (Figures 19.1 and 19.2).

19.1.1.1 Data Volume

The most interesting data for any organization to tap into today is social media data. The amount of data generated by consumers every minute provides extremely important insights into choices, opinions, influences, connections, brand loyalty, brand management,

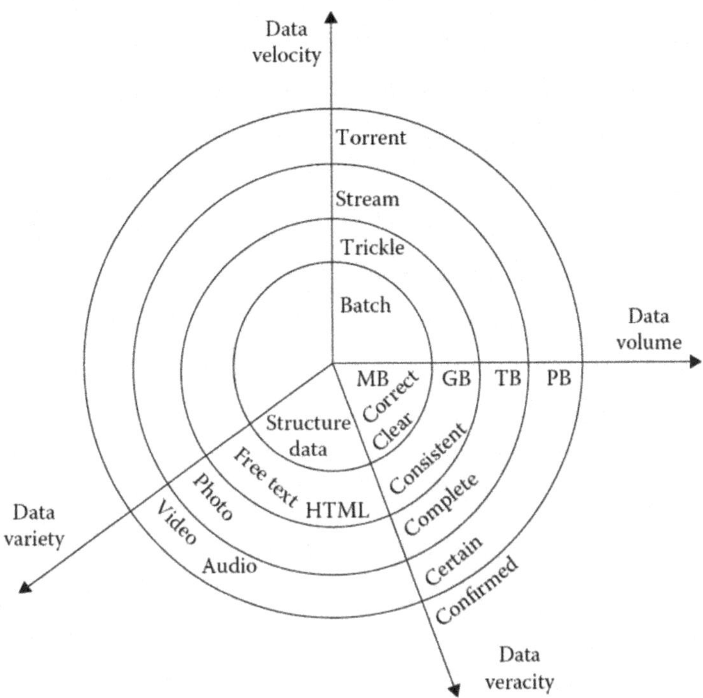

FIGURE 19.1
4V characteristics of big data.

and much more. Social media sites provide not only consumers' perspectives but also competitive positioning, trends, and access to communities formed by common interest. Organizations today leverage social media pages to personalize the marketing of products and services to each customer.

Many additional applications are being developed and are slowly becoming a reality. These applications include remote sensing to detect underground sources of energy, environmental monitoring, traffic monitoring, and regulation by automatic sensors mounted on vehicles and roads, remote monitoring of patients using special scanners and equipment, and tighter control and replenishment of inventories using RFID and other technologies. All these developments will come with a large volume of data. Social networks such as Twitter and Facebook have hundreds of millions of subscribers worldwide who generate new data with every message they send or post they make.

Every enterprise has massive amounts of e-mails that are generated by its employees, customers, and executives on a daily basis. These e-mails are all considered an asset of the corporation and need to be managed as such. After Enron and the collapse of many audits in enterprises, the U.S. government mandated that all enterprises should have a clear life-cycle management of e-mails, and that e-mails should be available and auditable on a case-by-case basis. There are several examples that come to mind, such as insider trading, intellectual property, competitive analysis, and much more, to justify the governance and management of e-mails.

If companies can analyze petabytes of data (equivalent to 20 million four-drawer file cabinets filled with text files or 13.3 years of HDTV content) with acceptable performance to discern patterns and anomalies, businesses can begin to make sense of data in new ways. Table 19.1 indicates the escalating scale of data.

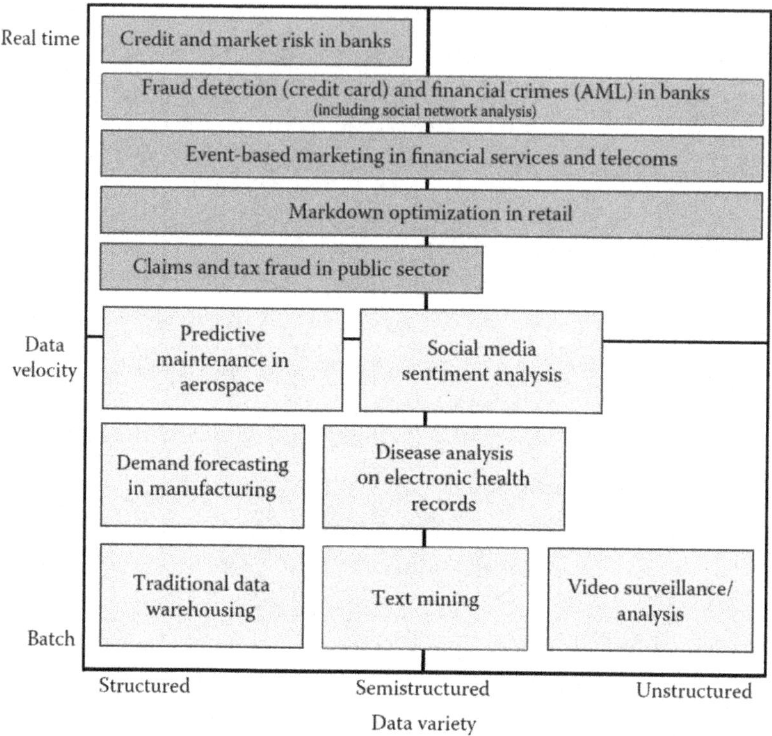

FIGURE 19.2
Use cases for big data computing.

TABLE 19.1
Scale of Data

Size of Data	Scale of Data
1,000 megabytes	1 gigabyte (GB)
1,000 gigabytes	1 terabyte (TB)
1,000 terabytes	1 petabyte (PB)
1,000 petabytes	1 exabyte (EB)
1,000 exabytes	1 zettabyte (ZB)
1,000 zettabytes	1 yottabyte (YB)

The list of features for handling data volume includes the following:

- Nontraditional and unorthodox data processing techniques need to be innovated
- to process this data type.
- Metadata is essential for processing this data successfully.
- Metrics and key performance indicators (KPIs) are key to provide visualization.
- Raw data does not need to be stored online to be accessed.
- The processed output needs to be integrated into an enterprise-level analytical ecosystem to provide better insights and visibility into the trends and outcomes of

business exercises, including customer relationship management (CRM), optimization of inventory, clickstream analysis, and more.
- The enterprise data warehouse (EDW) is needed for analytics and reporting.

19.1.1.2 Data Velocity

The business models adopted by Amazon, Facebook, Yahoo!, and Google, which have become the de facto business models for most web-based companies, operate on the fact that by tracking customer clicks and navigation on the website, you can deliver personalized browsing and shopping experiences. In this process of clickstreams, there are millions of clicks gathered from users every second, amounting to large volumes of data. This data can be processed, segmented, and modeled to study populations' behavior based on time of the day, geography, advertisement effectiveness, click behavior, and guided navigation response. The result sets of these models can be stored to create a better experience for the next set of clicks exhibiting similar behaviors. The velocity of data produced by user clicks on any website today is a prime example for big data velocity. Real-time data and streaming data are accumulated by the likes of Twitter and Facebook at very high velocity. Velocity is helpful in detecting trends among people that are tweeting a million tweets every three minutes. The processing of streaming data for analysis also involves the velocity dimension. Similarly, high velocity is attributed to data associated with the typical speed of transactions on stock exchanges; this speed reaches billions of transactions per day on certain days. If these transactions must be processed to detect potential fraud, or billions of call records on cell phones need processing in order to detect malicious activity, we are dealing with the velocity dimension.

The most popular way to share pictures, music, and data today is via mobile devices. The sheer volume of data that is transmitted by mobile networks provides insights to the providers on the performance of their network, the amount of data processed at each tower, the time of the day, the associated geographies, user demographics, location, latencies, and much more. The velocity of data movement is unpredictable, and sometimes can cause a network to crash. Studying data movement has enabled mobile service providers to improve the QoS, and associating this data with social media inputs has provided insights into competitive intelligence.

The list of features for handling data velocity includes the following:

- Systems must be elastic to handle data velocity along with volume.
- Systems must scale up and scale down as needed without increasing costs.
- Systems must be able to process data across the infrastructure in the lowest processing time.
- Systems' throughput should remain stable independently of data velocity.
- Systems should be able to process data on a distributed platform.

19.1.1.3 Data Variety

Data comes in multiple formats, as it ranges from e-mails to tweets to social media and sensor data. There is no control over the input data format or the structure of the data. The processing complexity associated with a variety of formats is the availability of appropriate metadata for identifying what is contained in the actual data. This is critical when we process images, audio, video, and large chunks of text. The absence of metadata or

TABLE 19.2
Value of Big Data across Industries

	Volume of Data	Velocity of Data	Variety of Data	Underutilized Data (*Dark Data*)	Big Data Value Potential
Banking and securities	High	High	Low	Medium	High
Communications and media services	High	High	High	Medium	High
Education	Very low	Very low	Very low	High	Medium
Government	High	Medium	Medium	High	High
Healthcare providers	Medium	High	High	Medium	High
Insurance	Medium	Medium	Medium	Medium	Medium
Manufacturing	High	High	High	High	High
Chemicals and natural resources	High	High	High	High	Medium
Retail	High	High	High	Low	High
Transportation	Medium	Medium	Medium	High	Medium
Utilities	Medium	Medium	Medium	Medium	Medium

partial metadata means processing delays from the ingestion of data to the production of the final metrics, and, more importantly, in the integration of the results with the data warehouse (Table 19.2). The sources of data in traditional applications were mainly transactions involving financial, insurance, travel, healthcare, and retail industries, and governmental and judicial processing. The types of sources have expanded dramatically and include Internet data (e.g., clickstream and social media), research data (e.g., surveys and industry reports), location data (e.g., mobile device data and geospatial data), images (e.g., surveillance, satellites, and medical scanning), e-mails, supply chain data (e.g., EDI—electronic data interchange, vendor catalogs), signal data (e.g., sensors and RFID devices), and videos (YouTube enters hundreds of minutes of video every minute). Big data includes structured, semistructured, and unstructured data in different proportions based on context.

The list of features for handling data variety includes the following:

- Scalability
- Distributed processing capabilities
- Image processing capabilities
- Graph processing capabilities
- Video and audio processing capabilities

19.1.1.4 Data Veracity

The veracity dimension of big data is a more recent addition than the advent of the Internet.

Veracity has two built-in features: The credibility of the source and the suitability of data for its target audience. It is closely related to trust; listing veracity as one of the dimensions of big data amounts to saying that data coming into the so-called big data applications has different levels of trustworthiness, and therefore, before we accept it for analytical or other applications, it must go through some degree of quality testing and credibility analysis.

Many sources generate data that is uncertain, incomplete, and inaccurate, therefore making its veracity questionable.

19.1.2 Common Characteristics of Big Data Computing Systems

There are several important common characteristics of big data computing systems that distinguish them from other forms of computing.

1. Principle of co-location of the data and programs or algorithms to perform the computation: To achieve high performance in big data computing, it is important to minimize the movement of data. This principle—"move the code to the data"—which was designed into the data parallel processing architecture implemented by Seisint in 2003, is extremely effective since the program size is usually small in comparison to the large data sets processed by big data systems, and results in much lower network traffic since the data can be read locally instead of across the network. In direct contrast to other types of computing and supercomputing that utilize data stored in a separate repository or servers and transfer the data to the processing system for computation, big data computing uses distributed data and distributed file systems in which the data is located across a cluster of processing nodes, and instead of moving the data, the program or algorithm is transferred to the nodes with the data that needs to be processed. This characteristic allows processing algorithms to execute on the nodes where the data resides, reducing system overhead and increasing performance.
2. Programming model utilized: Big data computing systems utilize a machine-independent approach in which applications are expressed in terms of high-level operations on data, and the runtime system transparently controls the scheduling, execution, load balancing, communications, and movement of programs and data across the distributed computing cluster. The programming abstraction and language tools allow the processing to be expressed in terms of data flows and transformations incorporating new dataflow programming languages and shared libraries of common data manipulation algorithms, such as sorting. Conventional supercomputing and distributed computing systems typically utilize machine-dependent programming models that can require low-level programmer control of processing and node communications, using conventional imperative programming languages and specialized software packages that add complexity to the parallel programming task and reduce programmer productivity. A machine-dependent programming model also requires significant tuning and is more susceptible to single points of failure.
3. Focus on reliability and availability: Large-scale systems with hundreds or thousands of processing nodes are inherently more susceptible to hardware failures, communications errors, and software bugs. Big data computing systems are designed to be fault resilient. This includes redundant copies of all data files on disk, storage of intermediate processing results on disk, automatic detection of node or processing failures, and selective recomputation of results. A processing cluster configured for big data computing is typically able to continue its operation with a reduced number of nodes following a node failure, with automatic and transparent recovery of incomplete processing.
4. Scalability: A final important characteristic of big data computing systems is the inherent scalability of the underlying hardware and software architecture. Big

data computing systems can typically be scaled in a linear fashion to accommodate virtually any amount of data, or to meet time-critical performance requirements by simply adding processing nodes to a system configuration in order to achieve billions of records per second processing rates (BORPS). The number of nodes and processing tasks assigned for a specific application can be variable or fixed depending on the hardware, software, communications, and distributed file system architecture. This scalability helps solve computing problems once considered to be intractable due to the amount of data or processing time required, and affords opportunities for new breakthroughs in data analysis and information processing.

One of the key characteristics of the cloud is elastic scalability: Users can add or subtract resources in almost real time based on changing requirements. The cloud plays an important role within the big data world. Dramatic changes happen when these infrastructure components are combined with the advances in data management. A horizontally expandable and optimized infrastructure supports the practical implementation of big data. CloudWare technologies such as virtualization increase the efficiency of the cloud that makes many complex systems easier to optimize. As a result, organizations have the performance and optimization to be able to access data that was previously either unavailable or very hard to collect. Big data platforms are increasingly used as sources of enormous amounts of data about customer preferences, sentiment, and behaviors. Companies can integrate this information with internal sales and product data to gain insights into customer preferences and make more targeted and personalized offers.

Appendix 19.A gives a comparison of compute-intensive big compute versus data-intensive big data computing.

19.2 Tools and Techniques of Big Data

19.2.1 Processing Approach

Current big data computing platforms use a "divide and conquer" parallel processing approach, combining multiple processors and disks in large computing clusters connected using high-speed communications switches, and networks that allow the data to be partitioned among the available computing resources and processed independently to achieve performance and scalability based on the amount of data. We define a cluster as "a type of parallel and distributed system, which consists of a collection of interconnected stand-alone computers working together as a single integrated computing resource."

This approach to parallel processing is often referred to as a "shared nothing" approach since each node consisting of processor, local memory, and disk resources shares nothing with other nodes in the cluster. In parallel computing, this approach is considered suitable for data-processing problems that are "embarrassingly parallel," that is, where it is relatively easy to separate the problem into a number of parallel tasks and there is no dependency or communication required between the tasks other than their overall management. These types of

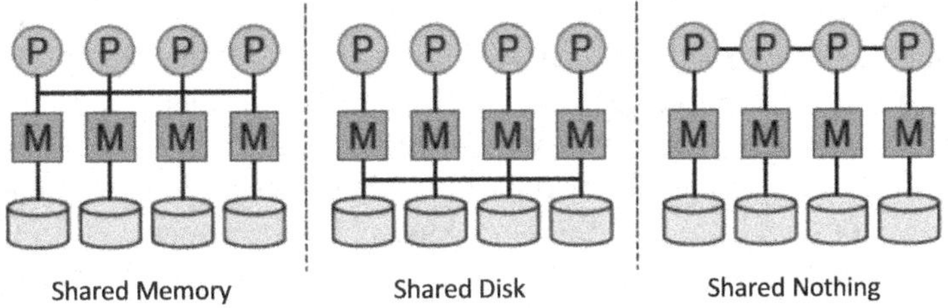

FIGURE 19.3
Parallel architectures.

data-processing problems are inherently adaptable to various forms of distributed computing, including clusters and data grids and cloud computing. Analytical environments are deployed in different architectural models. Even on parallel platforms, many databases are built on a shared-everything approach in which the persistent storage and memory components are all shared by the different processing units. Parallel architectures are classified by what shared resources each processor can directly access. There are important distinctions among shared memory, shared disk, and shared-nothing architectures (as depicted in Figure 19.3).

1. In a shared memory-system, all processors have direct access to all memory via a shared bus. Typical examples are the common symmetric multiprocessor systems, where each processor core can access the complete memory via the shared-memory bus. To preserve the abstraction, the processor's caches, buffering a subset of the data closer to the processor for fast access, have to be kept consistent with specialized protocols. Because disks are typically accessed via the memory, all processes also have access to all disks.
2. In a shared-disk architecture, all processes have their own private memory, but all disks are shared. A cluster of computers connected to a SAN is representative of this architecture.
3. In a shared-nothing architecture, each processor has its private memory and private disk. The data is distributed across all disks, and each processor is responsible only for the data on its own connected memory and disks. To operate on data that spans through different memories or disks, the processors have to explicitly send data to other processors. If a processor fails, the data held by its memory and disks is unavailable. Therefore, the shared-nothing architecture requires special considerations to prevent data loss.

When scaling out the system, the two main bottlenecks are typically the bandwidth of the shared medium and the overhead of maintaining a consistent view of the shared data in the presence of cache hierarchies. For this reason, the shared-nothing architecture is considered the most scalable one, because it has no shared medium and no shared data. While it is often argued that shared-disk architectures have certain advantages for transaction processing, the shared-nothing is the undisputed architecture of choice for analytical queries.

A shared-disk approach may have isolated processors, each with its own memory, but the persistent storage on disk is still shared across the system. These types of architectures are layered on top of SMP machines. While there may be applications that are suited to this approach, some bottlenecks exist due to the sharing, because all I/O and memory requests are transferred (and satisfied) over the same bus. As more processors are added, the synchronization and communication needs increase exponentially, and therefore the bus is less able to handle the increased need for bandwidth. This means that unless the need for bandwidth is satisfied, there will be limits to the degree of scalability.

In contrast, in a shared-nothing approach, each processor has its own dedicated disk storage. This approach, which maps nicely to an MPP architecture, is not only more suitable to the discrete allocation and distribution of the data, but it also enables more effective parallelization and, consequently, does not introduce the same kind of bus bottlenecks from which the SMP/shared-memory and shared-disk approaches suffer. Most big data appliances use a collection of computing resources, typically a combination of processing nodes and storage nodes.

19.2.2 Big Data System Architecture

A variety of system architectures have been implemented for big data and large-scale data analysis applications, including parallel and distributed relational database management systems that have been available to run on shared-nothing clusters of processing nodes for more than two decades. These include database systems from Teradata, Netezza, Vertica, Exadata/Oracle, and others that provide high-performance parallel database platforms. Although these systems have the ability to run parallel applications and queries expressed in the SQL language, they are typically not general-purpose processing platforms, and usually run as a back end to a separate front-end application processing system.

Although this approach offers benefits when the data utilized is primarily structured in nature, fits easily into the constraints of a relational database, and often excels for transaction processing applications, most of the data growth happens with data in unstructured form, so new processing paradigms with more flexible data models were needed. Internet companies such as Google, Yahoo!, Microsoft, Facebook, and others required a new processing approach to effectively deal with the enormous amount of web data for applications such as search engines and social networking. In addition, many government and business organizations were overwhelmed with data that could not be effectively processed, linked, and analyzed with traditional computing approaches.

Several solutions have emerged, including the MapReduce architecture pioneered by Google and now available in an open-source implementation called Hadoop used by Yahoo!, Facebook, and others (see KALE 2017).

19.2.2.1 BASE (Basically Available, Soft State, Eventual Consistency)

BASE follows an optimistic approach accepting stale data and approximate answers while favoring availability. This can be achieved by supporting partial failures without total system failures, decoupling updates on different tables (i.e., relaxing consistency), and using item-potent operations that can be applied multiple times with the same result. In this sense, BASE describes more a spectrum of architectural styles than a single model. The eventual state of consistency can be provided as a result of a read-repair, where any outdated data is refreshed with the latest version as a result of the system detecting stale data during a read operation. Another approach is that of weak consistency. In this case, the read operation will return the first value found, not checking for staleness. Any stale nodes discovered are simply marked for updating at some stage in the future. This is a performance-focused approach, but has the associated risk that the data retrieved may not be the most current. In the following sections, we will discuss several techniques for implementing services following the BASE principle.

Conventional storage techniques may not be adequate for big data and, hence, cloud applications. In order to scale storage systems to cloud scale, the basic technique is to partition and replicate the data over multiple independent storage systems. The word independent is emphasized, since it is well known that databases can be partitioned into mutually dependent subdatabases that are automatically synchronized for reasons of performance and availability. Partitioning and replication increase the overall throughput of the system, since the total throughput of the combined system is the aggregate of the individual storage systems. To scale both the throughput and the maximum size of the data that can be stored beyond the limits of traditional database deployments, it is possible to partition the data and store each partition in its own database. To scale the throughput only, it is possible to use replication. Partitioning and replication also increase the capacity of a storage system by reducing the amount of data that needs to be stored in each partition. However, this creates synchronization and consistency problems, and a discussion of this aspect is outside the scope of this book.

The other technology for scaling storage is known by the name NoSQL. NoSQL was developed as a reaction to the perception that conventional databases, focused on the need to ensure data integrity for enterprise applications, were too rigid to scale to cloud levels. As an example, conventional databases enforce a schema on the data being stored, and changing the schema is not easy. However, changing the schema may be a necessity in a rapidly changing environment like the cloud. NoSQL storage systems provide more flexibility and simplicity compared to relational databases. The disadvantage, however, is greater application complexity. NoSQL systems, for example, do not enforce a rigid schema. The trade-off is that applications have to be written to deal with data records of varying formats (schema). BASE is the NoSQL operating premise, in the same way that traditional transactionally focused databases use ACID: One moves from a world of certainty in terms of data consistency to a world where all we are promised is that all copies of the data will, at some point, be the same.

Partitioning and replication techniques used for scaling are as follows:

1. The first possible method is to store different tables in different databases (as in multidatabase systems, or MDBS).
2. The second approach is to partition the data within a single table onto different databases. There are two natural ways to partition the data from within a table: Storing different rows in different databases, and storing different columns in different databases (more common for NoSQL databases).

19.2.2.2 Functional Decomposition

As stated previously, one technique for partitioning the data to be stored is to store different tables in different databases, which leads to the storage of the data in a MDBS.

19.2.2.3 Master–Slave Replication

To increase the throughput of transactions from the database, it is possible to have multiple copies of the database. A common replication method is master–slave replication. The master and slave databases are replicas of each other. All writes go to the master and the master keeps the slaves in sync. However, reads can be distributed to any database. Since this configuration distributes the reads among multiple databases, it is a good technology for read-intensive workloads. For write-intensive workloads, it is possible to have multiple masters, but consistency must be ensured if multiple processes update different replicas simultaneously is a complex problem. Additionally, due to the necessity of writing to all masters and effecting the synchronization overhead between the masters rapidly, time to write increases becomes a limiting overhead.

19.2.3 Row Partitioning or Sharding

In cloud technology, sharding is used to refer to the technique of partitioning a table among multiple independent databases by row. However, the partitioning of data by row in relational databases is not new and is referred to as horizontal partitioning in parallel database technology. The distinction between sharding and horizontal partitioning is that horizontal partitioning is done transparently to the application by the database, whereas sharding is explicit partitioning done by the application. However, the two techniques have started converging, since traditional database vendors have started offering support for more sophisticated partitioning strategies. Since sharding is similar to horizontal partitioning, we will first discuss different horizontal partitioning techniques. It can be seen that a good sharding technique depends on both the organization of the data and the type of queries expected.

The different techniques of sharding are as follows:

1. Round-robin partitioning: The round-robin method distributes the rows in a round-robin fashion over different databases. As an example, we could partition the transaction table into multiple databases so that the first transaction is stored in the first database, the second in the second database, and so on. The advantage of round-robin partitioning is its simplicity. However, it also suffers from the disadvantage of losing associations (say) during a query, unless all databases are queried. Hash partitioning and range partitioning do not suffer from the disadvantage of losing record associations.
2. Hash partitioning method: In this method, the value of a selected attribute is hashed to find the database into which the tuple should be stored. If queries are frequently made on an attribute (say) Customer_Id, then associations can be preserved by using this attribute as the attribute that is hashed, so that records with the same value of this attribute can be found in the same database.
3. Range partitioning: The range partitioning technique stores records with "similar" attributes in the same database. For example, the range of Customer_Id could be partitioned between different databases. Again, if the attributes chosen for grouping are those on which queries are frequently made, record association is preserved and it is not necessary to merge results from different databases. Range partitioning can be susceptible to load imbalance, unless the partitioning is chosen carefully. It is possible to choose the partitions so that there is an imbalance in the amount of data stored in the partitions (data skew) or in the execution of queries across partitions (execution skew). These problems are less likely in round-robin and hash partitioning, since they tend to uniformly distribute the data over the partitions.

Thus, hash partitioning is particularly well suited to large-scale systems. Round robin simplifies a uniform distribution of records but does not facilitate the restriction of operations to single partitions. While range partitioning does supports this, it requires knowledge about the data distribution in order to properly adjust the ranges.

19.2.4 Row Versus Column-Oriented Data Layouts

Most traditional database systems employ a row-oriented layout, in which all the values associated with a specific row are laid out consecutively in memory. That layout may work well for transaction processing applications that focus on updating specific records associated with a limited number of transactions (or transaction steps) at a time. These are manifested as algorithmic scans performed using multiway joins; accessing whole rows at a time when only the values of a smaller set of columns are needed may flood the network with extraneous data that is not immediately needed and will ultimately increase the execution time.

Big data analytics applications scan, aggregate, and summarize over massive data sets. Analytical applications and queries will only need to access the data elements needed to satisfy join conditions. With row-oriented layouts, the entire record must be read in order to access the required attributes, with significantly more data read than is needed to satisfy the request. Also, the row-oriented layout is often misaligned with the characteristics of the different types of memory systems (core, cache, disk, etc.), leading to increased access latencies. Subsequently, row-oriented data layouts will not enable the types of joins or aggregations typical of analytic queries to execute with the anticipated level of performance.

Hence, a number of appliances for big data use a database management system that employs an alternate, columnar layout for data. This can help to reduce the negative performance impacts of data latency that plague databases with a row-oriented data layout. The values for each column can be stored separately, and because of this, for any query, the system is able to selectively access the specific column values requested to evaluate the join conditions. Instead of requiring separate indexes to tune queries, the data values themselves within each column form the index. This speeds up data access while reducing the overall database footprint, and dramatically improving query performance. The simplicity of the columnar approach provides many benefits, especially for those seeking a high-performance environment to meet the growing needs of extremely large analytic data sets.

19.2.5 NoSQL Data Management

NoSQL suggests environments that combine traditional SQL (or SQL-like query languages) with alternative means of querying and access. NoSQL data systems hold out the promise of greater flexibility in database management while reducing the dependence on more formal database administration. NoSQL databases have more relaxed modeling constraints, which may benefit both the application developer and the end-user analysts when their interactive analyses are not throttled by the need to cast each query in terms of a relational table-based environment.

Different NoSQL frameworks are optimized for different types of analyses. For example, some are implemented as key–value stores, which nicely align to certain big data programming models, while another emerging model is a graph database, in which a graph abstraction is implemented to embed both semantics and connectivity within its structure. In fact, the general concepts for NoSQL include schemaless modeling in which the semantics of the data are embedded within a flexible connectivity and storage model; this provides for automatic distribution of data and elasticity with respect to the use of computing, storage, and network bandwidth in ways that do not force specific binding of data to be persistently stored in particular physical locations. NoSQL databases also provide for integrated data caching that helps reduce data access latency and speed performance.

The key–value store does not impose any constraints on data typing or data structure—the value associated with the key is the value, and it is up to the consuming business applications to assert expectations about the data values and their semantics and interpretation. This demonstrates the schemaless property of the model.

A relatively simple type of NoSQL data store is a key–value store, a schemaless model in which distinct character strings called keys are associated with values (or sets of values, or even more complex entity objects)—not unlike hash table data structure. If you want to associate multiple values with a single key, you need to consider the representations of the objects and how they are associated with the key. For example, you may want to associate a list of attributes with a single key, which may suggest that the value stored with the key is yet another key–value store object itself.

Key–value stores are essentially very long, and presumably thin tables (in that there are not many columns associated with each row). The table's rows can be sorted by the key–value to simplify finding the key during a query. Alternatively, the keys can be hashed using a hash function that maps the key to a particular location (sometimes called a "bucket") in the table. The representation can grow indefinitely, which makes it good for storing large amounts of data that can be accessed relatively quickly, and also allows massive amounts of indexed data values to be appended to the same key–value table, which can then be sharded or distributed across the storage nodes. Under the right conditions, the table is distributed in a way that is aligned with the way the keys are organized, so that the hashing function that is used to determine where any specific key exists in the table can also be used to determine which node holds that key's bucket (i.e., the portion of the table holding that key).

NoSQL data management environments are engineered for the following two key criteria:

1. Fast accessibility, whether that means inserting data into the model or pulling it out via some query or access method.
2. Scalability for volume, so as to support the accumulation and management of massive amounts of data.

The different approaches are amenable to extensibility, scalability, and distribution, and these characteristics blend nicely with programming models (such as MapReduce) with straightforward creation and execution of many parallel processing threads. Distributing a tabular data store or a key–value store allows many queries/accesses to be performed simultaneously, especially when the hashing of the keys maps to different data storage nodes. Employing different data allocation strategies will allow the tables to grow indefinitely without requiring significant rebalancing. In other words, these data organizations are designed for high-performance computing of reporting and analysis.

The model will not inherently provide any kind of traditional database capabilities (such as atomicity of transactions, or consistency when multiple transactions are executed simultaneously)—those capabilities must be provided by the application itself.

19.3 NoSQL Databases

NoSQL databases have been classified into four subcategories:

1. *Column family stores*: An extension of the key–value architecture with columns and column families; the overall goal was to process distributed data over a pool of infrastructure, for example, HBase and Cassandra.

2. *Key–value pairs*: This model is implemented using a hash table where there is a unique key and a pointer to a particular item of data, creating a key–value pair, for example, Voldemort.
3. *Document databases*: This class of databases is modeled after Lotus Notes and is similar to key–value stores. The data is stored as a document and is represented in JSON or XML formats. The biggest design feature is the flexibility to list multiple levels of key–value pairs, for example, Riak and CouchDB.
4. *Graph databases*: Based on the graph theory, this class of database supports scalability across a cluster of machines. The complexity of representation for extremely complex sets of documents is evolving, for example, Neo4J.

19.3.1 Column-Oriented Stores or Databases

Hadoop HBase is the distributed database that supports the storage needs of the Hadoop distributed programming platform. HBase is designed by taking inspiration from Google BigTable; its main goal is to offer real-time read/write operations for tables with billions of rows and millions of columns by leveraging clusters of commodity hardware. The internal architecture and logic model of HBase are very similar to those of Google BigTable, and the entire system is backed by the Hadoop Distributed File System (HDFS), which mimics the structure and services of GFS.

19.3.2 Key–Value Stores (K–V Stores) or Databases

Apache Cassandra is a distributed object store for managing a large amount of structured data spread across many commodity servers. The system is designed to avoid a single point of failure and offers a highly reliable service. Cassandra was initially developed by Facebook; now, it is part of the Apache incubator initiative. In the initial years, Facebook used a leading commercial database solution for their internal architecture in conjunction with some Hadoop. Eventually, the tsunami of users led the company to start thinking in terms of unlimited scalability and focus on availability and distribution. The nature of the data and its producers and consumers did not mandate consistency but needed unlimited availability and scalable performance.

The team at Facebook built an architecture that combines the data model approaches of BigTable and the infrastructure approaches of Dynamo with scalability and performance capabilities, named Cassandra. Cassandra is often referred to as hybrid architecture since it combines the column-oriented data model from BigTable with Hadoop MapReduce jobs, and it implements the patterns from Dynamo like eventually consistent, gossip protocols, a master–master way of serving both read and write requests. Cassandra supports a full replication model based on NoSQL architectures.

The Cassandra team had a few design goals to meet, considering the architecture at the time of first development, and deployment was primarily being done at Facebook. The goals included

- High availability
- Eventual consistency
- Incremental scalability
- Optimistic replication

- Tunable trade-offs between consistency, durability, and latency
- Low cost of ownership
- Minimal administration

Amazon Dynamo is the distributed key–value store that supports the management of information of several of the business services offered by Amazon Inc. The main goal of Dynamo is to provide an incrementally scalable and highly available storage system. This goal helps in achieving reliability at a massive scale, where thousands of servers and network components build an infrastructure serving 10 million requests per day. Dynamo provides a simplified interface based on get/put semantics, where objects are stored and retrieved with a unique identifier (key). The main goal of achieving an extremely reliable infrastructure has imposed some constraints on the properties of these systems. For example, ACID properties on data have been sacrificed in favor of a more reliable and efficient infrastructure. This creates what is called an eventually consistent model (i.e., in the long term, all the users will see the same data).

19.3.3 Document-Oriented Databases

Document-oriented databases or document databases can be defined as a schemaless and flexible model of storing data as documents, rather than relational structures. The document will contain all the data it needs to answer specific query questions. The benefits of this model include:

- Ability to store dynamic data in unstructured, semistructured, or structured formats.
- Ability to create persisted views from a base document and store them for analysis.
- Ability to store and process large data sets.

The design features of document-oriented databases are as follows:

- Schema-free—there is no restriction on the structure and format of how the data need to be stored. This flexibility allows an evolving system to add more data and allows the existing data to be retained in the current structure.
- Document store—objects can be serialized and stored in a document, and there is no relational integrity to enforce and follow.
- Ease of creation and maintenance—a simple creation of the document allows complex objects to be created once, and there is minimal maintenance once the document is created.
- No relationship enforcement—documents are independent of each other and there is no foreign key relationship to worry about when executing queries. The effects of concurrency and performance issues related to the same are not an issue here.
- Open formats—documents are described using JSON, XML, or some derivative, making the process standard and clean from the start.
- Built-in versioning—documents can get large and messy with versions. To avoid conflicts and keep processing efficiencies, versioning is implemented by most solutions available today.

Document databases express the data as files in JSON or XML formats. This allows the same document to be parsed for multiple contexts and the results scrapped and added to the next iteration of the database data.

Apache CouchDB and MongoDB are two examples of document stores. Both provide a schemaless store whereby the primary objects are documents organized into a collection of key–value fields. The value of each field can be of type string, integer, float, date, or an array of values. The databases expose a RESTful interface and represent data in JSON format. Both allow querying and indexing data by using the MapReduce programming model, expose JavaScript as a base language for data querying and manipulation rather than SQL, and support large files as documents. From an infrastructure point of view, the two systems support data replication and high availability. CouchDB ensures ACID properties on data. MongoDB supports sharding, which is the ability to distribute the content of a collection among different nodes.

19.3.4 Graph Stores or Databases

Social media and the emergence of Facebook, LinkedIn, and Twitter have accelerated the emergence of the most complex NoSQL database, the graph database. The graph database is oriented toward modeling and deploying data that is graphical by construct. For example, to represent a person and their friends in a social network, we can either write code to convert the social graph into key–value pairs on a Dynamo or Cassandra, or simply convert them into a node-edge model in a graph database, where managing the relationship representation is much more simplified.

A graph database represents each object as a node and the relationships as an edge. This means person is a node and household is a node, and the relationship between them is an edge. Like for the classic ER model for RDBMS, we need to create an attribute model for a graph database. We can start by taking the highest level in a hierarchy as a root node (similar to an entity) and connect each attribute as its subnode. To represent different levels of the hierarchy, we can add a subcategory or subreference and create another list of attributes at that level. This creates a natural traversal model such as a tree traversal, which is similar to traversing a graph. Depending on the cyclic property of the graph, we can have a balanced or skewed model. Some of the most evolved graph databases include Neo4J, InfiniteGraph, GraphDB, and AllegroGraph.

19.4 Aadhaar Project

The Aadhaar project, undertaken by the Unique Identification Authority of India (UIDAI), has the mission of identifying 1.2 billion citizens of India uniquely and reliably to build the largest biometric identity repository in the world (while eliminating duplication and fake identities) and provide an online, anytime anywhere, multifactor authentication service. This makes it possible to identify any individual and get them authenticated at any time, from any place in India, in less than a second.

The UIDAI project is a Hadoop-based program that is well into production. At the time of this writing, over 700 million people have been enrolled and their identity information has been verified. The target is to reach a total of at least 1 billion enrolments during 2015.

Currently, the enrolment rate is about 10 million people every 10 days, so the project is well positioned to meet that target.

In India, there is no social security card, and much of the population lacks a passport. Literacy rates are relatively low, and the population is scattered across hundreds of thousands of villages. Without adequately verifiable identification, it has been difficult for many citizens to set up a bank account or otherwise participate in a modern economy.

For India's poorer citizens, this problem has even more dire consequences. The government has extensive programs to provide widespread relief for the poor—for example, through grain subsidies to those who are underfed and through government sponsored work programs for the unemployed. Yet many who need help do not have access to benefit programs, in part because of the inability to verify who they are and whether they qualify for the programs. In addition, there is a huge level of so-called "leakage" of government aid that disappears to apparent fraud. For example, it has been estimated that over 50% of funds intended to provide grain to the poor goes missing, and that fraudulent claims for "ghost workers" siphon off much of the aid intended to create work for the poor.

There are clearly immense benefits from a mechanism that uniquely identifies a person and ensures instant identity verification. The need to prove one's identity only once will bring down transaction costs. A clear identity number can transform the delivery of social welfare programs by making them more inclusive of those communities now cut off from such benefits due to their lack of identification. It also enables the government to shift from indirect to direct benefit delivery by directly reaching out to the intended beneficiaries. A single universal identity number is also useful in eliminating fraud and duplicate identities, since individuals can no longer represent themselves differently to different agencies. This results in significant savings to the state exchequer.

Aadhaar is in the process of creating the largest biometric database in the world, one that can be leveraged to authenticate identities for each citizen, even on site in rural villages. A wide range of mobile devices, from cell phones to microscanners, can be used to enrol people and to authenticate their identities when a transaction is requested. People will be able to make payments at remote sites via micro-ATMs. Aadhaar ID authentication will be used to verify qualification for relief food deliveries and to provide pension payments for the elderly. The implementation of this massive digital identification system is expected to save the equivalent of millions and perhaps billions of dollars each year by thwarting fraud attempts. While the UIDAI project will have broad benefits for the Indian society as a whole, the greatest impact will be for the poorest people.

All application components are built using open-source components and open standards.

The Aadhaar software currently runs across two of the data centers within India managed by UIDAI, and handles 1 million enrolments a day and at the peak, doing about 600 trillion biometric matches a day. The current system already has about 4 PB (4,000 terabytes) of raw data and continues to grow as new enrolments come in. The Aadhaar authentication service is built to handle 100 million authentications a day across both the data centers in an active–active fashion, and is benchmarked to provide sub-second response time. Central to the Aadhaar system is its biometric subsystem, which performs de-duplication and authentication in an accurate way.

Figure 19.4 presents the solution architecture for the Aadhaar project.

The application modules are built on a common technology platform that contains frameworks for persistence, security, messaging, etc. The platform standardizes on a technology stack based on open standards and using open source where prudent. A list of extensively used open-source technology stacks is as follows:

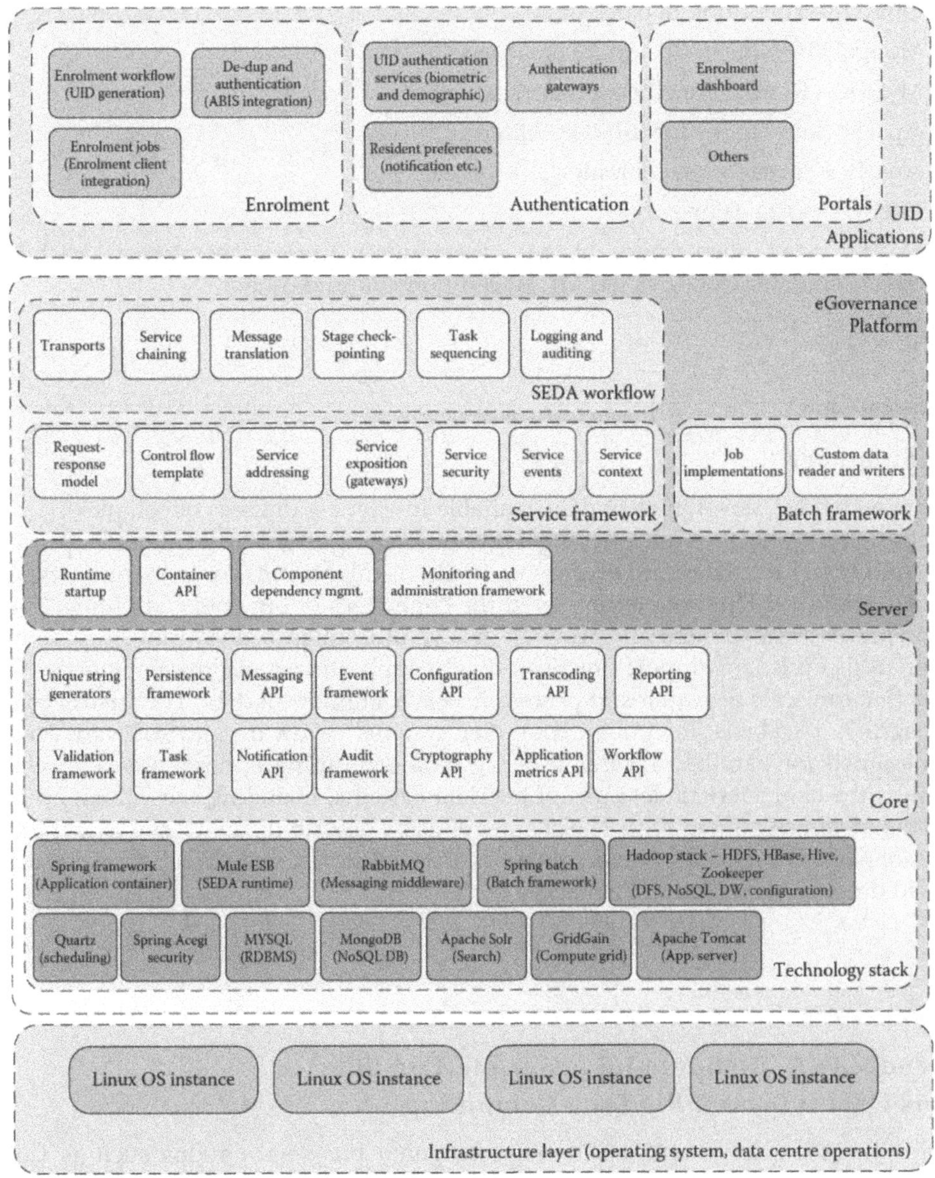

FIGURE 19.4
Solution architecture for the Aadhaar project.

- Spring framework—application container for all components and runtime
- Spring batch—runtime for various batch jobs
- Spring security—for all application security needs
- Mule ESB—runtime for loosely coupled SEDA stages of enrolment flow
- RabbitMQ—messaging middleware
- Hadoop stack—HDFS, Hive, HBase, Pig, and Zookeeper
- Pentaho—open source BI Solution

- Quartz—scheduling of batch jobs
- MongoDB—NoSQL document database
- MySQL—RDBMS for storing relational data
- Apache Solr—index for full-text search
- Apache Tomcat—web container
- Liferay—portal framework
- Several other open-source libraries for random number generation, hashing, advanced data structures, HTML UI components, and others.

19.5 Summary

Big data is defined as volumes of data available in varying degrees of complexity, generated at different velocities and varying degrees of ambiguity, which cannot be processed using traditional technologies, processing methods, algorithms, or any commercial off-the-shelf solutions. This chapter explored the challenges of big data computing: managing and processing exponentially growing data volumes; significantly reducing associated data analysis cycles to support practical, timely applications; and developing new algorithms that can scale to search and process massive amounts of data. The answer to these challenges is a scalable, integrated computer systems hardware and software architecture designed for parallel processing of big data computing applications. This chapter described the characteristic features of big data systems, including the volume, velocity, variety, and veracity of big data. The chapter ends by describing an overview of the major classes of NoSQL databases, namely, column-oriented stores, key–value stores, document-oriented databases, and graph databases.

Appendix 19.A: Compute-intensive Big Compute versus Data-intensive Big Data Computing

Simply processing large datasets is not considered big data. Groups such as Conseil Européen pour la Recherche Nucléaire (CERN) and Transnational Research in Oncology (TRIO) have been using high-performance computing (HPC) systems and scalable software to analyze very large datasets. Characteristically, this is compute-intensive processing and corresponding systems can be called big compute systems. Examples of big computer systems are computational fluid dynamics, image processing, and traditional genome analysis.

Compute-intensive processing involves the input of small quantities of data and generates large quantities of data while processing or as output. Typically, a mathematical algorithm is used to generate results from the data that forms the input. As the power and thermal limits of silicon are approached, multiple processors are grouped together to parallelize and speed up processing. Compute-intensive applications typically parallelize the processing by distributing the data and the instruction to multiple processors that can be as close as on the same chip or geographically remote and only accessible over the Internet.

Taking traditional HPC as an exemplar system, processing elements (PEs) are typically located across a tightly coupled local area network (LAN) operating at network speeds between 1 and 100 Gbps. The biggest bottleneck to a compute-intensive parallel program on a HPC system is the network. Complex programs are not able to scale to bigger systems due to large global communication operations. Therefore, input data cannot be distributed in the same manner as the instruction set, from one system across the entire parallel machine. A dedicated, fast, shared storage device is used to make the data available to all processing cores. As all the data is grouped together, even if the data domain is partitioned within the algorithm, each PE still needs to traverse the entire dataset to find the required subset.

Data-centric systems devote the majority of the running time to performing data manipulation and input/output (I/O) over numerical operations—the optimization of an algorithm is secondary to the data management. Within the MapReduce ecosystem, data locality is a major component of the concept of data centricity. Unlike the HPC systems, the data is not stored at a single point. At ingestion time, it is, in fact, divided and replicated across a distributed compute system, and stored local to the PEs. In this way, each PE only needs to deal with its local subset of data without needing to search for it. The PEs also do not need to compete with each other for bandwidth over the network. This creative distribution of data ensures that processing instructions only go to the PEs that have direct access to the relevant data. The replication of the data subsets ensures further and much enhanced parallelization. If two instructions require access to the same subset of data, the replication ensures that two separate PEs can run both instructions simultaneously without any contention for network or disk.

When designing a data-intensive big data system, the metrics to keep in mind are

- Size of PE level storage
- Speed of PE level storage
- Memory per PE
- Processor clock speed
- Network interconnect

HPC or big compute systems have large power overheads leading to high processor density, and require highly specialized networking components to deliver performance. In contrast, big data systems can be very efficient using high-quality workstations loosely coupled with commodity networking equipment (Table 19A.1).

The introduction of modern software and hardware has made the real-time processing of massive datasets a reality. Such real-time analysis is often called stream processing. In a stream processing model, data is processed, queried, and analyzed immediately as it arrives into the system. Increasingly, a data stream from a generation source is sent directly to a compute resource for processing before being archived for later access. This is in contrast to the batch processing method, where data is first stored and then processed in bulk at a later date. The Internet of things (IoT) big data stream processing is discussed in Chapter 20.

TABLE 19.A.1

Big Compute Systems versus Big Data Systems

Component	Big Compute	Big Data
Data	Centralized shared storage	Local storage managed centrally
Network	High bandwidth and low latency required for scalability	Latency plays minimal role, most bandwidth required during data loading and unloading phases
System design	Tightly coupled systems	Run on almost anything approach—PEs can be heterogeneous with consumer-grade networks
Task management	Task concurrency required. System can be divided among jobs but each job must run as a single unit	Task and data replication allows for out of order execution of tasks and jobs can also be split
Job resilience	If a PE involved in a job fails, the job fails and needs to be restarted	Replication of tasks allows for the failure of a PE without affecting the job
System resilience	Systems can cope with loss of a PE. Single points of failure: centralized storage, controller node (redundancy possible), internal networking	Built-in redundancy in nearly all components. Default operation includes replication. Single point of failure: internal networking
Programming model	Message-passing interface (MPI), symmetric multiprocessing (SMP), parallel virtual machine (PVM)	MapReduce, bulk synchronous parallel (BSP)

20

Big Data Stream Processing

With the advent of IoT, a new class of applications has emerged that requires managing data streams, i.e., data composed of a continuous, real-time sequence of items. Streaming applications have gained prominence due to both business and technical reasons. Businesses and government agencies increasingly want to perform analysis on data much sooner than it is possible with the traditional model, which entails storing data in a data warehouse and performing the analysis off-line. Additionally, data is now available from a wide variety of monitoring devices, including sensors that are extremely cheap. Data from such devices is potentially unbounded and needs to be processed in real time. Application domains requiring data stream management include military, homeland security, sensor networks, financial applications, network management, website performance tracking, real-time credit-card fraud detection, etc.

20.1 Big Data Stream Processing

A data stream is a possibly unbounded sequence of data items—streaming data sets grow continuously, and queries must be evaluated on such unbounded data sets. Such application domains require queries to be evaluated continuously as opposed to the one-time evaluation of a query for traditional applications. The monitoring aspect of many streaming applications requires support for reactive capabilities in real time from data management systems.

With sensors becoming cheaper, a whole area of applications is emerging where sensors distributed in the real world measure the state of some entities and generate streams of data from the measured values, e.g., such sensors may be monitoring temperature at weather stations, or traffic on highways. Consider a scenario where a sensor embedded along expressways reports on the current traffic on the road. The data reported by the sensors forms a continuous stream giving:

- The identity of the expressway and the segment and lane of the expressway on which the car is traveling, as well the direction in which the car is traveling.
- The identity of a car as well as its speed.

Various queries that can be evaluated over this data are as follows:

1. To manage the flow of traffic, a query would compute the average speed of cars over a segment. If the speed drops below a threshold, commuters about to travel on that segment can be notified to take alternative routes.
2. Based on the average speed of vehicles over a segment, the application might alert operators to possible accidents that are causing a delay on that segment.

3. On toll roads, the data stream is used to automatically deduct the toll from the account of those vehicle owners that have tags recognized by the sensors.
4. In advanced traffic management, a goal is to manage congestion by varying the toll rate. To achieve this goal, the application might deduct a toll as a function of the average speed on the expressway.

Database management systems (DBMS) were originally developed to support business applications. However, this model of a DBMS as a repository of relatively static data, which is queried as a result of human interaction, does not meet the challenges posed by streaming applications. Traditional DBMS are inadequate to meet the requirements of a new class of applications data stream management systems (DSMS), which require evaluating persistent long-running queries against a continuous, real-time stream of data items. A comparison of the capabilities of traditional DBMS and SDMS is shown in Table 20.1.

An incredible amount of *sensing* data is being generated around the world every second. The amount of data generated is so large that it is difficult not only to manage it but also to process it using traditional data management tools. Such data is referred as *big data*. To tackle the challenge of processing big data, the MapReduce framework was developed by Google. This system needs to process millions of webpages every second. Over the last five years, thanks to the availability of several open-source implementations of this framework, such as Hadoop, MapReduce has become a dominant framework for solving big data processing problems. Batch processing refers to the computational analysis of bounded data sets. In practical terms, this means that those data sets are available and retrievable as a whole from some form of storage. We know the size of the data set at the start of the computational process, and the duration of that process is limited in time.

However, it was observed that *volume* is not the only challenge when processing *sensing data* that is continuously being generated, and that the *velocity* of data generation is also an important challenge that needs to be tackled.

There are a number of applications where data is expected to be ingested not only in high *volume* but also with high *velocity*, requiring real-time analytics or data processing. These applications include: stock trading, network monitoring, social media–based business analytics, and so on.

TABLE 20.1

Comparison of the Capabilities of Traditional DSMS and DBMS

Feature	DBMS	DSMS
Model	*Persistent* data	*Transient* data
Table	*Set or bag* of tuples	*Infinite sequence* of tuples
Updates	All	Append only
Queries	Transient	Persistent
Query answer	Exact	Often approximate
Query evaluation	Multi-pass	One pass
Operators	Blocking and non-blocking	Non-blocking
Query plan	Fixed	Adaptive
Data processing	Synchronous	Asynchronous
Concurrency overhead	High	Low

There are two fundamental aspects that have changed the way data needs to be processed, which create the need for a complete paradigm shift:

- The size of data has evolved to the point that it has become intractable by existing data management systems.
- The rate of change in data is so rapid that processing also needs to be done in real time.

The limitation of the previous approach in managing and analyzing high-volume and velocity data in real time has led to the development of new and sophisticated distributed techniques and technologies. The processing of data with such features is defined as *data stream processing* or *stream processing*. Stream processing refers to the computational analysis of unbounded data sets; it is concerned with the processing of data as it arrives to the system. Given the unbounded nature of data streams, the stream processing systems need to run constantly for as long as the stream is delivering new data, which is theoretically forever.

Stream processing can be subdivided into three areas:

1. DSMS where online query languages have been explored.
2. Online data processing algorithms where the aim is to process the data in a single pass.
3. Stream processing platforms/engines, which enable implementation and scaling of stream processing–based applications.

The challenges posed by stream processing systems impose certain architectural and functional requirements on DSMS:

- The data model must include the notion of time, while the query mechanism should support definition of continuous queries over such data.
- Given the unbounded nature of streaming data and the fact that the data might be unreliable in certain cases, a stream processing system must be capable of computing answers based on incomplete or unreliable data.
- Since the queries are long standing, the stream processing system should be capable of coping with variations in conditions. This implies that query execution plans need to be adaptive and dynamic instead of traditional and static.
- A large number of stream processing systems are inherently distributed in nature. For instance, sensors for traffic monitoring would be distributed over a large area. This distribution makes bandwidth considerations important in query processing.
- An implication of the above requirement is that the stream processing system may not use blocking operators that process the entire stream before producing an answer. A trade-off has to be made between non-blocking operators capable of computing approximate answers and blocking operators computing exact answers.
- Stream processing systems need to have reactive capability. The challenge here is to build reactive capability that scales to possibly thousands of triggers, as opposed to the current systems that don't scale beyond a limited number of triggers.
- In many streaming systems, allied to this need of reactive capability is the requirement of providing this capability in (near) real-time. This requires that a stream processing system intelligently manage resources and provide QoS guarantees.

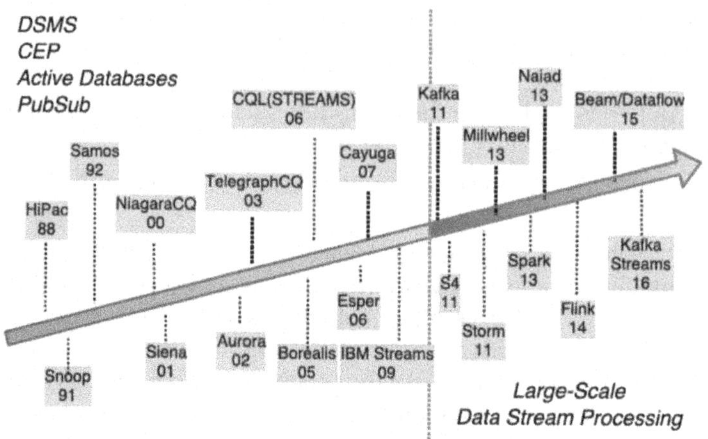

FIGURE 20.1
Evolution of data stream processing systems.

20.1.1 History of Data Stream Processing

Data stream processing systems (DSPS) are specially designed systems that are able to manage infinite streams of data with low latency and high throughput. They are widely employed in active database, complex event processing, and publish-subscribe system applications (Figure 20.1) and rooted in database systems, data warehouses, and information flow programming systems. Gradually, they have incorporated additional technological capabilities, including (Map-Reduce-like) scalability, declarativity, and expressivity (akin to relational programming models, such as SQL), beside the efficiency of data warehousing technologies.

1. Active database systems (ADS) are an explicit form of event-based database systems, implemented originally as extensions to existing DBMS. HiPac, Snoop, and Samos enriched traditional relational query support with event-based actions, conditionally applied to data upon ingestion time. The usage of ADS (and the heavy use of database triggers) ranged from basic extract-transform-load operations (ETL) to more sophisticated event-based detection tasks. The latter category of queries is also known as standing or continuous queries. These were typically used to monitor database entries for specific conditions. NiagaraCQ and OpenCQ are two noteworthy examples of systems supporting continuous queries.

   Drawbacks of ADS are as follows:

   a. They are limited to centralized, non-scalable execution engines, an inherent characteristic of the monolithic DBMS that hosted this technology; they were tightly coupled to specific DBMS, thus limiting broader adoption.
   b. They have limited expressivity when it comes to defining complex patterns for event processing, an ability that complex event processing (CEP) systems were created to cover.

ADS had a decisive role in the development of stream processing systems: many large-scale stream processing systems commit to a similar architecture, such as S-Store, which is an in-memory scalable stream processing system that is built on top of H-Store. The latter is a shared-nothing distributed relational database with strong transactional properties.

2. Complex Event Processing (CEP) systems are prevalent in several enterprise applications such as sensor-network monitoring, intrusion detection systems, and high-performance financial systems. In CEP systems, complex rule-based pattern matching is a prominent application with a plethora of open-source and proprietary solutions using declarative event-based language. One of the major contributions of the CEP ecosystem (e.g., Cayuga, Esper, and STREAMS) is the introduction of sliding window semantics: windows are used to group event sequences into evolving views or sets, upon which aggregations and patterns can be evaluated. Streaming windows are now an integral part of many stream processing systems. However, the architecture of most CEP systems remains monolithic and centralized, which renders it unsuitable for large-scale, highly available deployments in clusters environments.
3. Publish-subscribe systems were mainly developed and used as distributed messaging middleware, which routes messages from data producers to data consumers, i.e., subscribers. In addition to trivial topic-based routing, subscriptions in several publish-subscribe systems can be expressed through complex rules, such as event sequences and repetitions, or even through arbitrarily complex queries. Publish-subscribe systems serve as a basis for the development of large-scale event processing systems that run continuous queries. They heavily influenced the development of modern message queues and distributed log systems such as Apache Kafka, which adopt a similar subscription-based pattern for distributed data stream ingestion.
4. DSMS introduced many architectural primitives that reside at the core of several stream processing systems today. Systems such as Aurora, Borealis, and StreamBase allowed for distributed and managed deployments of stream processing pipelines, consisting of tasks and data dependencies in a dataflow graph (defined by the user through a graphical interface). Depending on dynamic properties such as the current workload, a scheduler managed the deployment of parallel tasks, which could be later re-optimised for improved latency or throughput. At the same time, other DSMS focused on expressivity and integration with DBMS by enriching SQL with windowing semantics, CQL being a noteworthy example of such an effort. In general, DSMS were mainly developed as research prototypes, yet, they went on to influence the emerging data stream processing field.

Historically, stream processing systems have been relegated to a somewhat niche market providing low-latency, inaccurate, or speculative results, often in conjunction with a more capable batch system to provide eventually correct results, i.e., Lambda architecture. The essential idea of Lambda architecture is that it runs a stream processing system alongside a batch system—both performing essentially the same calculation. The stream processing system gives a low-latency, inaccurate result (either because of the use of an approximation algorithm, or because the stream processing system itself does not provide correctness), and subsequently a separate batch system provides the correct output. Originally proposed by Twitter's Nathan Marz (creator of Storm), Lambda architecture successfully addressed the need of reconciling:

1. Stream processing engines challenged on the accuracy dimension.
2. Batch engines which were inherently unwieldy.

However, maintaining a Lambda system was a hassle to the extent that it entailed building, provisioning, and maintaining two independent versions of the processing pipelines that had to be reconciled at the end. This begged for a unified solution: A functioning stream processing system with the ability to effectively provide "batch processing" functionality on demand. Apache Flink is a noteworthy example (see Subsection 21.1.2.3 'Stream Processing Platforms/Engine').

20.1.2 Data Stream Processing

Due to different challenges and requirements posed by different application domains, several open-source platforms have emerged for real-time data stream processing. Although different platforms share the concept of handling data as continuous unbounded streams, and process it immediately as the data is collected, they follow different architectural models and offer different capabilities and features. Each platform offers very specific special features that make its architecture unique, and some features make a stream processing platform more applicable than others for different scenarios.

A taxonomy is derived after studying different open-source platforms, including DSMS), CEP systems, and stream processing systems such as Storm.

20.1.2.1 Data Stream Processing Systems

The aspects underlying stream processing platforms or engines consist of distributed computing, parallel computing, and message passing. Dataflow has always been the core element of stream processing systems. "Data streams" or "streams" in the stream processing context refers to the infinite dataflow within the system. Stream processing platforms are designed to run on top of distributed and parallel computing technologies such as clusters to process real-time streams of data. The cluster computing technology allows a collection of connected computers to work together providing adequate computing power for the processing of large data sets. Such a feature is so important for stream processing platforms that clusters have become one of its essential modules for processing high-velocity big data.

The performance of a stream processing system will be always limited by the capacity of the underlying cluster environment where real processing is done. None of the systems surveyed allows the use of cloud computing resources, which can scale up and down according to the volume and velocity of the data that needs to be processed.

The 1980s was a decade of booming development for the stream processing theory, during which another significant concept, namely synchronous concurrent computation, was introduced. This term is another way of saying "parallel computing." This technology further led to new advancements in data management technologies, such as reactive systems, which enhanced the efficiency of different queries.. Reactive systems used highly concurrent lightweight message passing to quickly respond to the input data events from sensors. The real-time behavior of data ingestion components in the reactive systems is one of the most remarkable characteristics of todays' stream processing platforms.

In the early 1990s, another development started to address the requirements of applications such as network traffic analysis, where:

- Data is generated in real time.
- Continuous queries are required.

This development led to the introduction of features such as continuous querying and temporal data models, which were integrated in the form of DSMS. These systems allow persistent queries on both continuous, real-time stream of data and standard database tables. Their key feature is that data can be queried on the fly before it is stored permanently.

The distinctive features of DSPS are:

i. Continuous uninterrupted execution. The ability of a system to execute a continuous query or stream topology without inducing additional delays such as queuing, re-scheduling, halting, etc. This is the norm in shared-nothing stream processing systems.

ii. Robustness: As with every distributed system, process or network failures are bound to happen, especially in a long-running operation. These failures need to be handled transparently to system users. Systems differ in terms of their assumptions (e.g., repeatable persistent sources) and in the guarantees they can offer to applications under failures. A plethora of techniques have been studied in the past in order to deal with failures in continuous processing, each of them imposing additional computational and resource overhead to ensure certain properties.

iii. Sustainable flow control. Network channels and in-memory buffers that reside within stream processors have a finite capacity, which places certain constraints on the ingestion throughput. In the most general case, data is being pulled at ingestion points in a pipeline (e.g., stream sources) and pushed throughout different computation tasks. In order to sustain an overall continuous ingestion, despite throughput imbalance among operators, a stream processing system can either discard events or trigger a flow control mechanism such as back-pressure.

Back-pressure allows stream processing systems to "keep up" with processing at sustainable rates. This is a highly important property, which is missing in several existing stream processing solutions (e.g., Apache Storm).

iv. Low latency. Data stream processing systems have the ability to process data and make incremental computations at ingestion rate. This drops end-to-end latency by orders of magnitude compared to batch executions or typical daily database integration jobs. Low-latency processing can serve critical applications where timely and thus actionable knowledge is paramount. For this reason, it serves as a major incentive for using stream processing systems today. Moreover, low latency or response time is considered as a common benchmarking measurement, and is used to stress and compare the performance of different stream processing systems.

v. Explicitsmanagement. State summarizes the results of computation in a stream processing system (e.g. a counter). From a systems perspective, state needs to be declared and managed explicitly in order to enable fault tolerance and repartitioning capabilities in a transparent manner. Alternatively, when state is managed in the application layer (e.g., when programming in Apache Storm v0.10), there is a need for custom synchronization with external storage systems. However, a state agnostic approach disables prospects for state reconfiguration and efficient native fault tolerance mechanisms.

vi. Efficient plan/topology execution. As with database queries, executing a continuous stream processing query in a stream processing system as declared by the user could lead to potentially redundant resource usage and inefficient pipelining of operators. Thus, several stream processing systems optimize the execution of certain queries in order to eliminate redundancy and increase the efficiency of resource utilization and throughput, while also reducing latency. As with programming languages, most optimizations are applied transparently upon query translation to physical dataflow operators or some other intermediate-level representation of the computation at hand. Typical optimisations that are adopted in several stream processing systems are:

- Operator fusion (also known as superbox scheduling)
- Operator reordering
- State sharing
- Batching

vii. Elasticity and dynamic reconfiguration. A stream processing system can potentially execute a job for weeks or years continuously. The workloads of such long-running jobs can change considerably over time. Thus, it is handy for such a system to be able to adapt resource consumption (e.g., workers, memory) dynamically, according to changing demands. This requires general support for reconfiguration and additional monitoring of several runtime parameters. Additionally, physical operators should allow for partitionable state (when that is applicable) in order to scale in or out according to the workload.

viii. Programming primitives. Systems provide primitives in their APIs that aid programmers with built-in implementations for common tasks. Most frameworks provide windowing primitives that group data points based on time. Frameworks are introducing more and more higher-level abstractions in their APIs for advanced expressivity.

For example, aggregations, such as summations, could be implemented with low-level dataflow API by using custom managed state. However, stream processing systems typically contain parts where values must be aggregated. Thus, some systems provide an aggregation primitive to aid the development process. There are similar primitives in many system APIs for other frequent cases, such as filtering or grouping by a key.

Flow versus state: The transition from a large-scale monolithic application design using a large database to transactionally update and access state to a streaming microservice architecture can be difficult. Much of the difficulty can be attributed to a switch from thinking of computer programs as state-oriented to thinking of them in terms of flows. Computation as a process that updates a global state is a very familiar idiom, but scaling such a system can be very difficult to do and often requires that a system be scaled up instead of scaled out—which is a very expensive proposition. Viewing computation as data flowing between independent processing elements is a less familiar idiom, but it has substantial benefits, perhaps most significantly that it is much easier to scale out such a system.

The key difference between the two systems is that state-based computation involves an idealized state that has a globally consistent value at any point in time. A simple example involves the question of the outside temperature at any given millisecond at many locations around the earth. We cannot actually know what the temperature is at all of these locations, if only because light can only travel about 300 km in a millisecond. In fact, if we want to have carefully reviewed and cross-checked temperatures reliable enough for scientific publication, we will have to wait a month or more. This means that we cannot build a computer program that assumes it knows all the current temperatures. However, we can still write a useful program that knows the current local temperature and the delayed temperature from other locations.

Similarly, it is not physically possible to actually have such a global state with modern computers without slowing computations to a crawl, but the illusion that such a state exists can often be maintained up to a certain size and at a certain time scale. Beyond that size or on a smaller time scale, maintaining the illusion becomes impossible (and also horrendously expensive). Flow-based computation gets rid of the concept of global state and prevents parts from even pretending that the system knows exactly what other parts are doing. This allows more work to be done without coordination.

While programming with streams, stateless functions deal with one element at a time, whereas aggregations take the entire stream into account. But none of these options is satisfactory if the interest is in hourly, daily, or maybe yearly statistics. For instance, with reference to counting the clicks that a certain webpage receives—the interest would be the number of clicks during some custom time periods of a certain granularity and not since the data processing application first started to operate. Windowing techniques are used to logically group records of an infinite stream into finite sets, upon which aggregations or other custom operations can be performed. Windows are typically declared in terms of predefined templates (e.g., time and count).

The input events of an application are usually created by an external source prior to their processing. Consequently, the two notions of time are:

- Event time: The time corresponding to when an event was generated externally. It is commonly provided by a timestamp field using the local clock of its source (e.g., a sensor).
- Processing time: The time corresponding to when a system processes the event (measured by the system local clock).

The event time of the records is a property of the input, whereas the exact processing time of events depends on the actual execution of the stream processing system, which can be affected by arbitrary network delays, system workload changes, and other factors. Consequently, processing time is not a consistent metric for progress in distributed stream processing due to an inherent absence of a global synchronized clock. Thus, given that there is a known clock skew among the sources of the data streams, event time is typically a preferable choice to specify time-based operations in a stream processing system; e.g., parallel time windows such as:

1. Tumbling time window, which specifies the window size in some time units. The stream is split into non-overlapping, adjacent time intervals that have a given size. For instance, if the objective is to get the sum of the prices of orders every three hours (or days, weeks, etc.), this can be obtained by specifying a tumbling window and then applying the sum aggregation on it (Figure 20.2a).
2. Sliding time window, which, in addition to a window size, also specifies a slide size, which declares the frequency of the window computation (Figure 20.2b). The windows might overlap if the slide size is smaller than the window size, or there might be "gaps" between the windows, if it is bigger. In fact, tumbling windows are a special case of sliding windows, where the slide size is the same as the window size.

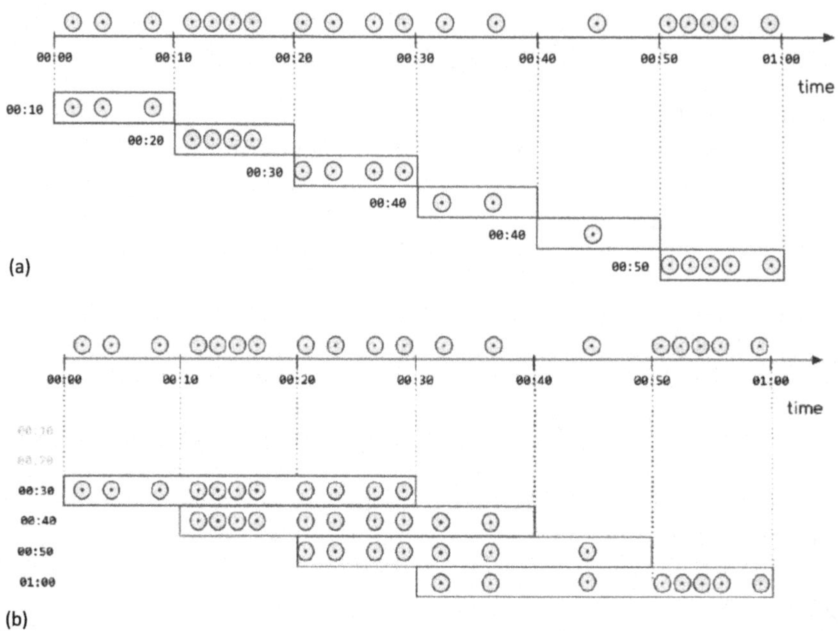

FIGURE 20.2
(a) Tumbling time window; (b) sliding time window.

20.1.2.2 DSMS

DSMS are the earliest version of the stream processing systems. They encompass the functions of a conventional DBMS, but further offer the ability to execute continuously incoming data queries to enable real-time data processing. The evolution of DSMS from DBMS is a result of the world's demand for high-velocity data querying, especially in the industries where sensors are heavily used.

There are several other DSMS that are developed for different purposes. For instance, there is a distributed spatiotemporal DSMS named PLACE which is used for monitoring moving objects, and XStream is used for the tracking and processing of signals. Other systems, such as Borealis, NILE, and Medusa, are designed as general purpose data query processing DSMS.

20.1.2.3 CEPs

CEPs handle events. Compared to generic queries answered by DSMS, events are higher-level analytics results that enable people to better understand their environments and take appropriate actions. CEP systems associate semantics with the data so that the system can detect, filter, and combine the data, or so-called event notifications from external sources to understand the events.

Though CEP is not capable of processing unstructured data compared to stream processing platforms, it is efficient in analyzing the structured or semistructured data. Currently, there are many CEP systems that are available for either business or research purpose, e.g., Oracle Event Processing, Microsoft StreamInsight, SQLStream s-Server, and StreamBase.

Besides the systems introduced above, there are other CEP platforms that share a similar set of characteristics, such as Esper, Cayuga, and Apama.

20.1.2.4 Stream Processing Platforms/Engine

While most stream processing systems essentially work with moving data (data streams) and do the processing in the memory, some of the allied requirements are orthogonal to each other, and the activity of guaranteed data safety and availability (Item 8 below) will raise the cost of computation and storage performance, which eventually compromises the throughput of dataflow. This leads to adverse effects on latency and real-time response (Items 2 and 3 below). These conflicting requirements result in differences in the way they were emphasized in different stream processing platforms.

A general set of requirements for data stream processing engines is as follows:

1. Partition and scale applications automatically: Distribute data and processes among multiple processors/CPUs/nodes.
2. Process and respond instantaneously: Achieve the real-time response with minimal overhead for high-volume data streams.
3. Keep the data moving: Keep latency at an absolute minimum by processing data as soon as it is captured.
4. Handle stream imperfections: Provide built-in features for handling missing or out-of-order data.
5. Query using SQL on streams: Allow SQL queries on data streams to build extensive operators.
6. Generate predictable outcomes: Be able to provide guaranteed repeatable and predictable results.
7. Integrate stored and streaming data: Be able to combine different data streams from external sources ingested with different speed.
8. Guarantee data safety and availability: Provide fault tolerance features to ensure the continuous processing of data.

A stream processing platform is a data-passing system; thus, the execution module of a stream process platform/engine can be modeled using the dataflow from the sources where data is ingested to the sink that will output the processed data. However, the dataflow in stream processing is quite different from that in batch processing. Stream processing systems cannot be designed using the conventional relation model for data management, which is more suitable for the management of static and stored content. Stream processing requires a dynamic model for data management and processing, since a stream processing system is by nature a message passing system, and its activities, such as programming, are driven by the data.

Consequently, a typical stream processing platform/engine consists of three fundamental elements with respect to the dynamic nature of stream processing systems (Figure 20.3):

1. A source that allows external data to pass into the system.
2. A processing node where computation activities are performed.
3. A sink that passes the processed data out of the system.

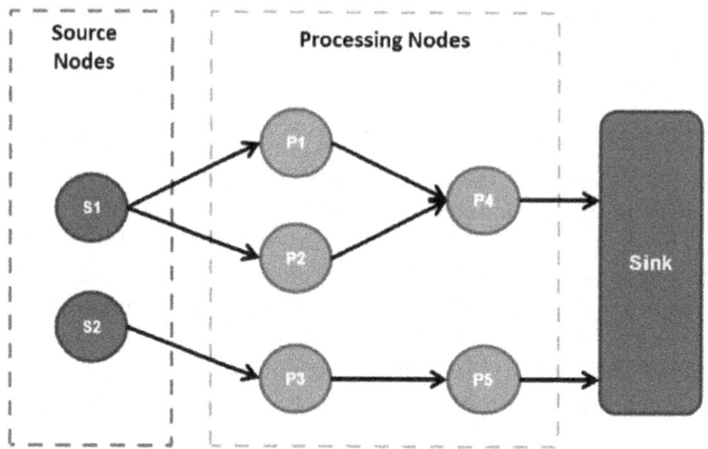

FIGURE 20.3
Dataflow model of a stream processing platform/engine.

20.2 Stream Processing System Implementations

There are several implementations of stream processing systems, which are implemented by different research and open-source groups as well as by commercial enterprises.

20.2.1 Academic or Research Prototype Systems

1. TelegraphCQ

TelegraphCQ is one of the earliest stream processing systems and was developed at the University of California, Berkeley. Its design is based on an earlier system built for an adaptive dataflow-processing Telegraph, and its implementation borrowed heavily from PostgreSQL. TelegraphCQ was designed to support continuous queries over a combination of tables and data streams. Its programming model relied on a declarative programming language, StreaQuel, with operators designed for stream relational processing directly inspired by SQL counterparts and extended with a rich windowing mechanism used to buffer and operate on groups of tuples.

TelegraphCQ also included a simple version of edge adaptation in the form of a user-defined wrapper designed to ingest data from external sources. StreaQuel's query plans were executed by a TelegraphCQ's distributed runtime with adaptive logic used to route data efficiently across operators and the distributed nodes of the runtime. The runtime environment was eventually optimized to handle queries combining real time with historical data by employing a framework in which multiple resolutions of summarization and sampling could be generated simultaneously.

2. STREAM

STREAM was developed at Stanford University. Its early prototype had targeted environments with streams that may be fast-paced and have load characteristics that can vary over time. Due to this variability, the STREAM system was designed to work under severe resource constraints and to support continuous adaptivity as an application runs. The STREAM programming model employs CQL, a declarative language with relational and stream processing operators whose abstract semantics is based on two basic constructs: Streams, which are bags (collections) of tuple–timestamp pairs, and relations, which are time-varying bags of tuples.

In the STREAM runtime environment, applications are expressed in terms of query plans. Owing to its database architectural roots, when a continuous query is registered with the STREAM system, a plan, comprising a tree of operators, is generated. This plan indicates how the actual processing is carried out and it employs queues to buffer tuples (or references to them) as they move between operators, and synopses to store the operator state as the execution progresses. When a query plan is executed, a *scheduler* selects operators to execute based on the (explicit) timestamps of the tuples it is supposed to process, ensuring that the order of execution has no effect on the query result.

STREAM's runtime employs a set of performance optimizations to speed up the execution of query plans, namely:

1. Synopsis sharing is used to reduce memory utilization when multiple synopses in a query plan materialize nearly identical relations.
2. Constraints exploitation is used when data or properties of its arrival can be harnessed to reduce the size of a synopsis.
3. Global operator scheduling is used to reduce memory utilization, particularly with queries that manipulate bursty input streams.

The STREAM runtime environment also includes a monitoring and adaptive query processing infrastructure, StreaMon. It manages the query plan, collects and maintains statistics about the streams and plan characteristics, and, more importantly, can re-optimize the query plan and the in-memory structures used in its execution. STREAM also makes use of load shedding techniques to probabilistically drop tuples under severe resource constraints.

STREAM includes a GUI-based query and system visualizer, the STREAM Visualizer, which allows system administrators and developers to inspect the system while it is running, as well as to experiment with adjustments.

The early STREAM prototype did not implement any support for distributed processing, nor did it provide any fault-tolerance mechanisms, but the STREAM researchers clearly identified these components as critical to a production-grade stream processing system.

3. Aurora

Aurora was developed jointly by a collaboration between Brandeis University, Brown University, and MIT. Aurora is a centralized stream processor that is fundamentally presented as a dataflow system and uses the popular boxes and arrows paradigm. In Aurora, a stream is modeled as an append-only sequence of tuples with uniform type (schema). In addition to application-specific data fields A1,..., An, each tuple in a stream has a timestamp (ts) that specifies its time of origin within the Aurora network. The Aurora data model supports out-of-order data arrival. Tuples flow through a loop-free, directed graph of processing operators (i.e., boxes). Ultimately, output streams are presented to applications, which must be constructed to handle the asynchronously arriving tuples in an output stream. Each operator accepts input streams, transforms them in some way, and produces one or more output streams. By default, queries are continuous in that they can potentially run forever over push-based inputs.

Aurora's programming model is built on an imperative and visual programming language named SQuAl. SQuAl uses a boxes and arrows paradigm, common in workflow and process flow systems, to specify applications as directed acyclic graphs (DAGs), where arrows represent stream connections between boxes representing operators. The Aurora Stream Query Algebra (SQuAl) supports seven operators which are used to construct Aurora networks queries. These operators are analogous to operators in the relational algebra. However, they differ in the way they address the special requirements of stream processing. They can be divided into two main sections:

- Order-agnostic operators (filter, map, and union)
- Order-sensitive operators (BSort, Aggregate, Join, and Resample).

Figure 20.4 illustrates the runtime architecture of Aurora. The basic purpose of an Aurora runtime network is to process dataflows through a potentially large workflow diagram where inputs from data sources and outputs from boxes are fed to the router, which forwards them either to external applications or to the storage manager to be placed on the proper queue. The storage manager is responsible for maintaining the box queues and managing the buffer.

When in execution, an Aurora network can accept input data, perform data filtering, computation, aggregation, and correlation, and, eventually, deliver output messages to client applications. In this network, every output can be optionally tagged with a QoS specification, indicating how much latency the connected application can tolerate as well as information on what to do if adequate responsiveness cannot be ensured. Conceptually, the scheduler picks a box for execution, ascertains what processing is required, and passes

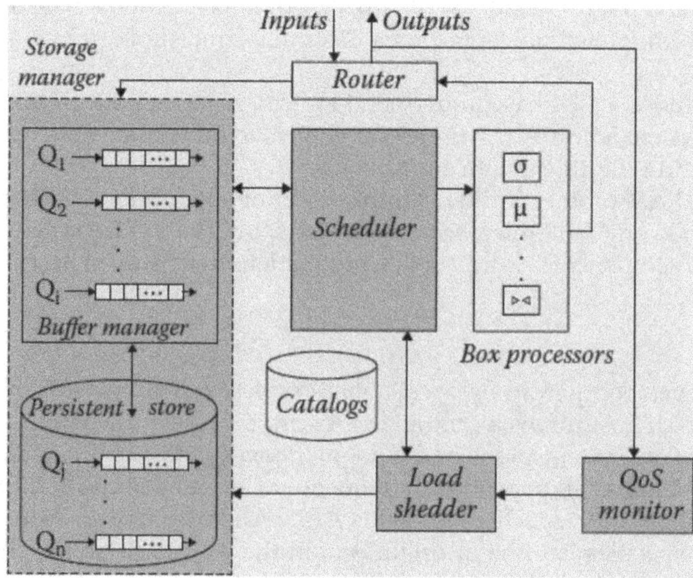

FIGURE 20.4
Runtime architecture of Aurora.

a pointer to the box description on to the multithreaded box processor. The box processor executes the appropriate operation and then forwards the output tuples to the router. The scheduler then ascertains the next processing step and the cycle is repeated.

Using the QoS tag, Aurora's optimizer can rearrange the physical structure of the network to meet the required QoS requirements. Along the same lines, at runtime, Aurora's scheduler makes decisions based on the form of the network, the QoS specifications, and the length of the various queues. These decisions include reordering flows, delaying or storing parts of the streaming data, and combining operators to minimize communication and processing overheads.

Medusa is a system designed to provide networking infrastructure for Aurora operations, based on which an Aurora network can be spread across any number of hosts, which can be either under the control of one entity or organized as a loosely coupled federation with different autonomous participants. Medusa provides a distributed naming scheme so that the output of an application from a host can be connected to another on a different host. Medusa also provides a distributed data transport layer, allowing the efficient delivery of messages between hosts. All of these functions are incorporated in contemporary commercial stream processing systems.

The Aurora platform led to the creation of StreamBase, which developed one of the earliest commercial stream processing systems.

4. Borealis

Borealis is a research offshoot created to address some of the limitations in Aurora's design.

Borealis inherited the core stream processing functionality from Aurora as well as the distributed functionality from Medusa. Due to its distributed architecture, a collection of queries submitted to the system can be seen as a network of operators whose processing occurs at multiple sites. To support this model, the Borealis' runtime added infrastructure to allow the dynamic deployment and adaptation of the applications running on the system, as well as capabilities to dynamically revise derived results, reflecting additional information gleaned from delayed data.

A Borealis application, which is a single connected diagram of processing boxes, is deployed on a network of N sites. Borealis optimization consists of multiple collaborating monitoring and optimization components. These components continuously optimize the allocation of query network fragments to processing sites. Monitors, in particular, are of two types:

1. Local monitor (LM) runs at each site and produces a collection of local statistics, which it forwards periodically to the end-point monitor (EM). LM maintains various box- and site-level statistics regarding utilization and queuing delays for various resources, including CPU, disk, bandwidth, and power (only relevant to sensor proxies).
2. End-point monitor (EM) runs at every site that produces Borealis outputs. EM evaluates QoS for every output message and keeps statistics on QoS for all outputs for the site.

In Borealis, the collection of continuous queries submitted to the system can be seen as one giant network of operator query diagrams whose processing is distributed to multiple sites. Each site runs a Borealis server where the query processor (QP) is a single-site processor. In the system architecture of Borealis, input streams are fed into the QP and results are pulled through I/O queues, which route tuples to and from remote Borealis nodes and clients. The QP is controlled by the admin module, which sets up locally running queries and takes care of moving query diagram fragments to and from remote Borealis nodes, when instructed to do so by another module. System control messages issued by the admin are fed into the local optimizer. The latter supplies performance-improving directions to major runtime components of the QP:

- Priority scheduler, which determines the order of box execution based on tuple priorities.
- Box processors, with one for each different type of box, which can change behavior on the fly based on control messages from the local optimizer.
- Load shedder, which discards low-priority tuples when the node is overloaded.

The QP also contains the storage manager, which is responsible for the storage and retrieval of data that flows through the arcs of the local query diagram. The local catalog stores query diagram descriptions and metadata, which are accessible by all the components.

5. IBM Systems and IBM SPADE

IBM System S is a large-scale, distributed data stream processing middleware that supports structured as well as unstructured data stream processing and can be scaled to a large number of compute nodes. The System S runtime can execute a large number of long-running queries that take the form of dataflow graphs. A data-flow graph consists of a set of processing elements (PEs) connected by streams, where each stream carries a series of tuples. The PEs implement data stream analytics and are basic execution containers which are distributed over the compute nodes. The compute nodes are organized as a shared-nothing cluster of workstations (COW). The PEs communicate with each other via their input and output ports, connected by streams. The PE ports as well as the streams connecting them are typed. PEs can be explicitly connected using hard-coded links or through implicit links that rely on type compatibility. System S also provides several other services, such as fault tolerance, scheduling, placement optimization, distributed job management, storage services, and security.

SPL is a stream processing language that allows the composition of streaming applications by assembling operators and expressing their stream interconnections. In SPL, operators can implement any logic (e.g., filtering, aggregation, image processing) and be arbitrarily interconnected. The language allows developers to define composite operators which represent a logically related subgraph that can be reused to assemble more complex graphs. These composite operators are important for application modularization. To execute an application, the SPL compiler places operators into PEs, which are runtime containers for one or more operators. During execution, each PE maps to an OS process, which can execute in any host available to the stream processing infrastructure. The compiler partitions operators into PEs based on performance measurements and following partition constraints informed by the developers. During runtime, PEs are distributed over hosts according to host placement constraints informed by developers as well as by the resource availability of hosts and load balance. The SPL compiler can also group operators that belong to different composites into the same PE. This means that the physical streaming graph layout does not reflect the fact that some operators are logically grouped.

When the SPL compiler builds an application, it generates C++ code for each used operator and a file with the application description called ADL.

20.2.2 Open-Source Systems

1. Apache Storm

Storm is a distributed stream processing platform that was originally created by Nathan Marz and then acquired by Twitter, who turned Storm into a free and open-source streaming engine. Currently the Storm project is undergoing incubation in the Apache Software Foundation, sponsored by the Apache Incubator.

Storm's architecture model is commonly known as topology, and mostly follows the general pattern mentioned in Figure 20.2:

- The source node in Storm is named "spout," and emits data into the cluster.
- The processing nodes in Storm are called "bolts."
- The data stream in Storm is an unbounded sequence of tuples with a formatted structure.

Storm topology is a parallel architecture in which nodes execute concurrently to perform different tasks. Users can specify the degree of parallelism for each node to optimize the resources spent on tasks with different complexity.

2. Yahoo! S4

S4 (Simple Scalable Stream Processing System) is a distributed real-time data processing system developed by Yahoo. Yahoo! S4 architecture is inspired by the MapReduce model. However, unlike MapReduce, which has a limitation on scaling, Yahoo! S4 is capable of scaling to a large cluster size to handle frequent real-time data.

Similarly to other distributed and parallel systems, Yahoo! S4 has a cluster consisting of computing machines, known as processing nodes (PNs). A PN is the host of PEs, which perform data processing tasks on events. The data stream within S4 is a sequence of events. The adapter is responsible for the conversion of raw data into events before delivering the events into the S4 cluster. When a processing node receives input events, it will assign them to associate PEs via the communication layer. ZooKeeper plays a role as PN coordinator by assigning and distributing events to different PEs in different stages.

3. Apache Samza

Samza is the stream processing framework of LinkedIn, and it is now another incubator project of the Apache Software Foundation. The platform is scalable, distributed, pluggable, and fault tolerant, and it has recently released its new version as an open-source project. However, the new version has some limitations on its fault tolerance semantics, according to the Samza development team. The framework is highly integrated with Hadoop YARN, the next-generation cluster manager, so that the architecture of Samza is very similar to that of Hadoop.

Samza consists of three layers:

- Streaming layer
- Execution layer
- Processing layer

Samza heavily relies on dynamic message passing and thus includes a message processing system like Kafka, adopted for data streaming.

4. Apache Streaming

Spark Streaming is an extended tool of the core Spark engine, used to enable this large-scale data processing engine to process live data streams. The role of Spark Streaming is very similar to that of the client adapter used by Yahoo! S4. Currently, Spark Streaming is developed by the Apache Software Foundation, which is responsible for the testing, updates, and release of each Spark version.

The data processing engine is called Apache Spark, but without Spark Streaming the engine cannot perform real-time data analytics. Spark Streaming runs as a filter of streams that divides the input streams into batches of data, and dispatches them into the Spark engine for further processing. The Spark engine consists of many machines that form a computing cluster, which is used in a similar manner to other surveyed platforms. The most special feature of Spark Streaming is how it treats data streams. The data streams within Spark Streaming are called discretized streams, or DStreams, which is, in fact, a continuous sequence of immutable data sets, known as Resilient Distributed Datasets (RDDs). All RDDs in a DStream contain data within a certain interval, so that they can be clearly separated and ordered for parallel processing.

5. Apache Flink

Apache Flink is a highly scalable, high-performance processing engine that can handle low latency as well as batch analytics. Flink is a relatively new project that originated as a joint effort of several German and Swedish universities under the name "Stratosphere." The project changed its name to Flink (meaning "agile" or "swift" in German) when it entered incubation as an Apache project in 2015. Flink became a top-level Apache project later that year and now has an international team of collaborators.

Flink has the capability to handle the low-latency, real-time analytics applications for which Storm is appropriate as well as batch processing. In fact, Flink treats batch as a special example of streaming. Flink programs are developer friendly; they are written in Java or Scala, and they deliver "exactly once" guarantees. Like Spark or Storm, Flink requires a distributed storage system. Flink has already demonstrated very high performance at scale, even while providing a real-time level of latency.

Appendix 20.A gives a brief on Spark.

20.2.3 Commercial Systems

20.2.3.1 Streambase

StreamBase is based on the Aurora/Borealis systems. It has been used in numerous application domains, including real-time algorithmic trading as well as order execution and routing in financial engineering applications.

The programming model of StreamBase has two language environments, namely, EventFlow, which is a visual language, and StreamSQL, which is a combined declarative SQL-like DDL and DML. Both languages include relational operators extended to be used with event- or time-based windows when manipulating streaming data. These operators perform a variety of functions, including filtering, aggregation, merging, and correlation of data from multiple streams as well as carrying out complex analytics. Due to its SQL roots, StreamSQL can seamlessly reference database-stored data. A StreamSQL query can also make use of external data sources via adapters, including a variety of market data feeds and financial data messaging interfaces. StreamSQL also includes a Drools operator, which relies on a Java-based rule management engine to support a simple pattern-matching language that can be used to implement typical transformation and detection tasks. Interestingly, this capability demonstrates an approach by which a CEP-like functionality can be made available as part of a stream process system.

The StreamBase runtime environment consists of one or more StreamBase servers (called sbd) that, in addition to hosting applications, provide tracing, debugging, logging, as well as profiling and monitoring services. StreamBase defines the notion of containers for organizing and connecting multiple applications. Each container runs a single application and serves as a handle for an application's resources. Hence, it is possible to run multiple simultaneous applications in a server by employing multiple containers. The container abstraction makes it possible to establish and maintain connections, including dynamic ones, between streams from different applications, as well as to tap into Java Message Service (JMS)-based messaging infrastructure for exchanging information with other components in a larger IT environment.

20.2.3.2 IBM InfoSphere Streams

IBM InfoSphere Streams is based on the System S research prototype. These design attributes have resulted in a manageable, scalable, extensible, and industrial-strength environments that can seamlessly integrate with existing enterprise computing environments.

Infosphere Streams is a component of the IBM big data analytics platform, which allows user-developed applications to quickly ingest, analyze, and correlate information as it arrives from thousands of data stream sources. The system is designed to handle up to millions of events or messages per second. It provides a programming model and IDE for defining data sources, and software analytic modules called "operators" which are fused into processing execution units. It also provides infrastructure to support the composition of scalable stream processing applications from these components.

The main platform components are as follows:

1. Runtime environment: This includes platform services and a scheduler for deploying and monitoring streams applications across a single host or set of integrated hosts.
2. Programming model: Streams applications are developed using the Streams Processing Language (SPL), which is a declarative language. Developers use it to state what they want, and the runtime environment accepts the responsibility for determining how best to service the request. In this model, a streams application is represented as a graph that consists of operators and the streams that connect them.
3. Monitoring tools and administrative interfaces: Streams applications process data at speeds that are much higher than those normal operating system monitoring utilities can efficiently handle. InfoSphere Streams provides tools that can deal with this environment.

SPL, the programming language for InfoSphere Streams, is a distributed dataflow composition language. It is an extensible and full-featured language that supports user-defined data types. An InfoSphere Streams continuous application describes a directed graph composed of individual operators that interconnect and operate on multiple data streams. Data streams can come from outside the system or be produced internally as part of an application.

The basic building blocks of SPL programs are:

1. Stream: An infinite sequence of structured tuples. It can be consumed by operators on a tuple-by-tuple basis or through the definition of a window.
2. Tuple: A structured list of attributes and their types. Each tuple on a stream has the form dictated by its stream type.
3. Stream type: Specifies the name and data type of each attribute in the tuple.
4. Window: A finite sequential group of tuples. It can be based on count, time, attribute value, or punctuation marks.
5. Operator: The fundamental building block of SPL; its operators process data from streams and can produce new streams.

In this architecture, an operator represents a reusable stream transformer that transforms some input streams into output streams. In SPL programs, operator invocation implements the specific use of an operator, with specific assigned input and output streams and with locally specified parameters and logic. Each operator invocation names the input and output streams.

20.2.3.3 TIBCO BusinessEvents

TIBCO BusinessEvents is a CEP system that provides reasonably sophisticated query and event pattern matching capabilities. TIBCO BusinessEvents has been used, for example, to process data from financial data feeds as well as from website-monitoring feeds. As a CEP platform, TIBCO BusinessEvents lacks many of the distributed processing, extensibility, and fault-tolerance capabilities provided by stream processing systems. Its major strengths are in its programming model and in its integration with messaging infrastructure, including other TIBCO software products and other vendors' products such as the JMS interface.

The TIBCO BusinessEvents programming model employs Unified Modeling Language (UML)-based models to describe applications, services, and servers. These models are used to define the causal and temporal relationships between events as well as the actions to be taken when a particular event occurs. The modeling task is performed using a rule editor, which is part of its TIBCO BusinessEvents Studio.

The SQL-like query language allows developers to craft both snapshot and continuous queries. These queries are executed by agents deployed on the platform's runtime environment. An agent can execute the query against a previously primed cache or listen to an event stream as if the data was hosted by regular database tables. Its pattern description language is simple and shares some similarities with both SQL and regular expression-based languages. It includes constructs for defining patterns and configuring them for deployment using the platform's pattern matcher.

20.2.3.4 Oracle CEP

Oracle CEP also includes a few features found in more sophisticated SPSs. Its primary analytical goals include filtering, processing, and correlating events in real time. Its main application development framework is an Event Processing Network (EPN), where the analytics are implemented as a combination of data adapters and continuous queries described in Oracle's CQL, which is not only fully compliant with ANSI SQL 99 standard, but also adds constructs to support streaming data.

An EPN makes use of three operational constructs:

- An event source is a data producer on which CQL queries operate. Practically, an event source can be an adapter connecting to a JMS messaging interface, a HyperText Transfer Protocol (HTTP) server, a file, a stream (or channel), a processor, a cache, or a relational database table.
- An event sink is a consumer of query results. An event sink can be an adapter, a channel, a processor, or a cache.
- A processor is where the analytical portion of an application resides, but it can also act as either an event source or a sink. A processor is associated with one or more CQL queries that operate on events arriving from multiple incoming channels. It is usually connected to one or more output channels where the results are written.

Oracle CEP's query execution engine works in-memory, and continuous queries listening on a stream are able to combine streaming events with data that has been previously stored. Oracle CEP's runtime environment hosts a server where containers for the EPN applications are used to manage their life cycle. This environment consists of a real-time JVM with deterministic garbage collection, providing services that include security, database access through a Java Data Base Connectivity (JDBC) interface, web connectivity via HTTP interfaces, connectivity to publish–subscribe systems, as well as logging and debugging infrastructures.

20.3 Summary

The chapter commenced by defining stream processing systems. It then provided an overview of systems that were significant milestones in the history of stream processing, namely, data stream processing systems, data stream management systems, complex event processing systems, and stream processing platforms/engines. The latter half of the chapter provides an overview of several stream processing system implementations. It describes academic or research prototype systems such as TelegraphCQ, STREAM, Aurora, Borealis, IBM System S, and IBM SPADE. It gives an overview of open-source systems such as Apache Storm, Yahoo! S4, Apache Samza, and Apache Streaming. In addition, gives briefs on commercial systems such as Streambase, IBM InfoSphere Streams, TIBCO BusinessEvents, and Oracle CEP.

Appendix 20.A: Spark

Spark is a fault-tolerant and distributed data analytics tool capable of implementing large-scale, data-intensive applications on commodity hardware. Hadoop and other technologies have already popularized acyclic dataflow techniques for building data-intensive applications on commodity clusters, but these are not suitable for applications that reuse a working dataset for multiple parallel operations such as iterative machine-learning algorithms and interactive data analysis tools. Spark is not only scalable and fault tolerant but also addresses these problems by introducing a data storage and processing abstraction called resilient distributed datasets (RDDs). An RDD is a read-only distribution of objects that are partitioned across a set of machines and can be rebuilt if a partition is lost.

While Spark is a fairly new framework, it is easy to use, extendable, highly supported, well designed, and fast. Spark is expected to eclipse MapReduce for most functionalities. Spark is already the best choice for machine-learning applications because of its ability to perform iterative operations on data-cached in memory. In addition to replacing MapReduce, Spark offers structured query language (SQL), graph processing, and streaming frameworks.

MapReduce revolutionized computation over huge datasets by offering a simple model for writing programs that could execute in parallel across hundreds to thousands of machines. The MapReduce engine achieves near linear scalability—as the data size increases, one can use more computers and see jobs complete in the same amount of time—and is resilient to the fact that failures that rarely occur on a single machine, occur all the time on clusters of thousands. It breaks up work into small tasks and can gracefully accommodate task failures without compromising the job to which they belong.

Hadoop users have a challenge in using MapReduce to address the following:

- Iterative jobs: Gradient descent is an excellent example of an algorithm that is repeatedly applied to the same dataset to optimize a parameter. While it is easy to represent each iteration as a MapReduce job, the data from each iteration has to be loaded from the disk, incurring a significant performance penalty.
- Interactive analytics: Interfaces such as Pig and Hive are commonly used to run SQL queries on large datasets using Hadoop. Ideally, this dataset is loaded into the memory and queried repeatedly; however, with Hadoop, every query is executed as a MapReduce job that incurs significant latency from disk read.

Distributed shared memory (DSM) is a mechanism by which processes can access shared data without interprocess communication. The challenges of implementing a DSM system include addressing problems such as data location, data access, sharing and locking data, and data coherence. These problems have connections with transactional models, data migrations, concurrent programming, distributed systems, etc. RDDs are an important abstraction in Spark that allows a read-only collection of objects capable of rebuilding lost partitions across clusters. These RDDs can be reused in multiple parallel operations through memory caching. RDDs use lineage information about the lost partition in the rebuilding process.

Systems such as MapReduce provide locality-aware scheduling, fault tolerance, and load balancing features that simplify distributed programming, allowing users to analyze large datasets using commodity clusters. However, RDDs are a distributed memory abstraction that allows users to write in-memory computations while still maintaining the advantages of current dataflow systems such as MapReduce. An RDD performs exceptionally well on iterative algorithms, machine learning, and interactive data mining, while the other dataflows become inadequate. This is possible because RDDs provide only read-only datasets, avoiding the need to checkpoint, which is common in other shared memory techniques.

RDDs are easy to program and capable of efficiently expressing computations. Fault tolerance is perhaps most difficult to support. Checkpointing datasets has a huge disadvantage as it requires replicating datasets across clusters. This can slow down the machines due to bandwidth and memory storage restrictions. RDDs ensure fault tolerance by supporting the stages of transformation. At any point in time, a partition can be recovered by repeating the transformation steps on the parent (lineage). RDDs are well suited for applications that require executing a single function on many data records such as graph and machine-learning algorithms.

Spark maintains MapReduce's linear scalability and fault tolerance, but extends it in a few important ways. First, rather than relying on a rigid map-then-reduce format, its engine can execute a more general directed acyclic graph (DAG) of operators. This means that, in situations where MapReduce must write out intermediate results to the distributed file system, Spark can pass them directly to the next step in the pipeline.

Spark extends its predecessors (such as MapReduce) with in-memory processing. An RDD enables developers to materialize any point in a processing pipeline into memory across the cluster, meaning that future steps that want to deal with the same dataset need not recompute it or reload it from disk. This capability opens up use cases that distributed processing engines could not previously approach. Spark is well suited for highly iterative algorithms that require multiple passes over a dataset, as well as reactive applications that quickly respond to user queries by scanning large in-memory datasets.

20.A.1 Spark Components

The components of Spark are as follows:

- Driver: The driver defines RDD objects and their relationships; it is the code that includes the "main" function and defines the resilient RDDs and their transformations.
- DAG scheduler: The DAG scheduler optimizes the code and arrives at an efficient DAG that represents the data processing steps in the application. The resulting DAG is sent to the cluster manager.
- Cluster manager: The cluster manager is responsible for assigning specific processing tasks to workers. The cluster manager has information about the workers, assigned threads, and the location of data blocks. The cluster manager is also the service that handles DAG playback in the case of worker failure. The cluster manager can be Yet Another Resource Negotiator (YARN), Mesos, or Spark's cluster manager.
- Worker: The worker receives units of work and data to manage. The worker executes its specific task without knowledge of the entire DAG, and its results are sent back to the driver application.

MapReduce has only two processing phases: map and/or reduce; with the MapReduce framework, it is only possible to build complete applications by stringing together sets of map and reduce tasks. These complex chains of tasks are known as directed acyclic graphs (DAGs). Thus, DAGs contain a series of actions connected to each other in a workflow. Oozie actually allows users to define these workflows of MapReduce tasks in XML and use an orchestration framework to monitor their execution.

Rather than the DAG being an abstraction added externally to the model, the Spark engine itself creates those complex chains of steps from the application's logic; this enables developers to express complex algorithms and data processing pipelines within the same job and allows the framework to optimize the job as a whole, leading to improved performance.

20.A.2 Spark Concepts

- Shared variables: Spark includes two types of variables that allow sharing information between the execution nodes, which are as follows:
  - Broadcast variables are sent to all remote execution nodes, where they can be used for data processing. This is similar to the role that configuration objects play in MapReduce.
  - Accumulator variables are also sent to the remote execution nodes, but unlike broadcast variables, they can also be "added" by the executors. Accumulators are somewhat similar to MapReduce counters.
- SparkContext is an object that represents the connection to a Spark cluster. It is used to create RDDs, broadcast data, and initialize accumulators.
- RDDs are collections of serializable elements that are partitioned so that they can be stored on multiple nodes. An RDD may reside in the memory or on disk. Spark uses RDDs to reduce input/output (I/O) and maintain the processed dataset in memory while still tolerating node failures without having to restart the entire job. RDDs are typically created from either of the following:
  - A Hadoop input format (e.g., a file on the Hadoop Distributed File System [HDFS]): Spark determines the number of partitions by the input format, very similar to the way splits are determined in MapReduce jobs.
  - Transformations applied on existing RDDs: Spark can shuffle the data and repartition it to any number of partitions.

RDDs store their "lineage," that is, the set of transformations that was used to create the current state, starting from the first input format that was used to create the RDD. If the data is lost, Spark will replay the lineage to rebuild the lost RDDs so that the job can continue.

- Transformations are functions that take one RDD and return another. RDDs are "immutable," so transformations will never modify their input, and only return the modified RDD. Transformations in Spark are always "lazy" in that they do not compute their own results. Instead, calling a transformation function only creates a new RDD with this specific transformation as part of its lineage; the complete set of transformations is executed only when an "action" is called. This improves Spark's efficiency and allows it to cleverly optimize the execution graph.

This can make debugging more challenging because exceptions are thrown when the action is called, far from the code that called the function that actually threw the exception. It is important that the exception handling code should not be placed around the action but around the function where the exception may be thrown.

There are many transformations in Spark, which are as follows:

- map()

  Applies a function on every element of an RDD to produce a new RDD. This is similar to the way the MapReduc emap() method is applied to every element in the input data.

  For example: lines.map(s=>s.length) takes an RDD of strings ("lines") and returns an RDD with the length of the strings.

- filter()

  Takes a Boolean function as a parameter, executes this function on every element of the RDD, and returns a new RDD containing only the elements for which the function returned true.

  For example, lines.filter(s=>(s.length>35)) returns an RDD containing only the lines with more than 35 characters.

- keyBy()

  Takes every element in an RDD and turns it into a key-value pair in a new RDD.

  For example, lines.keyBy(s=>s.length) returns an RDD of key-value pairs with the length of the line as the key, and the line as the value.

- join()

  Joins two key-value RDDs by their keys.

  For example, let us assume we have two RDDs: lines and more_lines. Each entry in both RDDs contains the line length as the key and the line as the value.

  lines.join(more_lines) will return for each line length a pair of strings, one from the lines RDD and one from the more_lines RDD.

  Each resulting element looks like <length,<line,more_line>>.

- groupByKey()

  Performs a group-by operation on an RDD by the keys.

  For example: lines.groupByKey() will return an RDD where each element has a length as the key and a collection of lines with that length as the value.

- sort()
- Performs a sort on an RDD and returns a sorted RDD.

• "Actions" are methods that take an RDD, perform a computation, and return the result to the driver application. Recall that transformations are "lazy" and are not executed when called. Actions trigger the computation of transformations. The result of the computation can be a collection of values printed to the screen, values saved to a file, or similar. However, an action will never return an RDD.

20.A.3 Benefits of Spark

- Interactive shell (REPL): Spark jobs can be easily deployed as an application, similar to how MapReduce jobs are executed. In addition, Spark also includes a shell called REPL (Read-Eval-Print-Loop). This allows for fast interactive experimentation with the data and easy validation of code. REPL enables quick access to data as well as interactive queries.
- Reduced disk I/O: MapReduce writes to the local disk at the end of the map phase and to the HDFS at the end of the reduce phase. This means that while processing 1 Tb of data, the system may write 4 Tb of data to disk and send 2 Tb of data over the network. When the application is stringing multiple MapReduce jobs together, the situation is even worse. Spark's RDDs can be stored in the memory and processed in multiple steps or iterations without additional I/O. Because there are no special map and reduce phases, data is typically read from disk when processing starts and written to disk only when there is a need to persist results.
- Storage: Spark gives developers flexibility to store RDDs:
  - In memory on a single node.
  - In memory but replicated to multiple nodes.
  - Persisted to disk.

An RDD can go through multiple stages of transformation (equivalent to multiple map and reduce phases) without storing anything to disk.

- Multilanguage: While Spark itself is developed in Scala (see Section 13.3.2.1: "Scala"), Spark application programming interfaces (APIs) are implemented for Java, Scala, and Python. This allows developers to use Spark in the language in which they are most productive. Hadoop developers often use Java APIs, whereas data scientists often prefer the Python implementation so that they can use Spark combined with Python's powerful numeric processing libraries.
- Resource manager independence: Spark supports both YARN and Mesos as resource managers, as well as in a stand-alone mode. Since each resource manager has its own strengths and limitations, Spark enables developers to use resource manager(s) of their choice. This allows Spark to be enabled for changes in resource managers in future.
- Simplicity: Spark APIs are significantly cleaner and simpler than those of MapReduce. The APIs are so usable that they obviate the need for any high-level abstractions on top of Spark like those that are essential for MapReduce, such as Hive or Pig. Consequently, Spark codes are significantly shorter than their MapReduce equivalents and are easily readable even by someone not familiar with Spark.
- Versatility: Spark was built from the ground up to be an extensible, general-purpose, parallel-processing framework. It is generic enough to support a stream processing framework called Spark streaming and a graph processing engine called GraphX. With this flexibility, Spark can be expected to see many new special-purpose libraries in the future.

Epilogue: Quantum Computing

As stated in the Preface, the requirements of massive parallelism envisaged in the future is achievable more effectively through quantum computing. This epilogue explores the very idea of quantum computing. In 1994, Peter Shor (a research scientist at AT&T Bell Laboratories) wrote a paper in which he described the first algorithm specifically intended for quantum computation. Shor's algorithm takes advantage of the power of quantum superposition to implement a set of mathematical operations that enable a machine to rapidly factor very large integers. Given a quantum computer of sufficient power, the factorization could be accomplished orders of magnitude faster than is possible with even the most advanced silicon-based computers. Although these computations seem trivial, they represent proofs of the concept of factorization, with staggering implications if the same algorithms can be run on quantum computers with many more qubits.

Conventional computers have increased by orders of magnitude in speed over their 70-plus years of existence. Much of this increase in speed and computing power has been made possible by continuing reductions in the sizes of the individual components used in their construction. The performance achievable with computers based on integrated circuits has historically followed a pattern known as Moore's Law: the number of transistors on a single integrated circuit would continue to double on approximately a yearly basis, with a corresponding doubling of computational power approximately every 18 to 24 months.

Ultimately, the semiconductor industry will reach a stopping point at which the transistors that make up the basic logic gates can be made no smaller while continuing to work as binary switches and thus, effectively, classical computer architectures can be made no faster. At this point, problems would arise because, on an atomic scale, the laws that govern device properties and behavior are those of quantum mechanics, not classical (Newtonian) physics. This observation led these researchers to wonder whether a new, radically different type of computer could be devised based on quantum principles.

Researchers who did early work on the idea included Richard Feynman of the California Institute of Technology, who conceived the idea of a quantum computer as a simulator for experiments in quantum physics, and David Deutsch of the University of Oxford, who expanded Feynman's idea and showed that any physical process could, in theory, be modeled by a quantum computer. A quantum computer is a device based not on Boolean algebra, but on the principles of quantum physics. These principles, in effect, allow the same physical device to simultaneously compute a vast number of possibilities as though it were massively parallel hardware.

A characteristic of all conventional computers, whether they are uniprocessor (SISD) or parallel (SIMD or MIMD) machines, is that the basic unit of information they store or process is a binary digit or bit. These bits may be grouped together to form bytes or words, but all the basic combinational and sequential logic devices (gates, latches, flip-flops, etc.) operate on or store individual bits. Quantum computers are different from all the other machines we have studied in that their basic unit of information is a *quantum bit* (*qubit*). Unlike a bit, which can take on only one or the other of two states (1 or 0, true or false, on or off, etc.) at a given time, a qubit is an entity that can assume not only the logical states corresponding to one or zero, but also other states corresponding to both 1 and 0 at the same time, or a superposition or blend of those states with a certain probability of being either.

In a quantum computer, the atoms (and the subatomic particles that comprise them) are essentially used as processors and memories at the same time. Even though there is only one set of some number of qubits in the machine, the qubits are not restricted to be in only one state at a time as the bits in a binary register would be. Although a 3-bit binary register can only take on one of the eight states 000 through 111 at any given time, a 3-qubit quantum register can be in all eight states at once in coherent superposition. Using quantum parallelism, a set of n qubits can store 2^n numbers at once, and once the quantum register is initialized to the superposition of states, operations can be performed on all the states simultaneously. In effect, in one time step an n-qubit quantum computer can perform the same calculation on 2^n values, something that would take 2^n time steps on a uniprocessor machine, or require an SIMD machine with 2^n processors to accomplish in one-time step.

One of the most significant problems in making practical applications of quantum computers is retrieving the results of the computations. Measuring the results of a quantum computation is problematic because interfering in any way with the atoms being used for computation can change their value, collapsing them back into the single state 1 or 0 instead of their coherent superposition of many states. One viable method for determining the states of the qubits uses the phenomenon of *quantum entanglement*. The quantum principle of entanglement allows one to apply an external force to a pair of atoms; once they are entangled, the second atom takes on the properties of the first atom but with opposite spin. This linkage allows the qubit value stored by a given atom to be read indirectly via the spin of its entangled partner by using techniques such as NMR. Thus, the results of a quantum computation can be read without interfering with the atom doing the computation. Another, more recently devised approach involves using the interference between quantum states, rather than entanglement, to retrieve information from the qubits.

Researchers at the IBM Almaden Research Center constructed a 5-qubit computer in 2000 and used it to compute a single-step solution to an "order-finding" equation that would have required repeated iterations to solve on a conventional machine. Since then, the same researchers have produced a 7-qubit machine that has run Shor's factoring algorithm—the first algorithm designed specifically for quantum computers—factoring the number 15 into the numbers 3 and 5. Although these computations seem trivial, the difficulty of using conventional computers to factor large integers is what makes present crypto-systems, such as RSA, extremely hard to crack. Given the ability of quantum computers to factor very large numbers, cryptography could very well turn out to be the "killer application" that drives the continued development of quantum computers.

The RSA algorithm, named for its inventors Rivest, Shamir, and Adelman, is the most widely used public key encryption method, and the principal technology behind secure transactions on the Internet.

A person, organization, or government with access to a powerful quantum computer could use Shor's (or some other) factoring algorithm to break into any encrypted message and recover the supposedly secure information; thus, today's encryption methods could be made obsolete. Conversely, quantum computers could potentially be used to implement new codes that would encode information with far stronger encryption than is possible with even the fastest supercomputers of today and thus be essentially impossible to crack.

But, in a quantum computer, errors can be introduced due to decoherence, or the tendency for unavoidable interactions with the surrounding environment to affect the qubits, destroying the constructive interference patterns that are used in the computation and decaying the quantum state to an incoherent mixed state. This tends to break down the information stored in the quantum computer and induce errors in computations. Substantial progress in fighting decoherence and other potential error sources will need to be made before robust quantum computers, capable of solving computationally difficult problems, can be built.

References

H. C. M. Andrade, B. Gedik and D. S. Turaga, *Fundamentals of Stream Processing: Application Design, Systems, and Analytics* (Cambridge University Press, Cambridge, UK, 2014).

T. J. Anthony, *Systems Programming: Designing and Developing Distributed Applications* (Elsevier, Amsterdam, the Netherlands, 2016).

A. Arora, *Analysis and Design of Algorithms* (Cognella Academic Publication, 2015).

C. C. Aggarwal (Ed.), *Data Streams: Models and Algorithms* (Springer, Boston, MA, 2007).

H. Attiya and J. Wlech, *Distributed Computing: Fundamentals, Simulations and Advanced Topics* (Wiley, Hoboken, NJ, 2nd Ed., 2004).

B. Borowik, M. Karpinskyy, V. Lahno and O. Petrov, *Theory of Digital Automata* (Springer Science+Business Media, Dordrecht, 2013).

R. R. Brooks and S. S. Iyengar, *Multi-Sensor Fusion: Fundamentals and Applications with Software* (Prentice-Hall, New Jersey, 1998).

Sharma Chakravarthy and Q. Jiang, *A Quality of Service Perspective, Modeling, Scheduling, Load Shedding, and Complex Event Processing* (Springer, New York, NY, 2009).

Z. J. Czech, *Introduction to Parallel Computing* (Cambridge University Press, Cambridge, UK, 2016).

M. Drozdowski, *Scheduling for Parallel Processing* (Springer-Verlag, Berlin, Heidelberg, 2009).

M. Dubois, M. Annavaram and P. Stenstrom, *Parallel Computer Organization and Design* (Cambridge University Press, Cambridge, UK, 2012).

J. D. Dumas II, *Computer Architecture: Fundamentals and Principles of Computer Design* (CRC Press, Boca Raton, FL, 2017).

M. J. Flynn, Very high-speed computing systems. *Proceedings of the IEEE*, 54 (12): 1901–1909, 1966.

M. J. Flynn and W. Luk, *Computer System Design: System-On-Chip* (Wiley, Hoboken, NJ, 2011).

I. Foster, *Designing and Building Parallel Programs: Concepts and Tools for Parallel Software Engineering* (Pearson, 2003).

R. M. Fujimoto, *Parallel and Distributed Simulation Systems* (Wiley, Hoboken, NJ, 2000).

J. Gama and M. M. Gaber, *Learning from Data Streams: Processing Techniques in Sensor Networks* (Springer-Verlag, Berlin, Heidelberg, 2007).

S. Ghosh, *Distributed Systems: An Algorithmic Approach* (CRC Press, Boca Raton, FL, 2007).

M. Garofalakis, J. Gehrke and R. Rastogi (Eds.), *Data Stream Management: Processing High-Speed Data Streams* (Springer-Verlag, Berlin Heidelberg, 2016).

G. W. Greenwood and A. M. Tyrrell, *Introduction to Evolvable Hardware-A Practical Guide for Designing Adaptive Systems* (Wiley, Hoboken, NJ, 2007).

G. Hager and G. Wellein, *Introduction to High Performance Computing for Scientists and Engineers* (CRC Press, Boca Raton, FL, 2011).

Hui-Huang Hsu, Chuan-Yu Chang and Ching-Hsien Hsu, *Big Data Analytics for Sensor-Network Collected Intelligence* (Elsevier, Amsterdam, The Netherlands, 2017).

V. Kale, *Creating Smart Enterprises: Leveraging Cloud, Big Data, Web, Social Media, Mobile and IoT Technologies* (CRC Press, Boca Raton, FL, 2018).

V. Kale, *Big Data Computing: A Guide for Business and Technology Managers* (CRC Press, Boca Raton, FL, 2016).

L. N. Kanal, V. Kumar, H. Kitano and C. B. Suttner (Eds.), *Parallel Processing for Artificial Intelligence* (Elsevier, Amsterdam, The Netherlands, 1994).

P. K. Kapur, U. Kumar and A. K. Verma (Eds.), *Quality, IT and Business Operations Modeling and Optimization* (Springer Nature, Singapore, 2018).

L. Kirischian, *Reconfigurable Computer Systems Engineering: Virtualization of Computing Architecture* (CRC Press, Boca Raton, FL, 2016).

J. Levesque and A. Vose, *Programming for Hybrid Multi/Manycore MPP Systems* (CRC Press, Boca Raton, FL, 2018).

K. Li, H. Jiang, L. T. Yang and A. Cuzzocrea (Eds.), *Big Data: Algorithms, Analytics and Applications* (CRC Press, Boca Raton, FL, 2015).

M. McCool, A. D. Robison and J. Reinders, *Structured Parallel Programming: Patterns for Efficient Computation* (Elsevier, Amsterdam, the Netherlands, 2012).

R. Miller and L. Boxer, *Algorithms: Sequential and Parallel: A Unified Approach* (Cengage Learning, Boston, MA, 3rd ed., 2013).

V. Milutinovic, J. Salom, N. Trifunovic and R. Giorgi, *Guide to DataFlow Supercomputing: Basic Concepts, Case Studies and a Detailed Example* (Springer, Cham, Switzerland, 2015).

I. Mistrik, R. Bahsoon, N. Ali, M. Heisel and B. Maxim (Eds.), *Software Architecture for Big Data and Cloud* (Elsevier, Cambridge, MA, 2017).

S. B. Mitchell, *Data Fusion: Concepts and Ideas* (Springer-Verlag, Berlin, Heidelberg, 2012).

A. Osseyran and M. Giles (Eds.), *Industrial Applications of High-Performance Computing: Best Global Practices* (CRC Press, Boca Raton, FL, 2015).

P. Pacheco, *An Introduction to Parallel Programming* (Elsevier, Amsterdam, the Netherlands, 2011).

V. Pankratius, A. Adl-Tabatabai and W. Tichy (Eds.), *Fundamentals of Multicore Software Development* (CRC Press, Boca Raton, FL, 2016).

B. Pharhami, *Introduction to Parallel Processing Algorithms and Architectures* (Kluwer Academic Publishers, New York, 2002).

S. Pllana and F. Xhafa (Eds.), *Programming Multicore and Many-Core Computing Systems* (Wiley, Hoboken, NJ, 2017).

T. Rauber and G. Rünger, *Parallel Programming for Multicore and Cluster Systems* (Springer-Verlag, Berlin Heidelberg, 2nd ed., 2013).

A. Rahimi, L. Benini and R. K. Gupta, *From Variability Tolerance to Approximate Computing in Parallel Integrated Architectures and Accelerators* (Springer, Cham, Switzerland, 2017).

D. A. Reed and R. M. Fujimoto, *Multicomputer Networks: Message-Based Parallel Processing* (The MIT Press, Cambridge, MA, 1987).

M. Raynal, *Distributed Algorithms for Message-Passing Systems* (Springer-Verlag, Berlin Heidelberg, 2013).

P. Sanders, K. Mehlorn, M. Dietzfelbinger and R. Dementiev, *Sequential and Parallel Algorithms and Data Structures: The Basic Toolbox* (Springer Nature, Singapore, 2019).

S. G. Shiva, *Advanced Computer Architectures* (CRC Press, Boca Raton, FL, 2006).

O. Sinnen, *Task Scheduling for Parallel Systems* (John Wiley, 2007).

R. Trobec, B. Slivnik, P. Bulić and B. Robič, *Introduction to Parallel Computing: From Algorithms to Programming on State-of-the-Art Platforms* (Springer, 2018).

R. Trobec, M. Vajteršic and P. Zinterhof (Eds.), *Parallel Computing: Numerics, Applications, and Trends* (Springer-Verlag London Limited, 2009).

P. Veríssimo and L. Rodrigues, *Distributed Systems for System Architects* (Springer, New York, 2001).

G. L. Vert, S. S. Iyengar and S. S. Phoha, *Introduction to Contextual Processing: Theory and Applications* (CRC Press, Boca Raton, FL, 2011).

S. Wang and R. S. Ledley, *Computer Architecture and Security: Fundamentals of Designing Secure Computer Systems* (Wiley, Singapore, 2013).

C. Xavier and S. S. Iyengar, *Introduction to Parallel Algorithms* (Wiley-Interscience, 1998).

F. Xhafa, L. Barolli, A. Barolli and P. Papajorgji (Eds.), *Modeling and Processing for Next-Generation Big-Data Technologies: With Applications and Case Studies* (Springer, Cham, Switzerland, 2015).

Index

E

K

L

M

Q

R

S

T